The Slow Cooker COOKBOOK

1001 Slow Cooker Recipes

for Balanced Meals and Healthy Living.

14-Day Meal Plan

Ruth K. Miller

CONTENTS

INTRODUCTION **13**

Not every slow cooker recipe is equally healthy 13
Ingredient substitutions that can make any slow cooker recipe healthier 13

10 TOP TIPS FOR USING A SLOW COOKER **13**

14-DAY MEAL PLAN **15**

BREAKFAST RECIPES **16**

1. Radish Bowl 16
2. Apple Crumble 16
3. Bacon and Egg Casserole 16
4. Ham Omelet 16
5. Breakfast Casserole 16
6. Peach, Vanilla and Oats Mix 16
7. Omelet with Greens 16
8. Egg Bake 17
9. Shrimp Omelet 17
10. Lentils and Quinoa Mix 17
11. Mayo Sausage Rolls 17
12. Milk Oatmeal 17
13. Hash Brown and Bacon Casserole 17
14. French Breakfast Pudding 17
15. Cheesy Eggs 18
16. Leek Bake 18
17. Italian Style Scrambled Eggs 18
18. Creamy Asparagus Chicken 18
19. Hash Browns Casserole 18
20. Butter Oatmeal 18
21. Zesty Pumpkin Cubes 18
22. French Toast 19
23. Bacon Potatoes 19
24. Eggs and Sausage Casserole 19
25. Cinnamon French Toast 19
26. Chicken Cabbage Medley 19
27. Chorizo Eggs 19
28. Cocoa and Berries Quinoa 19
29. Breakfast Pork Ground 19
30. Cauliflower Casserole 20
31. Creamy Shrimp Bowls 20
32. Cranberry Maple Oatmeal 20
33. Herbed Egg Scramble 20
34. Almond and Quinoa Bowls 20
35. Morning Muesli 20
36. Baked Eggs 20
37. Apple Breakfast Rice 20
38. Squash Bowls 21
39. Artichoke Pepper Frittata 21
40. Kale & Feta Breakfast Frittata 21
41. Sausage Frittata 21
42. Jalapeno Muffins 21
43. Mixed Egg and Sausage Scramble 21
44. Creamy Yogurt 21
45. Mushroom Chicken Casserole 22
46. Raspberry Chia Porridge 22
47. Apricot Butter 22
48. Butternut Squash Pate 22
49. Cheddar Eggs 22
50. Turkey Breakfast Casserole 22
51. Ham Pockets 22
52. Baby Carrots In Syrup 22
53. Pork and Eggplant Casserole 23
54. Oats Granola 23
55. Meat Buns 23
56. Potato Omelet 23
57. Fried Apple Slices 23
58. Squash Butter 23
59. Cheesy Egg Bake 23
60. Cheese and Turkey Casserole 23
61. Dates Quinoa 24
62. Creamy Breakfast 24
63. Cranberry Quinoa 24
64. Chocolate French Toast 24
65. Cinnamon Pumpkin Oatmeal 24
66. Vanilla Quinoa 24
67. Leek Eggs 24
68. Chocolate Toast 24
69. Cheesy Cauliflower Hash 25
70. Quinoa Cauliflower Medley 25
71. Hot Eggs Mix 25
72. Bacon Tater 25
73. Quinoa Oats Bake 25
74. Bacon Eggs 25
75. Tofu Eggs 25
76. Quinoa and Oats Mix 26
77. Raspberry Oatmeal 26
78. Raisins and Rice Pudding 26
79. Nutmeg Banana Oatmeal 26
80. Breakfast Butterscotch Pudding 26
81. Quinoa Bars 26
82. Morning Pie 26

83.... Strawberry Yogurt Oatmeal.... 27
84.... Eggs with Spinach and Yogurt.... 27
85.... Peach Oats.... 27
86.... Sausage and Eggs Mix.... 27
87.... Apricots Bread Pudding.... 27
88.... Baguette Boats.... 27
89.... Lamb and Eggs Mix.... 27
90.... Carrot Oatmeal.... 28
91.... Leek Casserole.... 28
92.... Asparagus Egg Casserole.... 28
93.... Sweet Quinoa.... 28
94.... Ginger Apple Bowls.... 28
95.... Breakfast Zucchini Oatmeal.... 28
96.... Creamy Quinoa with Nuts.... 28
97.... Cauliflower Rice Pudding.... 28
98.... Saucy Sriracha Red Beans.... 29
99.... Veggies Casserole.... 29
100.. Crock-pot Breakfast Casserole.... 29
101... Chicken- Pork Meatballs.... 29

LUNCH & DINNER RECIPES.... 29

102.. Beef and Veggie Stew.... 29
103.. Carne Adovada.... 29
104.. Chinese Hot Pot.... 30
105.. Curried Beef Short Ribs.... 30
106.. Fennel Tomato Pasta Sauce.... 30
107... Mixed Pork and Beans.... 30
108.. Parsnip Butternut Squash Stew.... 30
109.. Mexican Shredded Chicken.... 30
110... Spiced Butter Chicken.... 31
111.... Lemon Chicken.... 31
112... White Chicken Cassoulet.... 31
113... Asiago Chickpea Stew.... 31
114... Mushroom Pork Stew.... 31
115... Chicken and Brussels Sprouts Mix.... 31
116... Blue Cheese Chicken.... 31
117... Curry Braised Chicken.... 32
118... Whole Roasted Cauliflower.... 32
119... Wild Mushroom Barley Risotto.... 32
120.. Tomato Sauce Pork Roast.... 32
121... Tofu Chickpea Curry.... 32
122... Pork and Tomatoes Mix.... 32
123... Bavarian Beef Roast.... 32
124... Chicken Tacos.... 33
125... Cauliflower Mashed Sweet Potato.... 33
126... Bean and Spinach Enchilada Sauce.... 33
127... Balsamic Braised Chicken with Swiss Chard.... 33
128.. Three Pepper Roasted Pork Tenderloin.... 33
129... Seafood Soup.... 33
130.. Classic Osso Buco.... 33
131... Chicken Cauliflower Gratin.... 34
132... Beans-rice Mix.... 34
133... Lamb and Onion Stew.... 34
134... Pear Roasted Chicken.... 34
135... Honey Orange Glazed Tofu.... 34
136... Soy Braised Chicken.... 34
137... Eggplant Tapenade.... 34
138.. Buttered Broccoli.... 35
139... Lemon Vegetable Pork Roast.... 35
140.. Beans Chili.... 35
141... Artichoke Soup.... 35
142... Lentils Soup.... 35
143... Chili Verde.... 35
144... Hamburger Beef Casserole.... 35
145... Slow Cooker Jambalaya.... 36
146... Vegetable Pot Pie.... 36
147... Turnip and Beans Casserole.... 36
148.. Italian Style Pork Shoulder.... 36
149... Creamy Chicken Soup.... 36
150.. Vegetable Beef Roast with Horseradish.... 36
151... Cuban Flank Steaks.... 37
152... Three Bean Cornbread Casserole.... 37
153... Onion Pork Chops with Creamy Mustard Sauce.... 37
154... Bourbon Baked Beans.... 37
155... Sweet Glazed Chicken Drumsticks.... 37
156... Asparagus Barley Stew.... 37
157... Honey Apple Pork Chops.... 37
158... Beans and Peas Bowl.... 38
159... Cheesy Chicken Pasta.... 38
160.. Beef Lentil Stew with Goat Cheese.... 38
161... Mustard Pork Chops and Carrots.... 38
162... Spinach Potato Stew.... 38
163... Dumplings with Polenta.... 38
164... Tempeh Carnitas.... 38
165... Chickpea Tikka Masala.... 38
166... Cheesy Chicken Chili.... 39
167... Beef Stroganoff.... 39
168.. Creamed Sweet Corn.... 39
169... Layered Spinach Ricotta Lasagna.... 39
170... Fruity Veal Shanks.... 39
171... Pork and Chorizo Lunch Mix.... 39
172... Tomato Bulgur.... 39
173... Chicken with Corn and Wild Rice.... 40
174... Collard Greens Stew.... 40
175... Honey Orange Glazed Chicken Drumsticks.... 40
176... Chicken with Couscous.... 40
177... Squash and Chicken Soup.... 40
178... Cashew Chicken.... 40
179... Madras Lentils.... 41
180.. Indian Spiced Quinoa Stew.... 41
181... Lentils Curry.... 41
182.. Greek Orzo Chicken.... 41
183.. Pork Stew.... 41
184.. Cheesy Three Bean Chili.... 41
185... Chickpeas Stew.... 41
186.. Corned Beef with Sauerkraut.... 42
187... Bacon Chicken Stew.... 42
188.. Shrimp Stew.... 42
189.. Jamaican Jerk Chicken.... 42

190.. Chicken Layered Potato Casserole.......... 42
191... Beef Barbacoa.......... 42
192... Lime Bean Stew.......... 42
193... Tangy Italian Shredded Beef.......... 43
194... Cinnamon Pork Ribs.......... 43
195... Barley and Bean Tacos.......... 43
196... Chicken Thighs Mix.......... 43
197... Parmesan Biscuit Pot Pie.......... 43
198.. Red Salsa Chicken.......... 43
199... Quinoa Tofu Veggie Stew.......... 43
200.. Chicken and Rice.......... 44
201.. Orange Marmalade Glazed Carrots.......... 44

APPETIZERS RECIPES.......... 44

202.. Carne Asada Nachos.......... 44
203.. Bacon New Potatoes.......... 44
204.. Cheeseburger Meatballs.......... 44
205.. Goat Cheese Stuffed Mushrooms.......... 44
206.. Green Vegetable Dip.......... 45
207.. Spicy Monterey Jack Fondue.......... 45
208.. Quick Layered Appetizer.......... 45
209.. Cranberry Sauce Meatballs.......... 45
210.. Baba Ganoush.......... 45
211... Bacon Wrapped Chicken Livers.......... 45
212... Roasted Bell Peppers Dip.......... 45
213... Spicy Enchilada Dip.......... 46
214... Queso Verde Dip.......... 46
215... Cheesy Mushroom Dip.......... 46
216... Sausage Dip.......... 46
217... Bacon Black Bean Dip.......... 46
218.. Molasses Lime Meatballs.......... 46
219... Ranch Turkey Bites.......... 46
220.. Chipotle BBQ Meatballs.......... 47
221... Four Cheese Dip.......... 47
222.. Candied Kielbasa.......... 47
223.. Creamy Potatoes.......... 47
224.. Honey Glazed Chicken Drumsticks.......... 47
225.. Bacon Chicken Sliders.......... 47
226.. Quick Parmesan Bread.......... 47
227.. Eggplant Caviar.......... 47
228.. Party Mix.......... 48
229.. Stuffed Artichokes.......... 48
230.. Mediterranean Dip.......... 48
231... Cheeseburger Dip.......... 48
232.. Hoisin Chicken Wings.......... 48
233.. Mexican Chili Dip.......... 48
234.. Mixed Olive Dip.......... 48
235.. Spanish Chorizo Dip.......... 49
236.. Boiled Peanuts with Skin On.......... 49
237.. Spicy Asian Style Mushroom.......... 49
238.. Cocktail Meatballs.......... 49
239.. Ham and Swiss Cheese Dip.......... 49
240.. Three Cheese Artichoke Sauce.......... 49
241... Artichoke Bread Pudding.......... 49
242.. Creamy Chicken Dip.......... 50
243.. Oriental Chicken Bites.......... 50
244.. Mexican Dip.......... 50
245.. Chili Corn Cheese Dip.......... 50
246.. Caramelized Onion Dip.......... 50
247.. Pizza Dip.......... 50
248.. Spicy Glazed Pecans.......... 50
249.. Curried Chicken Wings.......... 51
250.. Sweet Corn Jalapeno Dip.......... 51
251... French Onion Dip.......... 51
252.. Cheese and Beer Fondue.......... 51
253.. Bourbon Glazed Sausages.......... 51
254.. Glazed Peanuts.......... 51
255.. Artichoke Dip.......... 51
256.. Cheesy Bacon Dip.......... 51
257.. Taco Dip.......... 52
258.. Bacon Wrapped Dates.......... 52
259.. Bacon Baked Potatoes.......... 52
260.. Marmalade Glazed Meatballs.......... 52
261... Turkey Meatloaf.......... 52
262.. Balsamico Pulled Pork.......... 52
263.. Spicy Chicken Taquitos.......... 52
264.. Beer BBQ Meatballs.......... 53
265.. Chili Chicken Wings.......... 53
266.. Pretzel Party Mix.......... 53
267.. Tahini Cheese Dip.......... 53
268.. Blue Cheese Chicken Wings.......... 53
269.. Tropical Meatballs.......... 53
270.. Five-spiced Chicken Wings.......... 54
271... Spiced Buffalo Wings.......... 54
272.. Classic Bread In A Slow Cooker.......... 54
273.. Bean Queso.......... 54
274.. Zesty Lamb Meatballs.......... 54
275.. White Bean Hummus.......... 54
276.. Mozzarella Stuffed Meatballs.......... 54
277... Charred Tomato Salsa.......... 55
278.. Sausage and Pepper Appetizer.......... 55
279.. Pork Ham Dip.......... 55
280.. Bacon Crab Dip.......... 55
281.. Creamy Spinach Dip.......... 55

BEEF, PORK & LAMB RECIPES.......... 55

282.. Burgers.......... 55
283.. BBQ Beer Beef Tenderloin.......... 56
284.. Sausages In Sweet Currant Sauce.......... 56
285.. Cinnamon Lamb.......... 56
286.. Beef Casserole.......... 56
287.. Pork and Chilies Mix.......... 56

288.. Tomato Beef Chowder....56
289.. Rosemary Lamb Shoulder....56
290.. BBQ Bratwurst....56
291... Cider Pork Roast....56
292.. Beef Soup....57
293.. Beef Stuffing....57
294.. Hot Lamb Strips....57
295.. Chinese Mushroom Pork....57
296.. Soy Sauce Marinated Meatballs....57
297.. Brisket Turnips Medley....57
298.. Italian Pork Chops....57
299.. Sour Cream Roast....58
300.. Beef Roast with Cauliflower....58
301.. Cajun Beef....58
302.. Coconut Beef....58
303.. Cucumber and Pork Cubes Bowl....58
304.. Beef and Pancetta....58
305.. Herbed and Cinnamon Beef....58
306.. Naked Beef Enchilada in A Slow Cooker....59
307.. Jalapeno Mississippi Roast....59
308.. Peppercorn Beef Steak....59
309.. Egg Salad with Ground Pork....59
310.. Salsa Meat....59
311... Balsamic Beef Cheeks....59
312... Lamb Leg and Sweet Potatoes....59
313... Succulent Pork Ribs....59
314... Garlic Lamb Chilli....60
315... Scalloped Potato Casserole....60
316... Pork and Beans Mix....60
317... Cocoa Pork Chops....60
318.. Thyme Beef....60
319... Lavender and Orange Lamb....60
320.. Filet Mignon with Fresh Basil Rub....60
321... Beef with Yams....61
322.. Ginger and Rosemary Pork Ribs....61
323.. Slow Cooker Beef Rendang....61
324.. Lamb and Lime Zucchinis....61
325.. Pickled Pulled Beef....61
326.. Beef Mac & cheese....61
327.. Corned Beef....61
328.. Simple Pork Chop Casserole....62
329.. Pork Roast with Apples....62
330.. Beef and Sauce....62
331... Pork Chops Stuffed with Olives....62
332.. Onion and Bison Soup....62
333.. Pesto Pork Chops....62
334.. Winter Pork with Green Peas....62
335.. Mexican Carne Adovada....62
336.. Pork Roast in Slow Cooker....62
337.. Lamb Cashews Tagine....63
338.. Lamb and Kale....63
339.. London Broil....63
340.. Balsamic Beef....63
341... Mayo Pork Salad....63
342.. Pork Tomatoes....63
343.. Bacon Potatoes with Cheese Inside....63
344.. Cumin Pork Chops....64
345.. Slow Cooker Gingered Pork Stew....64
346.. Rich Lamb Shanks....64
347.. Mussaman Curry....64
348.. Schweinshaxe....64
349.. Easy Slow Cooker Pulled Pork....64
350.. Beef Saute with Endives....64
351... Mexican Pork Roast....64
352.. Onion Beef....65
353.. Pork Sirloin Salsa Mix....65
354.. Lamb Meatballs....65
355.. Beef and Peas....65
356.. Lettuce and Pork Wraps....65
357.. Beef Brisket and Turnips Mix....65
358.. Slow Cooker Pork Carnitas....65
359.. Beef Burger....65
360.. Balsamic Lamb Mix....66
361... Lamb Leg and Mushrooms Mix....66
362.. Garlic Pork Ribs....66
363.. Ginger Beef....66
364.. Beef and Parsnip Saute....66
365.. Slow Cooker Mexican Beef Stew....66
366.. Beef Brisket In Orange Juice....66
367.. Soy Beef Steak....66
368.. Roast with Pepperoncini....67
369.. Parmesan Rosemary Potato....67
370.. Mexican Lamb Fillet....67
371... Caribbean Pork Chop....67
372.. Pork Chops Under Peach Blanket....67
373.. Jamaican Pork Shoulder....67
374.. Lamb Shanks....67
375.. Lamb and Cabbage....68
376.. Beef In Sauce....68
377... Cocktail Beef Meatballs....68
378.. Pork Loin Roast In Slow Cooker....68
379.. Oregano Pork Chops....68
380.. Turkish Meat Saute....68
381.. Bacon Swiss Pork Chops....68

POULTRY RECIPES....69

382.. Horseradish Chicken Wings....69
383.. Turkey with Plums....69
384.. Duck Saute....69
385.. Cilantro Chicken and Eggplant Mix....69
386.. Sauce Goose....69
387.. Mediterranean Chicken....69
388.. Turkey with Olives and Corn....69
389.. Chicken Stroganoff....69
390.. Chopped Chicken Liver Balls....70
391... Oregano Turkey and Tomatoes....70

392.. Citrus Glazed Chicken....70
393.. Chicken and Apples Mix....70
394.. Slow Cooker Salsa Chicken....70
395.. Slow Cooker Fajita Chicken....70
396.. Coriander and Turmeric Chicken....71
397.. Chicken Curry....71
398.. Slow Cooker Caesar Chicken....71
399.. Sun-dried Tomato Chicken....71
400.. Chocolate Chicken Mole....71
401.. Orange Duck Fillets....71
402.. Chicken and Tomatillos....71
403.. Chicken Pepper Chili....72
404.. Duck and Mushrooms....72
405.. Bourbon Honey Chicken....72
406.. Chicken In Apricots....72
407.. Creamy Turkey Mix....72
408.. BBQ Pulled Chicken....72
409.. Cinnamon and Cumin Chicken Drumsticks....72
410.. Chicken Chowder....73
411.. Asian Sesame Chicken....73
412.. Chicken Potato Sandwich....73
413.. Creamy Bacon Chicken....73
414.. Poultry Stew....73
415.. Chili Chicken Liver....73
416.. Mustard Chicken Mix....73
417.. Parsley Chicken Mix....74
418.. Zucchini Chicken....74
419.. Chicken and Beans....74
420.. Goose Mix....74
421.. Sichuan Chicken....74
422.. Chicken and Peppers....74
423.. Chicken Thighs and Mushrooms....74
424.. Chicken Cacciatore....74
425.. Saucy Chicken Thighs....75
426.. Cream Chicken with Spices....75
427.. Turkey Wings and Sauce....75
428.. Chicken and Chickpeas....75
429.. Turkey with Leeks and Radishes....75
430.. Maple Ginger Chicken....75
431.. Cheesy Chicken Breasts....75
432.. Paprika Chicken and Artichokes....76
433.. Chicken Stuffed with Beans....76
434.. Chicken Tomato Salad....76
435.. Cannellini Chicken....76
436.. Turkey Cranberry Stew....76
437.. Chicken Bowl....77
438.. Pulled Maple Chicken....77
439.. Chicken with Vegetables....77
440.. Wine Chicken....77
441.. Garlic Chipotle Lime Chicken....77
442.. Corn and Chicken Saute....77
443.. Chicken Vegetable Pot Pie....77
444.. Ginger Turkey....77
445.. Chicken Parm....78
446.. Spicy Almond-crusted Chicken Nuggets....78
447.. Creamy Duck Breast....78
448.. Lime and Pepper Chicken....78
449.. Curry Drumsticks....78
450.. Parsley Turkey Breast....78
451.. Bacon Chicken....78
452.. Slow Cooked Turkey Delight....79
453.. Ginger Turkey Mix....79
454.. Milk and Lemon Chicken....79
455.. Goose with Mushroom Cream....79
456.. Sheriff Chicken Wings....79
457.. Spinach and Artichoke Chicken....79
458.. Simple Chicken and Vegetables....79
459.. Russian Chicken....80
460.. Apple Chicken Bombs....80
461.. Chicken Stew In A Slow Cooker....80
462.. Cauliflower Chicken....80
463.. Citrus Chicken....80
464.. Creamy Mexican Slow Cooker Chicken....80
465.. Chicken and Asparagus....81
466.. Buffalo Chicken....81
467.. Stuffed Chicken Fillets....81
468.. Duck Breast and Veggies....81
469.. Moscow Bacon Chicken....81
470.. Chicken Casserole....81
471.. Basil Chicken Wings....81
472.. Chicken Thighs Delight....82
473.. Okra Chicken Saute....82
474.. Turkey with Rice....82
475.. Basil Chicken....82
476.. Chicken In Onion Rings....82
477.. Jerk Chicken....82
478.. Chicken Broccoli Casserole....82
479.. Lemongrass Chicken Thighs....83
480.. Slow Cooker Chicken Breasts....83
481.. Turkey and Avocado....83

FISH & SEAFOOD RECIPES....83

482.. Butter Crab....83
483.. Cilantro Salmon....83
484.. Slow Cooker Greek Snapper....83
485.. Indian Fish....83
486.. Parsley Salmon....83
487.. Chili Tamarind Mackerel....84
488.. Five-spice Tilapia....84
489.. Seafood Chowder....84
490.. Butter Dipped Crab Legs....84
491.. Shrimp, Salmon and Tomatoes Mix....84
492.. Spiced Mackerel....84
493.. Shrimp Mix....84
494.. Snapper Ragout....85
495.. Cream White Fish....85

496.. Chinese Cod....85
497.. Lamb Bacon Stew....85
498.. Spicy Cajun Scallops....85
499.. Tabasco Halibut....85
500.. Tuna Loin Mix....85
501.. Creamy Onion Casserole....86
502.. Salmon Croquettes....86
503.. Mustard-crusted Salmon....86
504.. Milky Fish....86
505.. Bacon-wrapped Salmon....86
506.. Prosciutto-wrapped Scallops....86
507.. Thyme Mussels....86
508.. Slow Cooker Smoked Trout....87
509.. Creamy Tuna and Scallions....87
510.. Vinaigrette Dipped Salmon....87
511... Slow Cooker Tuna Spaghetti....87
512... Nutmeg Trout....87
513... Simple Slow Cooker Steamed Crab....87
514... Mussels, Clams and Chorizo Mix....87
515... Jambalaya....87
516... Salmon Salad....88
517... Dill Shrimp Mix....88
518... Mackerel and Lemon....88
519... Fish Pudding....88
520.. Onion Cod Fillets....88
521... Butter Crab Legs....88
522.. Shrimp and Rice Mix....88
523.. Chives Shrimp....89
524.. Fish Pie....89
525.. Shrimp and Pineapple Bowls....89
526.. Mustard Cod....89
527.. Cheesy Fish Dip....89
528.. Salmon, Tomatoes and Green Beans....89
529.. Maple Mustard Salmon....89
530.. Thai Style Flounder....89
531... Cod with Asparagus....90
532.. Shrimp and Mango Mix....90
533.. Sweet and Mustard Tilapia....90
534.. Cod and Broccoli....90
535.. Broiled Tilapia....90
536.. Hot Calamari....90
537.. Poached Cod and Pineapple Mix....90
538.. Fish Hot Dog Sticks....91
539.. Fish Mix....91
540.. Alaska Salmon with Pecan Crunch Coating....91
541... Sage Shrimps....91
542.. Seabass Ragout....91
543.. Teriyaki Tilapia....91
544.. Turmeric Coconut Squid....91
545.. Chinese Mackerel....92
546.. Thyme and Sesame Halibut....92
547.. Taco Shrimps....92
548.. Tuna and Chimichurri....92
549.. Spicy Creole Shrimp....92
550.. Shrimps Boil....92
551... Thai Salmon Cakes....93
552.. Pesto Salmon....93
553.. Fish Pie....93
554.. Dill Crab Cutlets....93
555.. Italian Trout Croquettes....93
556.. Rice Stuffed Squid....93
557... BBQ Shrimps....93
558.. Herbed Shrimps....94
559.. Salmon Chickpea Fingers....94
560.. Octopus and Veggies Mix....94
561... Japanese Cod Fillet....94
562.. Easy Salmon and Kimchi Sauce....94
563.. Mackerel Stuffed Tacos....94
564.. Cod Sticks....95
565.. Shrimp and Peas Soup....95
566.. Tuna and Brussels Sprouts....95
567.. Creamy Shrimp....95
568.. Salmon and Berries....95
569.. Salmon Picatta....95
570.. Coconut Catfish....95
571... Shrimps and Carrot Saute....96
572.. Bigeye Jack Saute....96
573.. Flounder Cheese Casserole....96
574.. Pineapple Milkfish....96
575... Mussels Tomato Soup....96
576.. Shrimp and Avocado....96
577... Cod and Clams Saute....96
578.. Shrimp Chicken Jambalaya....96
579.. Chili Shrimp and Zucchinis....97
580.. Sriracha Shrimp....97
581... Fish Tart....97

SOUPS & STEWS RECIPES....97

582.. Split Pea Sausage Soup....97
583.. Fish Sweet Corn Soup....97
584.. Tomato and Turkey Chili....97
585.. Ham and White Bean Soup....98
586.. Paprika Noddle Soup....98
587.. Herbed Chickpea Soup....98
588.. Shredded Beef Soup....98
589.. Chicken Sausage Rice Soup....98
590.. Leek Potato Soup....98
591... Mussel Stew....98
592.. Lobster Stew....99
593.. Hungarian Goulash Soup....99
594.. Hot Lentil Soup....99
595.. Curried Corn Chowder....99
596.. Salmon Fennel Soup....99
597.. Tuscan Kale and White Bean Soup....99
598.. Crock-pot Low-carb Taco Soup....99
599.. Smoked Sausage Stew....100

600..Celery Soup with Ham 100
601.. Fennel Stew 100
602..Coconut Squash Soup 100
603..Posole Soup 100
604..Mexican Style Stew 100
605..Roasted Garlic Soup 100
606..Tomato Beef Soup 101
607..Chunky Pumpkin and Kale Soup 101
608..Butternut Squash Soup 101
609..Ham and Sweet Potato Soup 101
610..Mexican Style Soup 101
611...Barley Stew 101
612...Cream Of Broccoli Soup 101
613...Black Bean Soup 102
614...Lamb Stew 102
615...Tuscan White Bean Soup 102
616...Chicken Wild Rice Soup 102
617...Summer Vegetable Soup 102
618.. Tomato Chickpeas Stew 102
619...Bacon Cheeseburger Soup 102
620..Broccoli Cheese Soup 103
621...Creamy Edamame Soup 103
622.. Beans Stew 103
623..Creamy Potato Soup 103
624..Beef Liver Stew 103
625..Mexican Beef Soup 103
626..Spicy Black Bean Soup 104
627.. Garlicky Spinach Soup with Herbed Croutons 104
628..Jamaican Stew 104
629..Hearty Turkey Chili 104
630..Creamy Tortellini Soup 104
631...Paprika Hominy Stew 104
632.. Lentil Soup with Garlic Topping 104
633..Clam Soup 105
634..Creamy Spinach Tortellini Soup 105
635..Cabbage Stew 105
636..Chicken Chili 105
637..Chunky Potato Ham Soup 105
638..Lemony Salmon Soup 105
639..Hot and Sour Soup 105
640..Lentil Stew 106
641...Light Zucchini Soup 106
642..Mexican Chicken Stew 106
643..French Onion Soup 106
644..Beef Chili 106
645..Tomato Fish Soup 106
646..Ginger and Sweet Potato Stew 106
647..Barley Soup 107
648..Chorizo Soup 107
649..Summer Squash Chickpea Soup 107
650..Indian Cauliflower Creamy Soup 107
651...Shrimp Soup 107
652..Ham Potato Chowder 107
653..Beef Mushroom Soup 108
654..Taco Soup 108
655..Pork and Corn Soup 108
656..Southwestern Turkey Stew 108
657..Bean Medley Soup 108
658..Kielbasa Kale Soup 108
659..Thick Green Lentil Soup 108
660..Green Peas Chowder 109
661...Bouillabaisse Soup 109

VEGETABLE & VEGETARIAN RECIPES 109

662..Marinated Poached Aubergines 109
663..Rainbow Bake 109
664..White Beans Luncheon 109
665..Spicy Okra 109
666..Creamy Puree 110
667..Coconut Milk Lentils Bowl 110
668..Cauliflower Mac and Cheese 110
669..Sweet Potato and Lentils Pate 110
670..Lentil Rice Salad 110
671...Minestrone Zucchini Soup 110
672..Potato Balls 110
673..Creamy Corn Chili 110
674..Asian Broccoli Sauté 111
675..Bulgur Sauté 111
676..Cauliflower Curry 111
677..Cardamom Pumpkin Wedges 111
678..Mushroom Steaks 111
679..Spicy Eggplant with Red Pepper and Parsley 111
680..Couscous Halloumi Salad 111
681..Teriyaki Kale 111
682..Jalapeno Corn 112
683..Oat Fritters 112
684..Shredded Cabbage Saute 112
685..Eggplant Salad 112
686..Zucchini Mash 112
687..Chorizo Cashew Salad 112
688..Garam Masala Potato Bake 112
689..Broccoli Fritters 113
690..Vegan Kofte 113
691...Pumpkin Hummus 113
692..Sauteed Garlic 113
693..Rice Stuffed Apple Cups 113
694..Mung Beans Salad 113
695..Creamy Keto Mash 113
696..Chili Dip 114
697..Eggplant Mini Wraps 114
698..Zucchini Spinach Lasagne 114
699..Collard Greens Saute 114
700..Corn Pudding 114
701...Braised Root Vegetables 114
702..Slow Cooker Mediterranean Eggplant Salad 114
703..Bulgur Mushroom Chili 114

704.. Warming Butternut Squash Soup 115
705.. Rice Cauliflower Casserole 115
706.. Sweet Pineapple Tofu 115
707.. Mushroom Saute 115
708.. Sweet Onions 115
709.. Potato Parmesan Pie 115
710... Braised Swiss Chard 116
711... Potato Bake 116
712... Garlic Gnocchi 116
713... Sweet Potato Tarragon Soup 116
714... Mushroom Risotto 116
715... Chili Okra 116
716... Carrot Strips 116
717... Rainbow Carrots 117
718... Yam Fritters 117
719... Cauliflower Stuffing 117
720.. Arugula and Halloumi Salad 117
721... Zucchini Basil Soup 117
722.. Stuffed Okra 117
723.. Hot Sauce Oysters Mushrooms 117
724.. Sautéed Endives 117
725.. Fragrant Jackfruit 118
726.. Eggplant Casserole 118
727... Sweet Potato Puree 118
728.. Fragrant Appetizer Peppers 118
729.. Spaghetti Cheese Casserole 118
730.. Vegetable Bean Stew 118
731... Onion Chives Muffins 119
732.. Creamy White Mushrooms 119
733.. Paprika Okra 119
734.. Quinoa Fritters 119
735.. Tofu and Cauliflower Bowl 119
736.. Pumpkin Chili 119
737... Butter Hasselback Potatoes 119
738.. Parsnip Balls 119
739.. Swedish Style Beets 120
740.. Fennel Lentils 120
741... Curry Couscous 120
742.. Zucchini Soup with Rosemary and Parmesan 120
743.. Thyme Tomatoes 120
744.. Quinoa Casserole 120
745.. Pumpkin Bean Chili 120
746.. Marinated Jalapeno Rings 120
747.. Tri-bean Chili 121
748.. Butter Asparagus 121
749.. Honey Carrot Gravy 121
750.. Zucchini Caviar 121
751... Broccoli Egg Pie 121
752.. Vegan Pepper Bowl 121
753.. Pinto Beans with Rice 122
754.. French Vegetable Stew 122
755... Squash Noodles 122
756.. Beet and Capers Salad 122
757... Rice Stuffed Eggplants 122
758.. Brussel Sprouts 122
759.. Ranch Broccoli 122
760.. Aromatic Marinated Mushrooms 123
761... Spinach with Halloumi Cheese Casserole 123

SNACK RECIPES 123

762.. Bean Dip 123
763.. Tacos 123
764.. Tomato and Mushroom Salsa 123
765.. Nuts Bowls 123
766.. Chickpeas Spread 123
767.. Rice Snack Bowls 124
768.. Carrot Broccoli Fritters 124
769.. Jalapeno Poppers 124
770.. Creamy Mushroom Bites 124
771... Simple Salsa 124
772... Salsa Snack 124
773... Garlicky Bacon Slices 125
774.. Apple Jelly Sausage Snack 125
775... White Cheese & Green Chilies Dip 125
776.. Cheeseburger Cream Dip 125
777... Cheese Stuffed Meat Balls 125
778.. Eggplant Dip 125
779.. Salsa Corn Dip 126
780.. Cheesy Potato Dip 126
781... Chicken Meatballs 126
782.. Crock-pot Coconut Cake 126
783.. Curry Pork Meatballs 126
784.. Bulgur and Beans Salsa 126
785.. Broccoli Dip 126
786.. Chicken Taco Nachos 127
787.. Peanut Snack 127
788.. Chicken Salad 127
789.. Crock-pot Citrus Cake 127
790.. Beef and Chipotle Dip 127
791... Lentils Dip 127
792.. Zucchini Spread 128
793.. Zucchini Sticks 128
794.. Macadamia Nuts Snack 128
795.. Stuffed Peppers Platter 128
796.. Calamari Rings Bowls 128
797.. Mixed Nuts 128
798.. Spicy Mussels 128
799.. Piquant Mushrooms 129
800. Almond Spread 129
801.. Black Bean Salsa Salad 129
802.. Apple Sausage Snack 129
803.. Black Eyes Peas Dip 129
804.. Mozzarella Basil Tomatoes 129
805.. Fava Bean Onion Dip 129
806.. Potato Cups 130
807.. Cauliflower Bites 130

808.. Wild Rice Pilaf....130
809.. Potato Onion Salsa....130
810.. Almond Bowls....130
811... Caramel Corn....130
812.. Eggplant Salsa....130
813.. Queso Dip....131
814.. Cauliflower Dip....131
815... Cashew Dip....131
816.. Cheesy Corn Dip....131
817... Lemony Artichokes....131
818.. Lentils Hummus....131
819.. Buffalo Meatballs....131
820.. Thyme Pepper Shrimp....132
821.. Cinnamon Pecans Snack....132
822.. Onion Dip....132
823.. Veggie Spread....132
824.. Stuffed Mushrooms....132
825.. Crab Dip....132
826.. Beef Meatballs....132
827.. Sweet Potato Dip....132
828.. Jalapeno Onion Dip....133
829.. Paprika Cod Sticks....133
830.. Spicy Dip....133
831.. Potato Salsa....133
832.. Mushroom Salsa....133
833.. Butter Stuffed Chicken Balls....133
834.. Tostadas....134
835.. Hummus....134
836.. Ginger Chili Peppers....134
837.. Crumbly Chickpeas Snack....134
838.. Spinach Dip....134
839.. White Bean Spread....134
840.. Pork Stuffed Tamales....134
841.. Tamales....135

SIDE DISH RECIPES....135

842.. Green Beans with Mushrooms....135
843.. Berry Wild Rice....135
844.. Herbed Balsamic Beets....135
845.. Tomato and Corn Mix....136
846.. Zucchini Casserole....136
847.. Italian Black Beans Mix....136
848.. Barley Mix....136
849.. Cauliflower Rice and Spinach....136
850.. Chicken with Sweet Potato....136
851... Slow-cooked White Onions....136
852.. Okra and Corn....137
853.. Summer Squash Mix....137
854.. Marjoram Rice Mix....137
855.. Summer Squash Medley....137
856.. Cream Cheese Macaroni....137
857.. Saucy Macaroni....137
858.. Paprika Green Beans and Zucchinis....137
859.. Peas and Carrots....138
860.. White Beans Mix....138
861.. Cabbage and Kale Mix....138
862.. Sweet Potato and Cauliflower Mix....138
863.. Zucchini Mix....138
864.. Savoy Cabbage Mix....138
865.. Carrot and Beet Side Salad....138
866.. Tangy Red Potatoes....139
867.. Ramen Noodles....139
868.. Mexican Rice....139
869.. Cinnamon Applesauce....139
870.. Rice with Artichokes....139
871... Balsamic Okra Mix....139
872.. Cauliflower and Broccoli Mix....139
873.. Parsley Mushroom Mix....140
874.. Glazed Baby Carrots....140
875.. Mexican Avocado Rice....140
876.. Spinach Mix....140
877.. Carrot Beet Salad....140
878.. Veggies Rice Pilaf....140
879.. Mint Farro Pilaf....140
880.. Cornbread Cream Pudding....140
881.. Zucchini Crackers Casserole....141
882.. Potatoes and Leeks Mix....141
883.. Garlic Squash Mix....141
884.. Garlic Mushrooms....141
885.. Butter Green Beans....141
886.. Beets Side Salad....141
887.. Okra Side Dish....142
888.. Stewed Okra....142
889.. Maple Brussels Sprouts....142
890.. Minty Peas and Tomatoes....142
891.. Scalloped Potatoes....142
892.. Butternut Squash and Eggplant Mix....142
893.. Balsamic Cauliflower....142
894.. Hot Zucchini Mix....142
895.. Thai Side Salad....143
896.. Nut and Berry Side Salad....143
897.. Mashed Potatoes....143
898.. Veggie Medley....143
899.. Cider Dipped Farro....143
900.. Apples and Potatoes....143
901.. Farro....143
902.. Cabbage Mix....144
903.. Spinach Rice....144
904.. BBQ Beans....144
905.. Eggplants with Mayo Sauce....144
906.. Lime Beans Mix....144
907.. Zucchini Onion Pate....144
908.. Parmesan Spinach Mix....144
909.. Sweet Potatoes with Bacon....145
910.. Thyme Mushrooms and Corn....145
911... Italian Eggplant....145

912...Nut Berry Salad......145
913...Corn and Bacon......145
914...Mustard Brussels Sprouts......145
915...Mac Cream Cups......145
916...Corn Sauté......146
917...Kale Mix......146
918.. Orange Squash......146
919...Mashed Potatoes......146
920.. Bean Medley......146
921...Italian Squash and Peppers Mix......146

DESSERT RECIPES......146

922.. Lavender Blackberry Crumble......146
923.. Granola Apples......147
924.. Grain Free Chocolate Cake......147
925.. Pumpkin Bars......147
926.. Chia Muffins......147
927.. Lemon Poppy Seed Cake......147
928.. Raisin-flax Meal Bars......147
929.. Prune Bake......148
930.. Dark Chocolate Almond Cake......148
931...Coconut Poached Pears......148
932.. Peach Cobbler......148
933.. Lemon Cream......148
934.. Cardamom Plums......148
935.. Orange and Apricot Jam......148
936.. Cinnamon Rice Milk Cocktail......148
937.. Matcha Shake......149
938.. Cinnamon Rolls......149
939.. Rhubarb Stew......149
940.. Raspberry Nutmeg Cake......149
941...Greek Cream......149
942.. Citron Vanilla Bars......149
943.. Berry Marmalade......150
944.. Apricot and Peaches Cream......150
945.. Mint Summer Drink......150
946.. Dark Cherry Chocolate Cake......150
947.. Fudgy Raspberry Chocolate Bread Pudding......150
948.. Banana Cake......150
949.. Red Muffins......150
950.. Hazelnut Liqueur Cheesecake......150
951...Coconut and Macadamia Cream......151
952.. Creamy Rhubarb and Plums Bowls......151
953.. Berries Salad......151
954.. Cottage Cheese Ramekins......151
955.. Spiced Plum Butter......151
956.. Cardamom Lemon Pie......151
957.. Amaranth Bars......151
958.. Apricot Spoon Cake......151
959.. Butterscotch Self Saucing Pudding......152
960.. Chocolate Cake......152
961...Vanilla Bean Caramel Custard......152
962.. Monkey Bread......152
963.. Pears and Sauce......152
964.. Mint Cookies......152
965.. Cinnamon Plum Jam......153
966.. Chocolate Mocha Bread Pudding......153
967.. Creamy Dark Chocolate Dessert......153
968.. Coffee Cinnamon Roll......153
969.. Caramelized Bananas......153
970.. Cardamom Rice Porridge......153
971...Golden Syrup Pudding......153
972.. Cherry Dump Cake......153
973.. Honey Yogurt Cake......154
974.. Mocha Chocolate Brioche Pudding......154
975.. Banana Muffins......154
976.. Butternut Squash Pudding......154
977.. Classic Apple Pie......154
978.. Mango Cream......154
979.. Lemony Orange Marmalade......154
980.. Rich Bread Pudding......154
981.. Pear Crumble......155
982.. Fig Bars......155
983.. Milk Fondue......155
984.. Pear Apple Jam......155
985.. Summer Fruits Compote......155
986.. Cherry Bowls......155
987.. Baked Goat Cheese Balls......155
988.. Sweet Milk Souffle......155
989.. Quinoa Pudding......156
990.. Spongy Banana Bread......156
991...Cinnamon Apples......156
992.. Saucy Peach and Apple Dessert......156
993.. Caramel Apple Crisp......156
994.. Pavlova......156
995.. Pumpkin Croissant Pudding......156
996.. Vanilla Buns......157
997.. Classic Banana Foster......157
998.. Blueberry Tapioca Pudding......157
999.. Bread and Berries Pudding......157
1000. Peanut Sweets......157
1001. Cranberry Cookies......157

Recipe Index 158

Introduction

A slow cooker is a great cooking method for someone who's busy and wants to prepare easy meals without having to spend a lot of time in the kitchen. It's the "set it and forget it" kind of meal preparation method that cooks your food for multiple hours, hence the name "slow cooker."

Most slow cookers have timers that allow for a meal to be slow cooked throughout the day — but not overcooked — and then switched to a "warm" setting so the food remains hot and safe to eat. To maximize the taste and texture of your meal and to avoid overcooking, it's important to follow the indicated cooking times on the recipe you're following. But, if you get delayed for an hour or so, your slow cooker meal is probably okay for a couple of hours if it defaults to the warm setting once it is finished cooking.

Not every slow cooker recipe is equally healthy

Like every cooking method, there's almost always a way to make a meal that trends toward unhealthy — slow cooker cooking included.

When scanning a slow cooker recipe, watch out for too many:

- High-fat ingredients, such as cream-based soups, cream cheese and butter
- High-sodium ingredients, such as canned vegetables, broths, soups or beans
- High-carb, low-veggie ingredient lists, such as pastas or casserole-like dishes

In addition, if you choose a slow cooker recipe that's meat-heavy, such as pulled pork, be sure to have plenty of veggies as a side to complete your well-balanced meal.

The good news, however, is that — with a little planning — almost any recipe can be modified to reduce its fat, sodium, sugar or carbohydrate content.

Ingredient substitutions that can make any slow cooker recipe healthier

If you stumble on a slow cooker recipe you want to try, but it contains some of the unhealthier ingredients above, you can almost always make some healthier substitutions!

Here are some substitutions and other ideas to help boost the healthfulness of your slow cooker dish:

- Choose whole-grain options over refined carbohydrates. For instance, swap white pasta with whole-grain pasta or beans. Whole-grain choices add both fiber and protein to your dish.
- Rinse and drain canned vegetables and beans. Canned items are typically high in sodium, and draining the liquid can help lower the sodium content.
- Replace mayonnaise with Greek yogurt. Given their similar textures and cooking behaviors, this swap gives you less fat and more protein.
- Cut the cheese. Many recipes call for multiple cups of cheese, but you can typically cut this amount, and therefore the fat (and sodium) content, by half.
- More herbs, less salt. To help pack a flavorful punch while staying healthy, opt for fresh or dried herbs instead of more salt.

10 top tips for using a slow cooker

Slow cookers are cheap to buy, economical to use and they're great for making the most of budget ingredients. They offer a healthier, low-fat method of cooking and require the minimum amount of effort. Really, what's not to love?

1. Cut down your prep time

One of the main attractions for many people is the ease of a slow cooker, so when you're looking for recipes, avoid those that suggest a lot of pre-preparation. For many dishes, particularly soups and stews, you really can just throw all the ingredients in. It can be nice to cook the onions beforehand, as the flavour is different to when you put them in raw, but experiment both ways as you may find you prefer one. It can also be good to brown meat to give it some colour, but again, this is not essential.

2. Prepare for slow cooking the night before

If you're short on time in the morning, prepare everything you need for your slow-cooked meal the night before, put it into the slow-cooker dish, cover and store in the fridge overnight. Ideally the dish should be as close to room temperature as possible, so get it out of the fridge when you wake up and leave it for 20 minutes before turning the cooker on. If you need to heat your dish beforehand, then put the ingredients in a different container and transfer them in the morning.

3. Choose cheap cuts

Slow cookers are great for cooking cheaper cuts like beef brisket, pork shoulder, lamb shoulder and chicken thighs. You can also use less meat, as slow cooking really extracts a meaty flavour that permeates the whole dish. Bulk up with vegetables instead.

4. Trim fat from meat before slow cooking

You don't need to add oil to a slow cooker – the contents won't catch as long as there's enough moisture in there. You don't need a lot of fat on your meat either. Normally when you fry meat, a lot of the fat drains away, but this won't happen in a slow cooker so trim it off – otherwise you might find you have pools of oil in your stew. Removing the fat will give you a healthier result, and it'll still be tasty.

5. Reduce liquid when using a slow cooker

Because your slow cooker will have a tightly sealed lid, the liquid won't evaporate so if you're adapting a standard recipe, it's best to reduce the liquid by roughly a third. It should just cover the meat and vegetables. Don't overfill your slow cooker, or it may start leaking out the top, and the food won't cook so well. Half to two-thirds full is ideal – certainly no more than three-quarters.

6. Use flour to thicken sauces

Just as the liquid doesn't reduce, it also doesn't thicken. You can roll meat in a small amount of seasoned flour before adding it to the slow cooker or use a little cornflour at the end. If you want to do the latter, take a teaspoon or two of cornflour and mix it to a paste with a little cold water. Stir into your simmering slow cooker contents, then replace the lid.

7. Use the slow cooker low setting

Use the 'Low' setting as much as you can, finding that most dishes really benefit from a slow, gentle heat to really bring out the flavours. This also means you won't need to worry if you're heading out for the day – it'll take care of itself.

8. Leave your slow cooker recipe alone

Slow cookers are designed to do their own thing, so you don't need to keep checking the contents. Every time you take the lid off it will release some of the heat, so if you keep doing this you'll have to increase the cooking time.

9. Add all ingredients at the start (most of the time)

Ideally you want to choose recipes where most, if not all, of the ingredients can be added at the beginning, leaving you free to do other things. However, in most cases, pasta, rice and fresh herbs will need to be added towards the end.

10. How long should I cook a slow cooker recipe?

If a dish usually takes:

- 15-30 mins, cook it for 1-2 hours on High or 4-6 hours on Low
- 30 mins – 1 hour, cook it for 2-3 hours on High or 5-7 hours on Low
- 1-2 hours, cook it for 3-4 hours on High or 6-8 hours on Low
- 2-4 hours, cook it for 4-6 hours on High or 8-12 hours on Low

Root vegetables can take longer than meat and other vegetables so put these near the heat source, at the bottom of the pot.

14-Day Meal Plan

Meal Plan	Breakfast	Lunch	Dinner
Day-1	Breakfast Casserole	Cilantro Salmon	Beef and Veggie Stew
Day-2	Shrimp Omelet	Shrimp Mix	Cauliflower Mac and Cheese
Day-3	Milk Oatmeal	Creamy Puree	Asiago Chickpea Stew
Day-4	Italian Style Scrambled Eggs	Chili Tamarind Mackerel	BBQ Beer Beef Tenderloin
Day-5	Butter Oatmeal	Spicy Okra	Bavarian Beef Roast
Day-5	Zesty Pumpkin Cubes	Hot Lamb Strips	Chicken Tacos
Day-7	French Toast	Wild Mushroom Barley Risotto	Five-spice Tilapia
Day-8	Eggs and Sausage Casserole	Cauliflower Curry	Salmon Croquettes
Day-9	Breakfast Pork Ground	Squash and Chicken Soup	Asian Broccoli Sauté
Day-10	Cauliflower Casserole	Cream White Fish	Eggplant Salad
Day-11	Cranberry Maple Oatmeal	Salsa Meat	Chicken Layered Potato Casserole
Day-12	Herbed Egg Scramble	Horseradish Chicken Wings	Indian Fish
Day-13	Jalapeno Muffins	Mexican Shredded Chicken	Mushroom Steaks
Day-14	Raspberry Chia Porridge	Couscous Halloumi Salad	Mustard Pork Chops and Carrots

Breakfast Recipes

Radish Bowl

Servings:4 Cooking Time: 1.5 Hrs.

Ingredients:

2 cups radish, halved
1 tbsp. olive oil
1/4 tsp. salt
1 tbsp. dried dill
4 eggs, beaten
1/4 cup milk

Directions:

Mix radish with dried dill, olive oil, salt, and milk and transfer in the Slow Cooker.
Cook the radish on High for 30 Min.
Then shake the vegetables well and add eggs. Mix the mixture gently and close the lid.
Cook the meal on High for 1 Hr.

Apple Crumble

Servings:2 Cooking Time: 5 Hrs.

Ingredients:

1 tbsp. liquid honey
4 oz. granola
1 tbsp. almond butter
2 Granny Smith apples
4 tbsps. water
1 tsp. vanilla extract

Directions:

Cut the apple into small wedges.
Remove the seeds from the apples and chop them into small pieces.
Put them in the Slow Cooker.
Add water, almond butter, vanilla extract, and honey.
Cook the apples for 5 Hrs. on Low.
Then stir them carefully.
Put the cooked apples and granola one-by-one in the serving glasses.

Bacon and Egg Casserole

Servings: 8 Cooking Time: 5 Hrs.

Ingredients:

20 oz. hash browns
1/2 cup milk
8 oz. cheddar cheese, shredded
6 green onions, chopped
Cooking spray
12 eggs
8 bacon slices, cooked and chopped
Salt and black pepper to the taste

Salsa for serving

Directions:

Grease your Slow Cooker with cooking spray, spread hash browns, cheese, bacon and green onions and toss.
In a bowl, mix the eggs with salt, pepper and milk and whisk really well.
Pour this over hash browns, cover and cook on Low for 5 Hrs.
Divide between plates and serve with salsa on top.

Ham Omelet

Servings: 2 Cooking Time: 3 Hrs.

Ingredients:

Cooking spray
1 tbsp. sour cream
1 small yellow onion, chopped
1/2 cup cheddar cheese, shredded
A pinch of salt and black pepper
4 eggs, whisked
2 spring onions, chopped
1/2 cup ham, chopped
1 tbsp. chives, chopped

Directions:

Grease your Slow Cooker with the cooking spray and mix the eggs with the sour cream, spring onions and the other ingredients inside.
Toss the mix, spread into the pot, put the lid on and cook on High for 3 Hrs.
Divide the mix between plates and serve for breakfast right away.

Breakfast Casserole

Servings:5 Cooking Time: 7 Hrs.

Ingredients:

1 cup Cheddar cheese, shredded
1/2 cup carrot, grated
1/2 tsp. cayenne pepper
5 oz. ham, chopped
1 potato, peeled, diced
1 tsp. ground turmeric
5 eggs, beaten
1/2 cup bell pepper, chopped

Directions:

Make the layer from potato in the Slow Cooker mold.
Then put the layer of carrot over the potatoes.
Sprinkle the vegetables with ground turmeric and cayenne pepper.
Then add ham and bell pepper.
Pour the beaten eggs over the casserole and top with shredded cheese.
Cook the meal on LOW for 7 Hrs.

Peach, Vanilla and Oats Mix

Servings: 2 Cooking Time: 8 Hrs.

Ingredients:

1/2 cup steel cut oats
1/2 cup peaches, pitted and roughly chopped
1 tsp. cinnamon powder
2 cups almond milk
1/2 tsp. vanilla extract

Directions:

In your Slow Cooker, mix the oats with the almond milk, peaches and the other ingredients, toss, put the lid on and cook on Low for 8 Hrs.
Divide into bowls and serve for breakfast right away.

Omelet with Greens

Servings:2 Cooking Time: 2 Hrs.

Ingredients:

3 eggs, beaten
1 cup baby arugula, chopped
1 tsp. avocado oil
1/4 cup milk
1/2 tsp. salt

Directions:

In the bowl mix eggs with milk, salt, and arugula.
Then sprinkle the Slow Cooker with avocado oil from inside.
Pour the omelet egg mixture in the Slow Cooker and close the lid.

Cook the meal on High for 2 Hrs.

Egg Bake

Servings: 8 Cooking Time: 8 Hrs.

Ingredients:

20 oz. tater tots
6 oz. bacon, chopped
12 eggs
1 cup milk
4 tbsps. white flour
2 yellow onions, chopped
2 cups cheddar cheese, shredded
1/4 cup parmesan, grated
Salt and black pepper to the taste
Cooking spray

Directions:

Grease your Slow Cooker with cooking spray and layer half of the tater tots, onions, bacon, cheddar and parmesan.
Continue layering the rest of the tater tots, bacon, onions, parmesan and cheddar.
In a bowl, mix the eggs with milk, salt, pepper and flour and whisk well.
Pour this into the Slow Cooker, cover and cook on Low for 8 Hrs.
Slice, divide between plates and serve for breakfast.

Shrimp Omelet

Servings:4 Cooking Time: 3.5 Hrs.

Ingredients:

4 eggs, beaten
1/2 tsp. ground turmeric
1/4 tsp. salt
4 oz. shrimps, peeled
1/2 tsp. ground paprika
Cooking spray

Directions:

Mix eggs with shrimps, turmeric, salt, and paprika.
Then spray the Slow Cooker bowl with cooking spray.
After this, pour the egg mixture inside. Flatten the shrimps and close the lid.
Cook the omelet for 3.5 Hrs. on High.

Lentils and Quinoa Mix

Servings: 6 Cooking Time: 8 Hrs.

Ingredients:

3 garlic cloves, minced
1 celery stalk, chopped
12 oz. canned tomatoes, chopped
1 cup lentils
2 tbsps. chili powder
1 tbsps. oregano, chopped
1 yellow onion, chopped
2 red bell peppers, chopped
4 cups veggie stock
14 oz. pinto beans
1/2 cup quinoa
2 tsp. cumin, ground

Directions:

In your Slow Cooker, mix garlic with the onion, celery, bell peppers, tomatoes, stock, lentils, pinto beans, chili powder, quinoa, oregano and cumin, stir, cover, cook on Low for 8 Hrs., divide between plates and serve for breakfast

Mayo Sausage Rolls

Servings: 11 Cooking Time: 3 Hrs.

Ingredients:

1 lb. puff pastry
1 tbsp. mustard
10 oz. breakfast sausages
1 tbsp. mayo
2 tbsp. flour
1 egg, whisked
1 tsp. paprika

Directions:

Spread the puff pastry with a rolling pin and drizzle flour over it.
Slice the puff pastry into long thick strips.
Spread mustard, mayonnaise, and paprika on top of each pastry strip.
Place one sausage piece at one end of each strip.
Roll the puff pastry strip and brush the rolls with whisked egg.
Cover the base of your Slow Cooker with a parchment sheet.
Place the puff pastry rolls in the cooker.
Put the cooker's lid on and set the cooking time to 3 Hrs. on High settings.
Serve fresh.

Milk Oatmeal

Servings:4 Cooking Time: 2 Hrs.

Ingredients:

2 cups oatmeal
1 cup milk
1 tsp. vanilla extract
1/4 tsp. ground cinnamon
1 cup of water
1 tbsp. liquid honey
1 tbsp. coconut oil

Directions:

Put all ingredients except liquid honey in the Slow Cooker and mix.
Close the lid and cook the meal on High for 2 Hrs.
Then stir the cooked oatmeal and transfer in the serving bowls.
Top the meal with a small amount of liquid honey.

Hash Brown and Bacon Casserole

Servings: 2 Cooking Time: 3 Hrs.

Ingredients:

5 oz. hash browns, shredded
1/4 cup mozzarella cheese, shredded
1/4 cup sour cream
1 tbsp. olive oil
2 bacon slices, cooked & chopped
2 eggs, whisked
1 tbsp. cilantro, chopped
A pinch of salt and black pepper

Directions:

Grease your Slow Cooker with the oil, add the hash browns mixed with the eggs, sour cream and the other ingredients, toss, put the lid on and cook on High for 4 Hrs.
Divide the casserole into bowls and serve.

French Breakfast Pudding

Servings: 4 Cooking Time: 1 Hr. and 30 Min

Ingredients:

3 egg yolks
1 tsp. vanilla extract
6 oz. double cream
2 tbsps. caster sugar

Directions:

In a bowl, mix the egg yolks with sugar and whisk well.
Add cream and vanilla extract, whisk well, pour into your 4 ramekins, place them in your Slow Cooker, add some water to the Slow Cooker, cover and cook on High for 1 Hr. and 30 Min.
Leave aside to cool down and serve.

Cheesy Eggs

Servings: 2 Cooking Time: 3 Hrs.

Ingredients:

4 eggs, whisked
1 tbsp. oregano, chopped
2 oz. feta cheese, crumbled
Cooking spray
¼ cup spring onions, chopped
1 cup milk
A pinch of salt and black pepper

Directions:

In a bowl, combine the eggs with the spring onions and the other ingredients except the cooking spray and whisk.
Grease your Slow Cooker with cooking spray, add eggs mix, stir , put the lid on and cook on Low for 3 Hrs.
Divide between plates and serve for breakfast.

Leek Bake

Servings:3 Cooking Time: 8 Hrs.

Ingredients:

2 cups leek, chopped
¼ cup ground chicken
½ cup chicken stock
3 oz. Cheddar cheese, shredded
1 tsp. dried thyme

Directions:

Pour the chicken stock in the Slow Cooker.
Put the leek in the chicken stock and sprinkle it with dried thyme and ground chicken.
Then top the chicken with Cheddar cheese and close the lid.
Cook the leek bake on low for 8 Hrs.

Italian Style Scrambled Eggs

Servings:4 Cooking Time: 4 Hrs.

Ingredients:

4 eggs, beaten
¼ cup milk
¼ tsp. salt
3 oz. Mozzarella, shredded
1 tsp. Italian seasonings
1 tsp. butter, melted

Directions:

Mix eggs with milk, Italian seasonings, and salt.
Pour butter and milk mixture in the Slow Cooker and close the lid.
Cook the meal on high for 1 Hr.
Then open the lid and scramble the eggs.
After this, top the meal with cheese and cook the eggs on low for 3 Hrs. more.

Creamy Asparagus Chicken

Servings: 7 Cooking Time: 8 Hrs.

Ingredients:

1 cup cream
1 tsp. chili powder
1 tsp. oregano
1 tsp. sriracha
1 tsp. sage
2 lb. chicken breast, skinned, boneless, sliced
3 tbsp. flour
1 tsp. ground white pepper
6 oz. asparagus

Directions:

Whisk chili powder, oregano, sage, white pepper, and flour in a shallow tray.
Add the chicken slices to this spice mixture and coat them well.
Now add cream, chopped veggies, and Sriracha to the Slow Cooker.
Place the coated chicken slices in the cooker.
Put the cooker's lid on and set the cooking time to 8 Hrs. on Low settings.
Serve warm.

Hash Browns Casserole

Servings: 12 Cooking Time: 4 Hrs.

Ingredients:

30 oz. hash browns
8 oz. mozzarella cheese, shredded
6 green onions, chopped
12 eggs
Salt and black pepper to the taste
1 lb. sausage, browned and sliced
8 oz. cheddar cheese, shredded
½ cup milk
Cooking spray

Directions:

Coat the base of your Slow Cooker with cooking spray.
Spread half of the hash browns, mozzarella, sausage, green onions, and cheddar to the cooker.
Beat eggs with milk, black pepper, and salt in a bowl.
Pour half of this egg-milk mixture over the layer of hash browns.
Top it with the remaining half of the hash browns, sausages, cheddar, green onions, and mozzarella.
Pour in the remaining egg-milk mixture.
Put the cooker's lid on and set the cooking time to 4 Hrs. on High settings.
Slice and serve warm.

Butter Oatmeal

Servings:4 Cooking Time: 10 Min

Ingredients:

1 tbsp. liquid honey
1 tsp. vanilla extract
½ cup heavy cream
2 tbsps. butter
1 tbsp. coconut shred
1 cup of water
1 cup oatmeal

Directions:

Put butter, oatmeal, heavy cream, water, vanilla extract, and coconut shred in the Slow Cooker.
Carefully stir the ingredients and close the lid.
Cook the meal on Low for 5 Hrs.
Then add liquid honey, stir it, and transfer in the serving bowls.

Zesty Pumpkin Cubes

Servings: 4 Cooking Time: 10 Hrs.

Ingredients:

2 tbsp. lemon juice
1 tbsp. ground cinnamon
1 tbsp. lemon zest
1 lb. pumpkin, peeled and cubed
3 tbsp. honey
1 tbsp. brown sugar
2 tbsp. water

Directions:

Toss the pumpkin cubes with lemon juice, water, honey, cinnamon, sugar, lemon zest in a large bowl.
Spread the pumpkin with sugar mixture in the Slow Cooker.
Put the cooker's lid on and set the cooking time to 10 Hrs. on Low settings.
Toss well and serve.

French Toast

Servings:2 Cooking Time: 3.5 Hrs.

Ingredients:

2 white bread slices
1 tsp. white sugar
1/4 cup milk
1 tsp. cream cheese
1 egg, beaten
1 tbsp. butter

Directions:

Put butter in the Slow Cooker.
Add cream cheese, white sugar, egg, and milk. Stir the mixture.
Then put the bread slices in the Slow Cooker and close the lid.
Cook the toasts for 3.5 Hrs. on High.

Bacon Potatoes

Servings:4 Cooking Time: 5 Hrs.

Ingredients:

4 russet potatoes
4 tsps. olive oil
1 tsp. dried thyme
4 bacon slices

Directions:

Cut the potatoes into halves and sprinkle with dried thyme and olive oil.
After this, cut every bacon slice into halves.
Put the potatoes in the Slow Cooker bowl and top with bacon slices.
Close the lid and cook them for 5 Hrs. on High.

Eggs and Sausage Casserole

Servings: 4 Cooking Time: 8 Hrs.

Ingredients:

8 eggs, whisked
1 lb. pork sausage, chopped
1 tbsp. garlic powder
1 yellow bell pepper, chopped
1 yellow onion, chopped
2 tsps. basil, dried
Salt and black pepper to the taste
1 tsp. olive oil

Directions:

Grease your Slow Cooker with the olive oil, add eggs, onion, pork sausage, basil, garlic powder, salt, pepper and yellow bell pepper, toss, cover and cook on Low for 8 Hrs.
Slice, divide between plates and serve for breakfast.

Cinnamon French Toast

Servings: 2 Cooking Time: 4 Hrs.

Ingredients:

1/2 French baguette, sliced
1 tbsp. brown sugar
3 tbsps. almond milk
1/2 tsp. cinnamon powder
Cooking spray
2 oz. cream cheese
1 egg, whisked
2 tbsps. honey
1 tbsp. butter, melted

Directions:

Spread the cream cheese on all bread slices, grease your Slow Cooker with the cooking spray and arrange the slices in the pot.
In a bowl, mix the egg with the cinnamon, almond milk and the remaining ingredients, whisk and pour over the bread slices.
Put the lid on, cook on High for 4 Hrs., divide the mix between plates and serve for breakfast.

Chicken Cabbage Medley

Servings: 5 Cooking Time: 4.5 Hrs.

Ingredients:

6 oz. ground chicken
1 white onion, sliced
1 tsp. sugar
1 tsp. ground black pepper
2 garlic cloves
10 oz. cabbage, chopped
1/2 cup tomato juice
1/2 tsp. salt
4 tbsp. chicken stock

Directions:

Whisk tomato juice with black pepper, salt, sugar, and chicken stock in a bowl.
Spread the onion slices, chicken, and cabbage in the Slow Cooker.
Pour the tomato-stock mixture over the veggies and top with garlic cloves.
Put the cooker's lid on and set the cooking time to 4 Hrs. 30 Min. on High settings.
Serve.

Chorizo Eggs

Servings:4 Cooking Time: 1.5 Hrs.

Ingredients:

5 oz. chorizo, sliced
2 oz. Parmesan, grated
4 eggs, beaten
1 tsp. butter, softened

Directions:

Grease the Slow Cooker bottom with butter.
Add chorizo and cook them on high for 30 Min.
Then flip the sliced chorizo and add eggs and Parmesan.
Close the lid and cook the meal on High for 1 Hr. more.

Cocoa and Berries Quinoa

Servings: 2 Cooking Time: 8 Hrs.

Ingredients:

Cooking spray
2 cups almond milk
1/4 cup blueberries
1 tbsp. brown sugar
1 cup quinoa
1/4 cup heavy cream
2 tbsps. cocoa powder

Directions:

Grease your Slow Cooker with the cooking spray, add the quinoa, berries and the other ingredients, toss, put the lid on and cook on Low for 8 Hrs.
Divide into 2 bowls and serve for breakfast.

Breakfast Pork Ground

Servings:4 Cooking Time: 7 Hrs.

Ingredients:

1 cup ground pork
1 red onion, diced
1 tsp. tomato paste
1/2 cup Mozzarella, shredded

½ cup corn kernels
1 tbsp. butter

Directions:

Mix ground pork with tomato paste, mozzarella, butter, and corn kernels.
Transfer the mixture in the Slow Cooker and cook on low for 7 Hrs.
Then transfer the cooked meal in the serving plates and top with diced onion.

Cauliflower Casserole

Servings: 2 Cooking Time: 5 Hrs.

Ingredients:

1 lb. cauliflower florets
1 red onion, sliced
½ tsp. turmeric powder
A pinch of salt and black pepper
3 eggs, whisked
½ tsp. sweet paprika
1 garlic clove, minced
Cooking spray

Directions:

Spray your Slow Cooker with the cooking spray, and mix the cauliflower with the eggs, onion and the other ingredients inside.
Put the lid on, cook on Low for 5 Hrs., divide between 2 plates and serve for breakfast.

Creamy Shrimp Bowls

Servings: 2 Cooking Time: 2 Hrs.

Ingredients:

½ cup chicken stock
1 carrot, peeled and cubed
¼ cup heavy cream
¼ tbsp. onion powder
A pinch of salt and black pepper
1 oz. cream cheese
½ lb. shrimp, peeled and deveined
½ cup baby spinach
¼ tbsp. garlic powder
¼ tsp. rosemary, dried
¼ cup cheddar cheese, shredded
1 tbsp. chives, chopped

Directions:

In your Slow Cooker, mix the shrimp with the stock, cream and the other ingredients, toss, put the lid on and cook on Low for 2 Hrs.
Divide into bowls, and serve for breakfast.

Cranberry Maple Oatmeal

Servings: 2 Cooking Time: 6 Hrs.

Ingredients:

1 cup almond milk
½ cup cranberries
1 tbsp. maple syrup
½ cup steel cut oats
½ tsp. vanilla extract
1 tbsp. sugar

Directions:

In your Slow Cooker, mix the oats with the berries, milk and the other ingredients, toss, put the lid on and cook on Low for 6 Hrs.
Divide into bowls and serve for breakfast.

Herbed Egg Scramble

Servings: 2 Cooking Time: 6 Hrs.

Ingredients:

4 eggs, whisked
¼ cup heavy cream
¼ cup mozzarella, shredded
1 tbsp. oregano, chopped
A pinch of salt and black pepper
1 tbsp. chives, chopped
1 tbsp. rosemary, chopped
Cooking spray

Directions:

Grease your Slow Cooker with the cooking spray, and mix the eggs with the cream, herbs and the other ingredients inside.
Stir well, put the lid on, cook for 6 Hrs. on Low, stir once again, divide between plates and serve.

Almond and Quinoa Bowls

Servings: 2 Cooking Time: 5 Hrs.

Ingredients:

1 cup quinoa
2 tbsps. butter, melted
A pinch of cinnamon powder
¼ cup almonds, sliced
2 cups almond milk
2 tbsps. brown sugar
A pinch of nutmeg, ground
Cooking spray

Directions:

Grease your Slow Cooker with the cooking spray, add the quinoa, milk, melted butter and the other ingredients, toss, put the lid on and cook on Low for 5 Hrs.
Divide the mix into bowls and serve for breakfast.

Morning Muesli

Servings:6 Cooking Time: 4 Hrs.

Ingredients:

1 cup oatmeal
1 tsp. sesame seeds
1 banana, chopped
2 cups of coconut milk
1 tbsp. raisins
1 tsp. dried cranberries
1 tsp. ground cinnamon

Directions:

Mix coconut milk with oatmeal, raisins, sesame seeds, dried cranberries, and ground cinnamon.
Transfer the ingredients in the Slow Cooker and cook on Low for 4 Hrs.
Then stir carefully and transfer in the serving bowls.
Top the muesli with chopped banana.

Baked Eggs

Servings:5 Cooking Time: 8 Hrs.

Ingredients:

5 oz. tater tots
3 oz. bacon, chopped, cooked
4 eggs, beaten
½ cup milk
2 white onion, diced
3 oz. provolone cheese, shredded
1 tsp. ground black pepper

Directions:

Make the layer of tater tots in the Slow Cooker bowl.
Then top it with onion, bacon, and cheese.
After this, mix milk, ground black pepper, and eggs.
Pour the liquid over the cheese and close the lid.
Cook the meal on Low for 8 Hrs.

Apple Breakfast Rice

Servings: 4 Cooking Time: 7 Hrs.

Ingredients:

4 apples, cored, peeled and chopped
2 tbsps. butter
2 tsps. cinnamon powder
1 and ½ cups brown rice
½ tsp. vanilla extract
A pinch of nutmeg, ground
5 cups milk

Directions:

Put the butter in your Slow Cooker, add apples, cinnamon, rice, vanilla, nutmeg and milk, cover, cook on Low for 7 Hrs., stir, divide into bowls and serve for breakfast.

Squash Bowls

Servings: 2 Cooking Time: 6 Hrs.

Ingredients:

2 tbsps. walnuts, chopped
2 cups squash, peeled and cubed
½ cup coconut cream
½ tsp. cinnamon powder
½ tbsp. sugar

Directions:

In your Slow Cooker, mix the squash with the nuts and the other ingredients, toss, put the lid on and cook on Low for 6 Hrs.
Divide into bowls and serve.

Artichoke Pepper Frittata

Servings: 4 Cooking Time: 3 Hrs.

Ingredients:

14 oz. canned artichokes hearts, drained and chopped
12 oz. roasted red peppers, chopped
8 eggs, whisked
¼ cup green onions, chopped
4 oz. feta cheese, crumbled
Cooking spray

Directions:

Coat the base of your Slow Cooker with cooking spray.
Add green onions, roasted peppers, and artichokes to the Slow Cooker.
Pour whisked eggs over the veggies and drizzle cheese on top.
Put the cooker's lid on and set the cooking time to 3 Hrs. on Low settings.
Slice and serve.

Kale & Feta Breakfast Frittata

Servings: 6 Cooking Time: 3 Hrs. and 5 Min

Ingredients:

2 cups kale, chopped
½ cup feta, crumbled
2 tsps. olive oil
Salt and pepper to taste
3 green onions, chopped
1 large green pepper, diced
8 eggs

Directions:

Heat the olive oil in Crock-Pot and sauté the kale, diced pepper, and chopped green onion for about 2-3 Min. Beat the eggs in a mixing bowl, pour over other ingredients, and stir. Add salt and pepper and sprinkle crumbled feta cheese on top. Cover and cook on LOW for 2-3 Hrs., or until the cheese has melted. Serve hot.

Sausage Frittata

Servings:5 Cooking Time: 4 Hrs.

Ingredients:

½ onion, diced
8 oz. sausages, chopped
1 tsp. coconut oil
1 cup Mozzarella, shredded
6 eggs, beaten
½ tsp. cayenne pepper

Directions:

Put sausages in the Slow Cooker.
Add onion and coconut oil.
Close the lid and cook the ingredients on high for 2 Hrs.
Then stir them well.
Add eggs, cayenne pepper, and shredded mozzarella.
Carefully stir the meal and close the lid.
Cook it on high for 2 Hrs.

Jalapeno Muffins

Servings:4 Cooking Time: 3 Hrs.

Ingredients:

4 tbsps. flour
4 jalapeno pepper, diced
2 eggs, beaten
2 tbsps. cream cheese
1 oz. Parmesan, grated
1 tsp. olive oil

Directions:

Brush the silicone muffin molds with olive oil.
Then mix all remaining ingredients in the mixing bowl. In the end, you will get a smooth batter.
Transfer the batter in the prepared muffin molds.
Then put the molds in the Slow Cooker and close the lid.
Cook the muffins on High for 3 Hrs.

Mixed Egg and Sausage Scramble

Servings: 6 Cooking Time: 6 Hrs.

Ingredients:

12 eggs
14 oz. sausages, sliced
1 cup milk
16 oz. cheddar cheese, shredded
A pinch of salt and black pepper
1 tsp. basil, dried
1 tsp. oregano, dried
Cooking spray

Directions:

Grease your Slow Cooker with cooking spray, spread sausages on the bottom, crack eggs, add milk, basil, oregano, salt and pepper, whisk a bit, sprinkle cheddar all over, cover and cook on Low for 6 Hrs.
Divide egg and sausage scramble between plates and serve.

Creamy Yogurt

Servings: 8 Cooking Time: 10 Hrs.

Ingredients:

3 tsps. gelatin
½ gallon milk
7 oz. plain yogurt
1 and ½ tbsps. vanilla extract
½ cup maple syrup

Directions:

Put the milk in your Slow Cooker, cover and cook on Low for 3 Hrs.
In a bowl, mix 1 cup of hot milk from the Slow Cooker with the gelatin, whisk well, pour into the Slow Cooker, cover and leave aside for 2 Hrs.

Combine 1 cup of milk with the yogurt, whisk really well and pour into the pot.
Also add vanilla and maple syrup, stir, cover and cook on Low for 7 more Hrs.
Leave yogurt aside to cool down and serve it for breakfast.

Mushroom Chicken Casserole

Servings: 5 Cooking Time: 8 Hrs.

Ingredients:

8 oz. mushrooms, sliced
1 carrot, peeled and grated
7 oz. chicken fillet, sliced
1 tsp. fresh rosemary
½ tsp. coriander
1 cup cream
6 oz. Cheddar cheese, shredded
1 tsp. butter
1 tsp. salt

Directions:

Add the mushroom slices, grated carrot in the Slow Cooker.
Season the chicken strips with coriander and rosemary.
Place these chicken slices in the cooker and top it with cream, butter, salt, and cheese.
Put the cooker's lid on and set the cooking time to 8 Hrs. on Low settings.
Serve.

Raspberry Chia Porridge

Servings:4 Cooking Time: 4 Hrs.

Ingredients:

1 cup raspberry
1 cup chia seeds
3 tbsps. maple syrup
4 cups of milk

Directions:

Put chia seeds and milk in the Slow Cooker and cook the mixture on low for 4 Hrs.
Meanwhile, mix raspberries and maple syrup in the blender and blend the mixture until smooth.
When the chia porridge is cooked, transfer it in the serving bowls and top with blended raspberry mixture.

Apricot Butter

Servings:4 Cooking Time: 7 Hrs.

Ingredients:

1 cup apricots, pitted, chopped
1 tsp. ground cinnamon
3 tbsps. butter
1 tsp. brown sugar

Directions:

Put all ingredients in the Slow Cooker and stir well
Close the lid and cook them on Low for 7 Hrs.
Then blend the mixture with the help of the immersion blender and cool until cold.

Butternut Squash Pate

Servings:7 Cooking Time: 4 Hrs.

Ingredients:

8 oz. butternut squash puree
1 tsp. cinnamon
1 tbsp. lemon juice
1 tbsp. honey
¼ tsp. ground clove
2 tbsps. coconut oil

Directions:

Put all ingredients in the Slow Cooker, gently stir, and cook on Low for 4 Hrs.

Cheddar Eggs

Servings:4 Cooking Time: 2 Hrs.

Ingredients:

1 tsp. butter, softened
½ tsp. salt
4 eggs
1/3 cup Cheddar cheese, shredded

Directions:

Grease the Slow Cooker bowl with butter and crack the eggs inside.
Sprinkle the eggs with salt and shredded cheese.
Close the lid and cook on High for 2 Hrs.

Turkey Breakfast Casserole

Servings: 8 Cooking Time: 8 Hrs. 30 Min

Ingredients:

1-pound turkey sausages, cooked and drained
1 (30 oz) package shredded hash browns, thawed
2 cups Colby Jack cheese, shredded
1 tsp. salt
4 tbsps. flour
1 dozen eggs
1 yellow onion, chopped
1 cup milk
½ tsp. red pepper flakes, crushed
½ tsp. black pepper

Directions:

Grease a Slow Cooker and layer with 1/3 of the hash browns, onions, sausages and cheese.
Repeat these layers twice ending with the layer of cheese.
Whisk together the rest of the ingredients in a large mixing bowl.
Transfer this mixture into the Slow Cooker and cover the lid.
Cover and cook on LOW for about 8 Hrs.
Dish out to serve the delicious breakfast.

Ham Pockets

Servings:4 Cooking Time: 1 Hr.

Ingredients:

4 pita breads
4 ham slices
1 tsp. dried dill
½ cup Cheddar cheese, shredded
1 tbsp. mayonnaise

Directions:

Mix cheese with mayonnaise and dill.
Then fill the pita bread with sliced ham and cheese mixture.
Wrap the stuffed pitas in the foil and place it in the Slow Cooker.
Cook them on High for 1 Hr.

Baby Carrots In Syrup

Servings:5 Cooking Time: 7 Hrs.

Ingredients:

3 cups baby carrots
2 tbsps. brown sugar
1 cup apple juice
1 tsp. vanilla extract

Directions:

Mix apple juice, brown sugar, and vanilla extract.
Pour the liquid in the Slow Cooker.
Add baby carrots and close the lid.

Cook the meal on Low for 7 Hrs.

Pork and Eggplant Casserole

Servings: 2 Cooking Time: 6 Hrs.

Ingredients:

1 red onion, chopped
½ lb. pork stew meat, ground
½ tsp. chili powder
1 tbsp. sweet paprika
1 eggplant, cubed
3 eggs, whisked
½ tsp. garam masala
1 tsp. olive oil

Directions:

In a bowl, mix the eggs with the meat, onion, eggplant and the other ingredients except the oil and stir well.
Grease your Slow Cooker with oil, add the pork and eggplant mix, spread into the pot, put the lid on and cook on Low for 6 Hrs.
Divide the mix between plates and serve for breakfast.

Oats Granola

Servings: 8 Cooking Time: 2 Hrs.

Ingredients:

5 cups old-fashioned rolled oats
2/3 cup honey
½ cup peanut butter
2 tsps. cinnamon powder
Cooking spray
1/3 cup coconut oil
½ cup almonds, chopped
1 tbsp. vanilla
1 cup craisins

Directions:

Grease your Slow Cooker with cooking spray, add oats, oil, honey, almonds, peanut butter, vanilla, craisins and cinnamon, toss just a bit, cover and cook on High for 2 Hrs., stirring every 30 Min.
Divide into bowls and serve for breakfast.

Meat Buns

Servings:4 Cooking Time: 6 Hrs.

Ingredients:

1 cup ground pork
1 tbsp. semolina
1 tsp. butter, melted
½ cup ground chicken
1 tsp. dried oregano
1 tsp. salt

Directions:

Mix ground pork with ground chicken.
Add semolina, dried oregano, and salt.
Then add butter and stir the meat mixture until homogenous.
Transfer it in the silicon bun molds.
Put the molds with buns in the Slow Cooker.
Close the lid and cook them on Low for 6 Hrs.

Potato Omelet

Servings:4 Cooking Time: 6 Hrs.

Ingredients:

1 cup potatoes, sliced
6 eggs, beaten
1 tsp. salt
1 onion, sliced
2 tbsps. olive oil
½ tsp. ground black pepper

Directions:

Mix potatoes with ground black pepper and salt.
Transfer them in the Slow Cooker, add olive oil and cook on high for 30 Min.
Then mix the potatoes and add onion and eggs.
Stir the mixture and cook the omelet on Low for 6 Hrs.

Fried Apple Slices

Servings: 6 Cooking Time: 6 Hrs. 10 Min

Ingredients:

1 tsp. ground cinnamon
3 lbs. Granny Smith apples
1 cup sugar, granulated
3 tbsps. cornstarch
¼ tsp. nutmeg, freshly grated
2 tbsps. butter

Directions:

Put the apple slices in the Slow Cooker and stir in nutmeg, cinnamon, sugar and cornstarch.
Top with butter and cover the lid.
Cook on LOW for about 6 Hrs., stirring about halfway.
Dish out to serve hot.

Squash Butter

Servings:4 Cooking Time: 2 Hrs.

Ingredients:

1 cup butternut squash puree
4 tbsps. applesauce
1 tsp. cornflour
1 tsp. allspices
2 tbsps. butter

Directions:

Put all ingredients in the Slow Cooker and mix until homogenous.
Then close the lid and cook the butter on High for 2 Hrs.
Transfer the cooked squash butter in the plastic vessel and cool it well.

Cheesy Egg Bake

Servings: 8 Cooking Time: 8 Hrs.

Ingredients:

20 oz. tater tots
6 oz. bacon, chopped
12 eggs
1 cup milk
4 tbsp. white flour
2 yellow onions, chopped
2 cups cheddar cheese, shredded
¼ cup parmesan, grated
Salt and black pepper to the taste
Cooking spray

Directions:

Coat the base of your Slow Cooker with cooking spray.
Spread tater tots, bacon, onions, parmesan, and cheddar in the cooker.
Beat eggs with milk, flour, salt, and black pepper in a bowl.
Pour this mixture over the tater tots' layer.
Put the cooker's lid on and set the cooking time to 8 Hrs. on Low settings.
Serve fresh.

Cheese and Turkey Casserole

Servings:4 Cooking Time: 6 Hrs.

Ingredients:

8 oz. ground turkey
5 oz. Monterey jack cheese, shredded
1 tsp. chili powder
¼ cup of water
1 tsp. butter
1 tbsp. dried parsley
1 red onion, diced

Directions:

Put all ingredients in the Slow Cooker and mix carefully.
Close the lid and cook the casserole on low for 6 Hrs.

Dates Quinoa

Servings: 4 Cooking Time: 3 Hrs.

Ingredients:

1 cup quinoa
3 cups milk
¼ cup pepitas
1 tsp. vanilla extract
4 medjol dates, chopped
1 apple, cored and chopped
2 tsps. cinnamon powder
¼ tsp. nutmeg, ground

Directions:

In your Slow Cooker, mix quinoa with dates, milk, apple, pepitas, cinnamon, nutmeg and vanilla, stir, cover and cook on High for 3 Hrs.
Stir again, divide into bowls and serve.

Creamy Breakfast

Servings: 1 Cooking Time: 3 Hrs.

Ingredients:

1 tsp. cinnamon powder
½ cup almonds, chopped
1 and ½ cup heavy cream
¼ tsp. cloves, ground
½ tsp. nutmeg, ground
1 tsp. sugar
¼ tsp. cardamom, ground

Directions:

In your Slow Cooker, mix cream with cinnamon, nutmeg, almonds, sugar, cardamom and cloves, stir, cover, cook on Low for 3 Hrs., divide into bowls and serve for breakfast

Cranberry Quinoa

Servings: 4 Cooking Time: 2 Hrs.

Ingredients:

3 cups coconut water
1 cup quinoa
1/8 cup almonds, sliced
¼ cup cranberries, dried
1 tsp. vanilla extract
3 tsps. honey
1/8 cup coconut flakes

Directions:

In your Slow Cooker, mix coconut water with vanilla, quinoa, honey, almonds, coconut flakes and cranberries, toss, cover and cook on High for 2 Hrs.
Divide quinoa mix into bowls and serve.

Chocolate French Toast

Servings: 4 Cooking Time: 4 Hrs.

Ingredients:

Cooking spray
¾ cup brown sugar
1 and ½ cups milk
¾ cup chocolate chips
1 loaf of bread, cubed
3 eggs
1 tsp. vanilla extract
1 tsp. cinnamon powder

Directions:

Grease your Slow Cooker with the cooking spray and arrange bread cubes inside.
In a bowl, mix the eggs with milk, sugar, vanilla, cinnamon and chocolate chips, whisk well, add to the Slow Cooker, cover and cook on Low for 4 Hrs.
Divide into bowls and serve for breakfast.

Cinnamon Pumpkin Oatmeal

Servings: 4 Cooking Time: 9 Hrs.

Ingredients:

Cooking spray
½ cup milk
2 tbsp. brown sugar
½ tsp. cinnamon powder
A pinch of ginger, grated
A pinch of nutmeg, ground
1 cup steel-cut oats
4 cups of water
½ cup pumpkin puree
A pinch of cloves, ground
A pinch of allspice, ground

Directions:

Layer the base of Slow Cooker with cooking spray.
Stir in milk, sugar, water, oats, cinnamon, cloves, sugar, pumpkin puree, ginger, nutmeg, and allspice.
Put the cooker's lid on and set the cooking time to 9 Hrs. on Low settings.
Serve.

Vanilla Quinoa

Servings:2 Cooking Time: 4 Hrs.

Ingredients:

½ cup quinoa
1 tsp. vanilla extract
2 cups of milk
1 tbsp. butter

Directions:

Put quinoa, milk, and vanilla extract in the Slow Cooker.
Cook it for 4 Hrs. on Low.
Then add butter and stir the quinoa carefully.

Leek Eggs

Servings:4 Cooking Time: 2.5 Hrs.

Ingredients:

10 oz. leek, sliced
1 tsp. olive oil
3 oz. Cheddar cheese, shredded
4 eggs, beaten
½ tsp. cumin seeds

Directions:

Mix leek with olive oil and eggs.
Then transfer the mixture in the Slow Cooker.
Sprinkle the egg mixture with Cheddar cheese and cumin seeds.
Close the lid and cook the meal on High for 2.5 Hrs.

Chocolate Toast

Servings:4 Cooking Time:40 Min

Ingredients:

4 white bread slices
2 tbsps. Nutella
1 tbsp. coconut oil
1 tbsp. vanilla extract
1 banana, mashed
¼ cup full-fat milk

Directions:

Mix vanilla extract, Nutella, mashed banana, coconut oil, and milk.
Pour the mixture in the Slow Cooker and cook on High for 40 Min.
Make a quick pressure release and cool the chocolate mixture.
Spread the toasts with cooked mixture.

Cheesy Cauliflower Hash

Servings: 5 Cooking Time: 8 Hrs.

Ingredients:

7 eggs
1 tsp. salt
½ tsp. ground mustard
¼ tsp. chili flakes
½ onion, chopped
¼ cup milk
1 tsp. ground black pepper
10 oz. cauliflower, shredded
5 oz. breakfast sausages, chopped
5 oz. Cheddar cheese, shredded

Directions:

First, beat the eggs with milk, mustard, black pepper, salt, onion, and chili flakes in a bowl.
Spread the cauliflower shreds in the Slow Cooker.
Pour the egg-milk mixture over the cauliflower shreds.
Drizzle cheese and chopped sausages on top.
Put the cooker's lid on and set the cooking time to 8 Hrs. on Low settings.
Slice and serve.

Quinoa Cauliflower Medley

Servings: 7 Cooking Time: 9 Hrs.

Ingredients:

8 oz. potato, peeled and cubed
1 cup onion, chopped
1 cup tomatoes, chopped
3 cup chicken stock
1/3 tbsp. miso
2 tsp. curry paste
7 oz. cauliflower, cut in florets
7 oz. chickpea, canned
13 oz. almond milk
8 tbsp. quinoa
1 tsp. minced garlic

Directions:

Spread the chopped potatoes, tomatoes, and onion in the Slow Cooker.
Whisk curry paste with chicken stock and miso in a separate bowl.
Pour this mixture over the layer of the veggies.
Now top this mixture with chickpeas, cauliflower florets, quinoa, garlic, and almond milk.
Put the cooker's lid on and set the cooking time to 9 Hrs. on Low settings.
Serve.

Hot Eggs Mix

Servings: 2 Cooking Time: 2 Hrs.

Ingredients:

Cooking spray
¼ cup sour cream
½ tsp. chili powder
½ red bell pepper, chopped
2 cherry tomatoes, cubed
4 eggs, whisked
A pinch of salt and black pepper
½ tsp. hot paprika
½ yellow onion, chopped
1 tbsp. parsley, chopped

Directions:

In a bowl, mix the eggs with the cream, salt, pepper and the other ingredients except the cooking spray and whisk well.
Grease your Slow Cooker with cooking spray, pour the eggs mix inside, spread, stir, put the lid on and cook on High for 2 Hrs.
Divide the mix between plates and serve.

Bacon Tater

Servings: 4 Cooking Time: 8 Hrs. 10 Min

Ingredients:

½ lb. Canadian bacon, diced
½ cup whole milk
1 lb. package frozen tater tot potatoes
1½ cups Cheddar cheese, shredded
2 tbsps. flour
¼ cup Parmesan cheese, grated
Salt and black pepper, to taste
2 onions, chopped
6 eggs

Directions:

Grease a Slow Cooker and layer 1/3 of the tater tots, bacon, onions, and cheeses.
Repeat the layers twice, ending with cheeses.
Mix together eggs, milk, flour, salt and black pepper in a medium mixing bowl.
Drizzle this mixture over the layers in the Slow Cooker and cover the lid.
Cook on LOW about for 8 Hrs. and dish out to serve.

Quinoa Oats Bake

Servings: 6 Cooking Time: 7 Hrs.

Ingredients:

½ cup quinoa
4 and ½ cups of almond milk
4 tbsp. brown sugar
Cooking spray
1 and ½ cups steel cut oats
2 tbsp. maple syrup
1 and ½ tsp. vanilla extract

Directions:

Coat the base of your Slow Cooker with cooking spray.
Stir in oats, quinoa, maple syrup, vanilla extract, sugar, and almond milk.
Put the cooker's lid on and set the cooking time to 7 Hrs. on Low settings.
Serve.

Bacon Eggs

Servings:2 Cooking Time: 2 Hrs.

Ingredients:

2 bacon slices
¼ tsp. ground black pepper
½ tsp. dried thyme
2 eggs, hard-boiled, peeled
1 tsp. olive oil

Directions:

Sprinkle the bacon with ground black pepper and dried thyme.
Then wrap the eggs in the bacon and sprinkle with olive oil.
Put the eggs in the Slow Cooker and cook on High for 2 Hrs.

Tofu Eggs

Servings:4 Cooking Time: 7 Hrs.

Ingredients:

4 eggs, beaten
½ tsp. curry paste
1 tsp. olive oil
4 oz. tofu, chopped
2 tbsps. coconut milk
½ tsp. butter, melted

Directions:

Mix coconut milk with curry paste.
Then sprinkle the tofu with curry mixture.

After this, pour butter in the Slow Cooker.
Add eggs, olive oil, and tofu mixture.
Close the lid and cook the meal on Low for 7 Hrs.

Quinoa and Oats Mix

Servings: 6 Cooking Time: 7 Hrs.

Ingredients:

½ cup quinoa
4 and ½ cups almond milk
4 tbsps. brown sugar
Cooking spray
1 and ½ cups steel cut oats
2 tbsps. maple syrup
1 and ½ tsps. vanilla extract

Directions:

Grease your Slow Cooker with cooking spray, add quinoa, oats, almond milk, maple syrup, sugar and vanilla extract, cover and cook on Low for 7 Hrs.
Stir, divide into bowls and serve for breakfast.

Raspberry Oatmeal

Servings: 4 Cooking Time: 8 Hrs.

Ingredients:

2 cups water
1 cup steel cut oats
1 cup milk
1 cup raspberries
1 tbsp. coconut oil
1 tbsp. sugar
½ tsp. vanilla extract
4 tbsps. walnuts, chopped

Directions:

In your Slow Cooker, mix oil with water, oats, sugar, milk, vanilla and raspberries, cover and cook on Low for 8 Hrs.
Stir oatmeal, divide into bowls, sprinkle walnuts on top and serve for breakfast.

Raisins and Rice Pudding

Servings:4 Cooking Time: 6 Hrs.

Ingredients:

1 cup long-grain rice
2 tbsps. cornstarch
2 tbsps. raisins, chopped
2.5 cups organic almond milk
1 tsp. vanilla extract

Directions:

Put all ingredients in the Slow Cooker and carefully mix.
Then close the lid and cook the pudding for 6 Hrs. on Low.

Nutmeg Banana Oatmeal

Servings: 6 Cooking Time: 7 Hrs.

Ingredients:

Cooking spray
1 cup steel-cut oats
½ cup of water
2 tbsp. brown sugar
½ tsp. cinnamon powder
1 tbsp. flaxseed, ground
2 bananas, sliced
28 oz. canned coconut milk
1 tbsp. butter
¼ tsp. nutmeg, ground
½ tsp. vanilla extract

Directions:

Coat the base of your Slow Cooker with cooking spray.
Spread oats, banana slices, water, coconut milk, sugar, butter, cinnamon, flaxseed, and vanilla in this cooker.
Put the cooker's lid on and set the cooking time to 7 Hrs. on Low settings.
Serve fresh.
Enjoy.

Breakfast Butterscotch Pudding

Servings: 6 Cooking Time: 1 Hr. and 40 Min

Ingredients:

4 oz. butter, melted
7 oz. flour
1 tsp. vanilla extract
2 tbsps. maple syrup
1 egg
2 oz. brown sugar
¼ pint milk
Zest of ½ lemon, grated
Cooking spray

Directions:

In a bowl, mix butter with sugar, milk, vanilla, lemon zest, maple syrup and eggs and whisk well.
Add flour and whisk really well again.
Grease your Slow Cooker with cooking spray, add pudding mix, spread, cover and cook on High for 1 Hr. and 30 Min.
Divide between plates and serve for breakfast.

Quinoa Bars

Servings: 8 Cooking Time: 4 Hrs.

Ingredients:

2 tbsp. maple syrup
Cooking spray
1 cup almond milk
½ cup raisins
1/3 cup almonds, toasted and chopped
2 tbsp. chia seeds
2 tbsp. almond butter, melted
½ tsp. cinnamon powder
2 eggs
1/3 cup quinoa
1/3 cup dried apples, chopped

Directions:

Mix quinoa with almond butter, cinnamon, milk, maple syrup, eggs, apples, chia seeds, almonds, and raisins in a suitable bowl.
Coat the base of your Slow Cooker with cooking spray and parchment paper.
Now evenly spread the quinoa-oats mixture over the parchment paper.
Put the cooker's lid on and set the cooking time to 4 Hrs. on Low settings.
Slice and serve.

Morning Pie

Servings:6 Cooking Time: 3 Hrs.

Ingredients:

½ cup oatmeal
1 cup butternut squash, diced
½ tsp. ground cinnamon
4 pecans, crushed
1 cup full-fat milk
1 tsp. vanilla extract
1 tsp. sesame oil

Directions:

Mix oatmeal and milk in the Slow Cooker.
Add diced butternut squash, vanilla extract, and ground cinnamon.
Then add sesame oil and pecans.
Carefully mix the ingredients and close the lid.
Cook the pie on Low for 3 Hrs.
Then cool the pie and cut it into servings.

Strawberry Yogurt Oatmeal

Servings: 8   Cooking Time: 8 Hrs.

Ingredients:

6 cups of water
2 cups steel-cut oats
1 tsp. cinnamon powder
1 tsp. vanilla extract
2 cups of milk
1 cup Greek yogurt
2 cups strawberries, halved

Directions:

Add oats, milk, cinnamon, yogurt, water, vanilla, and strawberries to the Slow Cooker.
Put the cooker's lid on and set the cooking time to 8 Hrs. on Low settings.
Serve.

Eggs with Spinach and Yogurt

Servings:4   Cooking Time: 3 Hrs.

Ingredients:

1 clove of garlic, minced
2 tbsps. grass-fed butter, unsalted
1 tsp. fresh oregano, chopped
2 tbsps. olive oil
1/4 tsp. red pepper flakes, crushed
2/3 cup plain Greek yogurt
4 large eggs, beaten
Salt and pepper to taste
10 cups fresh spinach, chopped
2 tbsp. scallions, chopped

Directions:

In a mixing bowl, combine garlic, yogurt, butter, and eggs. Stir in oregano and season with salt and pepper to taste.
Grease the bottom of the Slow Cooker with olive oil.
Arrange the spinach and pour over the egg mixture.
Sprinkle with pepper flakes and scallions on top.
Close the lid and cook on high for 2 Hrs. or on low for 3 Hrs.

Peach Oats

Servings:3   Cooking Time: 7 Hrs.

Ingredients:

1/2 cup steel cut oats
1/2 cup peaches, pitted, chopped
1 cup milk
1 tsp. ground cardamom

Directions:

Mix steel-cut oats with milk and pour the mixture in the Slow Cooker.
Add ground cardamom and peaches. Stir the ingredients gently and close the lid.
Cook the meal on low for 7 Hrs.

Sausage and Eggs Mix

Servings: 2   Cooking Time: 8 Hrs. and 10 Min

Ingredients:

4 eggs, whisked
1/4 tsp. rosemary, dried
1/2 lb. pork sausage, sliced
1 tsp. basil, dried
Cooking spray
1 red onion, chopped
1/2 tsp. turmeric powder
1/2 tbsp. garlic powder
A pinch of salt and black pepper

Directions:

Grease a pan with the cooking spray, heat it up over medium-high heat, add the onion and the pork sausage, toss and cook for 10 Min.
Transfer this to the Slow Cooker, also add the eggs mixed with the remaining ingredients, toss everything, put the lid on and cook on Low for 8 Hrs.
Divide between plates and serve right away for breakfast.

Apricots Bread Pudding

Servings: 9   Cooking Time: 5 Hrs.

Ingredients:

10 oz. French bread
10 oz. milk
4 tbsp. butter
1 tsp. vanilla sugar
1/2 tsp. ground cardamom
4 tbsp. brown sugar
6 tbsp. dried apricots
3 eggs, beaten
1/2 tsp. salt
1/2 tsp. ground nutmeg
1/4 cup whipped cream

Directions:

Melt butter by heating in a saucepan then add milk.
Cook until warm, then stir in vanilla sugar, salt, ground cardamom, ground nutmeg, and brown sugar.
Continue mixing the milk mixture until sugar is fully dissolved.
Spread French bread and dried apricots in the Slow Cooker.
Beat eggs in a bowl and add to the milk mixture.
Stir in cream and mix well until fully incorporated.
Pour this milk-cream mixture over the bread and apricots in the Slow Cooker.
Put the cooker's lid on and set the cooking time to 5 Hrs. on Low settings.
Serve.

Baguette Boats

Servings:4   Cooking Time: 3 Hrs.

Ingredients:

6 oz. baguette (2 baguettes)
1 tsp. minced garlic
1 tsp. olive oil
4 ham slices
1/2 cup Mozzarella, shredded
1 egg, beaten

Directions:

Cut the baguettes into the halves and remove the flesh from the bread.
Chop the ham and mix it with egg, Mozzarella, and minced garlic.
Fill the baguettes with ham mixture.
Then brush the Slow Cooker bowl with olive oil from inside.
Put the baguette boats in the Slow Cooker and close the lid.
Cook them for 3 Hrs. on High.

Lamb and Eggs Mix

Servings: 2   Cooking Time: 6 Hrs.

Ingredients:

1 lb. lamb meat, ground
1 tbsp. basil, chopped
1 tbsp. chili powder
1 tbsp. olive oil
4 eggs, whisked
1/2 tsp. cumin powder
1 red onion, chopped
A pinch of salt and black pepper

Directions:

Grease the Slow Cooker with the oil and mix the lamb with the eggs, basil and the other ingredients inside.
Toss, put the lid on, cook on Low for 6 Hrs., divide into bowls and serve for breakfast.

Carrot Oatmeal

Servings:4 Cooking Time: 6 Hrs.

Ingredients:

1 cup oatmeal
1 tbsp. raisins
2 cups of water
1 cup carrot, shredded
1 tbsp. maple syrup
1 tsp. butter

Directions:

Put all ingredients in the Slow Cooker.
Close the lid and cook the oatmeal on low for 6 Hrs.
Carefully mix the cooked meal.

Leek Casserole

Servings: 2 Cooking Time: 4 Hrs.

Ingredients:

1 cup leek, chopped
1/2 cup mozzarella, shredded
4 eggs, whisked
1 tbsp. cilantro, chopped
Cooking spray
1 garlic clove, minced
1 cup beef sausage, chopped

Directions:

Grease the Slow Cooker with the cooking spray and mix the leek with the mozzarella and the other ingredients inside.
Toss, spread into the pot, put the lid on and cook on Low for 4 Hrs.
Divide between plates and serve for breakfast.

Asparagus Egg Casserole

Servings:4 Cooking Time: 2.5 Hrs.

Ingredients:

7 eggs, beaten
1 oz. Parmesan, grated
1 tsp. dried dill
4 oz. asparagus, chopped, boiled
1 tsp. sesame oil

Directions:

Pour the sesame oil in the Slow Cooker.
Then mix dried dill with parmesan, asparagus, and eggs.
Pour the egg mixture in the Slow Cooker and close the lid.
Cook the casserole on high for 2.5 Hrs.

Sweet Quinoa

Servings:4 Cooking Time: 3 Hrs.

Ingredients:

1 cup quinoa
3 cups of water
1/2 tsp. ground nutmeg
1/4 cup dates, chopped
1 apricot, chopped

Directions:

Put quinoa, dates, and apricot in the Slow Cooker.
Add ground nutmeg and mix the mixture.
Cook it on high for 3 Hrs.

Ginger Apple Bowls

Servings: 2 Cooking Time: 6 Hrs.

Ingredients:

2 apples, cored, peeled and cut into medium chunks
1 tbsp. ginger, grated
1/4 tsp. cinnamon powder
1/4 tsp. cardamom, ground
1 tbsp. sugar
1 cup heavy cream
1/2 tsp. vanilla extract

Directions:

In your Slow Cooker, combine the apples with the sugar, ginger and the other ingredients, toss, put the lid on and cook on Low for 6 Hrs.
Divide into bowls and serve for breakfast.

Breakfast Zucchini Oatmeal

Servings: 4 Cooking Time: 8 Hrs.

Ingredients:

1/2 cup steel cut oats
1 and 1/2 cups coconut milk
A pinch of cloves, ground
1/2 tsp. cinnamon powder
1/4 cup pecans, chopped
1 carrot, grated
1/4 zucchini, grated
A pinch of nutmeg, ground
2 tbsps. brown sugar

Directions:

In your Slow Cooker, mix oats with carrot, milk, zucchini, cloves, nutmeg, cinnamon and sugar, stir, cover and cook on Low for 8 Hrs.
Add pecans, toss, divide into bowls and serve.

Creamy Quinoa with Nuts

Servings:5 Cooking Time: 3 Hrs.

Ingredients:

1 oz. nuts, crushed
1 cup heavy cream
1 tsp. salt
1 oz. Parmesan, grated
2 cup quinoa
1 cup of water
1/4 tsp. chili flakes

Directions:

Put quinoa, heavy cream, water, salt, and chili flakes in the Slow Cooker.
Cook the ingredients on High for 3 Hrs.
Then add grated cheese and crushed nuts.
Stir the meal well and transfer in the serving plates.

Cauliflower Rice Pudding

Servings: 2 Cooking Time: 2 Hrs.

Ingredients:

1/4 cup maple syrup
1 cup cauliflower rice
3 cups almond milk
2 tbsps. vanilla extract

Directions:

Put cauliflower rice in your Slow Cooker, add maple syrup, almond milk and vanilla extract, stir, cover and cook on High for 2 Hrs.
Stir your pudding again, divide into bowls and serve for breakfast.

Saucy Sriracha Red Beans

Servings: 5 Cooking Time: 6 Hrs.

Ingredients:

1 cup red beans, soaked and drained
3 tbsp. tomato paste
1 tsp. salt
1 tsp. sriracha
1 tsp. turmeric
3 chicken stock
1 onion, sliced
1 chili pepper, sliced
1 tbsp. butter
1 cup green peas

Directions:

Spread the red beans in the Slow Cooker.
Add turmeric, salt, and chicken stock on its top.
Put the cooker's lid on and set the cooking time to 4 Hrs. on High settings.
Toss the sliced onion with Sriracha, butter, chili pepper, and sriracha in a separate bowl.
Spread this onion-pepper mixture over the cooked beans in the Slow Cooker.
Cover the beans again and slow cook for another 1 Hr. on Low setting.
Serve after a gentle stir.

Veggies Casserole

Servings: 8 Cooking Time: 4 Hrs.

Ingredients:

8 eggs
2 tsps. mustard
A pinch of salt and black pepper
1 yellow onion, chopped
4 bacon strips, chopped
4 egg whites
3/4 cup almond milk
2 red bell peppers, chopped
1 tsp. sweet paprika
6 oz. cheddar cheese, shredded
Cooking spray

Directions:

In a bowl, mix the eggs with egg whites, mustard, milk, salt, pepper and sweet paprika and whisk well.
Grease your Slow Cooker with cooking spray and spread bell peppers, bacon and onion on the bottom.
Add mixed eggs, sprinkle cheddar all over, cover and cook on Low for 4 Hrs.
Divide between plates and serve for breakfast.

Crock-pot Breakfast Casserole

Servings: 8 Cooking Time: 10-12 Hrs.

Ingredients:

1 lb. ground sausage, cooked, drained
1 dozen eggs
1/2 cup feta cheese, chopped
1 tsp. black pepper
1 1/2 cups spinach, fresh
1 green bell pepper, diced
4 cups daikon radish hashed browns
12-oz package bacon slices, crumbled, cooked, drained
1 cup heavy white cream
1 tsp. sea salt
2 cups Monterrey Jack cheese, shredded
1 1/2 cups mushrooms, fresh, sliced
1 medium sweet yellow onion, diced

Directions:

Place a layer of hashed browns on bottom of Crock-Pot. Follow with a layer of sausage and bacon, then add onions, spinach, green pepper, mushrooms and cheese. In a mixing bowl, beat the eggs, cream, salt, and pepper together. Pour over mixture in Crock-Pot. Cover and cook on LOW for 10-12 Hrs.

Chicken- Pork Meatballs

Servings: 8 Cooking Time: 7 Hrs.

Ingredients:

1 cup bread crumbs
9 oz. ground chicken
1 tsp. onion powder
1 tsp. ketchup
2 tbsp. sour cream
7 oz. ground pork
1 onion, chopped
1/4 tsp. olive oil

Directions:

Thoroughly mix ground chicken, onion powder, sour cream, ground pork, ketchup, and onion in a large bowl.
Add breadcrumbs to bind this mixture well.
Make small meatballs out of this mixture and roll them in extra breadcrumbs.
Brush the base of your Slow Cooker with olive oil.
Gently place the chicken-pork meatballs in the Slow Cooker.
Put the cooker's lid on and set the cooking time to 7 Hrs. on Low settings.
Serve warm.

Lunch & Dinner Recipes

Beef and Veggie Stew

Servings: 8 Cooking Time: 6 Hrs. and 30 Min

Ingredients:

3 potatoes, cubed
10 oz. canned tomato soup
3 and 3/4 cups water
1 yellow onion, chopped
1 garlic clove, minced
1 tsp. sugar
1/4 cup cornstarch
1 and 1/2 lb. beef chuck roast, boneless and cubed
1 and 1/2 cup baby carrots
1 celery rib, chopped
2 tbsps. Worcestershire sauce
Salt and black pepper to the taste
2 cups peas

Directions:

In your Slow Cooker, mix potatoes with beef cubes, tomato soup, baby carrots, 3 cups water, celery, onion, Worcestershire sauce, garlic, salt, pepper and sugar, stir, cover and cook on Low for 6 Hrs.
Add cornstarch mixed with the rest of the water and the peas, stir, cover and cook on Low for 30 Min. more.
Divide into bowls and serve for lunch.

Carne Adovada

Servings: 6 Cooking Time: 6 Hrs. 20 Min

Ingredients:

12 hot New Mexico red chili pods
3 cups chicken broth
1 tsp. ground cumin
2 garlic cloves, minced

½ tsp. salt
2 lbs. boneless pork shoulder, chunked
1/8 cup canola oil
1 tsp. Mexican oregano

Directions:

Put canola oil and pork shoulder in a pan over medium heat and cook for about 2 Min. on each side.
Transfer to a Slow Cooker and stir in the remaining ingredients.
Cover and cook on LOW for about 6 Hrs.
Dish out and serve hot.

Chinese Hot Pot

Servings: 6 Cooking Time: 2 1/4 Hrs.

Ingredients:

1 tbsp. canola oil
1 tsp. grated ginger
1 carrot, cut into sticks
1 cup chopped chestnuts
10 oz. firm tofu, cubed
2 red bell peppers, cored and sliced
1 tsp. tamarind paste
1/2 tsp. sesame oil
2 garlic cloves, chopped
1 shallot, chopped
1 celery stalk, cut into sticks
1 cup vegetable stock
4 oz. shiitake mushrooms, chopped
1/4 tsp. chili flakes
2 tbsps. soy sauce

Directions:

Heat the oil in a skillet and add the garlic, ginger, shallot, carrot and celery. Cook for 2 Min. then transfer in your Slow Cooker.
Add the remaining ingredients and cook on high settings for 2 Hrs.
Serve the dish warm.

Curried Beef Short Ribs

Servings: 6 Cooking Time: 8 1/4 Hrs.

Ingredients:

4 lbs. beef short ribs
1 cup tomato sauce
1/2 tsp. garlic powder
1 tsp. grated ginger
Salt and pepper to taste
3 tbsps. red curry paste
1 tsp. curry powder
2 shallots, chopped
1 lime, juiced

Directions:

Mix the curry paste, tomato sauce, curry powder, garlic powder, shallots, ginger and lime juice in a Slow Cooker.
Add salt and pepper then place the ribs in the pot as well.
Coat the ribs well and cover with a lid. Cook on low settings for 8 Hrs.
Serve the ribs warm and fresh.

Fennel Tomato Pasta Sauce

Servings: 10 Cooking Time: 8 1/4 Hrs.

Ingredients:

2 tbsps. olive oil
4 garlic cloves, chopped
1 can (28 oz.) diced tomatoes
1 cup tomato sauce
1 bay leaf
Salt and pepper to taste
2 onions, chopped
1 large fennel bulb, chopped
2 tbsps. tomato paste
1 cup vegetable stock
1 thyme sprig

Directions:

Heat the oil in a skillet and add the onions and garlic. Cook for 5 Min. until softened and caramelized slightly. Transfer in your Slow Cooker.
Add the remaining ingredients, as well as salt and pepper.
Cook on low settings for 8 Hrs.
The sauce can be served warm or can be frozen into individual portions and used when needed. You can also leave it chunkier or puree it into a fine sauce.

Mixed Pork and Beans

Servings: 2 Cooking Time: 8 Hrs.

Ingredients:

1 cup canned black beans, drained
½ lb. pork shoulder, cubed
3 garlic cloves, minced
½ cup beef stock
1 tbsp. olive oil
1 cup green beans, trimmed and halved
Salt and black pepper to the taste
½ yellow onion, chopped
¼ tbsp. balsamic vinegar

Directions:

In your Slow Cooker, mix the beans with the pork and the other ingredients, toss, put the lid on and cook on Low for 8 Hrs.
Divide everything between plates and serve.

Parsnip Butternut Squash Stew

Servings: 6 Cooking Time: 4 1/2 Hrs.

Ingredients:

2 tbsps. olive oil
3 parsnips, diced
1 green apple, peeled and diced
1/2 tsp. cumin powder
1/2 tsp. fennel seeds
1 thyme sprig
Plain yogurt for serving
1 sweet onion, chopped
4 cups butternut squash cubes
1 cup diced tomatoes
1/2 tsp. ground coriander
1 pinch chili powder
Salt and pepper to taste

Directions:

Heat the oil in a skillet and add the onion and parsnips. Cook for 5 Min. until softened then transfer in your Slow Cooker.
Add the remaining ingredients and cook on low settings for 4 Hrs., adjusting the taste with salt and pepper as needed.
Serve the stew warm, topped with plain yogurt if you want.

Mexican Shredded Chicken

Servings: 8 Cooking Time: 8 1/4 Hrs.

Ingredients:

4 chicken breasts
1 red onion, sliced
2 red bell peppers, cored and sliced
1 tsp. taco seasoning
Salt and pepper to taste
1 can fire roasted tomatoes
2 chipotle peppers, chopped
1 can (10 oz.) sweet corn, drained
1 cup chicken stock

Directions:

Combine the chicken and the rest of the ingredients in your Slow Cooker, adding enough salt and pepper.
Cover and cook on low settings for 8 Hrs.
When done, shred the chicken finely and serve it warm or chilled.

Spiced Butter Chicken

Servings: 6 Cooking Time: 6 3/4 Hrs.

Ingredients:

6 chicken thighs
1 large onion, chopped
1 tsp. curry powder
1/2 tsp. cumin powder
1 1/2 cups coconut milk
1/2 cup plain yogurt for serving
2 tbsps. butter
4 garlic cloves, chopped
1 tsp. garam masala
1/4 tsp. chili powder
Salt and pepper to taste

Directions:

Heat the butter in your Slow Cooker. Add the chicken and cook on all sides until golden brown.
Transfer the chicken in your Slow Cooker and add the remaining ingredients.
Cook on low settings for 6 Hrs.
Serve the chicken warm and fresh.

Lemon Chicken

Servings: 6 Cooking Time: 5 Hrs.

Ingredients:

6 chicken breast halves, skinless and bone in
1 tsp. oregano, dried
2 tbsps. butter
2 garlic cloves, minced
2 tsps. parsley, chopped
Salt and black pepper to the taste
¼ cup water
3 tbsps. lemon juice
1 tsp. chicken bouillon granules

Directions:

In your Slow Cooker, mix chicken with salt, pepper, water, butter, lemon juice, garlic and chicken granules, stir, cover and cook on Low for 5 Hrs.
Add parsley, stir, divide between plates and serve for lunch.

White Chicken Cassoulet

Servings: 8 Cooking Time: 6 1/4 Hrs.

Ingredients:

4 chicken breasts, cubed
2 cans (15 oz. each) white beans, drained
2 carrots, sliced
2 garlic cloves, chopped
1 cup chicken stock
2 tbsps. canola oil
2 celery stalks, sliced
1 large onion, chopped
1/4 cup dry white wine
Salt and pepper to taste

Directions:

Heat the oil in a skillet and add the chicken. Cook on all sides for a few Min. until golden then transfer the chicken in your Slow Cooker.
Add the rest of the ingredients in your Slow Cooker and adjust the taste with salt and pepper.
Cook on low settings for 6 Hrs.
Serve the cassoulet warm and fresh.

Asiago Chickpea Stew

Servings: 4 Cooking Time: 2 1/4 Hrs.

Ingredients:

2 cans (15 oz. each) chickpeas, drained
1/2 cup vegetable stock
Salt and pepper to taste
1 cup grated Asiago cheese
2 ripe tomatoes, peeled and diced
1/2 cup light cream
1/2 tsp. dried oregano

Directions:

Combine the chickpeas, tomatoes, stock, cream, salt, pepper and oregano in your Slow Cooker.
Top with grated cheese and cook on high settings for 2 Hrs.
Serve the stew warm and fresh.

Mushroom Pork Stew

Servings: 6 Cooking Time: 5 1/4 Hrs.

Ingredients:

1 lb. pork roast, cubed
1 lb. button mushrooms
1 tbsp. cornstarch
1 thyme sprig
2 tbsps. canola oil
1 1/2 cups chicken stock
1 cup cream cheese
Salt and pepper to taste

Directions:

Heat the oil in a skillet and add the pork. Cook on all sides until golden then transfer in your Slow Cooker.
Add the remaining ingredients and season with salt and pepper.
Cook on low settings for 5 Hrs. and serve the stew warm and fresh.

Chicken and Brussels Sprouts Mix

Servings: 2 Cooking Time: 6 Hrs.

Ingredients:

1 lb. chicken breast, skinless, boneless and cubed
1 cup Brussels sprouts, trimmed and halved
½ cup tomato paste
1 garlic clove, crushed
1 tbsp. rosemary, chopped
1 red onion, sliced
1 cup chicken stock
A pinch of salt and black pepper
1 tbsp. thyme, chopped

Directions:

In your Slow Cooker, mix the chicken with the onion, sprouts and the other ingredients, toss, put the lid on and cook on Low for 6 Hrs.
Divide the mix between plates and serve for lunch.

Blue Cheese Chicken

Servings: 4 Cooking Time: 2 1/4 Hrs.

Ingredients:

4 chicken breasts
Salt and pepper to taste
1/2 cup chicken stock
1 tsp. dried oregano
1/2 cup crumbled blue cheese

Directions:

Season the chicken with salt and pepper and place it in your Slow Cooker.
Add the stock then top each piece of chicken with crumbled feta cheese.
Cook on high settings for 2 Hrs.
Serve the chicken warm.

Curry Braised Chicken

Servings: 6 Cooking Time: 8 1/4 Hrs.

Ingredients:

6 chicken thighs
1 tsp. curry powder
1/2 tsp. onion powder
1/4 tsp. chili powder
1 cup chicken stock
Cooked white rice for serving
1 tbsp. grated ginger
1 tsp. garlic powder
1/2 tsp. cumin powder
1/2 cup plain yogurt
Salt and pepper to taste

Directions:

Season the chicken with ginger, curry powder, garlic powder, onion, cumin and chili powder.
Place the chicken in your Slow Cooker then add the yogurt and stock.
Adjust the taste with salt and pepper and cook on low settings for 8 Hrs.
Serve the chicken warm over cooked white rice.

Whole Roasted Cauliflower

Servings: 4 Cooking Time: 6 1/4 Hrs.

Ingredients:

1 head cauliflower
1/4 tsp. garlic powder
1/2 tsp. dried thyme
1 pinch cayenne pepper
1 cup tomato sauce
1/4 tsp. onion powder
1/4 tsp. salt
1/2 cup vegetable stock

Directions:

Place the cauliflower in your Slow Cooker.
Combine the remaining ingredients in a bowl and pour this mixture over the cauliflower.
Cover with a lid and cook on low settings for 6 Hrs.
Serve the cauliflower warm and fresh.

Wild Mushroom Barley Risotto

Servings: 6 Cooking Time: 6 1/4 Hrs.

Ingredients:

2 tbsps. olive oil
1 celery stalk, diced
1 carrot, diced
2 cups vegetable stock
Salt and pepper to taste
1 shallot, chopped
1 garlic clove, minced
1 cup pearl barley
1/4 cup grated Parmesan
1 thyme sprig

Directions:

Heat the oil in a skillet and add the shallot, celery, garlic and carrot. Cook for 2 Min. until softened. Transfer in your Slow Cooker.
Add the remaining ingredients, except the Parmesan, and season with salt and pepper.
Cook on low settings for 6 Hrs.
When done, add the cheese and mix well.
Serve the risotto warm.

Tomato Sauce Pork Roast

Servings: 4 Cooking Time: 3 1/4 Hrs.

Ingredients:

2 lbs. pork roast, cubed
1/2 cup tomato sauce
2 tbsps. tomato paste
Salt and pepper to taste
2 tbsps. canola oil
1/2 cup chicken stock
1/4 tsp. cayenne pepper

Directions:

Combine all the ingredients in your Slow Cooker.
Add salt and pepper to taste and cook on high settings for 3 Hrs.
Serve the pork roast warm and fresh with your favorite side dish.

Tofu Chickpea Curry

Servings: 6 Cooking Time: 6 1/2 Hrs.

Ingredients:

12 oz. firm tofu, cubed
1 tsp. curry powder
2 garlic cloves, chopped
1 large sweet potato, peeled and cubed
1 cup diced tomatoes
1 cup vegetable stock
1 tsp. grated ginger
2 tbsps. olive oil
1 large onion, chopped
2 cups cauliflower florets
1 can (15 oz.) chickpeas, drained
1 cup coconut milk
1 kaffir lime leaf
Salt and pepper to taste

Directions:

Heat the oil in a skillet and add the tofu. Cook on all sides until golden and crusty.
Sprinkle with curry powder and fry just 1 additional minute.
Transfer in your Slow Cooker.
Add the remaining ingredients and season well.
Cook on low settings for 6 Hrs.
Serve the curry warm.

Pork and Tomatoes Mix

Servings: 2 Cooking Time: 8 Hrs.

Ingredients:

1 and ½ lbs. pork stew meat, cubed
1 cup tomato paste
½ tsp. sweet paprika
A pinch of salt and black pepper
1 cup cherry tomatoes, halved
1 tbsp. rosemary, chopped
½ tsp. coriander, ground
1 tbsp. chives, chopped

Directions:

In your Slow Cooker, combine the meat with the tomatoes, tomato paste and the other ingredients, toss, put the lid on and cook on Low for 8 Hrs.
Divide between plates and serve for lunch.

Bavarian Beef Roast

Servings: 6 Cooking Time: 10 1/4 Hrs.

Ingredients:

2 lbs. beef roast
2 tbsps. mustard seeds
1 cup apple juice
Salt and pepper to taste
2 tbsps. all-purpose flour
1 tsp. prepared horseradish
1/2 cup beef stock

Directions:

Season the beef with salt and pepper and sprinkle with flour.
Combine the beef roast and the rest of the ingredients in your Slow Cooker.
Add salt and pepper as needed and cook on low settings for 10 Hrs.
Serve the roast while still warm.

Chicken Tacos

Servings: 16 Cooking Time: 5 Hrs.

Ingredients:

2 mangos, peeled and chopped
1 and ½ cups pineapple chunks
2 small green bell peppers, chopped
2 green onions, chopped
4 lbs. chicken breast halves, skinless
32 taco shells, warm
¼ cup brown sugar
2 tomatoes, chopped
1 red onion, chopped
1 tbsp. lime juice
1 tsp. sugar
Salt and black pepper to the taste
¼ cup cilantro, chopped

Directions:

In a bowl, mix mango with pineapple, red onion, tomatoes, bell peppers, green onions and lime juice and toss.
Put chicken in your Slow Cooker, add salt, pepper and sugar and toss.
Add mango mix, cover and cook on Low for 5 Hrs.
Transfer chicken to a cutting board, cool it down, discard bones and shred meat.
Divide meat and mango mix between taco shells and serve them for lunch.

Cauliflower Mashed Sweet Potato

Servings: 6 Cooking Time: 6 1/4 Hrs.

Ingredients:

1 head cauliflower, cut into florets
1 shallot, chopped
1 cup vegetable stock
1 lb. sweet potatoes, peeled and cubed
2 garlic cloves, chopped
Salt and pepper to taste

Directions:

Combine all the ingredients in your Slow Cooker.
Add salt and pepper to taste and cook on low settings for 6 Hrs.
When done, mash the mix with a potato masher and serve warm.

Bean and Spinach Enchilada Sauce

Servings: 8 Cooking Time: 6 1/4 Hrs.

Ingredients:

1 can (15 oz.) black beans, drained
1 cup frozen corn
1/2 tsp. chili powder
1 can fire roasted tomatoes
Salt and pepper to taste
10 oz. frozen spinach, thawed and drained
1/2 tsp. cumin powder
1 cup tomato sauce
1/2 lime, juiced

Directions:

Combine all the ingredients in your Slow Cooker, adding salt and pepper as needed.
Cook on low settings for 6 Hrs.
Serve the enchilada sauce warm or keep cooking it after wrapping it in flour tortillas. The sauce can also be frozen into individual portions to serve later.

Balsamic Braised Chicken with Swiss Chard

Servings: 8 Cooking Time: 8 1/4 Hrs.

Ingredients:

2 tbsps. olive oil
4 garlic cloves, chopped
2 anchovy fillets
1/4 cup balsamic vinegar
2 bay leaves
1 cup chicken stock
1 bunch Swiss chard, shredded
1 large onion, sliced
1 tsp. dried thyme
1 tsp. red pepper flakes
1 can (15 oz.) diced tomatoes
8 chicken thighs
Salt and pepper to taste

Directions:

Heat the oil in a skillet and add the onion and garlic. sauté for 2 Min. until softened.
Add the rest of the ingredients and season with salt and pepper.
Cook on low settings for 8 Hrs.
Serve the chicken warm and fresh.

Three Pepper Roasted Pork Tenderloin

Servings: 8 Cooking Time: 8 1/4 Hrs.

Ingredients:

3 lbs. pork tenderloin
1/4 cup three pepper mix
1 cup chicken stock
2 tbsps. Dijon mustard
Salt and pepper to taste

Directions:

Season the pork with salt and pepper.
Brush the meat with mustard. Spread the pepper mix on your chopping board then roll the pork through this mixture, making sure to coat it well.
Place carefully in your Slow Cooker and pour in the stock.
Cook on low settings for 8 Hrs.
Serve the pork tenderloin sliced and warm with your favorite side dish.

Seafood Soup

Servings: 2 Cooking Time: 8 Hrs.

Ingredients:

2 cups chicken stock
1 sweet potato, cubed
1 bay leaf
½ tbsp. thyme, dried
½ lbs. salmon fillets, skinless, boneless cubed
1 tbsp. chives, chopped
1 cup coconut milk
½ yellow onion, chopped
1 carrot, peeled and sliced
Salt and black pepper to the taste
12 shrimp, peeled and deveined

Directions:

In your Slow Cooker, mix the carrot with the sweet potato, onion and the other ingredients except the salmon, shrimp and chives, toss, put the lid on and cook on Low for 6 Hrs.
Add the rest of the ingredients, toss, put the lid on and cook on Low for 2 more Hrs.
Divide the soup into bowls and serve for lunch.

Classic Osso Buco

Servings: 4 Cooking Time: 7 1/4 Hrs.

Ingredients:

4 veal shanks
2 tbsp. butter
1 can (15 oz.) diced tomatoes
1 tsp. dried thyme
1/2 tsp. garlic powder
2 tbsps. all-purpose flour
2 red onions, chopped
1/4 cup red wine
1/4 tsp. cayenne pepper
Salt and pepper to taste

Directions:

Season the veal shanks with salt and pepper and sprinkle them with flour.
Melt the butter in a frying pan and add the veal shanks. Cook on all sides until golden.
Mix the remaining ingredients in your Slow Cooker then place the veal shanks on top.
Cover with a lid and cook on low settings for 7 Hrs.
Serve the osso bucco and the sauce formed in the pot warm and fresh.

Chicken Cauliflower Gratin

Servings: 6 Cooking Time: 6 1/4 Hrs.

Ingredients:

1 head cauliflower, cut into florets
1/2 tsp. garlic powder
1 can condensed cream of chicken soup
1 1/2 cups grated Cheddar
2 chicken breasts, cubed
1 pinch cayenne pepper
Salt and pepper to taste

Directions:

Combine the cauliflower, chicken, garlic powder, cayenne pepper, chicken soup, salt and pepper in your Slow Cooker.
Top with grated cheese and cook on low settings for 6 Hrs.
Serve the gratin warm and fresh.

Beans-rice Mix

Servings:4 Cooking Time: 3 Hrs.

Ingredients:

5 oz. red kidney beans, canned
¼ tsp. ground coriander
2 cups chicken stock
1 tsp. garlic powder
½ cup long-grain rice

Directions:

Put long-grain rice in the Slow Cooker.
Add chicken stock, ground coriander, and garlic powder.
Close the lid and cook the rice for 2.5 Hrs. on High.
Then add red kidney beans, stir the mixture, and cook for 30 Min. in High.

Lamb and Onion Stew

Servings: 2 Cooking Time: 8 Hrs.

Ingredients:

1 lb. lamb meat, cubed
3 spring onions, sliced
1 tbsp. olive oil
¼ tsp. thyme, dried
½ cup baby carrots, peeled
1 tbsp. cilantro, chopped
1 red onion, sliced
Salt and black pepper to the taste
½ tsp. rosemary, dried
1 cup water
½ cup tomato sauce

Directions:

In your Slow Cooker, mix the lamb with the onion, spring onions and the other ingredients, toss, put the lid on and cook on Low for 8 Hrs.
Divide the stew between plates and serve hot.

Pear Roasted Chicken

Servings: 6 Cooking Time: 8 1/4 Hrs.

Ingredients:

6 chicken thighs
1 fennel bulb, sliced
1 cup apple cider
1 thyme sprig
2 ripe pears, cored and sliced
2 shallots, sliced
1 bay leaf
Salt and pepper to taste

Directions:

Combine the chicken with the remaining ingredients in your Slow Cooker.
Add salt and pepper to taste and cook on low settings for 8 Hrs.
Serve the chicken warm and fresh.

Honey Orange Glazed Tofu

Servings: 4 Cooking Time: 4 1/4 Hrs.

Ingredients:

12 oz. firm tofu, cubed
1 garlic clove, minced
2 tbsps. soy sauce
1/4 cup vegetable stock
1 tbsp. grated ginger
1 orange, zested and juiced
1 tsp. Worcestershire sauce

Directions:

Combine all the ingredients in your Slow Cooker.
Cover and cook on low settings for 4 Hrs.
The tofu is best served warm with your favorite side dish.

Soy Braised Chicken

Servings: 6 Cooking Time: 3 1/4 Hrs.

Ingredients:

6 chicken thighs
2 garlic cloves, chopped
1/4 cup soy sauce
1 tbsp. brown sugar
Salt and pepper to taste
2 shallots, sliced
1/4 cup apple cider
1 bay leaf
1/2 tsp. cayenne pepper
Cooked white rice for serving

Directions:

Combine the chicken, shallots, garlic cloves, apple cider, soy sauce, leaf, brown sugar and cayenne pepper in your Slow Cooker.
Adjust the taste with salt and pepper if needed and cook on high settings for 3 Hrs.
Serve the chicken warm.

Eggplant Tapenade

Servings: 6 Cooking Time: 4 1/4 Hrs.

Ingredients:

1 large eggplant, peeled and diced
1 cup green olives, pitted and sliced
1 can fire roasted tomatoes
1 cup vegetable stock
1/4 tsp. dried basil
1 tbsp. olive oil
1/2 cup black olives, pitted and sliced
2 artichoke hearts, diced
Salt and pepper to taste
1/4 tsp. dried oregano

Directions:

Combine the eggplant, olive oil, olives, tomatoes, stock and herbs in your Slow Cooker.

Add salt and pepper to taste and cook on low settings for 2 Hrs. then on high for 2 additional Hrs.
Serve the tapenade warm or chilled.

Buttered Broccoli

Servings: 4 Cooking Time: 1 1/2 Hrs.

Ingredients:

2 heads broccoli, cut into florets
1 shallot, sliced
2 garlic cloves, chopped
4 tbsps. butter
Salt and pepper to taste

Directions:

Combine all the ingredients in your Slow Cooker.
Add enough salt and pepper and cook the broccoli on high settings for 1 1/4 Hrs.
Serve the broccoli warm and fresh.

Lemon Vegetable Pork Roast

Servings: 8 Cooking Time: 8 1/4 Hrs.

Ingredients:

1 large onion, sliced
4 lbs. pork roast, cut into quarters
1/2 lbs. baby carrots
2 cups snap peas
2 parsnips, sliced
2 large potatoes, peeled and cubed
1 cup vegetable stock
1 tbsp. molasses
1/4 cup red wine vinegar
2 tbsps. soy sauce
2 tbsp. ketchup
1 tsp. garlic powder
1/4 tsp. cayenne pepper
Salt and pepper to taste
1 lemon, sliced

Directions:

Combine the onion, pork roast, baby carrots, snap peas, parsnips, potatoes, stock, molasses, vinegar, soy sauce, ketchup, garlic powder and cayenne pepper in your Slow Cooker.
Add salt and pepper to taste and cover with lemon slices. Cover the pot with its lid.
Cook on low settings for 8 Hrs.
Serve the roast warm and fresh.

Beans Chili

Servings: 2 Cooking Time: 3 Hrs.

Ingredients:

½ red bell pepper, chopped
½ green bell pepper, chopped
1 garlic clove, minced
½ cup yellow onion, chopped
½ cup roasted tomatoes, crushed
1 cup canned red kidney beans, drained
1 cup canned white beans, drained
1 cup canned black beans, drained
½ cup corn
Salt and black pepper to the taste
1 tbsp. chili powder
1 cup veggie stock

Directions:

In your Slow Cooker, mix the peppers with the beans and the other ingredients, toss, put the lid on and cook on High for 3 Hrs.
Divide into bowls and serve right away.

Artichoke Soup

Servings: 2 Cooking Time: 5 Hrs.

Ingredients:

2 cups canned artichoke hearts, drained and halved
1 small carrot, chopped
1 small yellow onion, chopped
1 garlic clove, minced
¼ tsp. oregano, dried
¼ tsp. rosemary, dried
A pinch of red pepper flakes
A pinch of garlic powder
A pinch of salt and black pepper
3 cups chicken stock
1 tbsp. tomato paste
1 tbsp. cilantro, chopped

Directions:

In your Slow Cooker, mix the artichokes with the carrot, onion and the other ingredients, toss, put the lid on and cook on Low for 5 Hrs.
Ladle into bowls and serve.

Lentils Soup

Servings: 2 Cooking Time: 4 Hrs.

Ingredients:

2 garlic cloves, minced
1 carrot, chopped
1 red onion, chopped
3 cups veggie stock
1 cup brown lentils
½ tsp. cumin, ground
1 bay leaf
1 tbsp. lime juice
1 tbsp. cilantro, chopped
Salt and black pepper to the taste

Directions:

In your Slow Cooker, mix the lentils with the garlic, carrot and the other ingredients, toss, put the lid on and cook on High for 4 Hrs.
Ladle the soup into bowls and serve.

Chili Verde

Servings: 8 Cooking Time: 7 1/4 Hrs.

Ingredients:

2 lbs. pork shoulder, cubed
2 tbsps. canola oil
2 lbs. tomatillos, peeled and chopped
1 large onion, chopped
4 garlic cloves, chopped
1 tsp. dried oregano
1 tsp. cumin powder
1/2 tsp. smoked paprika
1/4 tsp. chili powder
1 bunch cilantro, chopped
2 green chilis, chopped
1 1/2 cups chicken stock
Salt and pepper to taste

Directions:

Heat the oil in a skillet and add the pork shoulder. Cook for a few Min. on all sides until golden then transfer in your Slow Cooker.
Add the rest of the ingredients in your pot as well and season with salt and pepper.
Cook on low settings for 7 Hrs.
Serve the chili warm.

Hamburger Beef Casserole

Servings: 6 Cooking Time: 7 1/2 Hrs.

Ingredients:

1 1/2 lbs. beef sirloin, cut into thin trips
2 large potatoes, peeled and finely sliced
1 celery stalk, sliced
2 onions, sliced
1 cup green peas
1 can condensed cream of mushroom soup
Salt and pepper to taste
1 cup processed meat, shredded

1 cup grated Cheddar cheese

Directions:

Mix the beef, potatoes, celery stalk, green peas, mushroom soup, salt and pepper in your Slow Cooker.
Top with both cheeses and cover with a lid.
Cook on low settings for 7 Hrs.
Serve the casserole preferably warm.

Slow Cooker Jambalaya

Servings: 8 Cooking Time: 6 1/2 Hrs.

Ingredients:

2 tbsps. olive oil
1 large onion, chopped
2 garlic cloves, chopped
2 ripe tomatoes, peeled and diced
1 large sweet potato, peeled and cubed
1 1/4 cups vegetable stock
8 oz. firm tofu, cubed
2 red bell peppers, cored and diced
1/2 tsp. Cajun seasoning
1/2 head cauliflower, cut into florets
1 tbsp. tomato paste
Salt and pepper to taste

Directions:

Heat the oil in a skillet and add the tofu. Cook on low settings for a few Min. until golden brown.
Transfer in your Slow Cooker and add the rest of the ingredients, adjusting the taste with salt and pepper.
Cook on low settings for 6 Hrs.
Serve the jambalaya warm and fresh.

Vegetable Pot Pie

Servings: 6 Cooking Time: 6 1/2 Hrs.

Ingredients:

1 celery stalk, diced
1 red bell pepper, cored and diced
1/2 tsp. dried oregano
1 cup green peas
1 cup vegetable stock
6 oz. biscuit dough
1 carrot, diced
1 onion, chopped
1 tbsp. all-purpose flour
1 cup chopped green beans
Salt and pepper to taste

Directions:

Combine the celery, carrot, bell pepper, onion, oregano and flour in a bowl and mix well.
Transfer the mix in your Slow Cooker and add the green peas, beans and stock, as well as salt and pepper.
Top with biscuit dough and cook on low settings for 6 Hrs.
Serve the pot pie warm.

Turnip and Beans Casserole

Servings:4 Cooking Time: 6 Hrs.

Ingredients:

½ cup turnip, chopped
¼ cup of coconut milk
¼ cup potato, chopped 1 carrot, diced
½ cup Cheddar cheese, shredded
1 tsp. chili powder
1 tsp. coconut oil
1 cup red kidney beans, canned

Directions:

Grease the Slow Cooker bottom with coconut oil.
Then put the turnip and potato inside.
Sprinkle the vegetables with chili powder and coconut mil.
After this, top the with red kidney beans and Cheddar cheese.
Close the lid and cook the casserole on Low for 6 Hrs.

Italian Style Pork Shoulder

Servings: 6 Cooking Time: 7 1/4 Hrs.

Ingredients:

2 lbs. pork shoulder
4 garlic cloves, chopped
2 ripe tomatoes, peeled and diced
1 tsp. dried thyme
1 thyme sprig
1 large onion, sliced
2 celery stalks, sliced
1/4 cup white wine
1 tsp. dried basil
Salt and pepper to taste

Directions:

Combine all the ingredients in your Slow Cooker, adjusting the taste with enough salt and pepper.
Cover with a lid and cook on low settings for 7 Hrs.
Serve the pork shoulder warm and fresh with your favorite side dish.

Creamy Chicken Soup

Servings: 6 Cooking Time: 6 Hrs.

Ingredients:

2 chicken breasts, skinless and boneless
1 cup peas
1 cup carrots, chopped
4 oz. cream cheese, soft
4 cups chicken stock
3 cups heavy cream
1 cup yellow corn
1 celery stalk, chopped
2 gold potatoes, cubed
1 yellow onion, chopped
2 tsps. garlic powder
Salt and black pepper to the taste

Directions:

In your Slow Cooker, mix chicken with corn, peas, carrots, potatoes, celery, cream cheese, onion, garlic powder, stock, heavy cream, salt and pepper, stir, cover and cook on Low for 6 Hrs.
Transfer chicken to a cutting board, shred meat using2 forks, return to the Slow Cooker, stir, ladle soup into bowls and serve for lunch.

Vegetable Beef Roast with Horseradish

Servings: 8 Cooking Time: 6 1/2 Hrs.

Ingredients:

4 lbs. beef roast, trimmed of fat
2 large carrots, sliced
2 cups sliced mushrooms
1 celery root, peeled and cubed
1 cup water
1/4 cup prepared horseradish for serving
4 large potatoes, peeled and halved
2 onions, quartered
2 cups snap peas
1 cup beef stock
Salt and pepper to taste

Directions:

Mix all the ingredients in your Slow Cooker, adding salt and pepper to taste.
Cook on low settings for 6 Hrs.
When done, serve the roast warm with prepared horseradish as sauce.

Cuban Flank Steaks

Servings: 6 Cooking Time: 8 1/4 Hrs.

Ingredients:

6 beef flank steaks
1 tsp. cumin seeds
1 tsp. dried oregano
1 chipotle pepper, chopped
Salt and pepper to taste
2 red onions, sliced
1 tsp. chili powder
1 cup beef stock
2 limes, juiced

Directions:

Combine the steaks in your Slow Cooker and add salt and pepper.
Cover and cook for 8 Hrs. on low settings.
Serve the steaks warm.

Three Bean Cornbread Casserole

Servings: 8 Cooking Time: 6 1/2 Hrs.

Ingredients:

1 can (15 oz.) black beans, drained
1 can (15 oz.) white beans, drained
2 red bell peppers, cored and diced
1 cup frozen corn
1 cup vegetable stock
1/2 cup yellow cornmeal
1 tsp. baking powder
1/2 cup whole milk
Salt and pepper to taste
1 can (15 oz.) red beans, drained
1 cup fire roasted tomatoes
2 tbsps. tomato sauce
1 jalapeno pepper, chopped
1/2 tsp. dried thyme
1/2 cup all-purpose flour
1/2 cup buttermilk
1/4 tsp. cumin seeds

Directions:

Combine the beans, tomatoes, bell peppers, tomato sauce, corn, jalapeno pepper, stock and thyme in your Slow Cooker.
Add salt and pepper to taste.
In a bowl, mix the cornmeal, flour, baking powder, buttermilk, milk, salt and pepper. Give it a quick mix.
Spoon the batter over the vegetable mix and cook on low settings for 6 Hrs.
Serve the dish warm.

Onion Pork Chops with Creamy Mustard Sauce

Servings: 4 Cooking Time: 5 1/4 Hrs.

Ingredients:

4 pork chops, bone in
4 garlic cloves, minced
1/4 tsp. cayenne pepper
1/2 cup white wine
1/2 cup heavy cream
2 onions, finely chopped
1 tsp. dried mustard
1 tbsp. apple cider vinegar
2 tbsps. Dijon mustard
Salt and pepper to taste

Directions:

Combine the chops, onions, garlic, mustard, cayenne pepper, vinegar, wine and cream in your Slow Cooker.
Add salt and pepper to taste and cook on low settings for 5 Hrs.
Serve the dish warm and fresh.

Bourbon Baked Beans

Servings: 8 Cooking Time: 10 1/4 Hrs.

Ingredients:

1 lb. dried black beans, rinsed
1/4 cup maple syrup
2 cups vegetable stock
1 tsp. mustard seeds
1 tbsp. apple cider vinegar
Salt and pepper to taste
1 cup bourbon
1 cup BBQ sauce
1/2 cup ketchup
1 tbsp. molasses
1 tsp. Worcestershire sauce

Directions:

Combine the black beans, bourbon, maple syrup, BBQ sauce, stock, ketchup, seeds, molasses, Worcestershire sauce and vinegar in your Slow Cooker.
Add salt and pepper to taste and cook on low settings for 10 Hrs.
Serve the beans warm or chilled.

Sweet Glazed Chicken Drumsticks

Servings: 4 Cooking Time: 5 1/4 Hrs.

Ingredients:

2 lbs. chicken drumsticks
1 cup pineapple juice
2 tbsps. brown sugar
2 green onions, chopped
White rice for serving
1 tsp. grated ginger
2 tbsps. soy sauce
1/4 tsp. chili powder
1/4 cup chicken stock

Directions:

Combine the drumsticks, ginger, pineapple juice, soy sauce, brown sugar, chili, stock and green onions in your Slow Cooker.
Add salt and pepper to taste and cook on low settings for 5 Hrs.
Serve the dish warm, over cooked white rice.

Asparagus Barley Stew

Servings: 6 Cooking Time: 6 1/4 Hrs.

Ingredients:

1 bunch asparagus, trimmed and chopped
1 garlic clove, chopped
1 cup pearl barley
Salt and pepper to taste
1 shallot, chopped
1/2 tsp. fennel seeds
2 cups vegetable stock
1/2 cup grated Parmesan

Directions:

Combine the asparagus, shallot, garlic, fennel seeds, pearl barley and stock in your Slow Cooker.
Add salt and pepper to taste and cook on low settings for 6 Hrs.
When done, stir in the Parmesan and serve the stew warm and fresh.

Honey Apple Pork Chops

Servings: 4 Cooking Time: 5 1/4 Hrs.

Ingredients:

4 pork chops
1 shallot, chopped
1 tbsp. olive oil
1 heirloom tomato, peeled and diced
2 tbsps. honey
2 red, tart apples, peeled, cored and cubed
2 garlic cloves, chopped
1 red chili, chopped
1 cup apple cider
Salt and pepper to taste

Directions:

Mix all the ingredients in your Slow Cooker.
Add salt and pepper to taste and cook on low settings for 5 Hrs.
Serve the chops warm and fresh.

Beans and Peas Bowl

Servings:4 Cooking Time: 6 Hrs.

Ingredients:

½ cup black beans, soaked
4 cups of water
1 tsp. sriracha
1 cup green peas
1 tbsp. tomato paste

Directions:

Pour water in the Slow Cooker.
Add black beans and cook them for 5 Hrs. on High.
Then add green peas, tomato paste, and sriracha.
Stir the ingredients and cook the meal for 1 Hr. on High.

Cheesy Chicken Pasta

Servings: 6 Cooking Time: 6 1/4 Hrs.

Ingredients:

2 cups fusilli pasta
2 cups chicken stock
1 cup cream cheese
1/2 cup grated Parmesan
2 chicken breasts, diced
2 celery stalks, sliced
1 cup grated Cheddar
Salt and pepper to taste

Directions:

Combine all the ingredients in your Slow Cooker.
Season with salt and pepper if needed and cook on low settings for 6 Hrs.
Serve the pasta warm.

Beef Lentil Stew with Goat Cheese

Servings: 6 Cooking Time: 5 1/4 Hrs.

Ingredients:

1 lb. beef roast, cut into thin strips
2 tbsps. canola oil
1 large onion, chopped
2 garlic cloves, minced
1 cup brown lentils
1/4 cup red lentils
1/2 tsp. chili powder
1/2 tsp. fennel seeds
1 cup diced tomatoes
1 cups beef stock
1 bay leaf
1 thyme sprig
Salt and pepper to taste
Crumbled goat cheese for serving

Directions:

Heat the canola oil in a skillet and add the beef. Cook for a few Min. on all sides then transfer in your Slow Cooker.
Add the rest of the ingredients and season with salt and pepper.
When done, pour the stew into serving plates and top with crumbled goat cheese while still warm. Serve right away.

Mustard Pork Chops and Carrots

Servings: 2 Cooking Time: 4 Hrs.

Ingredients:

1 tbsp. butter
2 carrots, sliced
½ tbsp. honey
1 tbsp. lime zest, grated
1 lb. pork chops, bone in
1 cup beef stock
½ tbsp. lime juice

Directions:

In your Slow Cooker, mix the pork chops with the butter and the other ingredients, toss, put the lid on and cook on High for 4 Hrs.
Divide between plate sand serve.

Spinach Potato Stew

Servings: 6 Cooking Time: 4 1/4 Hrs.

Ingredients:

2 lbs. potatoes, peeled and cubed
1 shallot, chopped
1/4 tsp. cumin powder
1/4 tsp. fennel seeds
1 cup vegetable stock
2 tbsps. olive oil
2 garlic cloves, chopped
1/4 tsp. coriander powder
4 cups spinach
Salt and pepper to taste

Directions:

Heat the oil in a skillet and add the shallot and garlic. Cook for 2 Min. until softened then add the spices and sauté just for 30 seconds to release flavors.
Transfer in your Slow Cooker and add the remaining ingredients.
Season with salt and pepper and cook on low settings for 4 Hrs.
Serve the stew warm.

Dumplings with Polenta

Servings:6 Cooking Time: 45 Min

Ingredients:

3 oz. polenta
2 oz. Cheddar cheese, shredded
1 egg, beaten
3 oz. flour
½ cup of coconut milk
3 oz. water, hot

Directions:

Mix polenta and flour. Add egg and coconut milk. Mix the ingredients well.
Add cheddar cheese and knead the soft dough.
Cut the dough into 6 pieces and roll them into balls.
Pour water in the Slow Cooker.
Add polenta balls and cook them for 45 Min. on HIGH.
Drain the water and transfer the dumplings in the serving plates.

Tempeh Carnitas

Servings: 6 Cooking Time: 6 1/2 Hrs.

Ingredients:

1 lb. tempeh, cut into thin strips
4 garlic cloves, minced
1/2 tsp. dried oregano
1 cup vegetable stock
2 tbsps. canola oil
1 large onion, finely chopped
1/2 tsp. dried basil
Salt and pepper to taste

Directions:

Heat the oil in a skillet and add the tempeh. Cook on all sides until golden then transfer in your Slow Cooker.
Add the remaining ingredients and cook on low settings for 6 Hrs.
Serve the dish warm.

Chickpea Tikka Masala

Servings: 6 Cooking Time: 6 1/2 Hrs.

Ingredients:

2 tbsps. olive oil
4 garlic cloves, chopped
1 tsp. garam masala
1/2 tsp. red chili, sliced
1 can diced tomatoes
Salt and pepper to taste
1 large onion, chopped
1 tsp. grated ginger
1/2 tsp. turmeric powder
2 cans (15 oz. each) chickpeas, drained
1 cup coconut milk
Chopped cilantro for serving

Directions:

Heat the oil in a skillet and stir in the onion and garlic. Cook for 2 Min. until softened and translucent then transfer in your Slow Cooker.

Add the remaining ingredients and season well with salt and pepper.

Cover and cook on low settings for 6 Hrs.

The chickpea tikka masala is best served warm.

Cheesy Chicken Chili

Servings: 10 Cooking Time: 8 1/4 Hrs.

Ingredients:

2 lbs. boneless, skinless chicken breasts, cubed
2 tbsps. canola oil
4 bacon slices, chopped
2 cups red salsa
1 can (15 oz.) black beans, drained
1 can (15 oz.) kidney beans, drained
1 can (15 oz.) sweet corn, drained
2 celery stalks, sliced
2 large red onions, chopped
1 cup tomato sauce
1 tsp. chili powder
1tsp cumin powder
1 tsp. garlic powder
1 1/2 cups chicken stock
Salt and pepper to taste
Grated Cheddar cheese for serving

Directions:

Heat the oil in a skillet and add the bacon. Cook until crisp then stir in the chicken and cook for a few Min. on all sides until golden.

Transfer the chicken in your Slow Cooker and add the remaining ingredients.

Season with salt and pepper and cook on low settings for 8 Hrs.

Serve the chili warm, topped with grated cheese.

Beef Stroganoff

Servings: 6 Cooking Time: 6 1/4 Hrs.

Ingredients:

1 1/2 lbs. beef stew meat, cubed
1 large onion, chopped
4 garlic cloves, minced
1 tbsp. Worcestershire sauce
1/2 cup water
1 cup cream cheese
Salt and pepper to taste
Cooked pasta for serving

Directions:

Mix all the ingredients in a Slow Cooker.

Add salt and pepper to taste and cook on low settings for 6 Hrs.

Serve the stroganoff warm and serve it with cooked pasta of your choice.

Creamed Sweet Corn

Servings: 6 Cooking Time: 3 1/4 Hrs.

Ingredients:

2 cans (15 oz.) sweet corn, drained
1 cup cream cheese
1 cup grated Cheddar cheese
1/2 cup heavy cream
Salt and pepper to taste
1 pinch nutmeg

Directions:

Combine the corn, cream cheese, Cheddar and cream in your Slow Cooker.

Add the nutmeg, salt and pepper and cook on low settings for 3 Hrs.

Serve the creamed corn warm.

Layered Spinach Ricotta Lasagna

Servings: 10 Cooking Time: 6 1/2 Hrs.

Ingredients:

16 oz. frozen spinach, thawed
1 cup ricotta cheese
1/2 tsp. dried marjoram
1/2 tsp. dried basil
2 garlic cloves, chopped
1/2 cup grated Parmesan
2 1/2 cups tomato sauce
Salt and pepper to taste
6 lasagna noodles
2 cups shredded mozzarella cheese

Directions:

Mix the spinach, ricotta, marjoram, basil, garlic, parmesan, salt and pepper in a bowl.

Begin layering the lasagna noodles, spinach and ricotta filling and the tomato sauce in your Slow Cooker.

Top with shredded mozzarella and cook on low settings for 6 Hrs.

Serve the lasagna warm.

Fruity Veal Shanks

Servings: 4 Cooking Time: 3 1/4 Hrs.

Ingredients:

4 veal shanks
1 orange, zested and juiced
1/2 cup dried apricots, chopped
1/4 cup dried cranberries
1 cup beef stock
1 cup diced tomatoes
1 rosemary sprig
1 thyme sprig
Salt and pepper to taste
2 sweet potatoes, peeled and cubed

Directions:

Season the veal shanks with salt and pepper.

Mix the orange juice, orange zest, apricots, cranberries, stock, tomatoes, rosemary and thyme in your Slow Cooker.

Add salt, pepper and the sweet potatoes and cook for 3 Hrs. on high settings.

The dish is best served warm, but it can also be re-heated.

Pork and Chorizo Lunch Mix

Servings: 8 Cooking Time: 4 Hrs.

Ingredients:

1 lb. chorizo, ground
1 lb. pork, ground
3 tbsps. olive oil
1 tomato, chopped
1 avocado, pitted, peeled and chopped
Salt and black pepper to the taste
1 small red onion, chopped
2 tbsps. enchilada sauce

Directions:

Heat up a pan with the oil over medium-high heat, add pork, stir, brown for a couple of Min, transfer to your Slow Cooker, add salt, pepper, chorizo, onion and enchilada sauce, stir, cover and cook on Low for 4 Hrs.

Divide between plates and serve with chopped tomato and avocado on top.

Tomato Bulgur

Servings:6 Cooking Time: 6 Hrs.

Ingredients:

1 cup bulgur
1 tbsp. tomato paste
1/4 cup bell pepper, diced
1 tbsp. sesame oil
2 cups of water
1/4 cup onion, diced
1 tsp. cayenne pepper

Directions:

Heat sesame oil in the skillet.
Add onion and bell pepper and roast them for 5 Min. on medium heat.
Then transfer the roasted vegetables in the Slow Cooker.
Add water and tomato paste. Stir the ingredients.
Then add bulgur and cayenne pepper.
Close the lid and cook the meal on Low for 6 Hrs.

Chicken with Corn and Wild Rice

Servings: 2 Cooking Time: 6 Hrs.

Ingredients:

1 lb. chicken breast, skinless, boneless and cubed
1 cup chicken stock
Salt and black pepper to the taste
3 oz. canned roasted tomatoes, chopped
2 tbsps. cilantro, chopped
1 cup wild rice
1 tbsp. tomato paste
1/4 tsp. cumin, ground
1/4 cup corn

Directions:

In your Slow Cooker, mix the chicken with the rice, stock and the other ingredients, toss, put the lid on and cook on Low for 6 Hrs.
Divide everything between plates and serve.

Collard Greens Stew

Servings: 6 Cooking Time: 6 1/4 Hrs.

Ingredients:

1 tbsp. olive oil
1 cup dried black beans, rinsed
2 cups vegetable stock
Salt and pepper to taste
2 garlic cloves, chopped
1/2 cup tomato sauce
1 bunch collard greens, shredded
1 tbsp. chopped cilantro for serving

Directions:

Combine all the ingredients in your Slow Cooker, adding salt and pepper as needed.
Cook on low settings for 6 Hrs.
Serve the stew warm and fresh or chilled.

Honey Orange Glazed Chicken Drumsticks

Servings: 6 Cooking Time: 6 1/4 Hrs.

Ingredients:

2 lbs. chicken drumsticks
2 garlic cloves, minced
1/4 cup fresh orange juice
1/4 tsp. chili powder
2 tbsps. sesame seeds
1 tbsp. grated zest
2 tbsps. soy sauce
1 tsp. rice vinegar
1/4 cup chicken stock

Directions:

Combine all the ingredients in your Slow Cooker.
Cover with a lid and cook on low settings for 6 Hrs.
Serve the chicken warm with your favorite side dish.

Chicken with Couscous

Servings: 6 Cooking Time: 3 Hrs.

Ingredients:

2 sweet potatoes, peeled and cubed
1 and 1/2 lbs. chicken breasts, skinless and boneless
Salt and black pepper to the taste
1/4 tsp. cinnamon powder
For the couscous:
1 cup water
1 sweet red pepper, chopped
13 oz. canned stewed tomatoes
1/4 cup raisins
1/4 tsp. cumin, ground
1 cup whole wheat couscous
Salt to the taste

Directions:

In your Slow Cooker, mix potatoes with red peppers, chicken, tomatoes, salt, pepper, raisins, cinnamon and cumin, toss, cover, cook on Low for 3 Hrs. and shred meat using 2 forks.
Meanwhile, heat up a pan with the water over medium-high heat, add salt, bring water to a boil, add couscous, stir, leave aside covered for 10 Min. and fluff with a fork.
Divide chicken mix between plates, add couscous on the side and serve.

Squash and Chicken Soup

Servings: 2 Cooking Time: 6 Hrs.

Ingredients:

1/2 lb. chicken thighs, skinless, boneless and cubed
1/2 red bell pepper, chopped
3 cups chicken stock
2 oz. canned green chilies, chopped
A pinch of salt and black pepper
1 tbsp. cilantro, chopped
1/2 small yellow onion, chopped
1/2 green bell pepper, chopped
1/2 cup butternut squash, peeled and cubed
1/2 tsp. oregano, dried
1/2 tbsp. lime juice

Directions:

In your Slow Cooker, mix the chicken with the onion, bell pepper and the other ingredients, toss, put the lid on and cook on High for 6 Hrs.
Ladle the soup into bowls and serve.

Cashew Chicken

Servings: 6 Cooking Time: 4 1/4 Hrs.

Ingredients:

3 chicken breasts, cut into strips
1 celery stalk, sliced
1 cup cashew nuts, soaked overnight
1 cup chicken stock
1 shallot, sliced
1 head broccoli, cut into florets
1/2 tsp. ginger powder
Salt and pepper to taste

Directions:

Combine the chicken, shallot, celery and broccoli in your Slow Cooker.
Mix the cashew nuts, ginger and stock in a blender. Pulse until smooth then pour this mixture over the chicken in the pot.
Season with salt and pepper.
Cook on low settings for 4 Hrs.

Serve the chicken warm and fresh.

Madras Lentils

Servings: 6 Cooking Time: 4 1/4 Hrs.

Ingredients:

1 cup dried red lentils, rinsed
1 cup tomato sauce
1 large potato, peeled and cubed
3 garlic cloves, chopped
1/2 tsp. dried oregano
1/2 cup coconut milk
1/2 cup brown lentils, rinsed
2 cups vegetable stock
1 shallot, chopped
1/2 tsp. cumin powder
Salt and pepper to taste

Directions:

Mix the lentils, tomato sauce, stock, potato, shallot, garlic, cumin powder, oregano and coconut milk in your Slow Cooker.
Add salt and pepper to taste and cook over low settings for 4 Hrs.
Serve the lentils warm or store them in an airtight container in the freezer until needed.

Indian Spiced Quinoa Stew

Servings: 6 Cooking Time: 7 1/4 Hrs.

Ingredients:

2 tbsps. olive oil
2 garlic cloves, chopped
1/2 cup red lentils, rinsed
1 turnip, peeled and cubed
1/2 tsp. garam masala
3 cups vegetable stock
2 shallots, chopped
1/2 cup red quinoa, rinsed
1 large sweet potato, peeled and cubed
1/2 tsp. turmeric powder
Salt and pepper to taste

Directions:

Combine all the ingredients in your Slow Cooker.
Add salt and pepper as needed and cook on low settings for 7 Hrs.
Serve the stew warm or chilled.

Lentils Curry

Servings: 16 Cooking Time: 8 Hrs.

Ingredients:

4 garlic cloves, minced
2 yellow onions, chopped
4 tbsps. olive oil
4 tbsps. red curry paste
1 and ½ tsps. turmeric powder
45 oz. canned tomato puree
1 tbsp. cilantro, chopped
4 cups brown lentils
1 tbsp. ginger, grated
1 tbsp. garam masala
2 tsps. sugar
A pinch of salt and black pepper
½ cup coconut milk

Directions:

In your Slow Cooker, mix lentils with onions, garlic, ginger, oil, curry paste, garam masala, turmeric, salt, pepper, sugar and tomato puree, stir, cover and cook on Low for 7 Hrs. and 20 Min.
Add coconut milk and cilantro, stir, cover, cook on Low for 40 Min, divide into bowls and serve for lunch.

Greek Orzo Chicken

Servings: 6 Cooking Time: 6 1/2 Hrs.

Ingredients:

1 cup orzo, rinsed
1 celery stalk, diced
1 tsp. dried oregano
1/2 tsp. dried parsley
2 cups chicken stock
Feta cheese for serving
2 chicken breasts, cubed
2 ripe tomatoes, peeled and diced
1/2 tsp. dried basil
1/4 cup pitted Kalamata olives
Salt and pepper to taste

Directions:

Combine the orzo and the remaining ingredients in your Slow Cooker.
Add salt and pepper to taste and cook on low settings for 6 Hrs.
Serve the chicken warm and fresh, topped with feta cheese.

Pork Stew

Servings: 8 Cooking Time: 5 Hrs.

Ingredients:

2 pork tenderloins, cubed
2 carrots, sliced
2 celery ribs, chopped
3 cups beef stock
1 rosemary spring
2 bay leaves
1/3 cup green olives, pitted and sliced
Salt and black pepper to the taste
1 yellow onion, chopped
2 tbsps. tomato paste
1/3 cup plums, dried, pitted and chopped
1 thyme spring
4 garlic cloves, minced
1 tbsp. parsley, chopped

Directions:

In your Slow Cooker, mix pork with salt, pepper, carrots, onion, celery, tomato paste, stock, plums, rosemary, thyme, bay leaves, garlic, olives and parsley, cover and cook on Low for 5 Hrs.
Discard thyme, rosemary and bay leaves, divide stew into bowls and serve for lunch.

Cheesy Three Bean Chili

Servings: 8 Cooking Time: 8 1/2 Hrs.

Ingredients:

2 tbsps. olive oil
4 garlic cloves, chopped
1 carrot, diced
1 cup kidney beans
1 can fire roasted tomatoes
2 cups vegetable stock
Salt and pepper to taste
2 sweet onions, chopped
1 celery stalk, sliced
1 cup dried black beans
1/2 cup red beans
2 bay leaves
2 cups water
1 cup grated Cheddar for serving

Directions:

Heat the oil in a skillet and stir in the onions, garlic, celery and carrot. Cook on low settings for 5 Min. until softened then transfer in your Slow Cooker.
Add the remaining ingredients and season with salt and pepper.
Cook on low settings for 8 Hrs. and serve the chili warm, topped with grated Cheddar.

Chickpeas Stew

Servings: 2 Cooking Time: 6 Hrs.

Ingredients:

½ tbsp. olive oil
2 garlic cloves, minced
¼ cup carrots, chopped
1 red onion, chopped
1 red chili pepper, chopped
6 oz. canned tomatoes,

chopped
6 oz. canned chickpeas, drained
½ cup chicken stock
1 bay leaf
½ tsp. coriander, ground
A pinch of red pepper flakes
½ tbsp. parsley, chopped
Salt and black pepper to the taste

Directions:

In your Slow Cooker, mix the chickpeas with the onion, garlic and the other ingredients, toss, put the lid on and cook on Low for 6 Hrs.
Divide into bowls and serve.

Corned Beef with Sauerkraut

Servings: 6 Cooking Time: 8 1/4 Hrs.

Ingredients:

3 lbs. corned beef brisket
4 large carrots, sliced
1 lb. sauerkraut, shredded
1 onion, sliced
1/2 tsp. cumin seeds
1 cup beef stock
Salt and pepper to taste

Directions:

Combine all the ingredients in your Slow Cooker.
Add salt and pepper to taste and cook on low settings for 8 Hrs.
Serve the beef sliced and warm, paired with the sauerkraut.

Bacon Chicken Stew

Servings: 6 Cooking Time: 6 1/2 Hrs.

Ingredients:

6 chicken thighs
6 bacon slices, chopped
1 sweet onion, chopped
2 garlic cloves, chopped
2 large carrots, sliced
2 celery stalks, sliced
1 cup green peas
2 cups sliced mushrooms
1/4 cup dry white wine
1 cup vegetable stock
1/2 cup heavy cream
Salt and pepper to taste
1 thyme sprig
1 rosemary sprig

Directions:

Heat a skillet over medium flame. Add the bacon and cook until crisp.
Transfer the bacon in your Slow Cooker and add the remaining ingredients.
Season with salt and pepper and cook on low settings for 6 Hrs.
Serve the chicken warm.

Shrimp Stew

Servings: 2 Cooking Time: 3 Hrs.

Ingredients:

1 garlic clove, minced
1 red onion, chopped
1 cup canned tomatoes, crushed
1 cup veggie stock
½ tsp. turmeric powder
1 lb. shrimp, peeled and deveined
½ tsp. coriander, ground
½ tsp. thyme, dried
½ tsp. basil, dried
A pinch of salt and black pepper
A pinch of red pepper flakes

Directions:

In your Slow Cooker, mix the onion with the garlic, shrimp and the other ingredients, toss, put the lid on and cook on High for 3 Hrs.
Divide the stew into bowls and serve.

Jamaican Jerk Chicken

Servings: 4 Cooking Time: 7 1/2 Hrs.

Ingredients:

4 chicken breasts
2 tbsps. jerk seasoning
2 tbsps. olive oil
1/2 cup chicken stock
1/4 cup brewed coffee
1 jalapeno pepper, chopped
Salt and pepper to taste

Directions:

Season the chicken with salt, pepper and jerk seasoning.
Combine the seasoned chicken, stock and coffee, as well as jalapeno pepper in your Slow Cooker.
Cover with a lid and cook on low settings for 7 Hrs.
Serve the chicken warm and fresh.

Chicken Layered Potato Casserole

Servings: 8 Cooking Time: 6 1/2 Hrs.

Ingredients:

2 lbs. potatoes, peeled and sliced
2 chicken breasts, cut into thin strips
1/4 tsp. chili powder
1/4 tsp. cumin powder
1/2 tsp. garlic powder
1/4 tsp. onion powder
1 cup heavy cream
1 1/2 cups whole milk
Salt and pepper to taste

Directions:

Combine the cream, milk, chili powder, cumin powder, garlic powder and onion powder.
Layer the potatoes and chicken in your Slow Cooker.
Pour the milk mix over the potatoes and chicken, seasoning with salt and pepper.
Cook on low settings for 6 Hrs.
Serve the casserole warm or chilled.

Beef Barbacoa

Servings: 8 Cooking Time: 6 1/2 Hrs.

Ingredients:

4 lbs. beef chuck roast
2 red onions, sliced
6 garlic cloves, chopped
3 tbsps. white wine vinegar
1 1/2 cups tomato sauce
1 1/2 tsps. chili powder
Salt and pepper to taste

Directions:

Mix all the ingredients in your Slow Cooker.
Add enough salt and pepper and cook on low settings for 6 Hrs.
Serve the beef barbacoa warm.

Lime Bean Stew

Servings: 8 Cooking Time: 6 1/4 Hrs.

Ingredients:

2 cups dried lime beans
2 carrots, sliced
2 celery stalks, sliced
1 head cauliflower, cut into florets
1 tsp. grated ginger
1 cup diced tomatoes

1 cup tomato sauce
1 bay leaf
Salt and pepper to taste
2 cups vegetable stock
1 thyme sprig

Directions:

Combine the beans, carrots, celery, cauliflower, ginger, tomatoes, tomato sauce, stock, salt and pepper, as well as bay leaf and thyme in your Slow Cooker.
Season with salt and pepper as needed and cook on low settings for 6 Hrs.
The stew is best served warm.

Tangy Italian Shredded Beef

Servings: 8 Cooking Time: 8 1/4 Hrs.

Ingredients:

4 lbs. beef sirloin roast, trimmed of fat
1/4 cup white wine
1 tsp. Italian seasoning
1/2 cup tomato juice
1 lemon, juiced
1 tbsp. honey
Salt and pepper to taste
1 rosemary sprig

Directions:

Mix all the ingredients in your Slow Cooker.
Add enough salt and pepper and cook on low settings for 8 Hrs.
Serve the beef warm, finely shredded. It can be used in sandwiches or wraps if you want.

Cinnamon Pork Ribs

Servings: 2 Cooking Time: 8 Hrs.

Ingredients:

2 lbs. baby back pork ribs
2 tbsps. olive oil
A pinch of salt and black pepper
1 tbsp. balsamic vinegar
1 tbsp. tomato paste
1 tbsp. cinnamon powder
½ tsp. allspice, ground
½ tsp. garlic powder
½ cup beef stock

Directions:

In your Slow Cooker, mix the pork ribs with the cinnamon, the oil and the other ingredients, toss, put the lid on and cook on Low for 8 Hrs.
Divide ribs between plates and serve for lunch with a side salad.

Barley and Bean Tacos

Servings: 10 Cooking Time: 6 1/4 Hrs.

Ingredients:

1 red onion, chopped
1 can (15 oz.) black beans, drained
1 cup pearl barley
1/2 tsp. cumin powder
Salt and pepper to taste
1/2 cup chopped cilantro for serving
1 cup frozen corn
1 cup fire roasted tomatoes
2 cups vegetable stock
1/2 tsp. chili powder
10-14 taco shells
2 limes for serving

Directions:

Combine the onion, corn, black beans, tomatoes, pearl barley, stock, cumin powder and chili powder in your Slow Cooker.
Add salt and pepper to taste and cook on low settings for 6 Hrs.
When done, spoon the mixture into taco shells and top with chopped cilantro.
Drizzle with lime juice and serve fresh.

Chicken Thighs Mix

Servings: 6 Cooking Time: 6 Hrs.

Ingredients:

2 and ½ lbs. chicken thighs, skinless and boneless
2 yellow onions, chopped
¼ tsp. cloves, ground
Salt and black pepper to the taste
A handful pine nuts
1 and ½ tbsp. olive oil
1 tsp. cinnamon powder
¼ tsp. allspice, ground
A pinch of saffron
A handful mint, chopped

Directions:

In a bowl, mix oil with onions, cinnamon, allspice, cloves, salt, pepper and saffron, whisk and transfer to your Slow Cooker.
Add the chicken, toss well, cover and cook on Low for 6 Hrs.
Sprinkle pine nuts and mint on top before serving,

Parmesan Biscuit Pot Pie

Servings: 8 Cooking Time: 7 1/2 Hrs.

Ingredients:

2 tbsps. olive oil
1 large onion, finely chopped
1 parsnip, diced
2 cups sliced mushrooms
Salt and pepper to taste
1/2 tsp. baking powder
1/4 cup butter, chilled and cubed
2 garlic cloves, chopped
2 carrots, diced
1 turnip, diced
1 cup green peas
1/2 cup all-purpose flour
1 cup grated Parmesan
1/2 cup buttermilk

Directions:

Combine the oil, garlic, onion, carrots, parsnip, turnip, mushrooms, green peas, salt and pepper in your Slow Cooker.
Combine the flour, baking powder and Parmesan in your Slow Cooker. Mix until sandy then stir in the buttermilk.
Spoon the batter over the vegetables and cook on low settings for 7 Hrs.
Serve the pot pie warm or chilled.

Red Salsa Chicken

Servings: 8 Cooking Time: 8 1/4 Hrs.

Ingredients:

8 chicken thighs
1/2 cup chicken stock
Salt and pepper to taste
2 cups red salsa
1 cup grated Cheddar cheese

Directions:

Combine the chicken with the salsa and stock in your Slow Cooker.
Add the cheese and cook on low settings for 8 Hrs.
Serve the chicken warm with your favorite side dish.

Quinoa Tofu Veggie Stew

Servings: 6 Cooking Time: 6 1/4 Hrs.

Ingredients:

6 oz. firm tofu, cubed
1 celery stalk, sliced
1 carrot, diced
1/2 cup quinoa, rinsed
1 parsnip, diced
1/2 cup green peas

1 cup cauliflower florets
1 tbsp. Pesto sauce
1 cup vegetable stock
1 cup broccoli florets
2 tbsps. green lentils
Salt and pepper to taste

Directions:

Combine all the ingredients in your Slow Cooker.
Add salt and pepper to taste and cook on low settings for 6 Hrs.
Serve the stew warm and fresh.

Chicken and Rice

Servings: 2 Cooking Time: 6 Hrs.

Ingredients:

1 lb. chicken breast, skinless, boneless and cubed
2 spring onions, chopped
1 cup wild rice
½ tsp. garam masala
1 tbsp. cilantro, chopped
1 red onion, sliced
Cooking spray
2 cups chicken stock
½ tsp. turmeric powder
A pinch of salt and black pepper

Directions:

Grease the Slow Cooker with the cooking spray, add the chicken, rice, onion and the other ingredients, toss, put the lid on and cook on Low for 6 Hrs.
Divide the mix into bowls and serve for lunch.

Orange Marmalade Glazed Carrots

Servings: 4 Cooking Time: 4 1/4 Hrs.

Ingredients:

20 oz. baby carrots
1/4 tsp. chili powder
2 tbsps. water
Salt and pepper to taste
1/4 cup orange marmalade
1 pinch nutmeg
1/4 tsp. cumin powder

Directions:

Combine the carrots and the remaining ingredients in your Slow Cooker.
Add salt and pepper and cover with a lid.
Cook on low settings for 4 Hrs.
Serve the glazed carrots warm or chilled.

Appetizers Recipes

Carne Asada Nachos

Servings: 8 Cooking Time: 10 1/2 Hrs.

Ingredients:

2 lbs. flanks steak
1 tsp. smoked paprika
2 tbsps. brown sugar
1 tsp. garlic powder
1 cup dark beer
1 cup red salsa
2 cups grated Monterey jack cheese
Chopped cilantro for serving
1 tsp. salt
1/2 tsp. chili powder
1 tsp. cumin powder
2 tbsps. canola oil
8 oz. tortillas chips
1 can sweet corn, drained
Sour cream for serving

Directions:

Mix the salt, paprika, chili powder, sugar, cumin powder and garlic powder in a bowl. Spread this mix over the steak and rub it well into the meat.
Heat the oil in a skillet and add the steak in the hot oil. Cook on all sides for 4-5 Min. just to sear it.
Transfer the meat in your Slow Cooker and pour the beer over.
Cook on low settings for 8 Hrs.
When done, remove from the pot and cut the flank steak into thin slices.
Clean the pot then place the tortilla chips on the bottom.
Cover the tortilla chips with red salsa, followed by flank steak, corn and cheese.
Cook on low settings for 2 additional Hrs.
Serve right away.

Bacon New Potatoes

Servings: 6 Cooking Time: 3 1/4 Hrs.

Ingredients:

3 lbs. new potatoes, washed and halved
2 tbsps. white wine
1 rosemary sprig
12 slices bacon, chopped
Salt and pepper to taste

Directions:

Place the potatoes, wine and rosemary in your Slow Cooker.
Add salt and pepper to taste and top with chopped bacon.
Cook on high settings for 3 Hrs.
Serve the potatoes warm.

Cheeseburger Meatballs

Servings 8 Cooking Time: 6 14 Hrs.

Ingredients:

2 lbs. ground pork
2 tbsps. beef stock
14 cup breadcrumbs
12 tsp. dried basil
2 cups shredded processed cheese
1 shallot, chopped
1 egg
1 tsp. Cajun seasoning
Salt and pepper to taste

Directions:

Mix the pork, shallot, beef stock, egg, breadcrumbs, Cajun seasoning and basil in a bowl.
Add salt and pepper to taste and mix well.
Form small meatballs and place them in the Slow Cooker.
Top with shredded cheese and cook on low settings for 6 Hrs.
Serve the meatballs warm.

Goat Cheese Stuffed Mushrooms

Servings: 6 Cooking Time: 4 1/4 Hrs.

Ingredients:

12 medium size mushrooms
1 egg
1 poblano pepper, chopped
6 oz. goat cheese
1/2 cup breadcrumbs
1 tsp. dried oregano

Directions:

Mix the goat cheese, egg, breadcrumbs, pepper and oregano in a bowl.

Stuff each mushroom with the goat cheese mixture and place them all in a Slow Cooker.
Cover the pot and cook on low settings for 4 Hrs.
Serve the mushrooms warm or chilled.

Green Vegetable Dip

Servings: 12 Cooking Time: 2 1/4 Hrs.

Ingredients:

10 oz. frozen spinach, thawed and drained
1 cup chopped parsley
1 cup sour cream
1/2 cup feta cheese, crumbled
1/4 tsp. garlic powder
1 jar artichoke hearts, drained
1 cup cream cheese
1/2 cup grated Parmesan cheese
1/2 tsp. onion powder

Directions:

Combine all the ingredients in your Slow Cooker and mix gently.
Cover with its lid and cook on high settings for 2 Hrs.
Serve the dip warm or chilled with crusty bread, biscuits or other salty snacks or even vegetable sticks.

Spicy Monterey Jack Fondue

Servings: 6 Cooking Time: 4 1/4 Hrs.

Ingredients:

1 garlic clove
2 cups grated Monterey Jack cheese
1 red chili, seeded and chopped
1/2 cup milk
1 pinch salt
1 cup white wine
1/2 cup grated Parmesan
1 tbsp. cornstarch
1 pinch nutmeg
1 pinch ground black pepper

Directions:

Rub the inside of your Slow Cooker's pot with a garlic clove just to infuse it with aroma.
Add the white wine into the pot and stir in the cheeses, red chili, cornstarch and milk.
Season with nutmeg, salt and black pepper and cook on low heat for 4 Hrs.
The fondue is best served warm with bread sticks or vegetables.

Quick Layered Appetizer

Servings: 10 Cooking Time: 7 1/2 Hrs.

Ingredients:

4 chicken breasts, cooked and diced
1 tsp. dried oregano
1/4 tsp. chili powder
4 tomatoes, sliced
2 cups shredded mozzarella
1 tsp. dried basil
1 cup cream cheese
Salt and pepper to taste
4 large tortillas

Directions:

Mix the chicken, basil, oregano, cream cheese, chili powder, salt and pepper in a bowl.
Begin layering the chicken mixture, tomatoes, tortillas and mozzarella in your Slow Cooker.
Cover and cook on low settings for 7 Hrs.
Allow to cool then slice and serve.

Cranberry Sauce Meatballs

Servings: 12 Cooking Time: 7 1/2 Hrs.

Ingredients:

3 lbs. ground pork
1 egg
1 shallot, chopped
Salt and pepper to taste
1 cup BBQ sauce
1 thyme sprig
1 lb. ground turkey
1/2 cup breadcrumbs
1/2 tsp. ground cloves
2 cups cranberry sauce
1 tsp. hot sauce

Directions:

Mix the ground pork, turkey, egg, breadcrumbs, shallot, ground cloves, salt and pepper and mix well.
In the meantime, combine the cranberry sauce, BBQ sauce, hot sauce and thyme sprig in your Slow Cooker.
Form small meatballs and drop them in the sauce.
Cook on low settings for 7 Hrs.
Serve the meatballs warm or chilled.

Baba Ganoush

Servings: 4 Cooking Time: 4 1/4 Hrs.

Ingredients:

1 large eggplant, halved
2 tbsps. olive oil
1 tbsp. lemon juice
Salt and pepper to taste
2 garlic cloves, minced
1 tbsp. tahini paste
1 tbsp. chopped parsley

Directions:

Spread the garlic over each half of eggplant. Season them with salt and pepper and drizzle with olive oil.
Place the eggplant halves in your Slow Cooker and cook on low settings for 4 Hrs.
When done, scoop out the eggplant flesh and place it in a bowl.
Mash it with a fork.
Stir in the tahini paste, lemon juice and parsley and mix well.
Serve the dip fresh.

Bacon Wrapped Chicken Livers

Servings: 6 Cooking Time: 3 1/2 Hrs.

Ingredients:

2 lbs. chicken livers
Bacon slices as needed

Directions:

Wrap each chicken liver in one slice of bacon and place all the livers in your Slow Cooker.
Cook on high heat for 3 Hrs.
Serve warm or chilled.

Roasted Bell Peppers Dip

Servings: 8 Cooking Time: 2 1/4 Hrs.

Ingredients:

4 roasted red bell peppers, drained
1/2 cup water
4 garlic cloves, minced
2 tbsps. lemon juice
2 cans chickpeas, drained
1 shallot, chopped
Salt and pepper to taste
2 tbsps. olive oil

Directions:

Combine the bell peppers, chickpeas, water, shallot and garlic in a Slow Cooker.
Add salt and pepper as needed and cook on high settings for 2 Hrs.
When done, puree the dip in a blender, adding the lemon juice and olive oil as well.
Serve the dip fresh or store it in the fridge in an airtight container for up to 2 days.

Spicy Enchilada Dip

Servings: 8 Cooking Time: 6 1/4 Hrs.

Ingredients:

1 lb. ground chicken
1 shallot, chopped
1 red bell pepper, cored and diced
1 cup tomato sauce
1 1/2 cups grated Cheddar cheese
1/2 tsp. chili powder
2 garlic cloves, chopped
2 tomatoes, diced
Salt and pepper to taste

Directions:

Combine the ground chicken with chili powder, shallot and garlic in your Slow Cooker.
Add the remaining ingredients and cook on low settings for 6 Hrs.
Serve the dip warm with tortilla chips.

Queso Verde Dip

Servings: 12 Cooking Time: 4 1/4 Hrs.

Ingredients:

1 lb. ground chicken
2 tbsps. olive oil
1 cup cream cheese
2 poblano peppers, chopped
4 garlic cloves, minced
Salt and pepper to taste
2 shallots, chopped
2 cups salsa verde
2 cups grated Cheddar
1 tbsp. Worcestershire sauce
1/4 cup chopped cilantro

Directions:

Combine all the ingredients in your Slow Cooker.
Add salt and pepper to taste and cook on low heat for 4 Hrs.
The dip is best served warm.

Cheesy Mushroom Dip

Servings: 16 Cooking Time: 4 1/4 Hrs.

Ingredients:

1 can condensed cream of mushroom soup
1 tsp. Worcestershire sauce
1/2 tsp. chili powder
1 cup grated Swiss cheese
1 lb. mushrooms, chopped
1/4 cup evaporated milk
1 cup grated Cheddar cheese

Directions:

Mix the cream of mushroom soup, mushrooms, Worcestershire sauce, evaporated milk and chili powder in your Slow Cooker.
Top with grated cheese and cook on low settings for 4 Hrs.
Serve the dip warm or re-heated.

Sausage Dip

Servings: 8 Cooking Time: 6 1/4 Hrs.

Ingredients:

1 lb. fresh pork sausages
1 cup cream cheese
2 poblano peppers, chopped
1 lb. spicy pork sausages
1 can diced tomatoes

Directions:

Combine all the ingredients in a Slow Cooker.
Cook on low settings for 6 Hrs.
Serve warm or chilled.

Bacon Black Bean Dip

Servings: 6 Cooking Time: 6 1/4 Hrs.

Ingredients:

6 bacon slices
2 shallots, sliced
1 cup red salsa
1 tbsp. brown sugar
1/2 tsp. chili powder
2 tbsps. Bourbon
2 cans black beans, drained
1 garlic clove, chopped
1/2 cup beef stock
1 tbsp. molasses
1 tbsp. apple cider vinegar
Salt and pepper to taste

Directions:

Heat a skillet over medium flame and add the bacon. Cook until crisp then transfer the bacon and its fat in your Slow Cooker.
Stir in the remaining ingredients and cook on low settings for 6 Hrs.
When done, partially mash the beans and serve the dip right away.

Molasses Lime Meatballs

Servings: 10 Cooking Time: 8 1/4 Hrs.

Ingredients:

3 lbs. ground beef
1 shallot, chopped
1/2 tsp. cumin powder
1 egg
1/2 cup molasses
2 tbsps. lime juice
1 tbsp. Worcestershire sauce
2 garlic cloves, minced
1/2 cup oat flour
1/2 tsp. chili powder
Salt and pepper to taste
1/4 cup soy sauce
1/2 cup beef stock

Directions:

Combine the molasses, soy sauce, lime juice, stock and Worcestershire sauce in your Slow Cooker.
In a bowl, mix the ground beef, garlic, shallot, oat flour, cumin powder, chili powder, egg, salt and pepper and mix well.
Form small balls and place them in the sauce.
Cover the pot and cook on low settings for 8 Hrs.
Serve the meatballs warm or chilled.

Ranch Turkey Bites

Servings: 6 Cooking Time: 7 1/4 Hrs.

Ingredients:

2 lbs. turkey breast, cubed
1/2 tsp. garlic powder
1 tsp. hot sauce
Salt and pepper to taste
1 carrot, sliced
1 tbsp. Ranch dressing seasoning
1 cup tomato sauce

Directions:

Combine all the ingredients in a Slow Cooker.
Mix well until the ingredients are well distributed and adjust the taste with salt and pepper.
Cover with a lid and cook on low settings for 7 Hrs.

Serve the turkey bites warm or chilled.

Chipotle BBQ Meatballs

Servings: 10 Cooking Time: 7 1/2 Hrs.

Ingredients:

3 lbs. ground pork
2 shallots, chopped
Salt and pepper to taste
1/4 cup cranberry sauce
2 garlic cloves, minced
2 chipotle peppers, chopped
2 cups BBQ sauce
1 bay leaf

Directions:

Mix the ground pork, garlic, shallots, chipotle peppers, salt and pepper in a bowl.
Combine the BBQ sauce, cranberry sauce, bay leaf, salt and pepper in your Slow Cooker.
Form small meatballs and drop them in the sauce.
Cover the pot with its lid and cook on low settings for 7 Hrs.
Serve the meatballs warm or chilled with cocktail skewers or toothpicks.

Four Cheese Dip

Servings: 8 Cooking Time: 4 1/4 Hrs.

Ingredients:

1/2 lb. fresh Italian sausages, skins removed
1 cup tomato sauce
1 cup shredded mozzarella cheese
1 cup grated Cheddar cheese
1/2 tsp. dried basil
2 tbsps. olive oil
1 cup cottage cheese
1/2 cup grated Parmesan cheese
1/2 tsp. dried thyme
Salt and pepper to taste

Directions:

Heat the oil in a skillet and stir in the sausages. Cook for 5 Min, stirring often then transfer the sausages in a Slow Cooker.
Add the remaining ingredients and season with salt and pepper.
Cook on low settings for 4 Hrs.
The dip is best served warm.

Candied Kielbasa

Servings: 8 Cooking Time: 6 1/4 Hrs.

Ingredients:

2 lbs. kielbasa sausages
1 cup BBQ sauce
1/2 tsp. black pepper
1/2 cup brown sugar
1 tsp. prepared horseradish
1/4 tsp. cumin powder

Directions:

Combine all the ingredients in a Slow Cooker, adding salt if needed.
Cook on low settings for 6 Hrs.
Serve the kielbasa warm or chilled.

Creamy Potatoes

Servings: 6 Cooking Time: 6 1/4 Hrs.

Ingredients:

3 lbs. small new potatoes, washed
1 tsp. dried oregano
2 tbsps. olive oil
Salt and pepper to taste
2 green onions, chopped
4 bacon slices, chopped
1 shallot, chopped
2 garlic cloves, chopped
1 cup sour cream
2 tbsps. chopped parsley

Directions:

Combine the potatoes, bacon, oregano, shallot, olive oil and garlic in a Slow Cooker.
Add salt and pepper and mix until the ingredients are well distributed.
Cover the pot with its lid and cook on low settings for 6 Hrs.
When done, mix the cooked potatoes with sour cream, onions and parsley and serve right away.

Honey Glazed Chicken Drumsticks

Servings: 8 Cooking Time: 7 1/4 Hrs.

Ingredients:

3 lbs. chicken drumsticks
1/4 cup honey
1/2 tsp. sesame oil
1/2 tsp. dried Thai basil
1/4 cup soy sauce
1 tsp. rice vinegar
2 tbsps. tomato paste

Directions:

Combine all the ingredients in your Slow Cooker and toss them around until the drumsticks are evenly coated.
Cover the pot with its lid and cook on low settings for 7 Hrs.
Serve the chicken drumsticks warm or chilled.

Bacon Chicken Sliders

Servings: 8 Cooking Time: 4 1/2 Hrs.

Ingredients:

2 lbs. ground chicken
1/2 cup breadcrumbs
Salt and pepper to taste
1 egg
1 shallot, chopped
8 bacon slices

Directions:

Mix the chicken, egg, breadcrumbs and shallot in a bowl. Add salt and pepper to taste and give it a good mix.
Form small sliders then wrap each slider in a bacon slice.
Place the sliders in a Slow Cooker.
Cover with its lid and cook on high settings for 4 Hrs., making sure to flip them over once during cooking.
Serve them warm.

Quick Parmesan Bread

Servings: 8 Cooking Time: 1 1/4 Hrs.

Ingredients:

4 cups all-purpose flour
1/2 cup grated Parmesan cheese
2 cups buttermilk
1/2 tsp. salt
1 tsp. baking soda
2 tbsps. olive oil

Directions:

Mix the flour, salt, parmesan cheese and baking soda in a bowl.
Stir in the buttermilk and olive oil and mix well with a fork.
Shape the dough into a loaf and place it in your Slow Cooker.
Cover with its lid and cook on high heat for 1 Hr.
Serve the bread warm or chilled.

Eggplant Caviar

Servings: 6 Cooking Time: 3 1/4 Hrs.

Ingredients:

2 large eggplants, peeled and cubed
1 tsp. dried basil
4 tbsps. olive oil
1 tsp. dried oregano

1 lemon, juiced
Salt and pepper to taste
2 garlic cloves, minced

Directions:

Combine the eggplant cubes, olive oil, basil and oregano in a Slow Cooker.
Add salt and pepper to taste and cook on high settings for 3 Hrs.
When done, stir in the lemon juice, garlic, salt and pepper and mash the mix well with a potato masher.
Serve the dip chilled.

Party Mix

Servings: 20 Cooking Time: 1 3/4 Hrs.

Ingredients:

4 cups cereals
2 cups mixed nuts
1/2 cup butter, melted
1 tsp. hot sauce
1/2 tsp. cumin powder
4 cups crunchy cereals
1 cup mixed seeds
2 tbsps. Worcestershire sauce
1 tsp. salt

Directions:

Combine all the ingredients in your Slow Cooker and toss around until evenly coated.
Cook on high settings for 1 1/2 Hrs.
Serve the mix chilled.

Stuffed Artichokes

Servings: 6 Cooking Time: 6 1/2 Hrs.

Ingredients:

6 fresh artichokes
4 garlic cloves, minced
1 cup breadcrumbs
Salt and pepper to taste
6 anchovy fillets, chopped
2 tbsps. olive oil
1 tbsp. chopped parsley
1/4 cup white wine

Directions:

Cut the stem of each artichoke so that it sits flat on your chopping board then cut the top off and trim the outer leaves, cleaning the center as well.
In a bowl, mix the anchovy fillets, garlic, olive oil, breadcrumbs and parsley. Add salt and pepper to taste.
Top each artichoke with breadcrumb mixture and rub it well into the leaves.
Place the artichokes in your Slow Cooker and pour in the white wine.
Cook on low settings for 6 Hrs.
Serve the artichokes warm or chilled.

Mediterranean Dip

Servings: 20 Cooking Time: 6 1/4 Hrs.

Ingredients:

2 tbsps. canola oil
2 shallots, chopped
4 ripe tomatoes, peeled and diced
1/2 cup black olives, pitted and chopped
1 tsp. dried basil
1/2 cup tomato sauce
1 lb. ground beef
2 garlic cloves, chopped
1/2 cup Kalamata olives, pitted and chopped
1/2 tsp. dried oregano
1/4 cup white wine
Salt and pepper to taste

Directions:

Heat the oil in a skillet and stir in the beef. Cook for 5 Min. then add the shallots and garlic and cook for 5 additional Min.
Transfer the mixture in your Slow Cooker and add the remaining ingredients.
Season with salt and pepper and cook on low settings for 6 Hrs.
Serve the dip warm or chilled.

Cheeseburger Dip

Servings: 20 Cooking Time: 6 1/4 Hrs.

Ingredients:

2 lbs. ground beef
2 sweet onions, chopped
1/2 cup tomato sauce
2 tbsps. pickle relish
1 cup grated Cheddar
1 tbsp. canola oil
4 garlic cloves, chopped
1 tbsp. Dijon mustard
1 cup shredded processed cheese

Directions:

Heat the canola oil in a skillet and stir in the ground beef. Sauté for 5 Min. then add the meat in your Slow Cooker.
Stir in the remaining ingredients and cover with the pot's lid.
Cook on low settings for 6 Hrs.
The dip is best served warm.

Hoisin Chicken Wings

Servings: 8 Cooking Time: 7 1/4 Hrs.

Ingredients:

4 lbs. chicken wings
4 garlic cloves, minced
1 tsp. sesame oil
1 tsp. hot sauce
1/2 tsp. salt
2/3 cup hoisin sauce
1 tsp. grated ginger
1 tbsp. molasses
1/4 tsp. ground black pepper

Directions:

Mix the hoisin sauce, garlic, ginger, sesame oil, molasses, hot sauce, black pepper and salt in your Slow Cooker.
Add the chicken wings and toss them around until evenly coated.
Cover with a lid and cook on low settings for 7 Hrs.
Serve the wings warm or chilled.

Mexican Chili Dip

Servings: 20 Cooking Time: 2 1/4 Hrs.

Ingredients:

1 can black beans, drained
1 can diced tomatoes
1/2 tsp. chili powder
Salt and pepper to taste
1 can red beans, drained
1/2 tsp. cumin powder
1/2 cup beef stock
1 1/2 cups grated Cheddar

Directions:

Combine the beans, tomatoes, cumin powder, chili and stock in your Slow Cooker.
Add salt and pepper to taste and top with grated cheese.
Cook on high settings for 2 Hrs.
The dip is best served warm.

Mixed Olive Dip

Servings: 10 Cooking Time: 1 3/4 Hrs.

Ingredients:

1 lb. ground chicken
2 tbsps. olive oil

1 green bell pepper, cored and diced
1/2 cup Kalamata olives, pitted and chopped
1/2 cup green olives, chopped
1/2 cup black olives, pitted and chopped
1 cup green salsa
1/2 cup chicken stock
1 cup grated Cheddar cheese
1/2 cup shredded mozzarella

Directions:

Combine all the ingredients in your Slow Cooker.
Cover with its lid and cook on high settings for 1 1/2 Hrs.
The dip is best served warm.

Spanish Chorizo Dip

Servings: 8 Cooking Time: 6 1/4 Hrs.

Ingredients:

8 chorizo links, diced
1 can diced tomatoes
1 chili pepper, chopped
1 cup cream cheese
2 cups grated Cheddar cheese
1/4 cup white wine

Directions:

Combine all the ingredients in your Slow Cooker.
Cook the dip on low settings for 6 Hrs.
Serve the dip warm.

Boiled Peanuts with Skin On

Servings: 8 Cooking Time: 7 1/4 Hrs.

Ingredients:

2 lbs. uncooked, whole peanuts
1/2 cup salt
4 cups water

Directions:

Combine all the ingredients in your Slow Cooker.
Cover and cook on low settings for 7 Hrs.
Drain and allow to cool down before servings.

Spicy Asian Style Mushroom

Servings: 8 Cooking Time: 2 1/4 Hrs.

Ingredients:

1/4 cup hoisin sauce
1/4 cup soy sauce
2 garlic cloves, minced
1/2 tsp. red pepper flakes
2 lbs. fresh mushrooms, cleaned

Directions:

Mix the hoisin sauce, soy sauce, garlic and red pepper flakes in a bowl.
Place the mushrooms in your Slow Cooker and drizzle them with the sauce.
Cook on high settings for 2 Hrs.
Allow the mushrooms to cool in the pot before serving.

Cocktail Meatballs

Servings: 10 Cooking Time: 6 1/2 Hrs.

Ingredients:

2 lbs. ground pork
1 lb. ground beef
4 garlic cloves, minced
1 shallot, chopped
1 egg
1/4 cup breadcrumbs
2 tbsps. chopped parsley
1 tbsp. chopped cilantro
1/2 tsp. chili powder
2 tbsps. cranberry sauce
1 cup BBQ sauce
1/2 cup tomato sauce
1 tsp. red wine vinegar
1 bay leaf
Salt and pepper to taste

Directions:

Combine the cranberry sauce, BBQ sauce, tomato sauce and vinegar, as well as bay leaf, salt and pepper in your Slow Cooker.
In a bowl, mix the two types of meat, garlic, shallot, egg, breadcrumbs, parsley, cilantro and chili powder. Add salt and pepper to taste.
Form small meatballs and place them all in the sauce in the Slow Cooker.
Cover and cook on low settings for 6 Hrs.
Serve the meatballs warm or chilled with cocktail skewers.

Ham and Swiss Cheese Dip

Servings: 6 Cooking Time: 4 1/4 Hrs.

Ingredients:

1 lb. ham, diced
1 cup cream cheese
1 can condensed cream of mushroom soup
1 can condensed onion soup
2 cups grated Swiss cheese
1/2 tsp. chili powder

Directions:

Combine all the ingredients in a Slow Cooker.
Cook on low settings for 4 Hrs.
Serve the dip preferably warm.

Three Cheese Artichoke Sauce

Servings: 16 Cooking Time: 4 1/4 Hrs.

Ingredients:

1 jar artichoke hearts, drained and chopped
1 shallot, chopped
2 cups shredded mozzarella
1 cup grated Parmesan
1 cup grated Swiss cheese
1/2 tsp. dried thyme
1/4 tsp. chili powder

Directions:

Combine all the ingredients in your Slow Cooker.
Cover the pot with its lid and cook on low setting for 4 Hrs.
The sauce is great served warm with vegetable sticks or biscuits or even small pretzels.

Artichoke Bread Pudding

Servings: 10 Cooking Time: 6 1/2 Hrs.

Ingredients:

6 cups bread cubes
6 artichoke hearts, drained and chopped
1/2 cup grated Parmesan
4 eggs
1/2 cup sour cream
1 cup milk
4 oz. spinach, chopped
1 tbsp. chopped parsley
2 tbsps. olive oil
Salt and pepper to taste
1/2 tsp. dried oregano
1/2 tsp. dried basil

Directions:

Combine the bread cubes, artichoke hearts and Parmesan in your Slow Cooker. Add the spinach and parsley as well.
In a bowl, mix the eggs, sour cream, milk, oregano and basil, as well as salt and pepper.

Pour this mixture over the bread and press the bread slightly to make sure it soaks up all the liquid.
Cover the pot with its lid and cook on low settings for 6 Hrs.
The bread can be served both warm and chilled.

Creamy Chicken Dip

Servings: 6 Cooking Time: 3 1/4 Hrs.

Ingredients:

1 cup cream cheese
1 1/2 cups cooked and diced chicken
2 cups shredded Monterey Jack cheese
1/4 cup white wine
1 lime, juiced
1/4 tsp. cumin powder
2 garlic cloves, chopped
Salt and pepper to taste

Directions:

Combine all the ingredients in your Slow Cooker.
Add salt and pepper to taste and cook on low settings for 3 Hrs.
The dip is best served warm with tortilla chips or bread sticks.

Oriental Chicken Bites

Servings: 10 Cooking Time: 7 1/4 Hrs.

Ingredients:

4 chicken breasts, cubed
2 sweet onions, sliced
1 tsp. grated ginger
4 garlic cloves, minced
1/2 tsp. cinnamon powder
1 tsp. smoked paprika
1 tsp. cumin powder
1 cup chicken stock
1/2 lemon, juiced
2 tbsps. olive oil
Salt and pepper to taste

Directions:

Combine all the ingredients in your Slow Cooker.
Add salt and pepper to taste and mix well until the ingredients are evenly distributed.
Cover and cook on low settings for 7 Hrs.
Serve the chicken bites warm or chilled.

Mexican Dip

Servings: 10 Cooking Time: 4 1/4 Hrs.

Ingredients:

2 lbs. ground beef
1 can black beans, drained
1 can diced tomatoes
2 poblano peppers, chopped
1/2 tsp. chili powder
2 cups grated Cheddar cheese
Salt and pepper to taste

Directions:

Combine all the ingredients in a Slow Cooker.
Adjust the taste with salt and pepper if needed.
Cook on high settings for 4 Hrs.
The dip is best served warm.

Chili Corn Cheese Dip

Servings: 8 Cooking Time: 2 1/4 Hrs.

Ingredients:

1 lb. ground beef
2 tbsps. olive oil
1 shallot, chopped
1 can sweet corn, drained
1 can kidney beans, drained
1/2 cup beef stock
1 cup diced tomatoes
1/2 cup black olives, pitted and chopped
1 tsp. dried oregano
1/2 tsp. chili powder
1/2 tsp. cumin powder
1/4 tsp. garlic powder
2 cups grated Cheddar cheese
Tortilla chips for serving

Directions:

Heat the oil in a skillet and stir in the ground beef. Cook for 5-7 Min, stirring often.
Transfer the meat in a Slow Cooker and add the remaining ingredients.
Add salt and pepper to taste and cover with its lid.
Cook on high settings for 2 Hrs.
Serve the dip warm with tortilla chips.

Caramelized Onion Dip

Servings: 12 Cooking Time: 4 1/2 Hrs.

Ingredients:

4 red onions, sliced
2 tbsps. butter
1 tbsp. canola oil
1 cup beef stock
1 tsp. dried thyme
1/2 cup white wine
2 garlic cloves, chopped
2 cups grated Swiss cheese
1 tbsp. cornstarch
Salt and pepper to taste

Directions:

Heat the butter and oil in a skillet. Add the onions and cook over medium flame until the onions begin to caramelize.
Transfer the onions in your Slow Cooker and add the remaining ingredients.
Season with salt and pepper and cook on low settings for 4 Hrs.
Serve the dip warm with vegetable sticks or your favorite crunchy snacks.

Pizza Dip

Servings: 20 Cooking Time: 6 1/4 Hrs.

Ingredients:

1 lb. spicy sausages, sliced
1/2 lb. salami, diced
1 red bell pepper, cored and diced
1 yellow bell pepper, cored and sliced
1 onion, chopped
2 garlic cloves, minced
2 cups tomato sauce
1/2 cup grated Parmesan
1 cup shredded mozzarella
1/2 tsp. dried basil
1/2 tsp. dried oregano

Directions:

Layer all the ingredients in your Slow Cooker.
Cook on low settings for 6 Hrs., mixing once during the cooking time to ensure an even distribution of ingredients.
Serve the dip warm.

Spicy Glazed Pecans

Servings: 10 Cooking Time: 3 1/4 Hrs.

Ingredients:

2 lbs. pecans
1/2 cup butter, melted
1 tsp. chili powder
1 tsp. smoked paprika
1 tsp. dried basil
1 tsp. dried thyme
1/4 tsp. cayenne pepper
1/2 tsp. garlic powder
2 tbsps. honey

Directions:

Combine all the ingredients in your Slow Cooker.

Mix well until all the ingredients are well distributed and the pecans are evenly glazed.
Cook on high settings for 3 Hrs.
Allow them to cool before serving.

Curried Chicken Wings

Servings: 10 Cooking Time: 7 1/4 Hrs.

Ingredients:

4 lbs. chicken wings
1/4 cup red curry paste
2 shallots, chopped
Salt and pepper to taste
1 cup tomato sauce
1/2 cup coconut milk
1/2 tsp. dried basil

Directions:

Combine all the ingredients in a Slow Cooker and toss around until evenly coated.
Adjust the taste with salt and pepper and cook on low settings for 7 Hrs.
Serve the chicken wings warm or chilled.

Sweet Corn Jalapeno Dip

Servings: 10 Cooking Time: 2 1/4 Hrs.

Ingredients:

4 bacon slices, chopped
4 jalapenos, seeded and chopped
1 cup grated Cheddar cheese
1 pinch nutmeg
3 cans sweet corn, drained
1 cup sour cream
1/2 cup cream cheese
2 tbsps. chopped cilantro

Directions:

Combine the corn, jalapenos, sour cream, Cheddar, cream cheese and nutmeg in a Slow Cooker.
Cook on high settings for 2 Hrs.
When done, stir in the cilantro and serve the dip warm.
Store it in an airtight container in the fridge for up to 2 days. Reheat it when need it.

French Onion Dip

Servings: 10 Cooking Time: 4 1/4 Hrs.

Ingredients:

4 large onions, chopped
1 tbsp. butter
1 pinch nutmeg
2 tbsps. olive oil
1 1/2 cups sour cream
Salt and pepper to taste

Directions:

Combine the onions, olive oil, butter, salt, pepper and nutmeg in a Slow Cooker.
Cover and cook on high settings for 4 Hrs.
When done, allow to cool then stir in the sour cream and adjust the taste with salt and pepper.
Serve the dip right away.

Cheese and Beer Fondue

Servings: 10 Cooking Time: 2 1/4 Hrs.

Ingredients:

4 tbsps. butter
2 garlic cloves, minced
2 poblano peppers, chopped
1 shallot, chopped
2 tbsps. all-purpose flour
1 cup milk
1 cup light beer
1/2 tsp. chili powder
2 cups grated Cheddar

Directions:

Melt the butter in a saucepan and stir in the shallot and garlic.
Sauté for 2 Min. then add the flour and cook for 2 additional Min.
Stir in the milk and cook until thickened, about 5 Min.
Pour the mixture in your Slow Cooker and stir in the remaining ingredients.
Cook on high settings for 2 Hrs. and serve the fondue warm with biscuits or other salty snacks.

Bourbon Glazed Sausages

Servings: 10 Cooking Time: 4 1/4 Hrs.

Ingredients:

3 lbs. small sausage links
1/4 cup maple syrup
1/2 cup apricot preserves
2 tbsps. Bourbon

Directions:

Combine all the ingredients in your Slow Cooker.
Cover with its lid and cook on low settings for 4 Hrs.
Serve the glazed sausages warm or chilled, preferably with cocktail sticks.

Glazed Peanuts

Servings: 8 Cooking Time: 2 1/4 Hrs.

Ingredients:

2 lbs. raw, whole peanuts
1/2 tsp. garlic powder
1 tbsp. Cajun seasoning
1/4 cup coconut oil
1/4 cup brown sugar
2 tbsps. salt
1/2 tsp. red pepper flakes

Directions:

Combine all the ingredients in your Slow Cooker.
Cover and cook on high settings for 2 Hrs.
Serve chilled.

Artichoke Dip

Servings: 20 Cooking Time: 6 1/4 Hrs.

Ingredients:

2 sweet onions, chopped
2 garlic cloves, chopped
1 cup cream cheese
2 oz. blue cheese, crumbled
1 red chili, chopped
1 jar artichoke hearts, drained and chopped
1 cup heavy cream
2 tbsps. chopped cilantro

Directions:

Mix the onions, chili, garlic, artichoke hearts, cream cheese, heavy cream and blue cheese in a Slow Cooker.
Cook on low settings for 6 Hrs.
When done, stir in the cilantro and serve the dip warm or chilled.

Cheesy Bacon Dip

Servings: 20 Cooking Time: 4 1/4 Hrs.

Ingredients:

1 sweet onions, chopped
1 tsp. Dijon mustard
10 bacon slices, chopped
1 tsp. Worcestershire sauce
1 cup cream cheese
1 cup grated Gruyere

1/2 cup whole milk
Salt and pepper to taste

Directions:

Combine all the ingredients in a Slow Cooker.
Adjust the taste with salt and pepper and cover with its lid.
Cook on low settings for 4 Hrs.
Serve the dip warm or chilled with vegetable sticks, biscuits or other salty snacks.

Taco Dip

Servings: 20 Cooking Time: 6 1/2 Hrs.

Ingredients:

2 lbs. ground beef
1 can black beans, drained
1 cup tomato sauce
2 cups Velveeta cheese, shredded
2 tbsps. canola oil
1/2 cup beef stock
1 tbsp. taco seasoning

Directions:

Heat the oil in a skillet and add the beef. Cook for 10 Min, stirring often.
Transfer the beef in your Slow Cooker.
Add the remaining ingredients and cook on low settings for 6 Hrs.
Serve the dip warm.

Bacon Wrapped Dates

Servings: 8 Cooking Time: 1 3/4 Hrs.

Ingredients:

16 dates, pitted
16 slices bacon
16 almonds

Directions:

Stuff each date with an almond.
Wrap each date in bacon and place the wrapped dates in your Slow Cooker.
Cover with its lid and cook on high settings for 1 1/4 Hrs.
Serve warm or chilled.

Bacon Baked Potatoes

Servings: 8 Cooking Time: 3 1/4 Hrs.

Ingredients:

3 lbs. new potatoes, halved
1 tsp. dried rosemary
Salt and pepper to taste
8 slices bacon, chopped
1/4 cup chicken stock

Directions:

Heat a skillet over medium flame and stir in the bacon. Cook until crisp.
Place the potatoes in a Slow Cooker. Add the bacon bits and its fat, as well as rosemary, salt and pepper and mix until evenly distributed.
Pour in the stock and cook on high heat for 3 Hrs.
Serve the potatoes warm.

Marmalade Glazed Meatballs

Servings: 8 Cooking Time: 7 1/2 Hrs.

Ingredients:

2 lbs. ground pork
4 garlic cloves, minced
1 egg
1 cup orange marmalade
1 bay leaf
Salt and pepper to taste
1 shallot, chopped
1 carrot, grated
Salt and pepper to taste
2 cups BBQ sauce
1 tsp. Worcestershire sauce

Directions:

Mix the ground pork, shallot, garlic, carrot, egg, salt and pepper in a bowl.
Form small meatballs and place them on your working surface.
For the sauce, mix the orange marmalade, sauce, bay leaf, Worcestershire sauce, salt and pepper in your Slow Cooker.
Place the meatballs in the sauce. Cover with its lid and cook on low settings for 7 Hrs.
Serve the meatballs warm.

Turkey Meatloaf

Servings: 8 Cooking Time: 6 1/4 Hrs.

Ingredients:

1 1/2 lbs. ground turkey
1 sweet potato, grated
1/4 cup breadcrumbs
Salt and pepper to taste
1 carrot, grated
1 egg
1/4 tsp. chili powder
1 cup shredded mozzarella

Directions:

Mix all the ingredients in a bowl and season with salt and pepper as needed.
Give it a good mix then transfer the mixture in your Slow Cooker.
Level the mixture well and cover with the pot's lid.
Cook on low settings for 6 Hrs.
Serve the meatloaf warm or chilled.

Balsamico Pulled Pork

Servings: 6 Cooking Time: 8 1/4 Hrs.

Ingredients:

2 lbs. boneless pork shoulder
1/4 cup balsamic vinegar
1 tbsp. Dijon mustard
2 garlic cloves, minced
2 tbsps. soy sauce
2 tbsps. honey
1/4 cup hoisin sauce
1/4 cup chicken stock
2 shallots, sliced

Directions:

Combine the honey, vinegar, hoisin sauce, mustard, stock, garlic, shallots and soy sauce in your Slow Cooker.
Add the pork shoulder and roll it in the mixture until evenly coated.
Cover the Slow Cooker and cook on low settings for 8 Hrs.
When done, shred the meat into fine pieces and serve warm or chilled.

Spicy Chicken Taquitos

Servings: 8 Cooking Time: 6 1/2 Hrs.

Ingredients:

4 chicken breasts, cooked and diced
1 cup cream cheese
2 jalapeno peppers, chopped
1/2 cup canned sweet corn, drained
1/2 tsp. cumin powder
4 garlic cloves, minced

16 taco-sized flour tortillas
2 cups grated Cheddar cheese

Directions:

In a bowl, mix the chicken, cream cheese, garlic, cumin, poblano peppers and corn. Stir in the cheese as well.
Place your tortillas on your working surface and top each tortilla with the cheese mixture.
Roll the tortillas tightly to form an even roll.
Place the rolls in your Slow Cooker.
Cook on low settings for 6 Hrs.
Serve warm.

Beer BBQ Meatballs

Servings: 10 Cooking Time: 7 1/2 Hrs.

Ingredients:

2 lbs. ground pork
1 lb. ground beef
1 carrot, grated
2 shallots, chopped
1 egg
1/2 cup breadcrumbs
1/2 tsp. cumin powder
Salt and pepper to taste
1 cup dark beer
1 cup BBQ sauce
1 bay leaf
1/2 tsp. chili powder
1 tsp. apple cider vinegar

Directions:

Mix the ground pork and beef in a bowl. Add the carrot, shallots, egg, breadcrumbs, cumin, salt and pepper and mix well. Form small meatballs and place them on your chopping board.
For the beer sauce, combine the beer, BBQ sauce, bay leaf, chili powder and vinegar in a Slow Cooker.
Place the meatballs in the pot and cover with its lid.
Cook on low settings for 7 Hrs.
Serve the meatballs warm or chilled.

Chili Chicken Wings

Servings: 8 Cooking Time: 7 1/4 Hrs.

Ingredients:

4 lbs. chicken wings
1/4 cup maple syrup
1 tsp. garlic powder
1 tsp. chili powder
2 tbsps. balsamic vinegar
1 tbsp. Dijon mustard
1 tsp. Worcestershire sauce
1/2 cup tomato sauce
1 tsp. salt

Directions:

Combine the chicken wings and the remaining ingredients in a Slow Cooker.
Toss around until evenly coated and cook on low settings for 7 Hrs.
Serve the chicken wings warm or chilled.

Pretzel Party Mix

Servings: 10 Cooking Time: 2 1/4 Hrs.

Ingredients:

4 cups pretzels
1 cup peanuts
1 cup pecans
1 cup crispy rice cereals
1/4 cup butter, melted
1 tsp. Worcestershire sauce
1 tsp. salt
1 tsp. garlic powder

Directions:

Combine the pretzels, peanuts, pecans and rice cereals in your Slow Cooker.
Drizzle with melted butter and Worcestershire sauce and mix well then sprinkle with salt and garlic powder.
Cover and cook on high settings for 2 Hrs., mixing once during cooking.
Allow to cool before serving.

Tahini Cheese Dip

Servings: 8 Cooking Time: 2 1/4 Hrs.

Ingredients:

1/2 cup tahini paste
1 cup whole milk
1/8 tsp. garlic powder
1/2 tsp. cumin powder
1/4 lb. grated Gruyere
1/4 cup grated Emmentaler cheese
Salt and pepper to taste
1 pinch nutmeg

Directions:

Combine all the ingredients in your Slow Cooker.
Add salt and pepper if needed and cover the pot with its lid.
Cook on high settings for 2 Hrs.
Serve the dip warm.

Blue Cheese Chicken Wings

Servings: 8 Cooking Time: 7 1/4 Hrs.

Ingredients:

4 lbs. chicken wings
1/2 cup buffalo sauce
1/2 cup spicy tomato sauce
1 tbsp. tomato paste
2 tbsps. apple cider vinegar
1 tbsp. Worcestershire sauce
1 cup sour cream
2 oz. blue cheese, crumbled
1 thyme sprig

Directions:

Combine the buffalo sauce, tomato sauce, vinegar, Worcestershire sauce, sour cream, blue cheese and thyme in a Slow Cooker.
Add the chicken wings and toss them until evenly coated.
Cook on low settings for 7 Hrs.
Serve the chicken wings preferably warm.

Tropical Meatballs

Servings: 20 Cooking Time: 7 1/2 Hrs.

Ingredients:

1 can pineapple chunks (keep the juices)
2 poblano peppers, chopped
1/4 cup brown sugar
2 tbsps. soy sauce
2 tbsps. cornstarch
1 tbsp. lemon juice
2 lbs. ground pork
1 lb. ground beef
4 garlic cloves, minced
1 tsp. dried basil
1 egg
1/4 cup breadcrumbs
Salt and pepper to taste

Directions:

Mix the pineapple, poblano peppers, brown sugar, soy sauce, cornstarch and lemon juice in a Slow Cooker.
Combine the ground meat, garlic, basil, egg and breadcrumbs in a bowl. Add salt and pepper to taste and mix well.
Form small meatballs and place them in the sauce.
Cover and cook on low settings for 7 Hrs.
Serve the meatballs warm or chilled.

Five-spiced Chicken Wings

Servings: 8 Cooking Time: 7 1/4 Hrs.

Ingredients:

1/2 cup plum sauce
2 tbsps. butter
1 tsp. salt
4 lbs. chicken wings
1/2 cup BBQ sauce
1 tbsp. five-spice powder
1/2 tsp. chili powder

Directions:

Combine the plum sauce and BBQ sauce, as well as butter, five-spice, salt and chili powder in a Slow Cooker.
Add the chicken wings and mix well until well coated.
Cover and cook on low settings fir 7 Hrs.
Serve warm or chilled.

Spiced Buffalo Wings

Servings: 8 Cooking Time: 8 1/4 Hrs.

Ingredients:

4 lbs. chicken wings
1/4 cup butter, melted
1 tsp. dried oregano
1 tsp. onion powder
1/2 tsp. cumin powder
1 tsp. hot sauce
1 cup BBQ sauce
1 tbsp. Worcestershire sauce
1 tsp. dried basil
1 tsp. garlic powder
1/2 tsp. cinnamon powder
1 tsp. salt

Directions:

Combine all the ingredients in a Slow Cooker.
Mix until the wings are evenly coated.
Cook on low settings for 8 Hrs.
Serve warm or chilled.

Classic Bread In A Slow Cooker

Servings: 8 Cooking Time: 1 1/2 Hrs.

Ingredients:

2 tsps. active dry yeast
1 cup warm water
1 egg
3 cups all-purpose flour
1 tsp. sugar
1/2 cup yogurt
2 tbsps. olive oil
1/2 tsp. salt

Directions:

Mix the yeast, sugar, warm water, yogurt, egg and olive oil in a bowl.
Stir in the flour and salt and mix well. Knead the dough for 5-10 Min. until even and non-sticky.
Place the dough in your Slow Cooker and cover with its lid.
Cook on high settings for 1 1/4 Hrs.
Serve the bread warm or chilled.

Bean Queso

Servings: 10 Cooking Time: 6 1/4 Hrs.

Ingredients:

1 can black beans, drained
1/2 cup red salsa
1/2 tsp. cumin powder
1 1/2 cups grated Cheddar
1 cup chopped green chiles
1 tsp. dried oregano
1 cup light beer
Salt and pepper to taste

Directions:

Combine the beans, chiles, oregano, cumin, salsa, beer and cheese in your Slow Cooker.
Add salt and pepper as needed and cook on low settings for 6 Hrs.
Serve the bean queso warm.

Zesty Lamb Meatballs

Servings: 10 Cooking Time: 7 1/4 Hrs.

Ingredients:

3 lbs. ground lamb
2 garlic cloves, minced
1/4 tsp. five-spice powder
1/4 tsp. cumin powder
1/2 cup raisins, chopped
Salt and pepper to taste
1 lemon, juiced
1 thyme sprig
1 shallot, chopped
1 tbsp. lemon zest
1/2 tsp. cumin powder
1/4 tsp. chili powder
1 tsp. dried mint
2 cups tomato sauce
1 bay leaf
1 red chili, chopped

Directions:

Mix the tomato sauce, lemon juice, bay leaf, thyme sprig and red chili in your Slow Cooker.
Combine the remaining ingredients in a bowl and mix well.
Season with salt and pepper and give it a good mix.
Form small balls and place them in the sauce.
Cover with its lid and cook on low settings for 7 Hrs.
Serve the meatballs warm or chilled.

White Bean Hummus

Servings: 8 Cooking Time: 8 1/4 Hrs.

Ingredients:

1 lb. dried white beans, rinsed
2 cups chicken stock
1 thyme sprig
Salt and pepper to taste
2 large sweet onions, sliced
2 cups water
1 bay leaf
4 garlic cloves, minced
2 tbsps. canola oil

Directions:

Combine the white beans, water, stock, bay leaf and thyme in your Slow Cooker.
Add salt and pepper to taste and cook the beans on low settings for 8 Hrs.
When done, drain the beans well (but reserve 1/4 cup of the liquid) and discard the bay leaf and thyme.
Transfer the bean in a food processor. Add the reserved liquid and pulse until smooth.
Season with salt and pepper and transfer in a bowl.
Heat the canola oil in a skillet and add the onions. Cook for 10 Min. over medium flame until the onions begin to caramelize.
Top the hummus with caramelized onions and serve.

Mozzarella Stuffed Meatballs

Servings: 8 Cooking Time: 6 1/2 Hrs.

Ingredients:

2 lbs. ground chicken
1/2 tsp. dried oregano
1/2 cup breadcrumbs
Mini-mozzarella balls as needed
1 tsp. dried basil
1 egg
Salt and pepper to taste
1/2 cup chicken stock

Directions:

Mix the ground chicken, basil, oregano, egg, breadcrumbs, salt and pepper in a bowl.
Take small pieces of the meat mixture and flatten it in your palm.
Place a mozzarella ball in the center and gather the meat around the mozzarella.
Shape the meatballs, making sure they are well sealed and place them in a Slow Cooker.
Add the chicken stock and cook on low settings for 6 Hrs.
Serve the meatballs warm or chilled.

Charred Tomato Salsa

Servings: 8 Cooking Time: 3 Hrs.

Ingredients:

4 ripe tomatoes, sliced
1 tsp. dried basil
2 shallots, chopped
1 can black beans, drained
1 bay leaf
2 tbsps. olive oil
1/2 tsp. dried mint
1 jalapeno pepper, chopped
1/4 cup chicken stock
Salt and pepper to taste

Directions:

Place the tomato slices in a baking tray and sprinkle with salt, pepper, basil and mint.
Drizzle with olive oil and cook in the preheated oven at 350F for 35-40 Min. until the slices begin to caramelize.
Transfer the tomatoes in a Slow Cooker and add the remaining ingredients.
Cook on high settings for 2 Hrs. and serve the salsa warm or chilled.

Sausage and Pepper Appetizer

Servings: 8 Cooking Time: 6 1/4 Hrs.

Ingredients:

6 fresh pork sausages, skins removed
1 can fire roasted tomatoes
1 poblano pepper, chopped
1 cup grated Provolone cheese
2 tbsps. olive oil
4 roasted bell peppers, chopped
1 shallot, chopped
Salt and pepper to taste

Directions:

Heat the oil in a skillet and stir in the sausage meat. Cook for 5 Min, stirring often.
Transfer the meat in your Slow Cooker and add the remaining ingredients.
Season with salt and pepper and cook on low settings for 6 Hrs.
Serve the dish warm or chilled.

Pork Ham Dip

Servings: 20 Cooking Time: 6 1/4 Hrs.

Ingredients:

2 cups diced ham
1 shallot, chopped
1 tsp. Dijon mustard
1/2 cup chili sauce
Salt and pepper to taste
1 lb. ground pork
2 garlic cloves, chopped
1 cup tomato sauce
1/2 cup cranberry sauce

Directions:

Heat a skillet over medium flame and add the ground pork. Cook for 5 Min, stirring often.
Transfer the ground pork in a Slow Cooker and add the remaining ingredients.
Adjust the taste with salt and pepper and cook on low settings for 6 Hrs.
Serve the dip warm or chilled.

Bacon Crab Dip

Servings: 20 Cooking Time: 2 1/4 Hrs.

Ingredients:

1 lb. bacon, diced
1/2 cup grated Parmesan cheese
1 tsp. Dijon mustard
1 tsp. hot sauce
1 cup cream cheese
1 tsp. Worcestershire sauce
1 can crab meat, drained and shredded

Directions:

Heat a skillet over medium flame and add the bacon. Sauté for 5 Min. until fat begins to drain out.
Transfer the bacon in a Slow Cooker.
Stir in the remaining ingredients and cook on high settings for 2 Hrs.
Serve the dip warm or chilled.

Creamy Spinach Dip

Servings: 30 Cooking Time: 2 1/4 Hrs.

Ingredients:

1 can crab meat, drained
2 shallots, chopped
1 cup grated Parmesan
1 cup sour cream
1 cup grated Cheddar cheese
2 garlic cloves, chopped
1 lb. fresh spinach, chopped
2 jalapeno peppers, chopped
1/2 cup whole milk
1 cup cream cheese
1 tbsp. sherry vinegar

Directions:

Combine all the ingredients in your Slow Cooker.
Cover with its lid and cook on high settings for 2 Hrs.
Serve the spinach dip warm or chilled with vegetable stick or your favorite salty snacks.

Beef, Pork & Lamb Recipes

Burgers

Servings:4 Cooking Time: 4 Hrs.

Ingredients:

10 oz. ground beef
1 tsp. dried dill
1 tsp. ground black pepper
1 tbsp. minced onion
2 tbsps. water
1/3 cup chicken stock

Directions:

Mix the minced beef with onion, dill, water, and ground black pepper.
Make 4 burgers and arrange them in the Slow Cooker bowl.
Add chicken stock and close the lid.
Cook the burgers on high for 4 Hrs.

BBQ Beer Beef Tenderloin

Servings:4 Cooking Time: 10 Hrs.

Ingredients:

¼ cup beer
½ cup BBQ sauce
1 tsp. olive oil
1-pound beef tenderloin
1 tsp. fennel seeds

Directions:

Mix BBQ sauce with beer, fennel seeds, and olive oil.
Pour the liquid in the Slow Cooker.
Add beef tenderloin and close the lid.
Cook the meal on Low for 10 Hrs.

Sausages In Sweet Currant Sauce

Servings:4 Cooking Time: 4.5 Hrs.

Ingredients:

1 tbsp. butter
1 tbsp. brown sugar
1-pound beef sausages
1 cup fresh currant
1 cup of water
1 tbsp. sunflower oil

Directions:

Mix currants with brown sugar and blend with the help of the immersion blender until smooth.
Pour the liquid in the Slow Cooker.
Add all remaining ingredients and close the lid.
Cook the sausages on High for 5 Hrs.

Cinnamon Lamb

Servings: 2 Cooking Time: 6 Hrs.

Ingredients:

1 lb. lamb chops
1 red onion, chopped
1 tbsp. oregano, chopped
1 tbsp. chives, chopped
1 tsp. cinnamon powder
1 tbsp. avocado oil
½ cup beef stock

Directions:

In your Slow Cooker, mix the lamb chops with the cinnamon and the other ingredients, toss, put the lid on and cook on Low for 6 Hrs.
Divide the chops between plates and serve with a side salad.

Beef Casserole

Servings:5 Cooking Time: 7 Hrs.

Ingredients:

7 oz. ground beef
½ cup cream
½ cup broccoli, chopped
1 cup Cheddar cheese, shredded
1 tsp. Italian seasonings

Directions:

Mix ground beef with Italian seasonings and put in the Slow Cooker.
Top the meat with broccoli and Cheddar cheese.
Then pour the cream over the casserole mixture and close the lid.
Cook the casserole on Low for 7 Hrs.

Pork and Chilies Mix

Servings: 2 Cooking Time: 7 Hrs.

Ingredients:

1 lb. pork stew meat, cubed
½ green bell pepper, chopped
½ red bell pepper, chopped
2 oz. canned green chilies, chopped
Salt and black pepper to the taste
1 tbsp. cilantro, chopped
1 tbsp. olive oil
1 red onion, sliced
1 garlic clove, minced
½ cup tomato passata
1 tbsp. chili powder

Directions:

In your Slow Cooker, mix the pork with the oil, bell pepper and the other ingredients, toss, put the lid on and cook on Low for 7 Hrs.
Divide into bowls and serve right away.

Tomato Beef Chowder

Servings:4 Cooking Time: 7 Hrs.

Ingredients:

1 cup potatoes, peeled, chopped
3 cups of water
12 oz. beef sirloin, chopped
1 tsp. salt
1 cup tomato juice
1 onion, chopped
1 tsp. fresh parsley, chopped

Directions:

Put all ingredients in the Slow Cooker.
Gently stir the mixture and close the lid.
Cook the chowder on Low for 7 Hrs.

Rosemary Lamb Shoulder

Servings:3 Cooking Time: 9 Hrs.

Ingredients:

9 oz. lamb shoulder
½ cup apple cider vinegar
1 cup of water
2 garlic cloves, peeled
1 tbsp. fresh rosemary
1 tbsp. olive oil
1 tsp. ground black pepper

Directions:

Rub the lamb shoulder with olive oil and fresh rosemary.
Then put the lamb shoulder in the apple cider vinegar and leave for 30 Min. to marinate.
After this, transfer the lamb shoulder in the Slow Cooker.
Add water, ground black pepper, and garlic cloves.
Close the lid and cook the meat on low for 9 Hrs.

BBQ Bratwurst

Servings:5 Cooking Time: 4 Hrs.

Ingredients:

1-pound bratwurst
1 tsp. olive oil
1 tsp. chili powder
4 tbsps. BBQ sauce
¼ cup of water

Directions:

Roast the bratwurst in the olive oil for 1 minute per side.
Then transfer the bratwurst in the Slow Cooker.
Add water and BBQ sauce.
Close the lid and cook the meal on High for 4 Hrs.

Cider Pork Roast

Servings:4 Cooking Time: 8 Hrs.

Ingredients:

1-pound pork roast
1 cup cider

1 apple, chopped
½ cup of water
1 tsp. peppercorns
1 tsp. chili flakes

Directions:

Put all ingredients in the Slow Cooker.
Close the lid and cook the meat on low for 8 Hrs.

Beef Soup

Servings: 4 Cooking Time: 6 Hrs.

Ingredients:

1 lb. beef, ground
1 cup yellow onion, chopped
15 oz. tomato sauce
3 cups beef stock
½ tsp. oregano, dried
Salt and black pepper to the taste
2 cups cauliflower, chopped
2 red bell peppers, chopped
15 oz. tomatoes, chopped
½ tsp. basil, dried
3 garlic cloves, minced

Directions:

In your Slow Cooker, mix beef with cauliflower, onion, bell peppers, tomato sauce, tomatoes, stock, basil, oregano, garlic, salt and pepper, stir, cover, cook on Low for 6 Hrs., ladle into bowls and serve.

Beef Stuffing

Servings:6 Cooking Time: 5 Hrs.

Ingredients:

½ tsp. cumin seeds
1 tsp. garam masala
2 oz. scallions, chopped
1 tbsp. butter
12 oz. ground beef
1 tsp. ginger paste
1 cup of water
1 tsp. salt

Directions:

Put all ingredients in the Slow Cooker and carefully mix the mixture.
Close the lid and cook the beef stuffing on High for 5 Hrs.

Hot Lamb Strips

Servings:6 Cooking Time: 5 Hrs.

Ingredients:

14 oz. lamb fillet, cut into strips
2 tbsps. butter, melted
½ cup of water
1 tsp. cayenne pepper
1 tbsp. hot sauce

Directions:

Mix lamb strips with hot sauce and cayenne pepper.
Transfer them in the Slow Cooker.
After this, add water and butter.
Close the lid and cook the lamb on High for 5 Hrs.

Chinese Mushroom Pork

Servings: 4 Cooking Time: 7 Hrs.

Ingredients:

2 and ½ lbs. pork shoulder
½ cup of soy sauce
2 tbsp. chili sauce
1 tbsp. ginger, grated
2 cups portabella mushrooms, sliced
4 cups chicken stock
¼ cup white vinegar
Juice of 1 lime
1 tbsp. Chinese 5 spice
Salt and black pepper to the taste
1 zucchini, sliced

Directions:

Add pork, stock, and all other ingredients to the insert of Slow Cooker.
Put the cooker's lid on and set the cooking time to 7 Hrs. on Low settings.
Shred the cooked pork with the help of two forks.
Return the pork shreds to the mushrooms sauce.
Serve warm.

Soy Sauce Marinated Meatballs

Servings:4 Cooking Time: 5 Hrs.

Ingredients:

¼ cup of soy sauce
1 onion, minced
½ tsp. dried mint
¼ cup of water
12 oz. ground beef
1 tsp. cayenne pepper
1 tbsp. coconut oil

Directions:

In the mixing bowl mix ground beef with minced onion, cayenne pepper, and dried mint.
Make the small balls.
Melt the coconut oil in the skillet.
Add meatballs and roast them for 3 Min. per side.
After this, transfer the meatballs in the Slow Cooker.
Add water and soy sauce.
Close the lid and cook the meatballs on low for 5 Hrs.

Brisket Turnips Medley

Servings: 6 Cooking Time: 8 Hrs.

Ingredients:

2 and ½ lbs. beef brisket
2 bay leaves
4 carrots, chopped
Salt and black pepper to the taste
4 cups veggie stock
3 garlic cloves, chopped
1 cabbage head cut into 6 wedges
3 turnips, cut into quarters

Directions:

Add beef, bay leaves, stock, carrots, garlic, salt, cabbage, black pepper, and turnips to the insert of the Slow Cooker.
Put the cooker's lid on and set the cooking time to 8 Hrs. on Low settings.
Serve warm.

Italian Pork Chops

Servings:6 Cooking Time: 10 Hrs.

Ingredients:

6 pork loin chops
3 cloves of garlic, minced
1 cup mozzarella cheese
1 onion, chopped
3 cups sugar-free pasta sauce

Directions:

Place pork loin, onion, and garlic in the Slow Cooker.
Pour in the sugar-free pasta sauce.
Add the mozzarella cheese on top.
Close the lid and cook for low in 10 Hrs. or on high for 7 Hrs.

Sour Cream Roast

Servings:4 Cooking Time: 4.5 Hrs.

Ingredients:

1-pound pork shoulder, boneless, chopped
4 tbsps. lemon juice
¼ cup of water
1 tbsp. lemon zest, grated
1 cup sour cream

Directions:

Sprinkle the pork shoulder with lemon zest and lemon juice.
Transfer the meat in the Slow Cooker.
Add sour cream and water.
Close the lid and cook it on high for 5 Hrs.

Beef Roast with Cauliflower

Servings: 6 Cooking Time: 8 Hrs. 30 Min

Ingredients:

4 lbs. beef chuck roast
1 tbsp. coconut oil
10 thyme sprigs
1 carrot, roughly chopped
2 celery ribs, roughly chopped
Salt and black pepper to the taste
1 cup veggie stock
1 bay leaf
4 garlic cloves, minced
1 yellow onion, roughly chopped
1 cauliflower head, florets separated

Directions:

Place a suitable pan over medium-high heat and add oil to it.
Toss in the beef and drizzle salt and black pepper over it.
Sear the seasoned beef for 5 Min. per side then transfer to the insert of the Slow Cooker.
Toss in the garlic, thyme springs, stock, bay leaf, celery, carrot, and onion.
Put the cooker's lid on and set the cooking time to 8 Hrs. on Low settings.
Stir in cauliflower then cover again to cook for 20 Min. on High settings.
Serve warm.

Cajun Beef

Servings:4 Cooking Time: 5 Hrs.

Ingredients:

1-pound beef ribs
3 tbsps. lemon juice
½ cup of water
1 tbsp. Cajun seasonings
1 tbsp. coconut oil, melted

Directions:

Rub the beef ribs with Cajun seasonings and sprinkle with lemon juice.
Then pour the coconut oil in the Slow Cooker.
Add beef ribs and water.
Close the lid and cook the beef on high for 5 Hrs.

Coconut Beef

Servings:5 Cooking Time: 8 Hrs.

Ingredients:

1 cup baby spinach, chopped
1-pound beef tenderloin, chopped
1 tsp. dried rosemary
1 cup of coconut milk
1 tsp. avocado oil
1 tsp. garlic powder

Directions:

Roast meat in the avocado oil for 1 minute per side on high heat.
Ten transfer the meat in the Slow Cooker.
Add garlic powder, dried rosemary, coconut milk, and baby spinach.
Close the lid and cook the meal on Low for 8 Hrs.

Cucumber and Pork Cubes Bowl

Servings:4 Cooking Time: 4 Hrs.

Ingredients:

3 cucumbers, chopped
1 red onion, diced
1 tbsp. olive oil
1 cup of water
1 jalapeno pepper, diced
3 tbsps. soy sauce
8 oz. pork tenderloin

Directions:

Pour water in the Slow Cooker.
Add pork tenderloin and cook it on High for 4 Hrs.
Meanwhile, mix the red onion with jalapeno pepper and cucumbers in the salad bowl.
In the shallow bowl mix soy sauce and olive oil.
When the pork is cooked, chop it roughly and add in the cucumber salad.
Sprinkle the salad with oil-soy sauce mixture and shake well.

Beef and Pancetta

Servings: 4 Cooking Time: 4 Hrs. and 10 Min

Ingredients:

8 oz. pancetta, chopped
4 garlic cloves, minced
2 tbsps. olive oil
4 cups beef stock
2 cinnamon sticks
A handful parsley, chopped
2 tbsps. butter
4 lbs. beef, cubed
2 brown onions, chopped
4 tbsps. red vinegar
2 tbsps. tomato paste
3 lemon peel strips
4 thyme springs
Salt and black pepper to the taste

Directions:

Heat up a pan with the oil over medium-high heat, add pancetta, onion and garlic, stir, cook for 5 Min, add beef, stir and brown for a few Min
Add vinegar, salt, pepper, stock, tomato paste, cinnamon, lemon peel, thyme and butter, stir, cook for 3 Min. more, transfer everything to your Slow Cooker, cook on High for 4 Hrs., discard cinnamon, lemon peel and thyme, add parsley, stir, divide between plates and serve.

Herbed and Cinnamon Beef

Servings: 6 Cooking Time: 5 Hrs.

Ingredients:

4 lbs. beef brisket
2 garlic cloves, minced
11 oz. celery, thinly sliced
3 bay leaves
Salt and black pepper to the taste
2 oranges, sliced
2 yellow onions, thinly sliced
1 tbsp. dill, dried
4 cinnamon sticks, cut into halves
17 oz. veggie stock

Directions:

In your Slow Cooker, mix beef with orange slices, garlic, onion, celery, dill, bay leaves, cinnamon, salt, pepper and stock, stir, cover and cook on High for 5 Hrs.
Divide beef mix between plates and serve.

Naked Beef Enchilada in A Slow Cooker

Servings:4 Cooking Time: 6 Hrs.

Ingredients:

1-pound ground beef
1 cup cauliflower florets
¼ cup cilantro, chopped
2 tbsps. enchilada spice mix
2 cups Mexican cheese blend, grated

Directions:

In a skillet, sauté the ground beef over medium flame for 3 Min.
Transfer to the Slow Cooker and add the enchilada spice mix and cauliflower.
Stir to combine.
Add the Mexican cheese blend on top.
Cook on low for 6 Hrs. or on high for 4 Hrs.
Sprinkle with cilantro on top.

Jalapeno Mississippi Roast

Servings:4 Cooking Time: 8 Hrs.

Ingredients:

3 pepperoncini
2 tbsps. flour
½ tsp. salt
2 cups of water
1-pound beef chuck roast
1 tsp. ground black pepper
2 tbsps. avocado oil

Directions:

Put all ingredients in the Slow Cooker.
Close the lid and cook the meal on Low for 8 Hrs.
Then open the lid and shred the beef.

Peppercorn Beef Steak

Servings:4 Cooking Time: 8 Hrs.

Ingredients:

4 beef steaks
1 tsp. peppercorns
1 cup of water
1 tsp. salt
1 tbsp. butter
1 tsp. dried rosemary

Directions:

Rub the beef steaks with salt and dried rosemary.
Then rub the meat with butter and transfer in the Slow Cooker.
Add water and peppercorns.
Close the lid and cook the beef steaks on Low for 8 Hrs.

Egg Salad with Ground Pork

Servings:2 Cooking Time: 4 Hrs.

Ingredients:

2 eggs, hard-boiled, peeled, chopped
1 tsp. ground turmeric
¼ cup plain yogurt
2 tomatoes, chopped
¼ cup ground pork
1 tsp. salt
1 tbsp. coconut oil

Directions:

Put the coconut oil in the Slow Cooker.
Add ground pork, ground turmeric, salt, and yogurt.
Close the lid and cook the meat on High for 4 Hrs.
After this, transfer the ground pork and all remaining liquid from the Slow Cooker in the salad bowl.
Add all remaining ingredients from the list above and mix the salad.

Salsa Meat

Servings:4 Cooking Time: 4 Hrs.

Ingredients:

1-pound pork sirloin, sliced
2 garlic cloves, diced
½ cup of water
1 cup tomatillo salsa
1 tsp. apple cider vinegar

Directions:

Put all ingredients in the Slow Cooker and carefully mix.
Then close the lid and cook the salsa meat on high for 4 Hrs.

Balsamic Beef Cheeks

Servings: 4 Cooking Time: 4 Hrs.

Ingredients:

4 beef cheeks, halved
Salt and black pepper to the taste
4 garlic cloves, minced
5 cardamom pods
3 bay leaves
2 vanilla beans, split
1 carrot, sliced
2 tbsps. olive oil
1 white onion, chopped
2 cup beef stock
1 tbsp. balsamic vinegar
7 cloves
1 and ½ tbsps. tomato paste

Directions:

In your Slow Cooker, mix beef cheeks with the oil, salt, pepper, onion, garlic, stock, cardamom, vinegar, bay leaves, cloves, vanilla beans, tomato paste and carrot, toss, cover, cook on High for 4 Hrs., divide between plates and serve.

Lamb Leg and Sweet Potatoes

Servings: 4 Cooking Time: 8 Hrs.

Ingredients:

2 tbsps. olive oil
1 garlic head, peeled and cloves separated
5 rosemary springs
Salt and black pepper to the taste
1 lamb leg, bone in
5 sweet potatoes, cubed
2 cups chicken stock

Directions:

Rub your lamb leg with the oil, salt and pepper.
Place the potatoes and the garlic cloves on the bottom of your Slow Cooker, add lamb leg, rosemary springs and stock, cover and cook lamb on Low for 8 Hrs.
Divide lamb and potatoes between plates and serve.

Succulent Pork Ribs

Servings:4 Cooking Time: 8 Hrs.

Ingredients:

12 oz. pork ribs, roughly chopped
1 cup of water
1 tsp. salt
¼ cup of orange juice
1 tsp. ground nutmeg

Directions:

Pour water and orange juice in the Slow Cooker.
Then sprinkle the pork ribs with ground nutmeg and salt.
Put the pork ribs in the Slow Cooker and close the lid.
Cook the meat on low for 8 Hrs.

Garlic Lamb Chilli

Servings: 7 Cooking Time: 10 Hrs.

Ingredients:

2 oz. fresh rosemary, chopped
½ cup fresh cilantro, chopped
¼ cup coriander leaves, chopped
2 lbs. lamb fillet
1 tsp. salt
1 tsp. black peas
1 tsp. chili flakes
1 cup garlic
1 tsp. garlic powder
6 cups of water

Directions:

Spread all the greens and lamb fillet in the insert of the Slow Cooker.
Stir in garlic, garlic powder, black peas, chili flakes, salt, and water.
Put the cooker's lid on and set the cooking time to 10 Hrs. on Low settings.
Strain the excess liquid from the lamb and serve warm.

Scalloped Potato Casserole

Servings:4 Cooking Time: 8 Hrs.

Ingredients:

2 pork chops, sliced
3 potatoes, sliced
1 egg, beaten
1 tbsp. butter, softened
2 tbsps. breadcrumbs
1 oz. Parmesan, grated
½ cup of coconut milk

Directions:

Grease the Slow Cooker bottom with butter.
Then put the pork chops inside.
Add sliced potatoes over the meat.
Then sprinkle the potatoes with egg and breadcrumbs.
Add parmesan and coconut milk.
Close the lid and cook the casserole on Low for 8 Hrs.

Pork and Beans Mix

Servings: 2 Cooking Time: 8 Hrs.

Ingredients:

1 red bell pepper, chopped
1 lb. pork stew meat, cubed
1 tbsp. olive oil
1 cup canned black beans, drained and rinsed
½ cup tomato sauce
1 yellow onion, chopped
1 tsp. Italian seasoning
Salt and black pepper to the taste
1 tbsp. oregano, chopped

Directions:

In your Slow Cooker, mix the pork with the bell pepper, oil and the other ingredients, toss, put the lid on and cook on Low for 8 Hrs.
Divide the mix between plates and serve.

Cocoa Pork Chops

Servings:4 Cooking Time: 2.5 Hrs.

Ingredients:

4 pork chops
1 tbsp. cocoa powder
½ cup cream
1 tbsp. butter
1 tsp. ground black pepper
½ tsp. salt
¼ cup of water

Directions:

Beat the pork chops gently with the help of the kitchen hammer.
Then sprinkle the meat with ground black pepper and salt.
Transfer it in the Slow Cooker.
After this, mix water with cocoa powder and cream and pour it in the Slow Cooker.
Add butter and close the lid.
Cook the pork chops on high for 2.5 Hrs.

Thyme Beef

Servings:2 Cooking Time: 5 Hrs.

Ingredients:

8 oz. beef sirloin, chopped
1 tbsp. dried thyme
1 tbsp. olive oil
½ cup of water
1 tsp. salt

Directions:

Preheat the skillet well.
Then mix beef with dried thyme and olive oil.
Put the meat in the hot skillet and roast for 2 Min. per side on high heat.
Then transfer the meat in the Slow Cooker.
Add salt and water.
Cook the meal on High for 5 Hrs.

Lavender and Orange Lamb

Servings: 4 Cooking Time: 7 Hrs.

Ingredients:

2 tbsps. rosemary, chopped
1 and ½ lbs. lamb chops
Salt and black pepper to the taste
1 tbsp. lavender, chopped
2 garlic cloves, minced
1 red orange, cut into halves
2 red oranges, peeled and cut into segments
2 small pieces of orange peel
1 tsp. butter

Directions:

In a bowl, mix lamb chops with salt, pepper, rosemary, lavender, garlic and orange peel, toss to coat and leave aside for a couple of Hrs. in the fridge.
Put the butter in your Slow Cooker, add lamb chops, squeeze 1 orange over them, add the rest of the oranges over the lamb, cover Slow Cooker and cook on Low for 7 Hrs.
Divide lamb and sauce all over and serve.

Filet Mignon with Fresh Basil Rub

Servings:4 Cooking Time: 7 Hrs.

Ingredients:

1 ½ tsp. fresh basil, minced
1 ½ tsp. thyme, minced
2 tsps. garlic, minced
Salt and pepper to taste

4 beef tenderloin steaks, cut to 1-inch thick

Directions:

Line the bottom of the Slow Cooker with foil.

In a mixing bowl, combine the basil, thyme, and garlic. Season with salt and pepper.

Rub the steaks with the spice rub. Allow to marinate for at least 30 Min.

Place inside the Slow Cooker and cook on high for 7 Hrs. or on low for 10 Hrs.

Beef with Yams

Servings:4 Cooking Time: 8 Hrs.

Ingredients:

- 2 cups yams, chopped
- 1 cup of water
- 1 tsp. salt
- 4 beef chops
- 2 tbsps. butter
- 1 tsp. peppercorns

Directions:

Pour water in the Slow Cooker.

Add peppercorns, salt, butter, and beef chops.

Then add yams and close the lid.

Cook the meal on Low for 8 Hrs.

Ginger and Rosemary Pork Ribs

Servings:4 Cooking Time: 12 Hrs.

Ingredients:

- 1/3 cup chicken broth
- 3 tbsps. ginger paste or powder
- Salt and pepper to taste
- 4 racks pork spare ribs
- 1 tsp. rosemary, dried

Directions:

Pour the broth into the Slow Cooker.

Season the spare ribs with ginger paste, rosemary, salt and pepper.

Place in the Slow Cooker.

Close the lid and cook on low for 12 Hrs. or on high for 8 Hrs.

Slow Cooker Beef Rendang

Servings:8 Cooking Time: 10 Hrs.

Ingredients:

- ½ cup desiccated coconut, toasted
- 1 tsp. ground cumin
- 1 tsp. turmeric powder
- 6 cloves of garlic, minced
- 1 tbsp. coconut oil
- 2 stalks lemon grass
- 1 beef shoulder, cut into chunks
- 6 dried birds eye chilies, chopped
- 2 tsp. ground coriander
- 1 tsp. salt
- ½ cup water
- 6 kafir lime leaves
- 1 cup coconut cream
- ½ cup cilantro leaves, chopped

Directions:

Place all ingredients except the cilantro leaves in the slow cooker.

Give a good stir.

Close the lid and cook on high for 8 Hrs. or on low for 10 Hrs.

Garnish with cilantro once cooked.

Lamb and Lime Zucchinis

Servings: 2 Cooking Time: 4 Hrs.

Ingredients:

- 1 lb. lamb stew meat, roughly cubed
- Juice of 1 lime
- 2 tbsps. avocado oil
- ½ cup beef stock
- A pinch of salt and black pepper
- 2 small zucchinis, cubed
- ½ tsp. rosemary, dried
- 1 red onion, chopped
- 1 tbsp. garlic, minced
- 1 tbsp. cilantro, chopped

Directions:

In your Slow Cooker, mix the lamb with the zucchinis, lime juice and the other ingredients, toss, put the lid on and cook on High for 4 Hrs.

Divide the mix between plates and serve.

Pickled Pulled Beef

Servings:4 Cooking Time: 5 Hrs.

Ingredients:

- 1 cup cucumber pickles, chopped
- 1 tsp. ground black pepper
- 2 cups of water
- 10 oz. beef sirloin
- 1 tsp. salt
- 2 tbsps. mayonnaise

Directions:

Pour water in the Slow Cooker.

Add beef sirloin, ground black pepper, and salt.

Close the lid and cook the beef on high for 5 Hrs.

Then drain water and chop the beef.

Put the beef in the big bowl.

Add chopped cucumber pickles and mayonnaise.

Mix the beef well.

Beef Mac & cheese

Servings:4 Cooking Time: 4.5 Hrs.

Ingredients:

- ½ cup macaroni, cooked
- ½ cup marinara sauce
- ½ cup of water
- 10 oz. ground beef
- 1 cup Mozzarella, shredded

Directions:

Mix the ground beef with marinara sauce and water and transfer in the Slow Cooker.

Cook it on High for 4 Hrs.

After this, add macaroni and Mozzarella.

Carefully mix the meal and cook it for 30 Min. more on high.

Corned Beef

Servings:4 Cooking Time: 8.5 Hrs.

Ingredients:

- 1 cup carrot, chopped
- 1-pound beef brisket
- 1 tsp. mustard seeds
- 4 cups of water
- ½ cup celery stalk, chopped
- 1 yellow onion, chopped
- 1 tbsp. salt
- 1 tsp. cloves

Directions:

Put all ingredients in the Slow Cooker and gently mix.

Close the lid and cook the corned beef for 8.5 Hrs. on Low.

Simple Pork Chop Casserole

Servings:4 Cooking Time: 10 Hrs.

Ingredients:

4 pork chops, bones removed and cut into bite-sized pieces
½ cup water
1 cup heavy cream
3 tbsps. minced onion
Salt and pepper to taste

Directions:

Place the pork chop slices, onions, and water in the Slow Cooker.
Season with salt and pepper to taste.
Close the lid and cook on low for 10 Hrs. or on high for 8 Hrs.
Halfway through the cooking time, pour in the heavy cream.

Pork Roast with Apples

Servings:4 Cooking Time: 8 Hrs.

Ingredients:

1-pound pork shoulder, boneless
1 tsp. allspices
1 cup apples, chopped
2 cups of water
1 tsp. brown sugar
1 tsp. thyme
1 yellow onion, sliced

Directions:

Sprinkle the pork shoulder with allspices, thyme, and brown sugar. Transfer it in the Slow Cooker.
Add all remaining ingredients and close the lid.
Cook the pork roast on Low for 8 Hrs.

Beef and Sauce

Servings: 2 Cooking Time: 8 Hrs.

Ingredients:

1 lb. beef stew meat, cubed
½ tsp. turmeric powder
1 cup beef stock
½ cup sour cream
1 tbsp. chives, chopped
1 tsp. garam masala
Salt and black pepper to the taste
1 tsp. garlic, minced
2 oz. cream cheese, soft

Directions:

In your Slow Cooker, mix the beef with the turmeric, garam masala and the other ingredients, toss, put the lid on and cook on Low for 8 Hrs.
Divide everything into bowls and serve.

Pork Chops Stuffed with Olives

Servings:4 Cooking Time: 4 Hrs.

Ingredients:

4 pork chops
4 tsps. sesame oil
1 tsp. dried parsley
4 kalamata olives, sliced
1 tsp. minced garlic
½ cup chicken stock

Directions:

Make the horizontal cut in every pork chop.
Then mix minced garlic with sliced olives and dried parsley.
Fill every pork chop with olive mixture and secure them with toothpicks.
Put the stuffed pork chops in the Slow Cooker.
Add all remaining ingredients from the list above and close the lid.
Cook the pork chops on high for 4 Hrs.

Onion and Bison Soup

Servings:8 Cooking Time: 10 Hrs.

Ingredients:

6 onions, julienned
3 cups beef stock
3 sprigs of thyme
2 tbsps. olive oil
2 lbs. bison meat, cubed
½ cup sherry
1 bay leaf
Salt and pepper to taste

Directions:

Place all ingredients in the slow cooker.
Give a good stir.
Close the lid and cook on high for 8 Hrs. or on low for 10 Hrs.

Pesto Pork Chops

Servings:4 Cooking Time: 8 Hrs.

Ingredients:

4 pork chops
4 tbsps. butter
4 tsps. pesto sauce

Directions:

Brush pork chops with pesto sauce.
Put butter in the Slow Cooker.
Add pork chops and close the lid.
Cook the meat on low for 8 Hrs.
Then transfer the cooked pork chops in the plates and sprinkle with butter-pesto gravy from the Slow Cooker.

Winter Pork with Green Peas

Servings:4 Cooking Time: 7 Hrs.

Ingredients:

1-pound pork shoulder, boneless, chopped
3 cups of water
1 tsp. chili powder
1 cup green peas
1 cup carrot, chopped
1 tsp. dried thyme

Directions:

Sprinkle the pork shoulder with chili powder and dried thyme.
Transfer the meat in the Slow Cooker.
Add carrot, water, and green peas.
Close the lid and cook the meal on low for 7 Hrs.

Mexican Carne Adovada

Servings:9 Cooking Time:12 Hrs.

Ingredients:

3 lbs. pork Boston butt
2 ancho peppers, chopped
2 cups homemade beef stock
6 cloves of garlic, minced
1 tsp. coriander
Salt and pepper to taste
2 dried chili peppers, chopped
2 guajillo peppers, chopped
1 onion, chopped
1 tsp. cumin
2 tsps. apple cider vinegar

Directions:

Place all ingredients in the slow cooker.
Give a good stir.
Close the lid and cook on high for 10 Hrs. or on low for 12 Hrs.

Pork Roast in Slow Cooker

Servings:8 Cooking Time: 12 Hrs.

Ingredients:

3 lbs. pork shoulder roast
1 cup onion, chopped
2 cups chicken broth
2 tbsps. herb mix of your choice
Salt and pepper to taste

Directions:

Combine everything in the Slow Cooker.
Close the lid and cook on low for 12 Hrs. or on high for 8 Hrs.

Lamb Cashews Tagine

Servings: 7 Cooking Time: 5 Hrs.

Ingredients:

2 lbs. lamb fillet, cubed
3 tbsp. cashews
2 cups red wine
1 tsp. salt
1 cup of water
½ cup dried apricots
1 jalapeno pepper
1 tbsp. sugar
1 tsp. ground white pepper

Directions:

Add lamb cubes, cashews, and all other ingredients to the Slow Cooker.
Put the cooker's lid on and set the cooking time to 5 Hrs. on Low settings.
Mix well and serve warm.

Lamb and Kale

Servings: 2 Cooking Time: 4 Hrs.

Ingredients:

1 lb. lamb shoulder, cubed
1 tbsp. olive oil
½ tsp. coriander, ground
½ tsp. sweet paprika
¼ cup beef stock
1 cup baby kale
1 yellow onion, chopped
½ tsp. cumin, ground
A pinch of salt and black pepper
1 tbsp. chives, chopped

Directions:

In your Slow Cooker, mix the lamb with the kale, oil, onion and the other ingredients, toss, put the lid on and cook on High for 4 Hrs.
Divide everything between plates and serve.

London Broil

Servings:6 Cooking Time: 8 Hrs.

Ingredients:

2-pounds London broil
1 onion, sliced
¼ cup of soy sauce
3 garlic cloves, crushed
3 cups of water
1 tsp. ground black pepper

Directions:

Preheat the grill skillet well.
Then put London broil in the hot skillet and roast it on high heat for 3 Min. per side.
After this, transfer the meat in the Slow Cooker.
Add all remaining ingredients from the list above.
Close the lid and cook the meal on Low for 8 Hrs.

Balsamic Beef

Servings:4 Cooking Time: 9 Hrs.

Ingredients:

1 lb. beef stew meat, cubed
1 tsp. cayenne pepper
4 tbsps. balsamic vinegar
2 tbsps. butter
½ cup of water

Directions:

Toss the butter in the skillet and melt it.
Then add meat and roast it for 2 Min. per side on medium heat.
Transfer the meat with butter in the Slow Cooker.
Add balsamic vinegar, cayenne pepper, and water.
Close the lid and cook the meal on Low for 9 Hrs.

Mayo Pork Salad

Servings:4 Cooking Time: 4 Hrs.

Ingredients:

7 oz. pork loin
1 cup of water
2 eggs, hard-boiled, peeled, chopped
1 tsp. salt
1 cup arugula, chopped
3 tbsps. mayonnaise

Directions:

Pour water in the Slow Cooker.
Add pork loin and close the lid.
Cook the meat on high for 4 Hrs.
After this, drain water and cut the pork loin into strips.
Put the pork strips in the big salad bowl.
Add arugula and chopped eggs.
Add mayonnaise and carefully mix the salad.

Pork Tomatoes

Servings:2 Cooking Time: 4.5 Hrs.

Ingredients:

2 tomatoes
¼ cup of rice, cooked
1 tbsp. cream cheese
½ cup of water
¼ cup ground pork
2 oz. Parmesan
½ tsp. chili powder

Directions:

Cut the caps from tomatoes and remove the flesh to get the tomato cups.
After this, mix ground pork with rice, cream cheese, and chili pepper.
Fill the tomato cups with ground pork mixture.
Grate the parmesan.
Top the tomato cups with parmesan and put in the Slow Cooker.
Add water and cook on High for 4.5 Hrs.

Bacon Potatoes with Cheese Inside

Servings:4 Cooking Time: 3.5 Hrs.

Ingredients:

2 russet potatoes, halved
4 Cheddar cheese slices
4 tbsps. plain yogurt
4 bacon slices, roasted
4 tsps. butter, softened
½ cup of water

Directions:

Pour water in the Slow Cooker.
Then arrange the potato halves in the Slow Cooker in one layer.
Mix butter with plain yogurt.
Top the potato halves with bacon and cheese and close the lid.
Cook the potatoes on High for 3.5 Hrs.

Then transfer them in the plates and top with butter-yogurt mixture.

Cumin Pork Chops

Servings: 2 Cooking Time: 5 Hrs.

Ingredients:

1 lb. pork chops
2 tbsps. balsamic vinegar
½ cup beef stock
1 tbsp. chives, chopped
2 tbsps. olive oil
½ tsp. cumin, ground
A pinch of salt and black pepper

Directions:

In your Slow Cooker, mix the pork chops with the oil, vinegar and the other ingredients, toss, put the lid on and cook on High for 5 Hrs.
Divide everything between plates and serve.

Slow Cooker Gingered Pork Stew

Servings:9 Cooking Time: 12 Hrs.

Ingredients:

2 tbsps. ground cinnamon
1 tbsp. ground allspice
1 ½ tsps. ground cloves
3 lbs. pork shoulder, cut into cubes
Salt and pepper to taste
2 tbsps. ground ginger
1 tbsp. ground nutmeg
1 tbsp. paprika
2 cups homemade chicken broth

Directions:

Place all ingredients in the slow cooker.
Give a good stir.
Close the lid and cook on high for 10 Hrs. or on low for 12 Hrs.

Rich Lamb Shanks

Servings: 4 Cooking Time: 7 Hrs.

Ingredients:

4 lamb shanks
1 yellow onion, finely chopped
2 garlic cloves, minced
1 tsp. oregano, dried
4 oz. chicken stock
2 tbsps. olive oil
3 carrots, roughly chopped
2 tbsps. tomato paste
1 tomato, roughly chopped
Salt and black pepper to the taste

Directions:

In your Slow Cooker, mix lamb with oil, onion, garlic, carrots, tomato paste, tomato, oregano, stock, salt and pepper, stir, cover and cook on Low for 7 Hrs.
Divide into bowls and serve hot.

Mussaman Curry

Servings:4 Cooking Time: 5 Hrs.

Ingredients:

16 oz. beef sirloin, cubed
2 tbsps. coconut aminos
1 tbsp. sesame oil
¼ cup peanuts, chopped
1 tbsp. curry powder
2 tbsps. soy sauce
2 tbsps. peanut butter
1 cup coconut cream

Directions:

Mix curry powder with coconut aminos, soy sauce, sesame oil, and coconut cream.
After this, mix the curry mixture with beef and transfer in the Slow Cooker.
Add all remaining ingredients and mix well.
Close the lid and cook the curry on High for 5 Hrs.

Schweinshaxe

Servings:4 Cooking Time: 10 Hrs.

Ingredients:

1 tbsp. juniper berries
1-pound pork knuckle
1 lemon, halved
1 tbsp. sunflower oil
½ cup beer
½ tsp. sugar
2 cups of water

Directions:

Put all ingredients in the Slow Cooker and close the lid.
Cook the meal on Low for 10 Hrs.

Easy Slow Cooker Pulled Pork

Servings:4 Cooking Time: 12 Hrs.

Ingredients:

4 pork shoulder, trimmed from excess fat
Salt and pepper to taste
1 tsp. rosemary
1 small onion, sliced
1 cup water

Directions:

Place all ingredients in the slow cooker.
Cook on low for 12 Hrs. or on high for 8 Hrs.
Once cooked, use forks to shred the meat.

Beef Saute with Endives

Servings:4 Cooking Time: 8 Hrs.

Ingredients:

1-pound beef sirloin, chopped
1 tsp. peppercorns
1 onion, sliced
½ cup tomato juice
3 oz. endives, roughly chopped
1 carrot, diced
1 cup of water

Directions:

Mix beef with onion, carrot, and peppercorns.
Place the mixture in the Slow Cooker.
Add water and tomato juice.
Then close the lid and cook it on High for 5 Hrs.
After this, add endives and cook the meal for 3 Hrs. on Low.

Mexican Pork Roast

Servings: 6 Cooking Time: 8 Hrs.

Ingredients:

1 yellow onion, chopped
15 oz. canned tomato, roasted and chopped
1 tsp. coconut oil
A pinch of nutmeg, ground
Juice of 1 lemon
2 tbsps. sweet paprika
1 tsp. cumin, ground
Salt and black pepper to the taste
5 lbs. pork roast
¼ cup apple cider vinegar

Directions:

Heat up a pan with the oil over medium-high heat, add onions, brown them for a couple of Min, transfer them to your Slow Cooker, add paprika, tomato, cumin, nutmeg, lemon juice,

vinegar, salt, pepper and pork, toss coat and cook on Low for 8 Hrs.
Slice roast, arrange on plates and serve with tomatoes and onions mix.

Onion Beef

Servings:14 Cooking Time: 5.5 Hrs.

Ingredients:

4-pounds beef sirloin, sliced
3 cups of water
1 tsp. ground black pepper
1 bay leaf
2 cups white onion, chopped
½ cup butter
1 tsp. salt

Directions:

Mix beef sirloin with salt and ground black pepper and transfer in the Slow Cooker.
Add butter, water, onion, and bay leaf.
Close the lid and cook the meat on High for 5.5 Hrs.

Pork Sirloin Salsa Mix

Servings: 4 Cooking Time: 8 Hrs.

Ingredients:

2 lbs. pork sirloin roast, cut into thick slices
2 tsps. garlic powder
1 tbsp. olive oil
Salt and black pepper to the taste
2 tsps. cumin, ground
16 oz. green chili tomatillo salsa

Directions:

In your Slow Cooker, mix pork with cumin, salt, pepper and garlic powder and rub well.
Add oil and salsa, toss, cover and cook on Low for 8 Hrs.
Divide between plates and serve hot.

Lamb Meatballs

Servings:4 Cooking Time: 4 Hrs.

Ingredients:

2 tbsps. minced onion
1 tsp. Italian seasonings
1 tbsp. olive oil
½ cup of water
9 oz. lamb fillet, minced
1 tsp. flour
½ tsp. salt

Directions:

In the bowl mix minced lamb, minced onion, Italian seasonings, flour, and salt.
Make the small meatballs.
After this, preheat the olive oil in the skillet.
Add meatballs and roast them on high heat for 30 seconds per side.
Then transfer the meatballs in the Slow Cooker.
Add water and cook the meal on high for 4 Hrs.

Beef and Peas

Servings: 2 Cooking Time: 5 Hrs.

Ingredients:

1 lb. beef stew meat, cubed
½ tsp. coriander, ground
½ cup beef stock
1 tbsp. olive oil
½ tsp. sweet paprika
½ cup tomato sauce
1 cup fresh peas
A pinch of salt and black pepper
1 tbsp. lime juice
1 tbsp. dill, chopped

Directions:

In your Slow Cooker, mix the beef with the oil, coriander, peas and the other ingredients, toss, put the lid on and cook on High for 5 Hrs.
Divide everything between plates and serve.

Lettuce and Pork Wraps

Servings:2 Cooking Time: 3.5 Hrs.

Ingredients:

2 lettuce leaves
1 tsp. ketchup
3 tbsps. water
4 oz. ground pork
1 tbsp. butter
1 tsp. white pepper

Directions:

Mix ground pork with water, butter, and white pepper.
Put the meat mixture in the Slow Cooker.
Close the lid and cook it on High for 5 Hrs.
After this, mix ground pork with ketchup.
Fill the lettuce leaves with ground pork.

Beef Brisket and Turnips Mix

Servings: 6 Cooking Time: 8 Hrs.

Ingredients:

2 and ½ lbs. beef brisket
2 bay leaves
4 carrots, chopped
Salt and black pepper to the taste
4 cups veggie stock
3 garlic cloves, chopped
1 cabbage head cut into 6 wedges
3 turnips, cut into quarters

Directions:

In your Slow Cooker, mix beef with stock, bay leaves, garlic, carrots, cabbage, salt, pepper and turnips, stir, cover and cook on Low for 8 Hrs.
Divide beef brisket and turnips mix between plates and serve.

Slow Cooker Pork Carnitas

Servings:12 Cooking Time: 12 Hrs.

Ingredients:

4 lbs. pork shoulder
½ cup lemon juice, freshly squeezed
1 tbsp. garlic powder
1 tsp. ground coriander
1 tsp. cayenne pepper
½ cup lime juice, freshly squeezed
1 tbsp. ground cumin
½ tbsp. salt
1 tsp. black pepper

Directions:

Place all ingredients in the Slow Cooker.
Give a good stir.
Close the lid and cook on high for 10 Hrs. or on low for 12 Hrs.
Once cooked, shred the meat using two forks.

Beef Burger

Servings:4 Cooking Time: 6 Hrs.

Ingredients:

1 tsp. ground black pepper
1/4 cup Cheddar cheese, shredded
1 tbsp. sunflower oil
12 oz. ground beef
1 tsp. salt
1/4 cup cream

Directions:

Mix ground beef with salt, and ground black pepper.
Then add shredded cheese and carefully mix the meat mixture.
Pour sunflower oil in the Slow Cooker.
Then make the burgers and place them in the Slow Cooker.
Add cream and close the lid.
Cook the meal on Low for 6 Hrs.

Balsamic Lamb Mix

Servings: 2 Cooking Time: 7 Hrs.

Ingredients:

1 lb. lamb stew meat, cubed
1 tbsp. balsamic vinegar
A pinch of salt and black pepper
2 tsps. avocado oil
1/2 tsp. coriander, ground
1 cup beef stock

Directions:

In your Slow Cooker, mix the lamb with the oil, vinegar and the other ingredients, toss, put the lid on and cook on Low for 7 Hrs.
Divide the mix between plates and serve with a side salad.

Lamb Leg and Mushrooms Mix

Servings: 8 Cooking Time: 8 Hrs.

Ingredients:

1 and 1/2 lbs. lamb leg, bone-in
1/2 lbs. mushrooms, sliced
1 small yellow onion, chopped
2 tbsps. tomato paste
Salt and black pepper to the taste
2 carrots, sliced
4 tomatoes, chopped
6 garlic cloves, minced
1 tsp. olive oil
A handful parsley, chopped

Directions:

In your Slow Cooker, mix lamb with carrots, mushrooms, tomatoes, onion, garlic, tomato paste, oil, salt, pepper and parsley, toss, cover, cook on Low for 8 Hrs., divide between plates and serve.

Garlic Pork Ribs

Servings:3 Cooking Time: 5.5 Hrs.

Ingredients:

8 oz. pork ribs, chopped
1 tsp. avocado oil
1/2 cup of water
1 tsp. garlic powder
1/2 tsp. salt

Directions:

Preheat the skillet until hot.
Then sprinkle the pork ribs with garlic powder and avocado oil and put in the hot skillet.
Roast the ribs for 3 Min. per side or until they are light brown.
Then transfer the pork ribs in the Slow Cooker and sprinkle with salt.
Add water and cook the ribs on high for 5 Hrs.

Ginger Beef

Servings:2 Cooking Time: 4.5 Hrs.

Ingredients:

10 oz. beef brisket, sliced
1 tsp. ground coriander
1 tbsp. lemon juice
1 tsp. minced ginger
1 tbsp. olive oil
1 cup of water

Directions:

In the bowl mix lemon juice and olive oil.
Then mix beef brisket with ground coriander and minced ginger.
Sprinkle the meat with oil mixture and transfer in the Slow Cooker.
Add water and cook the meal on High for 5 Hrs.

Beef and Parsnip Saute

Servings:2 Cooking Time: 7 Hrs.

Ingredients:

1 cup parsnip, peeled, chopped
1 tbsp. tomato paste
1 tsp. salt
2 cups of water
6 oz. beef tenderloin, chopped
1 tsp. dried dill
1 tsp. chili powder

Directions:

Put all ingredients in the Slow Cooker and carefully mix with the help of the spoon.
Close the lid and cook the saute on Low for 7 Hrs.

Slow Cooker Mexican Beef Stew

Servings:4 Cooking Time: 10 Hrs.

Ingredients:

1-pound beef stew meat, cubed
5 cloves of garlic, minced
1/4 cup green chilies, diced
1 tsp. cumin powder
Salt and pepper to taste
1 red onion, chopped
3 beefsteak tomatoes, chopped
1 tsp. dried oregano
2 cups homemade beef broth or water

Directions:

Throw all ingredients in the Slow Cooker.
Give a good stir.
Close the lid and cook on high for 8 Hrs. or on low for 10 Hrs.

Beef Brisket In Orange Juice

Servings:4 Cooking Time: 5 Hrs.

Ingredients:

1 cup of orange juice
2 tbsps. butter
1/2 tsp. salt
2 cups of water
12 oz. beef brisket

Directions:

Toss butter in the skillet and melt.
Put the beef brisket in the melted butter and roast on high heat for 3 Min. per side.
Then sprinkle the meat with salt and transfer in the Slow Cooker.
Add orange juice and water.
Close the lid and cook the meat on High for 5 Hrs.

Soy Beef Steak

Servings:4 Cooking Time: 12 Hrs.

Ingredients:

2 lbs. beef tenderloin, sliced thinly
1/4 cup lemon juice
1 large red onion, sliced into rings
1/4 cup soy sauce
1 bay leaf

Directions:

Place all ingredients in the Slow Cooker.
Give a good stir.
Close the lid and cook on low for 12 Hrs. or on high for 10 Hrs.

Roast with Pepperoncini

Servings: 4 Cooking Time: 8 Hrs.

Ingredients:

5 lbs. beef chuck roast
10 pepperoncini's
2 tbsp. butter, melted
1 tbsp. soy sauce
1 cup beef stock

Directions:

Add beef roast and all other ingredients to the insert of Slow Cooker.
Put the cooker's lid on and set the cooking time to 8 Hrs. on Low settings.
Shred the cooked meat with the help of 2 forks and return to the cooker.
Mix gently and serve warm.

Parmesan Rosemary Potato

Servings: 5 Cooking Time: 4 Hrs.

Ingredients:

1 lb. small potato, peeled
7 oz. Parmesan, shredded
1 tsp. thyme
1/4 tsp. chili flakes
1 tsp. salt
1/2 cup fresh dill, chopped
1 tsp. rosemary
1 cup of water
3 tbsp. cream

Directions:

Add potatoes, salt, rosemary, chili flakes, thyme, and water to the Slow Cooker.
Put the cooker's lid on and set the cooking time to 2 Hrs. on High settings.
Drizzle the remaining ingredients over the potatoes.
Cover again and slow cook for another 2 Hrs. on High.
Serve warm.

Mexican Lamb Fillet

Servings: 4 Cooking Time: 8 Hrs.

Ingredients:

1 chili pepper, deseeded and chopped
1 cup sweet corn
14 oz. lamb fillet
1 tsp. ground black pepper
1 tsp. grated ginger
1 tbsp. white sugar
1 jalapeno pepper, deseeded and chopped
1 cup chicken stock
1 tsp. salt
1 tbsp. ground paprika
1 cup tomato juice

Directions:

Add the peppers, ginger, and ground paprika to the blender jug.
Blend this peppers mixture for 30 seconds until smooth.
Place the lamb fillet to the insert of the Slow Cooker.
Add pepper mixture, tomato juice, white sugar, black pepper, and salt to the lamb.
Lastly, add sweet corn and chicken stock.
Put the cooker's lid on and set the cooking time to 8 Hrs. on Low settings.
Shred the cooked lamb and return the cooker.
Mix well and serve warm.

Caribbean Pork Chop

Servings:4 Cooking Time: 10 Hrs.

Ingredients:

1 tbsp. curry powder
Salt and pepper to taste
1/2 cup chicken broth
1 tsp. cumin
1-pound pork loin roast, bones removed

Directions:

Place all ingredients in the Slow Cooker. Give a good stir.
Close the lid and cook on low for 8 to 10 Hrs. or on high for 7 Hrs.

Pork Chops Under Peach Blanket

Servings:4 Cooking Time: 4.5 Hrs.

Ingredients:

4 pork chops
1 tsp. salt
1 cup of water
2 tbsps. butter, softened
1 onion, sliced
1 cup peaches, pitted, halved

Directions:

Sprinkle the pork chops with salt.
Grease the Slow Cooker bottom with butter.
Put the pork chops inside in one layer.
Then top them with sliced onion and peaches.
Add water and close the lid.
Cook the meal on High for 4.5 Hrs.

Jamaican Pork Shoulder

Servings: 12 Cooking Time: 7 Hrs.

Ingredients:

1/2 cup beef stock
1/4 cup keto Jamaican spice mix
1 tbsp. olive oil
4 lbs. pork shoulder

Directions:

Add pork, Jamaican spice mix and all other ingredients to the Slow Cooker.
Put the cooker's lid on and set the cooking time to 7 Hrs. on Low settings.
Slice the roast and serve warm.

Lamb Shanks

Servings: 4 Cooking Time: 8 Hrs. and 10 Min

Ingredients:

4 lamb shanks, trimmed
1 onion, chopped
15 oz. canned tomatoes, chopped
2 celery stalks, chopped
2 cups veggie stock
1 tbsp. thyme, dried
3 tbsps. olive oil
2 carrots, chopped
2 garlic cloves, minced
2 tbsps. tomato paste
1 tbsp. rosemary, dried
1 tbsp. oregano, dried

Salt and black pepper to the taste

Directions:

Heat up a pan with 2 tbsps. oil over medium-high heat, add lamb shanks, brown them for 5 Min. on each side and transfer to your Slow Cooker.
Add the rest of the oil, onion, carrots, tomatoes, garlic, celery, tomato paste, stock, rosemary, thyme, salt and pepper, stir, cover and cook on Low for 8 Hrs.
Divide everything between plates and serve.

Lamb and Cabbage

Servings: 2 Cooking Time: 5 Hrs.

Ingredients:

2 lbs. lamb stew meat, cubed
1 cup beef stock
1 tsp. sweet paprika
A pinch of salt and black pepper
1 cup red cabbage, shredded
1 tsp. avocado oil
2 tbsps. tomato paste
1 tbsp. cilantro, chopped

Directions:

In your Slow Cooker, mix the lamb with the cabbage, stock and the other ingredients, toss, put the lid on and cook on High for 5 Hrs.
Divide everything between plates and serve.

Beef In Sauce

Servings:4 Cooking Time: 9 Hrs.

Ingredients:

1-pound beef stew meat, chopped
1 cup of water
1 tsp. garlic powder
1 tsp. garam masala
1 tbsp. flour
1 onion, diced

Directions:

Whisk flour with water until smooth and pour the liquid in the Slow Cooker.
Add garam masala and beef stew meat.
After this, add onion and garlic powder.
Close the lid and cook the meat on low for 9 Hrs.
Serve the cooked beef with thick gravy from the Slow Cooker.

Cocktail Beef Meatballs

Servings:4 Cooking Time: 3.5 Hrs.

Ingredients:

1 oz. walnuts, grinded
1 tsp. ground black pepper
1 tbsp. coconut oil
3 tbsps. breadcrumbs
12 oz. ground beef
½ cup of water

Directions:

Heat the coconut oil well in the skillet.
Then mix walnuts with breadcrumbs, ground black pepper, and ground beef.
Make the small meatballs and put them in the hot skillet.
Roast the meatballs for 2 Min. per side.
Transfer the meatballs in the Slow Cooker.
Add water and close the lid.
Cook the meatballs on High for 3.5 Hrs.

Pork Loin Roast In Slow Cooker

Servings:8 Cooking Time: 12 Hrs.

Ingredients:

2 lbs. pork loin
3 cups homemade beef stock
2 onions, chopped
Salt and pepper to taste

Directions:

Place all ingredients in the Slow Cooker.
Give a good stir.
Close the lid and cook on high for 10 Hrs. or on low for 12 Hrs.

Oregano Pork Chops

Servings: 4 Cooking Time: 8 Hrs.

Ingredients:

4 pork chops
2 garlic cloves, minced
15 oz. canned tomatoes, chopped
Salt and black pepper to the taste
1 tbsp. oregano, chopped
1 tbsp. olive oil
1 tbsp. tomato paste
¼ cup tomato juice

Directions:

In your Slow Cooker, mix pork with oregano, garlic, oil, tomatoes, tomato paste, salt, pepper and tomato juice, cover and cook on Low for 8 Hrs.
Divide everything between plates and serve.

Turkish Meat Saute

Servings:4 Cooking Time: 10 Hrs.

Ingredients:

1 cup green peas
2 cups of water
1 tsp. ground black pepper
1 tbsp. tomato paste
1 cup potatoes, chopped
10 oz. beef sirloin, chopped
1 tsp. salt

Directions:

Put all ingredients in the Slow Cooker and carefully mix.
Then close the lid.
Cook the saute on Low for 10 Hrs.

Bacon Swiss Pork Chops

Servings:8 Cooking Time: 10 Hrs.

Ingredients:

8 pork chops, bone in
4 cloves of garlic
1 cup Swiss cheese, shredded
2 tbsps. olive oil
12 bacon strips, cut in half

Directions:

Season the pork chops with salt and pepper to taste
In a skillet, heat the olive oil over medium flame and sauté the garlic until fragrant and slightly golden.
Transfer to the Slow Cooker.
Wrap the bacon strips around the pork chops.
Place in the Slow Cooker and sprinkle with shredded Swiss cheese.
Close the lid and cook on low for 10 Hrs. or on high for 8 Hrs.

Poultry Recipes

Horseradish Chicken Wings

Servings:4 Cooking Time: 6 Hrs.

Ingredients:

3 tbsps. horseradish, grated
1 tbsp. mayonnaise
1-pound chicken wings
1 tsp. ketchup
½ cup of water

Directions:

Mix chicken wings with ketchup, horseradish, and mayonnaise,
Put them in the Slow Cooker and add water.
Cook the meal on Low for 6 Hrs.

Turkey with Plums

Servings:5 Cooking Time: 8 Hrs.

Ingredients:

1-pound turkey fillet, chopped
1 tsp. ground cinnamon
1 tsp. ground black pepper
1 cup plums, pitted, halved
1 cup of water

Directions:

Mix the turkey with ground cinnamon and ground black pepper.
Then transfer it in the Slow Cooker.
Add water and plums.
Close the lid and cook the meal on Low for 8 Hrs.

Duck Saute

Servings:3 Cooking Time: 5 Hrs.

Ingredients:

8 oz. duck fillet, sliced
1 cup mushrooms, sliced
1 tsp. ground black pepper
1 cup of water
1 tsp. salt
1 tbsp. olive oil

Directions:

Heat the olive oil in the skillet well.
Add mushrooms and roast them for 3-5 Min. on medium heat.
Transfer the roasted mushrooms in the Slow Cooker.
Add duck fillet, and all remaining ingredients.
Close the lid and cook saute for 5 Hrs. on High.

Cilantro Chicken and Eggplant Mix

Servings: 2 Cooking Time: 7 Hrs.

Ingredients:

1 lb. chicken breasts, skinless, boneless and sliced
½ cup chicken stock
3 scallions, chopped
1 tsp. chili powder
2 eggplants, roughly cubed
½ cup tomato sauce
A pinch of salt and black pepper
1 tbsp. cilantro, chopped

Directions:

In your Slow Cooker, mix the chicken with the eggplant, stock and the other ingredients, toss, put the lid on, cook on Low for 7 Hrs., divide the mix between plates and serve.

Sauce Goose

Servings: 4 Cooking Time: 5 Hrs.

Ingredients:

1 goose breast half, skinless, boneless and cut into thin slices
1 sweet onion, chopped
Salt and black pepper to the taste
¼ cup olive oil
2 tsp. garlic, chopped
¼ cup sweet chili sauce

Directions:

Add goose, oil and all other ingredients to the Slow Cooker.
Put the cooker's lid on and set the cooking time to 5 Hrs. on Low settings.
Serve warm.

Mediterranean Chicken

Servings: 4 Cooking Time: 4 Hrs.

Ingredients:

1 and ½ lbs. chicken breast, skinless and boneless
1 rosemary spring, chopped
3 garlic cloves, minced
1 cucumber, chopped
¼ cup red onions, chopped
Juice of 2 lemons
¼ cup olive oil
A pinch of salt and black pepper
1 cup kalamata olives, pitted and sliced
2 tbsps. red vinegar

Directions:

In your Slow Cooker, mix chicken with lemon juice, rosemary, oil, garlic, salt and pepper, stir, cover and cook on High for 4 Hrs.
Transfer chicken to a cutting board, shred with 2 forks, transfer to a bowl, add cucumber, olives, onion and vinegar, toss, divide between plates and serve.

Turkey with Olives and Corn

Servings: 2 Cooking Time: 4 Hrs.

Ingredients:

1 lb. turkey breast, skinless, boneless and cubed
½ cup kalamata olives, pitted and halved
1 red onion, sliced
1 tbsp. parsley, chopped
1 tbsp. olive oil
1 cup corn
1 cup tomato passata

Directions:

In your Slow Cooker, mix the turkey with the olives, corn and the other ingredients, toss, put the lid on and cook on High for 4 Hrs.
Divide everything between plates and serve.

Chicken Stroganoff

Servings: 4 Cooking Time: 4 Hrs.

Ingredients:

2 garlic cloves, minced
¼ tsp. celery seeds, ground
1 cup coconut milk
1 lb. chicken breasts, cut into medium pieces
2 tbsps. parsley, chopped
8 oz. mushrooms, roughly chopped
1 cup chicken stock
1 yellow onion, chopped
1 and ½ tsps. thyme, dried
Salt and black pepper to the tasted

Already cooked pasta for serving

Directions:

Put chicken in your Slow Cooker, add salt, pepper, onion, garlic, mushrooms, coconut milk, celery seeds, stock, half of the parsley and thyme, stir, cover and cook on High for 4 Hrs.
Add the rest of the parsley and pasta, toss, divide between plates and serve.

Chopped Chicken Liver Balls

Servings:6 Cooking Time: 4 Hrs.

Ingredients:

1 egg, beaten
1 tsp. Italian seasonings
½ tsp. salt
1/3 cup water
3 tbsp. semolina
1 tbsp. flour
1-pound liver, minced

Directions:

Mix egg with semolina, Italian seasonings, flour, salt, and minced liver.
When the mixture is homogenous, make the medium size balls and put them in the Slow Cooker.
Add water and close the lid.
Cook the liver balls on High for 4 Hrs.

Oregano Turkey and Tomatoes

Servings: 4 Cooking Time: 7 Hrs.

Ingredients:

1 lb. turkey breast, skinless, boneless and sliced
1 cup chicken stock
1 tsp. turmeric powder
1 cup scallions, chopped
A pinch of salt and black pepper
1 tbsp. oregano, chopped
1 cup cherry tomatoes, halved
2 tbsps. olive oil
1 tsp. chili powder
½ cup tomato sauce

Directions:

In your Slow Cooker, mix the turkey with the oregano, stock and the other ingredients, toss, put the lid on and cook on Low for 7 Hrs.
Divide the mix between plates and serve.

Citrus Glazed Chicken

Servings: 4 Cooking Time: 4 Hrs.

Ingredients:

2 lbs. chicken thighs, skinless, boneless and cut into pieces
3 tbsp. olive oil
For the sauce:
1 and ½ tsp. orange extract
¼ cup of orange juice
1 tbsp. orange zest
2 tbsp. scallions, chopped
1 cup of water
2 tbsp. soy sauce
Salt and black pepper to the taste
¼ cup flour
2 tbsp. fish sauce
1 tbsp. ginger, grated
2 tsp. sugar
¼ tsp. sesame seeds
½ tsp. coriander, ground
¼ tsp. red pepper flakes

Directions:

Whisk flour with black pepper, salt, and chicken pieces in a bowl to coat well.
Add chicken to a pan greased with oil and sear it over medium heat until golden brown.
Transfer the chicken to the Slow Cooker.
Blend orange juice, fish sauce, soy sauce, ginger, water, coriander, orange extract, and stevia in a blender jug.
Pour this fish sauce mixture over the chicken and top it with orange zest, scallions, sesame seeds, and pepper flakes.
Put the cooker's lid on and set the cooking time to 4 Hrs. on High settings.
Serve warm.

Chicken and Apples Mix

Servings: 2 Cooking Time: 7 Hrs.

Ingredients:

1 lb. chicken breast, skinless, boneless and sliced
1 tsp. olive oil
1 tbsp. oregano, chopped
½ tsp. chili powder
A pinch of salt and black pepper
1 cup apples, cored and cubed
1 red onion, sliced
½ tsp. turmeric powder
1 cup chicken stock
1 tbsp. chives, chopped

Directions:

Grease the Slow Cooker with the oil, and mix the chicken with the apples, onion and the other ingredients inside.
Toss, put the lid on, cook on Low for 7 Hrs., divide the mix between plates and serve.

Slow Cooker Salsa Chicken

Servings:4 Cooking Time: 7 Hrs.

Ingredients:

6 roma tomatoes, cut into quarters
1 yellow onion, quartered
1 cup cilantro leaves
4 chicken breasts, skin and bones removed
Salt and pepper to taste
1 jalapeno, seeded
3 cloves of garlic, peeled
1 tsp. cumin
2 tbsps. oil
2 tbsp. lime juice, freshly squeezed

Directions:

Place in a food processor tomatoes, jalapeno, onion, garlic, cilantro, and cumin. Pulse until smooth.
Place the chicken breasts in the Slow Cooker. Add in the oil and season with salt and pepper to taste.
Pour the homemade salsa and add in the lime juice.
Close the lid and cook on high for 5 Hrs. or on low for 6 Hrs.

Slow Cooker Fajita Chicken

Servings:8 Cooking Time: 8 Hrs.

Ingredients:

2 ½ lbs. chicken thighs and breasts, skin and bones removed
1 onion, sliced
2 cups bell peppers, sliced
½ tsp. cumin
1 cup roma tomatoes, diced
4 cloves of garlic, minced
1 tsp. ground coriander
½ tsp. chipotle pepper, chopped
Salt and pepper to taste

Directions:

Place all ingredients in the Slow Cooker.
Close the lid and cook on high for 6 Hrs. or on low for 8 Hrs.
Shred the chicken meat using two forks.
Return to the Slow Cooker and cook on high for another 30 Min.
Garnish with chopped cilantro.

Coriander and Turmeric Chicken

Servings: 2 Cooking Time: 6 Hrs.

Ingredients:

1 lb. chicken breasts, skinless, boneless and cubed
1 tbsp. coriander, chopped
2 scallions, minced
1 tbsp. lime zest, grated
1 tbsp. chives, chopped
½ tsp. turmeric powder
1 tbsp. olive oil
1 cup lime juice
¼ cup tomato sauce

Directions:

In your Slow Cooker, mix the chicken with the coriander, turmeric, scallions and the other ingredients, toss, put the lid on and cook on Low for 6 Hrs.
Divide the mix between plates and serve right away.

Chicken Curry

Servings: 2 Cooking Time: 7 Hrs.

Ingredients:

1 lb. chicken breast, skinless, boneless and cubed
1 tbsp. yellow curry paste
1 tbsp. olive oil
1 tsp. black peppercorns, crushed
¼ cup coconut cream
1 tbsp. cilantro, chopped
1 yellow onion, chopped
1 tsp. basil, dried
1 cup chicken stock
1 tbsp. lime juice

Directions:

In your Slow Cooker, mix the chicken with the curry paste, onion and the other ingredients, toss, put the lid on and cook on Low for 7 Hrs.
Divide everything into bowls and serve hot.

Slow Cooker Caesar Chicken

Servings:4 Cooking Time: 8 Hrs.

Ingredients:

½ cup cashew nuts, soaked in water overnight
4 boneless chicken breasts, skin and bones removed
¼ cup parmesan cheese, divided
2 tbsp. Dijon mustard
Salt and pepper to taste

Directions:

In a blender, place the cashew nuts and Dijon mustard. Season with salt and pepper to taste. Blend until smooth. Set aside.
Season the chicken breasts with salt and pepper to taste.
Place in the Slow Cooker and add half of the parmesan cheese.
Pour over the sauce and mix until well combined.
Sprinkle the remaining parmesan cheese.
Close the lid and cook on low for 8 Hrs. or on high for 6 Hrs.

Sun-dried Tomato Chicken

Servings:10 Cooking Time: 8 Hrs.

Ingredients:

1 tbsp. butter
4 lbs. whole chicken, cut into pieces
Salt and pepper to taste
3 cloves of garlic, minced
1 cup sun-dried tomatoes in vinaigrette

Directions:

In a skillet, melt the butter and sauté the garlic until lightly browned.
Add the chicken pieces and cook for 3 Min. until slightly browned.
Transfer to the Slow Cooker and stir in the sun-dried tomatoes including the vinaigrette.
Season with salt and pepper to taste.
Close the lid and cook on low for 8 Hrs. or on high for 6 Hrs.

Chocolate Chicken Mole

Servings:6 Cooking Time: 7 Hrs.

Ingredients:

2 lbs. chicken pieces, skin and bones removed
2 tbsps. butter
4 cloves of garlic, minced
5 dried chili peppers, rehydrated then chopped
¼ cup unsweetened dark chocolate, shaved
½ tsp. cinnamon powder
1 onion, chopped
7 tomatoes chopped
¼ cup organic and unsweetened almond butter
1 tsp. cumin powder
Salt and pepper to taste

Directions:

Place all ingredients in the Slow Cooker.
Close the lid and cook on high for 6 Hrs. or on low for 7 Hrs.
Garnish with cilantro, avocado slices, lemon wedges, or sour cream.

Orange Duck Fillets

Servings: 4 Cooking Time: 8 Hrs.

Ingredients:

2 oranges, peeled and sliced
1 lb. duck fillet, sliced
½ tsp. ground black pepper
1 tsp. coriander, chopped
1 tbsp. chives, chopped
2 tbsp. butter
1 tbsp. honey
1 tsp. salt
½ tsp. cilantro, chopped
7 oz. celery stalk, chopped
¼ cup of water
1 tsp. cinnamon

Directions:

Add butter, duck, and all other ingredients to the Slow Cooker.
Put the cooker's lid on and set the cooking time to 8 Hrs. on Low settings.
Serve warm.

Chicken and Tomatillos

Servings: 6 Cooking Time: 4 Hrs.

Ingredients:

1 lb. chicken thighs, skinless and boneless
1 yellow onion, chopped
4 oz. canned green chilies, chopped
Salt and black pepper to the taste
5 oz. canned garbanzo beans,
2 tbsps. olive oil
1 garlic clove, minced
A handful cilantro, chopped
15 oz. canned tomatillos, chopped
15 oz. rice, cooked

drained
5 oz. tomatoes, chopped
4 oz. black olives, pitted and chopped
15 oz. cheddar cheese, grated

Directions:

In your Slow Cooker, mix oil with onions, garlic, chicken, chilies, salt, pepper, cilantro and tomatillos, stir, cover the Slow Cooker and cook on High for 3 Hrs.
Take chicken out of the Slow Cooker, shred, return to Slow Cooker, add rice, beans, cheese, tomatoes and olives, cover and cook on High for 1 more Hr.
Divide between plates and serve.

Chicken Pepper Chili

Servings: 4   Cooking Time: 7 Hrs.

Ingredients:

16 oz. salsa
1 yellow onion, chopped
1 red bell pepper, chopped
8 chicken thighs
16 oz. canned tomatoes, chopped
2 tbsp. chili powder

Directions:

Add salsa and all other ingredients to the Slow Cooker.
Put the cooker's lid on and set the cooking time to 7 Hrs. on Low settings.
Serve warm.

Duck and Mushrooms

Servings: 2   Cooking Time: 6 Hrs.

Ingredients:

1 lb. duck leg, skinless, boneless and sliced
1 cup chicken stock
½ tsp. rosemary, dried
½ cup heavy cream
¼ cup chives, chopped
1 cup white mushrooms, sliced
½ tsp. cumin, ground
1 tbsp. olive oil

Directions:

In your Slow Cooker, mix the duck with the stock, mushrooms and the other ingredients, toss, put the lid on and cook on Low for 6 Hrs.
Divide everything between plates and serve.

Bourbon Honey Chicken

Servings: 6   Cooking Time: 5 Hrs.

Ingredients:

4 oz. cup bourbon
1 tbsp. honey
3 oz. yellow onion, chopped
3 lb. chicken breast, skinless, boneless
1 tsp. salt
3 tbsp. soy sauce
1 tsp. ketchup
1 tsp. minced garlic
7 oz. water

Directions:

Add water, garlic, salt, ketchup, honey, and soy sauce in a bowl then mix well.
Arrange the chicken breast in the Slow Cooker and top it with honey mixture, bourbon, and onion.
Put the cooker's lid on and set the cooking time to 5 Hrs. on High settings.
Mix well and serve.

Chicken In Apricots

Servings:4   Cooking Time: 5 Hrs.

Ingredients:

4 chicken drumsticks
1 tsp. white pepper
1 tsp. chili pepper
1 tsp. butter
1 cup of water
1 tsp. smoked paprika
1 cup apricots, pitted, halved

Directions:

Put all ingredients in the Slow Cooker and gently stir them.
Close the lid and cook the chicken on low for 5 Hrs.

Creamy Turkey Mix

Servings: 2   Cooking Time: 7 Hrs.

Ingredients:

1 lb. turkey breast, skinless, boneless and cubed
1 tsp. turmeric powder
½ cup heavy cream
½ cup chicken stock
¼ cup chives, chopped
1 tbsp. chives, chopped
½ tsp. garam masala
1 red onion, chopped
4 garlic cloves, minced
A pinch of salt and black pepper

Directions:

In your Slow Cooker, mix the turkey with turmeric, garam masala and the other ingredients except the cream, toss, put the lid on and cook on Low for 6 Hrs.
Add the cream, toss, put the lid on again, cook on Low for 1 more Hr., divide everything between plates and serve.

BBQ Pulled Chicken

Servings:3   Cooking Time:8 Hrs.

Ingredients:

12 oz. chicken breast, skinless, boneless
½ cup BBQ sauce
1 cup of water
1 tsp. dried rosemary

Directions:

Pour water in the Slow Cooker.
Add chicken breast and dried rosemary. Cook the chicken on High for 5 Hrs.
Then drain the water and shred the chicken with the help of the fork.
Add BBQ sauce, carefully mix the chicken and cook it on Low for 3 Hrs.

Cinnamon and Cumin Chicken Drumsticks

Servings:4   Cooking Time: 6 Hrs.

Ingredients:

8 chicken drumsticks
1 tsp. ground cinnamon
1 tsp. salt
1 tsp. cumin seeds
1 onion, peeled, chopped
2 cups of water

Directions:

Put all ingredients in the Slow Cooker and carefully mix.
Close the lid and cook the chicken on low for 6 Hrs.

Chicken Chowder

Servings: 4 Cooking Time: 6 Hrs.

Ingredients:

3 chicken breasts, skinless and boneless and cubed
4 cups chicken stock
8 oz. canned green chilies, chopped
15 oz. coconut cream
4 bacon strips, cooked and crumbled
1 tbsp. parsley, chopped
1 sweet potato, cubed
1 yellow onion, chopped
1 tsp. garlic powder
A pinch of salt and black pepper

Directions:

In your Slow Cooker, mix chicken with stock, sweet potato, green chilies, onion, garlic powder, salt and pepper, stir, cover and cook on Low for 5 Hrs. and 40 Min.
Add coconut cream and parsley, stir, cover and cook on Low for 20 Min. more.
Ladle chowder into bowls, sprinkle bacon on top and serve.

Asian Sesame Chicken

Servings:12 Cooking Time: 8 Hrs.

Ingredients:

12 chicken thighs, bones and skin removed
2 tbsps. sesame oil
3 tbsps. soy sauce
3 tbsps. water
1 thumb-size ginger, sliced thinly

Directions:

Place all ingredients in the Slow Cooker.
Stir all ingredients to combine.
Close the lid and cook on low for 8 Hrs. or on high for 6 Hrs.
Once cooked, garnish with toasted sesame seeds.

Chicken Potato Sandwich

Servings: 4 Cooking Time: 8 Hrs.

Ingredients:

7 oz. chicken fillet
5 oz. mashed potato, cooked
4 slices French bread, toasted
1 cup of water
1 tsp. cayenne pepper
6 tbsp. chicken gravy
2 tsp. mayo

Directions:

Place the chicken fillet in the Slow Cooker and add chicken gravy, water, and cayenne pepper on top.
Put the cooker's lid on and set the cooking time to 8 Hrs. on Low settings.
Layer the French bread with mashed potato mixture.
Slice the cooked chicken into strips and return to its gravy.
Mix well, then serve the chicken over the mashed potato.
Serve warm.

Creamy Bacon Chicken

Servings: 4 Cooking Time: 12 Hrs.

Ingredients:

5 oz. bacon, cooked
1 garlic clove, peeled and chopped
1 cup heavy cream
8 oz. chicken breast
½ carrot, peeled and chopped
1 egg, beaten
1 tbsp. paprika
3 tbsp. chives, chopped
1 tsp. curry
3 oz. scallions, chopped

Directions:

Carve a cut in the chicken breasts from sideways.
Stuff the chicken with garlic clove and carrot.
Place the stuffed chicken in the Slow Cooker.
Mix egg with cream, paprika, curry, scallions, and paprika in a bowl.
Pour this curry mixture over the chicken and top it with chives and bacon.
Add the remaining ingredients to the cooker.
Put the cooker's lid on and set the cooking time to 12 Hrs. on Low settings.
Shred the slow-cooked chicken and return to the cooker.
Mix well and serve.

Poultry Stew

Servings: 6 Cooking Time: 8 Hrs.

Ingredients:

3 garlic cloves, peeled and minced
1 lb. chicken fillet, diced
1 tbsp. smoked paprika
1 tbsp. honey
1 tsp. fresh rosemary
2 cups of water
3 carrots, cut into 3 parts
1 lb. duck fillet, diced
¼ cup of soy sauce
1 tsp. nutmeg
1 tsp. black peas

Directions:

Add chicken, duck, and all other ingredients to the Slow Cooker.
Put the cooker's lid on and set the cooking time to 8 Hrs. on Low settings.
Serve warm.

Chili Chicken Liver

Servings:6 Cooking Time: 2.5 Hrs.

Ingredients:

1-pound chicken liver, diced
½ cup of water
1 tsp. butter
1 tsp. chili powder
1 onion, diced
1 tsp. salt

Directions:

Pour water in the Slow Cooker.
Add salt, butter, diced onion, chili powder, and diced chicken liver.
Close the lid and cook the meal on High for 2.5 Hrs.

Mustard Chicken Mix

Servings: 4 Cooking Time: 6 Hrs.

Ingredients:

1 lb. chicken breast, skinless, boneless and roughly cubed
1 tbsp. olive oil
¾ cup chicken stock
1 tsp. rosemary, dried
A pinch of salt and black pepper
2 tbsps. mustard
1 tsp. sweet paprika
1 tbsp. lemon juice
1 tbsp. chives, chopped

Directions:

In your Slow Cooker, mix the chicken with the oil, mustard and the other ingredients, toss, put the lid on and cook on Low for 6 Hrs.

Divide the mix into bowls and serve.

Parsley Chicken Mix

Servings: 2 Cooking Time: 5 Hrs.

Ingredients:

1 lb. chicken breast, skinless, boneless and sliced
½ cup parsley, chopped
1 tbsp. pine nuts
½ cup chicken stock
1 tsp. hot paprika
2 tbsps. olive oil
1 tbsp. lemon juice
¼ cup black olives, pitted and halved
A pinch of salt and black pepper

Directions:

In a blender, mix the parsley with the oil, pine nuts and lemon juice and pulse well.
In your Slow Cooker, mix the chicken with the parsley mix and the remaining ingredients, toss, put the lid on and cook on High for 5 Hrs.
Divide everything between plates and serve.

Zucchini Chicken

Servings:4 Cooking Time: Hrs.

Ingredients:

4 chicken drumsticks
1 cup of water
1 carrot, grated
3 large zucchinis, chopped
1 tsp. white pepper
1 tsp. salt

Directions:

Put all ingredients in the Slow Cooker.
Carefully mix the mixture and close the lid.
Cook the meal on Low for 6 Hrs.
When the time is finished, gently transfer the meal in the plates.

Chicken and Beans

Servings: 2 Cooking Time: 7 Hrs.

Ingredients:

1 cup canned black beans, drained and rinsed
½ cup canned kidney beans, drained and rinsed
1 lb. chicken breast, skinless, boneless and cubed
1 red onion, chopped
1 tbsp. olive oil
1 tbsp. chili powder
A pinch of salt and black pepper
2 garlic cloves, minced
½ tsp. sweet paprika
1 cup tomato sauce
1 tbsp. parsley, chopped

Directions:

In your Slow Cooker, mix the chicken with the beans, onion and the other ingredients, toss, put the lid on and cook on Low for 7 Hrs.
Divide the mix into bowls and serve hot.

Goose Mix

Servings: 5 Cooking Time: 5 Hrs.

Ingredients:

1 goose breast, fat trimmed off and cut into pieces
1 goose leg, skinless
Salt and black pepper to the taste
2 tsps. garlic, minced
12 oz. canned mushroom cream
1 goose thigh, skinless
3 and ½ cups water
1 yellow onion, chopped

Directions:

In your Slow Cooker mix goose breast, leg and thigh with onion, salt, pepper, water, garlic, and mushroom cream, stir, cover and cook on Low for 5 Hrs.
Divide into bowls and serve

Sichuan Chicken

Servings:4 Cooking Time: 4 Hrs.

Ingredients:

1 chili pepper, chopped
1 onion, chopped
3 oz. scallions, chopped
2 tbsps. mustard
1 oz. fresh ginger, chopped
1-pound chicken fillet, chopped
1 garlic clove, chopped
1 cup of water

Directions:

Mix mustard with chicken and leave for 10 Min. to marinate.
Meanwhile, put all remaining ingredients in the Slow Cooker.
Add marinated chicken and close the lid.
Cook the chicken on High for 4 Hrs.

Chicken and Peppers

Servings: 2 Cooking Time: 6 Hrs.

Ingredients:

1 lb. chicken breasts, skinless, boneless and cubed
¼ cup tomato sauce
1 tsp. olive oil
½ tsp. coriander, ground
A pinch of cayenne pepper
2 red bell peppers, cut into strips
½ tsp. rosemary, dried
1 tsp. Italian seasoning
1 cup chicken stock

Directions:

In your Slow Cooker, mix the chicken with the peppers, tomato sauce and the other ingredients, toss, put the lid on and cook on Low for 6 Hrs.
divide everything between plates and serve.

Chicken Thighs and Mushrooms

Servings: 4 Cooking Time: 4 Hrs.

Ingredients:

4 chicken thighs
¼ cup butter, melted
½ tsp. onion powder
½ cup water
1 tbsp. tarragon, chopped
2 cups mushrooms, sliced
Salt and black pepper to the taste
½ tsp. garlic powder
1 tsp. Dijon mustard

Directions:

In your Slow Cooker, mix chicken with butter, mushrooms, salt, pepper, onion powder, garlic powder, water, mustard and tarragon, toss, cover and cook on High for 4 Hrs.
Divide between plates and serve.

Chicken Cacciatore

Servings:2 Cooking Time: 7 Hrs.

Ingredients:

1 tsp. sesame oil
1 tsp. tomato paste
½ cup mushrooms, sliced
1 tsp. Italian seasonings
2 chicken thighs, skinless, boneless
1 carrot, sliced
1 cup of water
¼ cup green beans, canned

Directions:

Put all ingredients in the Slow Cooker and gently stir them.

Then close the lid and cook the meal on Low for 7 Hrs.

Saucy Chicken Thighs

Servings: 6 Cooking Time: 5 Hrs. and 20 Min

Ingredients:

6 garlic cloves, minced
1 cup veggie stock
2 tsp. sugar
1 tsp. ginger, minced
2 cups cabbage, shredded
4 scallions, sliced
1 tbsp. olive oil
1 tbsp. soy sauce
2 lbs. chicken thighs, skinless and boneless

Directions:

Add stock along with other ingredients except cabbage to the Slow Cooker.
Put the cooker's lid on and set the cooking time to 5 Hrs. on Low settings.
Toss in cabbage and cook for another 30 Min. on the low setting.
Serve warm.

Cream Chicken with Spices

Servings:4 Cooking Time: 7 Hrs.

Ingredients:

1 cup cream
1 tsp. dried sage
1 tsp. coriander seeds
1 tbsp. dried cilantro
1-pound chicken fillet, chopped
1 tsp. dried lemongrass
1 tsp. salt

Directions:

Pour cream in the Slow Cooker.
Add dried sage, dried lemongrass, coriander, seeds, salt, and dried cilantro.
Then add chicken and close the lid.
Cook the meal on Low for 7 Hrs.
Serve the chicken with fragrant cream gravy.

Turkey Wings and Sauce

Servings: 4 Cooking Time: 8 Hrs.

Ingredients:

4 turkey wings
2 tbsps. olive oil
Salt and black pepper to the taste
1 cup walnuts
1 bunch thyme, chopped
2 tbsps. butter, melted
1 and ½ cups cranberries, dried
1 yellow onion, roughly chopped
1 cup orange juice

Directions:

In your Slow Cooker mix butter with oil, turkey wings, cranberries, salt, pepper, onion, walnuts, orange juice and thyme, stir a bit, cover and cook on Low for 8 Hrs.
Divide turkey and orange sauce between plates and serve.

Chicken and Chickpeas

Servings: 4 Cooking Time: 4 Hrs.

Ingredients:

1 yellow onion, chopped
4 garlic cloves, minced
1 and ½ tsp. paprika
1 and ½ tsps. coriander, ground
Salt and black pepper to the taste
15 oz. canned tomatoes, crushed
1 lb. spinach, chopped
½ cup cilantro, chopped
15 oz. canned chickpeas, drained
2 tbsps. butter
1 tbsp. ginger, grated
1 tbsp. cumin, ground
1 tsp. turmeric, ground
A pinch of cayenne pepper
¼ cup lemon juice
3 lbs. chicken drumsticks and thighs
½ cup chicken stock
½ cup heavy cream

Directions:

Grease your Slow Cooker with the butter, add onion, garlic, ginger, paprika, cumin, coriander, turmeric, salt, pepper, cayenne, tomatoes, lemon juice, spinach, chicken, stock, chickpeas and heavy cream, cover and cook on High for 4 Hrs.
Add cilantro, stir everything, divide between plates and serve.

Turkey with Leeks and Radishes

Servings: 2 Cooking Time: 6 Hrs.

Ingredients:

1 lb. turkey breast, skinless, boneless and cubed
1 leek, sliced
1 red onion, chopped
A pinch of salt and black pepper
½ tsp. sweet paprika
1 tbsp. cilantro, chopped
1 cup radishes, sliced
1 tbsp. olive oil
1 cup chicken stock
½ tsp. coriander, ground

Directions:

In your Slow Cooker, combine the turkey with the leek, radishes, onion and the other ingredients, toss, put the lid on and cook on High for 6 Hrs.
Divide everything between plates and serve.

Maple Ginger Chicken

Servings: 4 Cooking Time: 15 Hrs.

Ingredients:

½ cup of soy sauce
1 tbsp. fresh ginger, grated
1 lb. chicken breast, diced
¼ tsp. ground cinnamon
1 tsp. maple syrup
1 tsp. salt
1 tsp. ground ginger
2 tbsp. red wine

Directions:

Toss chicken with maple syrup and all other ingredients in the Slow Cooker.
Leave it for 10 Min. to marinate.
Put the cooker's lid on and set the cooking time to 15 Hrs. on Low settings.
Serve warm.

Cheesy Chicken Breasts

Servings: 4 Cooking Time: 4 Hrs.

Ingredients:

6 chicken breasts, skinless and boneless
¼ cup jalapenos, chopped
8 oz. cream cheese
Salt and black pepper to the taste
5 bacon slices, chopped
¼ cup yellow onion, chopped

½ cup mayonnaise
1 cup cheddar cheese, grated
½ cup parmesan, grated

Directions:

Add chicken breasts, cream cheese and all other ingredients to the Slow Cooker.
Put the cooker's lid on and set the cooking time to 4 Hrs. on High settings.
Mix well and serve warm.

Paprika Chicken and Artichokes

Servings: 2 Cooking Time: 7 Hrs. and 10 Min

Ingredients:

1 lb. chicken breast, skinless, boneless and cut into strips
1 cup canned artichoke hearts, drained and halved
3 scallions, chopped
2 garlic cloves, minced
1 tbsp. olive oil
1 tbsp. sweet paprika
1 cup chicken stock
½ cup parsley, chopped

Directions:

Heat up a pan with the oil over medium-high heat, add the scallions, garlic and the chicken, brown for 10 Min. and transfer to the Slow Cooker.
Add the rest of the ingredients, toss, put the lid on and cook on Low for 7 Hrs.
Divide everything between plates and serve.

Chicken Stuffed with Beans

Servings: 12 Cooking Time: 10 Hrs.

Ingredients:

21 oz. whole chicken
1 cup soybeans, canned
1 carrot, peeled and diced
1 tsp. cilantro, chopped
1 tsp. apple cider vinegar
1 tbsp. dried basil
¼ tsp. ground red pepper
2 potatoes, peeled and diced
1 chili pepper, chopped
2 red onions, peeled and diced
1 tsp. onion powder
1 tsp. oregano
1 tsp. olive oil
1 tsp. paprika
½ cup fresh dill
4 tbsps. tomato sauce

Directions:

Blend chili pepper, onion powder, cilantro, oregano, olive oil, red pepper, tomato sauce, dill, paprika, basil, and vinegar in a blender.
Stuff the whole chicken with soybeans, and vegetables.
Brush it with the blender spice-chili mixture liberally.
Place the spiced chicken in the Slow Cooker and pour the remaining spice mixture over it.
Put the cooker's lid on and set the cooking time to 10 Hrs. on Low settings.
Slice and serve.

Chicken Tomato Salad

Servings: 2 Cooking Time: 3 Hrs.

Ingredients:

1 chicken breast, skinless and boneless
1 cup chicken stock
Salt and black pepper to the taste
3 garlic cloves, minced
2 cups of water
1 tbsp. mustard
1 tbsp. balsamic vinegar
1 tbsp. honey
Mixed salad greens
3 tbsp. olive oil
Handful cherry tomatoes halved

Directions:

Mix water with a pinch of salt in a bowl and chicken.
Soak the chicken and refrigerate for 45 Min.
Drain the chicken and transfer to a Slow Cooker.
Along with stock, black pepper, and salt.
Put the cooker's lid on and set the cooking time to 3 Hrs. on High settings.
Transfer the slow-cooked chicken to a cutting board then cut into strips.
Mix garlic, salt, black pepper, honey, mustard, olive oil, and vinegar in a bowl.
Toss in salad greens, tomatoes, and chicken strips.
Mix well and serve.

Cannellini Chicken

Servings:4 Cooking Time: 3 Hrs.

Ingredients:

1 cup cannellini beans, canned
1 tsp. lemon zest, grated
1 tsp. salt
1 tbsp. butter
12 oz. chicken fillet, chopped
1 tsp. dried oregano
1 cup of water
1 garlic clove, chopped

Directions:

Put the chopped chicken in the Slow Cooker.
Add lemon zest, salt, water, butter, and garlic.
Close the lid and cook the chicken on high for 2 Hrs.
Then add cannellini beans and stir the chicken well.
Close the lid and cook the chicken on High for 1 Hr.

Turkey Cranberry Stew

Servings: 4 Cooking Time: 8 Hrs.

Ingredients:

3 lbs. turkey breast, skinless and boneless
2 sweet potatoes, chopped
½ cup walnuts, chopped
2 tbsp. lemon juice
1 tsp. ginger, grated
1 tsp. cinnamon powder
1 tsp. poultry seasoning
1 cup cranberries, chopped
½ cup raisins
1 sweet onion, chopped
1 cup of sugar
½ tsp. nutmeg, ground
½ cup veggie stock
Salt and black pepper to the taste
3 tbsp. olive oil

Directions:

Take oil in a nonstick pan and place it over medium-high heat.
Stir in walnuts, onion, raisins, cranberries, sugar, lemon juice, cinnamon, nutmeg, ginger, black pepper, and stock.
Cook this mixture to a simmer on medium heat.
Now place the turkey and sweet potatoes in the Slow Cooker.
Top them with poultry seasoning and cranberries mixture.
Put the cooker's lid on and set the cooking time to 8 Hrs. on Low settings.
Slice the slow-cooked turkey and serve with sweet potato-cranberry sauce.
Enjoy.

Chicken Bowl

Servings:6 Cooking Time: 4 Hrs.

Ingredients:

1-pound chicken breast, skinless, boneless, chopped
1 cup sweet corn, frozen
1 tsp. onion powder
1 cup of water
1 tsp. ground paprika
1 cup tomatoes, chopped
1 tsp. olive oil

Directions:

Mix chopped chicken breast with ground paprika and onion powder. Transfer it in the Slow Cooker.
Add water and sweet corn. Cook the mixture on High for 4 Hrs.
Then drain the liquid and transfer the mixture in the bowl.
Add tomatoes and olive oil. Mix the meal.

Pulled Maple Chicken

Servings: 2 Cooking Time: 6 Hrs.

Ingredients:

2 tomatoes, chopped
2 chicken breasts, skinless and boneless
1 tbsp. maple syrup
1 tsp. basil, dried
1 tsp. cloves, ground
2 red onions, chopped
2 garlic cloves, minced
1 tsp. chili powder
3 tbsp. water

Directions:

Place chicken along with all other ingredients in the Slow Cooker.
Put the cooker's lid on and set the cooking time to 6 Hrs. on Low settings.
Shred the cooked chicken and serve with the veggies.
Enjoy.

Chicken with Vegetables

Servings:4 Cooking Time: 4 Hrs.

Ingredients:

1-pound chicken fillet, cut into slices
½ cup green peas, frozen
1 cup of water
½ tsp. peppercorns
1 cup broccoli, chopped
½ cup corn kernels, frozen
1 tsp. dried rosemary

Directions:

Put all ingredients in the Slow Cooker.
Close the lid and cook the meal on High for 4 Hrs.

Wine Chicken

Servings:4 Cooking Time: 3 Hrs.

Ingredients:

1 cup red wine
1 anise star
2 garlic cloves, crushed
1-pound chicken breast, skinless, boneless, chopped
1 tsp. cayenne pepper

Directions:

Pour red wine in the Slow Cooker.
Add anise star, cayenne pepper, and garlic cloves.
Then add chopped chicken and close the lid.
Cook the meal on High for 3 Hrs.
Serve the chicken with hot wine sauce.

Garlic Chipotle Lime Chicken

Servings:6 Cooking Time: 8 Hrs.

Ingredients:

1 ½ lbs. chicken breasts, bones and skin removed
2 tbsps. olive oil
2 tbsps. mild green chilies, chopped
3 tbsps. lime juice
1 ½ tsp. chipotle pepper, chopped
½ cup organic tomato sauce
2 cloves of garlic
1 tbsp. apple cider vinegar
1/3 cup fresh cilantro
Salt and pepper to taste

Directions:

Place all ingredients in the Slow Cooker.
Close the lid and cook on high for 5 Hrs. or on low for 8 Hrs.
Serve with lime wedges.

Corn and Chicken Saute

Servings:4 Cooking Time: 8 Hrs.

Ingredients:

1 cup carrot, chopped
1 cup of water
1 tsp. Italian seasonings
2 corns on cobs, roughly chopped
1-pound chicken fillet, chopped
1 tsp. salt

Directions:

Put all ingredients from the list above in the Slow Cooker.
Close the lid and cook the meal on Low for 8 Hrs.

Chicken Vegetable Pot Pie

Servings: 8 Cooking Time: 8 Hrs.

Ingredients:

8 oz. biscuit dough
1 cup green peas
1 cup white onion, chopped
1 carrot, chopped
1 tbsp. ground paprika
½ tsp. oregano
1 tbsp. salt
1 cup of water
1 cup sweet corn, frozen
11 oz. chicken fillets, chopped
8 oz. chicken creamy soup, canned
1 tsp. onion powder
1 tsp. cilantro
1 tsp. turmeric
1 tsp. butter

Directions:

Mix the chicken pieces with onion powder, oregano, cilantro, turmeric, and paprika in a Slow Cooker.
Stir in green peas, salt, carrot, onion, and sweet corn.
Pour in chicken soup, water, and butter.
Put the cooker's lid on and set the cooking time to 5 Hrs. on High settings.
Spread the biscuit dough and place it over the cooked chicken.
Put the cooker's lid on and set the cooking time to Hrs. on High settings.
Slice and serve.

Ginger Turkey

Servings: 4 Cooking Time: 5 Hrs.

Ingredients:

3 oz. fresh ginger, peeled and grated
9 oz. turkey fillet

1 tbsp. maple syrup
1/4 cup thyme leaves
1/2 tsp. ground celery
1 tsp. sesame oil
1/4 cup heavy cream
1 tsp. brown sugar
1 tsp. thyme
1 tsp. salt
1 tsp. ground ginger

Directions:

Blend heavy cream with the ginger ground, sesame oil, salt, ground celery, thyme, and thyme leaves in a blender.
Add maple syrup and brown sugar then mix well.
Rub the turkey with ginger and place it in the Slow Cooker.
Pour the cream-thyme mixture over this turkey.
Put the cooker's lid on and set the cooking time to 5 Hrs. on High settings.
Slice and serve

Chicken Parm

Servings:3 Cooking Time: 4 Hrs.

Ingredients:

9 oz. chicken fillet
3 oz. Parmesan, grated
1/3 cup cream
1 tsp. olive oil

Directions:

Brush the Slow Cooker bowl with olive oil from inside.
Then slice the chicken fillet and place it in the Slow Cooker.
Top it with Parmesan and cream.
Close the lid and cook the meal on High for 4 Hrs.

Spicy Almond-crusted Chicken Nuggets

Servings:6 Cooking Time: 8 Hrs.

Ingredients:

1/4 cup butter, melted
1 1/2 cups grated parmesan cheese
2 eggs, beaten
1 1/2 cups almond meal
1 1/2 lbs. boneless chicken breasts, cut into strips

Directions:

Place foil at the bottom of the Slow Cooker.
Combine the almond meal and parmesan cheese.
Dip the chicken strips into the eggs and dredge into the parmesan and cheese mixture.
Place carefully in the Slow Cooker.
Close the lid and cook on low for 8 Hrs. or on high for 6 Hrs.

Creamy Duck Breast

Servings: 1 Cooking Time: 4 Hrs.

Ingredients:

1 medium duck breast, skin scored
1 tbsp. sugar
1 tbsp. heavy cream
2 tbsps. butter, melted
1/2 tsp. orange extract
Salt and black pepper to the taste
1 cup baby spinach
1/4 tsp. sage, dried

Directions:

In your Slow Cooker, mix butter with duck breast, cream, sugar, orange extract, salt, pepper and sage, stir, cover and cook on High for 4 Hrs.
Add spinach, toss, leave aside for a few Min, transfer to a plate and serve.

Lime and Pepper Chicken

Servings:4 Cooking Time: 8 Hrs.

Ingredients:

1/2 cup lime juice
3 tbsps. sucralose or stevia sweetener
1 tbsp. olive oil
Salt and pepper to taste
4 chicken breasts, bones removed

Directions:

In a mixing bowl, combine the lime juice, salt, pepper, and sucralose.
Marinate the chicken breasts for a few Hrs. in the fridge.
Add the oil and give a good mix.
Close the lid and cook on low for 8 Hrs. or on high for 6 Hrs.

Curry Drumsticks

Servings:4 Cooking Time: 3 Hrs.

Ingredients:

8 chicken drumsticks
1 tsp. curry paste
1 cup cream
1 tsp. olive oil

Directions:

Mix the curry paste with cream and pour the liquid in the Slow Cooker.
Add olive oil and chicken drumsticks.
Close the lid and cook the chicken on High for 3 Hrs.

Parsley Turkey Breast

Servings: 4 Cooking Time: 8 Hrs.

Ingredients:

3 lbs. turkey breast, bone in
3 sweet potatoes, cut into wedges
2 white onions, cut into wedges
1/3 cup water
1 tsp. garlic powder
1 tsp. thyme, dried
1 tsp. paprika, dried
Black pepper to the taste
1 cup black figs
1/2 cup dried cherries, pitted
1/2 cup dried cranberries
1 tsp. onion powder
1 tsp. parsley flakes
1 tsp. sage, dried
A pinch of sea salt

Directions:

Put the turkey breast in your Slow Cooker, add sweet potatoes, figs, cherries, onions, cranberries, water, parsley, garlic and onion powder, thyme, sage, paprika, salt and pepper, toss, cover and cook on Low for 8 Hrs.
Discard bone from turkey breast, slice meat, divide between plates and serve with the veggies, figs, cherries and berries on the side.

Bacon Chicken

Servings:4 Cooking Time: 7 Hrs.

Ingredients:

4 bacon slices, cooked
1/2 cup of water
1 tsp. salt
4 chicken drumsticks
1/4 tomato juice
1/2 tsp. ground black pepper

Directions:

Sprinkle the chicken drumsticks with the salt and ground black pepper.
Then wrap every chicken drumstick in the bacon and arrange it in the Slow Cooker.
Add water and tomato juice.
Cook the meal on Low for 7 Hrs.

Slow Cooked Turkey Delight

Servings: 8 Cooking Time: 4 Hrs.

Ingredients:

4 cups zucchinis, cut with a spiralizer
1 egg, whisked
3 cups cabbage, shredded
3 cups turkey meat, cooked and shredded
½ cup turkey stock
½ cup cream cheese
1 tsp. poultry seasoning
2 cup cheddar cheese, grated
½ cup parmesan cheese, grated
Salt and black pepper to the taste
¼ tsp. garlic powder

Directions:

In your Slow Cooker, mix the egg, stock, cream, parmesan, cheddar cheese, salt, pepper, poultry seasoning and garlic powder and stir.
Add turkey meat, cabbage and zucchini noodles, cover and cook on High for 4 Hrs.
Divide between plates and serve.

Ginger Turkey Mix

Servings: 2 Cooking Time: 6 Hrs.

Ingredients:

1 lb. turkey breast, skinless, boneless and roughly cubed
1 tbsp. ginger, grated
2 tsps. olive oil
1 cup tomato passata
½ cup chicken stock
A pinch of salt and black pepper
1 tsp. chili powder
2 garlic cloves, minced
1 tbsp. cilantro, chopped

Directions:

Grease the Slow Cooker with the oil and mix the turkey with the ginger and the other ingredients inside.
Put the lid on, cook on High for 6 Hrs., divide between plates and serve.

Chicken Cooked in Coconut Milk and Lemon Grass

Servings:10 Cooking Time: 8 Hrs.

Ingredients:

10 chicken drumsticks, skin removed
1 stalk lemon grass, trimmed and cut into 5 inches long
4 cloves of garlic, chopped
1 thumb-size ginger, sliced thinly
1 cup coconut milk, unsweetened
2 tbsps. fish sauce
3 tbsps. soy sauce
1 tsp. five spice powder
1 onion, sliced
Salt and pepper to taste
¼ cup scallions, chopped

Directions:

Place all ingredients except for the scallions in the Slow Cooker.
Close the lid and cook on low high for 6 Hrs. or on low for 8 Hrs. until the chicken is tender.
An Hr. before the cooking time ends, add in the scallions.

Goose with Mushroom Cream

Servings: 5 Cooking Time: 5 Hrs.

Ingredients:

1 goose breast, Total Fat: trimmed off and cut into pieces
1 goose leg, skinless
1 goose thigh, skinless
Salt and black pepper to the taste
3 and ½ cups of water
2 tsp. garlic, minced
1 yellow onion, chopped
12 oz. canned mushroom cream

Directions:

Add good breast, leg, thigh, and all other ingredients to the Slow Cooker.
Put the cooker's lid on and set the cooking time to 5 Hrs. on Low settings.
Serve warm.

Sheriff Chicken Wings

Servings:4 Cooking Time: 3 Hrs.

Ingredients:

1-pound chicken wings
1 cup plain yogurt
¼ cup pickled cucumbers, grated
1 tbsp. lemon juice
1 tsp. white pepper
1 tsp. salt
1 tsp. cayenne pepper
1 cup of water

Directions:

Put chicken wings in the Slow Cooker.
Add cayenne pepper and salt.
Then add water and cook the chicken on High for 3 Hrs.
Meanwhile, mix plain yogurt with grated pickled cucumbers, and white pepper.
When the chicken wings are cooked, transfer them in the serving plates and top with plain yogurt sauce.

Spinach and Artichoke Chicken

Servings: 4 Cooking Time: 4 Hrs.

Ingredients:

4 oz. cream cheese
4 chicken breasts, boneless and skinless
10 oz. canned artichoke hearts, chopped
10 oz. spinach
½ cup parmesan, grated
1 tbsp. dried onion
1 tbsp. garlic, dried
Salt and black pepper to the taste
4 oz. mozzarella, shredded

Directions:

Add chicken, artichokes, and all other ingredients to the Slow Cooker.
Put the cooker's lid on and set the cooking time to 4 Hrs. on High settings.
Serve warm.

Simple Chicken and Vegetables

Servings:4 Cooking Time: 8 Hrs.

Ingredients:

1-pound chicken breasts, bones and skin removed

1 sweet red bell pepper, cut into cubes
1 zucchini, sliced
1 red onion, cut into wedges
2/3 cup sun-dried tomatoes in vinaigrette

Directions:

Place all ingredients in the Slow Cooker.
Give a good stir.
Season with salt and pepper to taste.
Close the lid and cook on low for 8 Hrs. or on high for 6 Hrs.

Russian Chicken

Servings:4 Cooking Time: 4 Hrs.

Ingredients:

2 tbsps. mayonnaise
1 tsp. minced garlic
1 tsp. sunflower oil
½ cup of water
4 chicken thighs, skinless, boneless
1 tsp. ground black pepper
1 tsp. salt

Directions:

In the bowl mix mayonnaise, minced garlic, ground black pepper, salt, and oil.
Then add chicken thighs and mix the ingredients well.
After this, pour water in the Slow Cooker. Add chicken thighs mixture.
Cook the meal on High for 4 Hrs.

Apple Chicken Bombs

Servings: 7 Cooking Time: 4 Hrs.

Ingredients:

2 green apples, peeled and grated
1 tsp. minced garlic
1 egg
1 tsp. onion powder
½ tsp. salt
1 tsp. butter
12 oz. ground chicken
1 tsp. turmeric
1 tbsp. flour
1 tsp. chili flakes
1 tsp. garlic powder
½ cup panko bread crumbs

Directions:

Mix garlic, flour, turmeric, chili flakes, onion powder, garlic powder, and salt in a bowl.
Whisk in egg, ground chicken, and apple, then mix well.
Make small meatballs out of this mixture and coat them with breadcrumbs.
Grease the insert of the Slow Cooker with butter.
Add the coated meatballs to the greased cooker.
Put the cooker's lid on and set the cooking time to 3 Hrs. on High settings.
Flip the chicken balls and cook for another 1 Hr. on High setting.
Serve.

Chicken Stew In A Slow Cooker

Servings:4 Cooking Time: 5 Hrs.

Ingredients:

2 cups homemade chicken stock
½ onion, diced
3 cloves of garlic, minced
¼ tsp. dried thyme
2 celery sticks, diced
4 chicken breasts, cut into small pieces
1 sprig of rosemary
Salt and pepper to taste
1 cup fresh spinach
½ cup heavy cream

Directions:

Place all ingredients except for the spinach and heavy cream in the Slow Cooker.
Close the lid and cook on high for 4 Hrs. or on low for 5 Hrs.
Halfway through the cooking time, add in the spinach and heavy cream.
Continue cooking until the chicken is cooked through.

Cauliflower Chicken

Servings:6 Cooking Time: 7 Hrs.

Ingredients:

2 cups cauliflower, chopped
1 tsp. chili powder
1 tsp. salt
3 tbsps. plain yogurt
1-pound ground chicken
1 tsp. ground turmeric
1 cup of water

Directions:

Mix ground chicken with chili powder, ground turmeric, and salt.
Then mix the chicken mixture with cauliflower and transfer in the Slow Cooker.
Add plain yogurt and water.
Close the lid and cook the meal on Low for 7 Hrs.

Citrus Chicken

Servings: 4 Cooking Time: 4 Hrs.

Ingredients:

2 lbs. chicken thighs, skinless, boneless and cut into pieces
Salt and black pepper to the taste
¼ cup flour
2 tbsps. fish sauce
1 tbsp. ginger, grated
2 tsps. sugar
¼ tsp. sesame seeds
½ tsp. coriander, ground
¼ tsp. red pepper flakes
3 tbsps. olive oil
For the sauce:
1 and ½ tsps. orange extract
¼ cup orange juice
1 tbsp. orange zest
2 tbsps. scallions, chopped
1 cup water
2 tbsps. soy sauce

Directions:

In a bowl, mix flour and salt and pepper, stir, add chicken pieces and toss to coat well.
Heat up a pan with the oil over medium heat, add chicken, cook until they are golden on both sides and transfer to your Slow Cooker.
In your blender, mix orange juice with ginger, fish sauce, soy sauce, stevia, orange extract, water and coriander and blend well.
Pour this over the chicken, sesame seeds, orange zest, scallions and pepper flakes, stir, cover and cook on High for 4 Hrs.
Divide between plates and serve.

Creamy Mexican Slow Cooker Chicken

Servings:6 Cooking Time: 8 Hrs.

Ingredients:

1 cup organic sour cream
1 cup tomatoes, diced
½ tsp. cumin
½ tsp. cayenne pepper
A sprig of cilantro, chopped
½ cup chicken stock
1 green chili, chopped
½ tsp. oregano
2 lbs. chicken breasts

Directions:

Place all ingredients except for the cilantro in the Slow Cooker. Close the lid and cook on high for 6 Hrs. or on low for 8 Hrs.
Garnish with cilantro.

Chicken and Asparagus

Servings: 2 Cooking Time: 5 Hrs.

Ingredients:

1 lb. chicken breast, skinless, boneless and cubed
1 cup asparagus, sliced
2 scallions, chopped
1 tsp. garam masala
1 cup tomatoes, cubed
1 tbsp. olive oil
A pinch of salt and black pepper
1 cup chicken stock
1 tbsp. parsley, chopped

Directions:

In your Slow Cooker, mix the chicken with the asparagus, oil and the other ingredients except the asparagus, toss, put the lid on and cook on High for 4 Hrs.
Add the asparagus, toss, cook on High for 1 more Hr., divide everything between plates and serve.

Buffalo Chicken

Servings: 12 Cooking Time: 4 Hrs.

Ingredients:

2 lbs. chicken breasts, skinless and boneless
2 garlic cloves, minced
½ cup chicken stock
1 tbsp. brown sugar
Salt and black pepper to the taste
1 cup cayenne sauce
½ packet ranch seasoning mix

Directions:

In your Slow Cooker, mix chicken with salt, pepper, garlic, cayenne sauce, stock, seasoning and sugar, toss, cover and cook on High for 4 Hrs.
Divide between plates and serve.

Stuffed Chicken Fillets

Servings:6 Cooking Time: 4 Hrs.

Ingredients:

½ cup green peas, cooked
16 oz. chicken fillets
1 tsp. Italian seasonings
½ cup long-grain rice, cooked
1 cup of water

Directions:

Make the horizontal cuts in chicken fillets.
After this, mix Italian seasonings with rice and green peas.
Fill the chicken fillet with rice mixture and secure them with toothpicks.
Put the chicken fillets in the Slow Cooker.
Add water and close the lid.
Cook the chicken on high for 4 Hrs.

Duck Breast and Veggies

Servings: 2 Cooking Time: 4 Hrs.

Ingredients:

2 duck breasts, skin on and thinly sliced
1 tbsp. olive oil
1 radish, chopped
Salt and black pepper to the taste
2 zucchinis, sliced
1 spring onion stack, chopped
2 green bell peppers, chopped

Directions:

In your Slow Cooker, mix duck with oil, salt and pepper and toss.
Add zucchinis, onion, radish and bell peppers, cover and cook on High for 4 Hrs.
Divide everything between plates and serve.

Moscow Bacon Chicken

Servings: 5 Cooking Time: 7 Hrs.

Ingredients:

6 oz. Russian dressing
1 tbsp. minced garlic
1 tsp. ground black pepper
1 tsp. salt
¼ cup of water
17 oz. chicken thighs
1 tsp. onion powder
4 oz. bacon, sliced
1 tsp. oregano

Directions:

Add bacon slices to a skillet and saute until brown from both the sides.
Mix garlic, onion powder, salt, oregano, and black pepper in a bowl.
Rub the chicken with garlic mixture and transfer to the Slow Cooker.
Add bacon and all other ingredients to the Slow Cooker.
Put the cooker's lid on and set the cooking time to 7 Hrs. on Low settings.
Serve warm.

Chicken Casserole

Servings:4 Cooking Time: 4 Hrs.

Ingredients:

4 jalapeno peppers, chopped
10 oz. ground chicken
1 cup of water
½ tsp. salt
1 onion, chopped
1 cup Cheddar cheese, shredded
1 tsp. olive oil

Directions:

Brush the Slow Cooker bottom with olive oil.
Then mix ground chicken with salt and jalapeno pepper.
Put the mixture in the Slow Cooker in one layer.
After this, top the ground chicken with chopped onion and Cheddar cheese.
Add water and close the lid.
Cook the casserole on High for 4 Hrs.

Basil Chicken Wings

Servings: 2 Cooking Time: 5 Hrs.

Ingredients:

1 lb. chicken wings, halved
1 tbsp. honey
A pinch of salt and black pepper
½ tsp. cumin, ground
1 tbsp. olive oil
1 cup chicken stock
1 tbsp. basil, chopped

Directions:

In your Slow Cooker, mix the chicken wings with the oil, honey and the other ingredients, toss, put the lid on and cook on High for 5 Hrs.
Divide the mix between plates and serve with a side salad.

Chicken Thighs Delight

Servings: 6 Cooking Time: 6 Hrs.

Ingredients:

2 lbs. chicken thighs, boneless and skinless
1 yellow onion, chopped
1/3 cup prunes, dried and halved
½ cup green olives, pitted
1 tsp. cinnamon, ground
2 tsps. ginger, grated
A pinch of salt and black pepper
3 carrots, chopped
3 garlic cloves, minced
2 tsp. sweet paprika
2 tsps. cumin, ground
1 cup chicken stock
1 tbsp. cilantro, chopped

Directions:

In your Slow Cooker, mix chicken with onion, carrots, prunes, garlic, olives, paprika, cinnamon, cumin, ginger, stock, salt and pepper, stir, cover and cook on Low for 6 Hrs.
Divide between plates, sprinkle cilantro on top and serve.

Okra Chicken Saute

Servings:6 Cooking Time: 8 Hrs.

Ingredients:

1 cup bell pepper, chopped
2 cups okra, chopped
1 tsp. salt
2 cups of water
1 cup tomatoes, chopped
1-pound chicken fillet, chopped
1 tsp. ground black pepper

Directions:

Put all ingredients in the Slow Cooker.
Close the lid and cook the saute on Low for 8 Hrs.

Turkey with Rice

Servings: 2 Cooking Time: 7 Hrs.

Ingredients:

1 lb. turkey breasts, skinless, boneless and cubed
1 cup wild rice
1 tbsp. cilantro, chopped
2 tbsps. green onions, chopped
½ tsp. rosemary, dried
A pinch of salt and black pepper
2 cups chicken stock
1 tbsp. oregano, chopped
½ tsp. coriander, ground
½ tsp. turmeric powder

Directions:

In your Slow Cooker, mix the turkey with the rice, stock and the other ingredients, toss, put the lid on and cook on Low for 7 Hrs.
Divide everything between plates and serve.

Basil Chicken

Servings:4 Cooking Time: 7 Hrs.

Ingredients:

2 tbsps. balsamic vinegar
1 tsp. dried basil
1-pound chicken fillet, sliced
1 cup of water
1 tsp. dried oregano
1 tsp. mustard

Directions:

Mix chicken fillet with mustard and balsamic vinegar.
Add dried basil, oregano, and transfer in the Slow Cooker.
Add water and close the lid.
Cook the chicken on low for 7 Hrs.

Chicken In Onion Rings

Servings:4 Cooking Time: 3.5 Hrs.

Ingredients:

1-pound chicken fillet, roughly chopped
2 tbsps. butter
1 cup of water
3 white onions, sliced into rings
1 oz. Parmesan, grated
1 tsp. sugar

Directions:

Put butter in the Slow Cooker.
Then make the layer of the onion rings and sprinkle them with sugar.
After this, add chicken fillet and Parmesan.
Add water and close the lid.
Cook the meal on high for 3.5 Hrs.

Jerk Chicken

Servings:4 Cooking Time: 7 Hrs.

Ingredients:

1 lemon
1 tbsp. taco seasoning
1 tsp. ground black pepper
1 tbsp. soy sauce
1-pound chicken breast, skinless, boneless
1 tsp. garlic powder
½ tsp. minced ginger
1 cup of water

Directions:

Chop the lemon and put it in the blender.
Add taco seasoning, garlic powder, ground black pepper, minced ginger, and soy sauce.
Blend the mixture until smooth.
After this, cut the chicken breast into the servings and rub with the lemon mixture carefully.
Transfer the chicken in the Slow Cooker, add water, and cook on Low for 7 Hrs.

Chicken Broccoli Casserole

Servings: 4 Cooking Time: 4 Hrs.

Ingredients:

3 cups cheddar cheese, grated
3 chicken breasts, skinless, boneless, cooked and cubed
1 tbsp. olive oil
Salt and black pepper to the taste
10 oz. broccoli florets
1 cup mayonnaise
1/3 cup chicken stock
Juice of 1 lemon

Directions:

Grease the base of your Slow Cooker with olive oil.
Add chicken pieces, broccoli florets, and half of the cheese to the cooker.
Mix salt, lemon juice, black pepper, and mayo in a bowl.
Spread this lemon mixture over the chicken pieces and add the remaining cheese on top.
Put the cooker's lid on and set the cooking time to 4 Hrs. on High settings.

Serve.

Lemongrass Chicken Thighs

Servings:6 Cooking Time: 4 Hrs.

Ingredients:

6 chicken thighs
1 tsp. salt
2 tbsps. sesame oil
1 tbsp. dried sage
1 tsp. ground paprika
1 cup of water

Directions:

Mix dried sage with salt, and ground paprika.
Then rub the chicken thighs with the sage mixture and transfer in the Slow Cooker.
Sprinkle the chicken with sesame oil and water.
Close the chicken on High for 4 Hrs.

Slow Cooker Chicken Breasts

Servings: 4 Cooking Time: 4 Hrs.

Ingredients:

6 chicken breasts, skinless and boneless
¼ cup jalapenos, chopped
8 oz. cream cheese
½ cup mayonnaise
1 cup cheddar cheese, grated
Salt and black pepper to the taste
5 bacon slices, chopped
¼ cup yellow onion, chopped
½ cup parmesan, grated

Directions:

Arrange chicken breasts in your Slow Cooker, add salt, pepper, jalapenos, bacon, cream cheese, onion, mayo, parmesan and cheddar, cover and cook on High for 4 Hrs.
Divide between plates and serve.

Turkey and Avocado

Servings: 2 Cooking Time: 6 Hrs.

Ingredients:

1 lb. turkey breasts, skinless, boneless and cubed
1 cup tomatoes, cubed
½ tsp. chili powder
¼ cup chicken stock
1 cup avocado, peeled, pitted and cubed
1 tbsp. chives, chopped
4 garlic cloves, minced

Directions:

In Slow Cooker, mix the turkey with the tomatoes, chives and the other ingredients except the avocado, toss, put the lid on and cook on Low for 5 Hrs. and 30 Min.
Add the avocado, toss, cook on Low for 30 Min. more, divide everything between plates and serve.

Fish & Seafood Recipes

Butter Crab

Servings:4 Cooking Time: 4.5 Hrs.

Ingredients:

1-pound crab meat, roughly chopped
1 tbsp. fresh parsley, chopped
3 tbsps. butter
2 tbsps. water

Directions:

Melt butter and pour it in the Slow Cooker.
Add water, parsley, and crab meat.
Cook the meal on Low for 4.5 Hrs.

Cilantro Salmon

Servings:4 Cooking Time: 3 Hrs.

Ingredients:

12 oz. salmon fillet
1 tbsp. butter
½ cup of coconut milk
1 tsp. dried cilantro
1 tsp. ground black pepper

Directions:

Toss butter in the skillet and melt it.
Add salmon fillet and sprinkle it with ground black pepper.
Roast the salmon on high heat for 1 minute per side.
Then put the fish in the Slow Cooker.
Add coconut milk and cilantro.
Cook the fish on high for 3 Hrs.

Slow Cooker Greek Snapper

Servings:8 Cooking Time: 4 Hrs.

Ingredients:

3 tbsps. olive oil
1 tbsp. Greek seasoning
Salt and pepper to taste
12 snapper fillets
24 lemon slices

Directions:

Line the bottom of the Slow Cooker with foil.
Grease the foil with olive oil
Season the snapper fillets with Greek seasoning, salt, and pepper.
Arrange lemon slices on top.
Close the lid and cook on high for 2 Hrs. and on low for 4 Hrs.

Indian Fish

Servings: 6 Cooking Time: 2 Hrs.

Ingredients:

6 white fish fillets, cut into medium pieces
14 oz. coconut milk
2 red bell peppers, cut into strips
6 curry leaves
1 tbsp. ginger, finely grated
2 tsps. cumin, ground
½ tsp. fenugreek, ground
2 tbsps. lemon juice
1 tomato, chopped
2 yellow onions, sliced
2 garlic cloves, minced
1 tbsps. coriander, ground
½ tsp. turmeric, ground
Salt and black pepper to the taste
1 tsp. hot pepper flakes

Directions:

In your Slow Cooker, mix fish with tomato, milk, onions, bell peppers, garlic cloves, curry leaves, coriander, turmeric, cumin, salt, pepper, fenugreek, pepper flakes and lemon juice, cover and cook on High for 2 Hrs.
Toss fish, divide the whole mix between plates and serve.

Parsley Salmon

Servings: 6 Cooking Time: 5 Hrs. 30 Min

Ingredients:

¼ tsp. ginger powder
24-oz salmon fillets
3 tbsps. fresh parsley, minced
2 tbsps. olive oil
Salt and black pepper, to taste

Directions:

Mix together all the ingredients except salmon fillets in a bowl.
Marinate salmon fillets in this mixture for about 1 Hr.
Transfer the marinated salmon fillets into the Slow Cooker and cover the lid.
Cook on LOW for about 5 Hrs. and dish out to serve hot.

Chili Tamarind Mackerel

Servings: 4 Cooking Time: 2 Hrs.

Ingredients:

18 oz. mackerel, cut into pieces
3 garlic cloves, minced
8 shallots, chopped
1 tsp. dried shrimp powder
1 tsp. turmeric powder
1 tbsp. chili paste
2 lemongrass sticks, cut into halves
1 small piece of ginger, chopped
6 stalks laksa leaves
3 and ½ oz. water
5 tbsp. vegetable oil
1 tbsp. tamarind paste mixed with 3 oz. water
Salt to the taste
1 tbsp. sugar

Directions:

Add shallots, garlic, chili paste, shrimp powder, and turmeric powder to a blender jug.
Blend it well then add the shallots mixture to the insert of the Slow Cooker.
Now add fish and all other ingredients to the cooker.
Put the cooker's lid on and set the cooking time to 2 Hrs. on High settings.
Serve warm.

Five-spice Tilapia

Servings:4 Cooking Time: 5 Hrs.

Ingredients:

4 tilapia fillets
1 tbsp. sesame oil
3 scallions, thinly sliced
1 tsp. Chinese five-spice powder
¼ cup gluten-free soy sauce

Directions:

Season the tilapia fillets with the Chinese five-spice powder.
Place sesame oil in the Slow Cooker and arrange the fish on top.
Cook on high for 2 Hrs. and on low for 4 Hrs.
Halfway through the cooking time, flip the fish to slightly brown the other side.
Once cooking time is done, add the soy sauce and scallion and continue cooking for another Hr.

Seafood Chowder

Servings: 4 Cooking Time: 8 Hrs. and 30 Min

Ingredients:

2 cups water
2 sweet potatoes, cubed
2 bay leaves
1 celery rib, chopped
½ fennel bulb, chopped
1 yellow onion, chopped
1 tbsp. thyme, dried
Salt and black pepper to the taste
1 bottle clam juice
1 cup coconut milk
5 sea scallops, halved
¼ cup parsley, chopped
2 tbsps. tapioca powder
1 lbs. salmon fillets, cubed
24 shrimp, peeled and deveined

Directions:

In your Slow Cooker, mix water with fennel, potatoes, onion, bay leaves, thyme, celery, clam juice, salt, pepper and tapioca, stir, cover and cook on Low for 8 Hrs.
Add salmon, coconut milk, scallops, shrimp and parsley, cook on Low for 30 Min. more, ladle chowder into bowls and serve.

Butter Dipped Crab Legs

Servings: 4 Cooking Time: 1 Hr. 30 Min

Ingredients:

4 lbs. king crab legs, broken in half
¼ cup butter, melted
3 lemon wedges
½ cup chicken stock

Directions:

Add crab legs, butter, and chicken stock to the insert of the Slow Cooker.
Put the cooker's lid on and set the cooking time to 1.5 Hrs. on High settings.
Serve warm with lemon wedges.

Shrimp, Salmon and Tomatoes Mix

Servings: 2 Cooking Time: 1 Hr. and 30 Min

Ingredients:

1 lb. shrimp, peeled and deveined
½ lb. salmon fillets, boneless and cubed
1 cup cherry tomatoes, halved
½ cup chicken stock
½ tsp. chili powder
½ tsp. rosemary, dried
A pinch of salt and black pepper
1 tbsp. parsley, chopped
2 tbsps. tomato sauce
2 garlic cloves, minced

Directions:

In your Slow Cooker, combine the shrimp with the salmon, tomatoes and the other ingredients, toss gently, put the lid on and cook on High for 1 Hr. and 30 Min.
Divide the mix into bowls and serve.

Spiced Mackerel

Servings:4 Cooking Time: 4 Hrs.

Ingredients:

1-pound mackerel, peeled, cleaned
1 tsp. ground black pepper
1 cup of water
1 tsp. salt
½ tsp. ground clove
1 tbsp. olive oil

Directions:

Sprinkle the fish with salt, ground black pepper, ground clove, and olive oil.
Then put the fish in the Slow Cooker. Add water.
Close the lid and cook the mackerel on high for 4 Hrs.

Shrimp Mix

Servings: 4 Cooking Time: 1 Hr. and 30 Min

Ingredients:

2 tbsps. olive oil
1/4 cup chicken stock
2 tbsps. parsley, chopped
Salt and black pepper to the taste
1 lb. shrimp, peeled and deveined
1 tbsp. garlic, minced
Juice of 1/2 lemon

Directions:

Put the oil in your Slow Cooker, add stock, garlic, parsley, lemon juice, salt and pepper and whisk really well.
Add shrimp, stir, cover, cook on High for 1 Hr. and 30 Min, divide into bowls and serve.

Snapper Ragout

Servings:6 Cooking Time:6 Hrs.

Ingredients:

1-pound snapper, chopped
1 cup onion, chopped
2 cups of water
1 tsp. salt
1 cup tomatoes, chopped
1 cup mushrooms, chopped
1/2 cup sour cream
1 tsp. chili powder

Directions:

Put all ingredients in the Slow Cooker.
Gently stir them with the help of the spoon.
Close the lid and cook the meal on low for 6 Hrs.

Cream White Fish

Servings: 6 Cooking Time: 2 Hrs.

Ingredients:

17 oz. white fish, skinless, boneless and cut into chunks
13 oz. potatoes, peeled and cut into chunks
Salt and black pepper to the taste
14 oz. water
1 yellow onion, chopped
13 oz. milk
14 oz. chicken stock
14 oz. half and half cream

Directions:

Add onion, fish, potatoes, water, stock, and milk to the insert of Slow Cooker.
Put the cooker's lid on and set the cooking time to 2 Hrs. on High settings.
Add half and half cream, black pepper, and salt to the fish.
Mix gently, then serve warm.

Chinese Cod

Servings: 4 Cooking Time: 2 Hrs.

Ingredients:

1 lb. cod, cut into medium pieces
2 green onions, chopped
3 tbsps. soy sauce
1 tbsp. balsamic vinegar
1/2 tsp. chili pepper, crushed
Salt and black pepper to the taste
3 garlic cloves, minced
1 cup fish stock
1 tbsp. ginger, grated

Directions:

In your Slow Cooker, mix fish with salt, pepper green onions, garlic, soy sauce, fish stock, vinegar, ginger and chili pepper, toss, cover and cook on High for 2 Hrs.
Divide everything between plates and serve.

Lamb Bacon Stew

Servings: 6 Cooking Time: 7 Hrs. and 10 Min

Ingredients:

2 tbsps. flour
1 and 1/2 lbs. lamb loin, chopped
1 garlic clove, minced
3 and 1/2 cups veggie stock
1 cup celery, chopped
1 tbsp. thyme, chopped
2 tbsps. olive oil
2 oz. bacon, cooked and crumbled
Salt and black pepper to the taste
1 cup yellow onion, chopped
1 cup carrots, chopped
2 cups sweet potatoes, chopped
1 bay leaf

Directions:

Thoroughly mix lamb meat with salt, black pepper, and flour in a bowl.
Take oil in a non-stick skillet and heat over medium-high heat.
Stir in lamb meat and sauté for 5 Min.
Transfer the sauteed meat to the Slow Cooker along with the rest of the ingredients to the cooker.
Put the cooker's lid on and set the cooking time to 7 Hrs. on Low settings.
Discard the bay leaf and serve warm.

Spicy Cajun Scallops

Servings:6 Cooking Time: 2 Hrs.

Ingredients:

2 lbs. scallops
2 tbsps. unsalted butter
Salt and pepper to taste
2 tsps. Cajun seasoning
1 tsp. cayenne pepper

Directions:

Place everything in the Slow Cooker.
Give a stir to combine all ingredients.
Close the lid and cook on low for 2 Hrs. or on high for 45 Min.

Tabasco Halibut

Servings: 4 Cooking Time: 2 Hrs.

Ingredients:

1/2 cup parmesan, grated
1/4 cup mayonnaise
6 garlic cloves, minced
4 halibut fillets, boneless
Juice of 1/2 lemon
1/4 cup butter, melted
2 tbsps. green onions, chopped
1/2 tsp. Tabasco sauce
Salt and black pepper to the taste

Directions:

Season halibut with salt, pepper and some of the lemon juice, place in your Slow Cooker, add butter, mayo, green onions, garlic, Tabasco sauce and lemon juice, toss a bit, cover and cook on High for 2 Hrs.
Add parmesan, leave fish mix aside for a few more Min, divide between plates and serve.

Tuna Loin Mix

Servings: 2 Cooking Time: 4 Hrs. and 10 Min

Ingredients:

1/2 lb. tuna loin, cubed
4 jalapeno peppers, chopped
3 red chili peppers, chopped
1 garlic clove, minced
1 cup olive oil
2 tsps. black peppercorns,

Salt and black pepper to the taste

ground

Directions:

Put the oil in your Slow Cooker, add chili peppers, jalapenos, peppercorns, salt, pepper and garlic, whisk, cover and cook on Low for 4 Hrs.

Add tuna, stir again, cook on High for 10 Min. more, divide between plates and serve.

Creamy Onion Casserole

Servings:6   Cooking Time: 3 Hrs.

Ingredients:

3 white onions, sliced
1-pound salmon fillet, chopped
¼ cup fresh parsley, chopped
1 cup cream
1 tsp. ground coriander
2 tbsps. breadcrumbs

Directions:

Sprinkle the salmon fillet with ground coriander and coat in the breadcrumbs.

Put the fish in the Slow Cooker.

Then top it with sliced onion and fresh parsley.

Add cream and close the lid.

Cook the casserole on High for 3 Hrs.

Salmon Croquettes

Servings:6   Cooking Time: 2 Hrs.

Ingredients:

1-pound salmon fillet, minced
2 tbsps. panko breadcrumbs
1 egg, beaten
½ cup of water
1 tbsp. mayonnaise
½ tsp. ground black pepper
1 tsp. smoked paprika

Directions:

In the bowl mix minced salmon with mayonnaise panko breadcrumbs, ground black pepper, egg, and smoked paprika.

Then make the small croquettes and place them in the Slow Cooker.

Add water and close the lid.

Cook the meal on high for 2 Hrs.

Mustard-crusted Salmon

Servings:4   Cooking Time: 4 Hrs.

Ingredients:

4 pieces salmon fillets
2 tsps. lemon juice
¼ cup full sour cream
salt and pepper to taste
2 tbsps. stone-ground mustard

Directions:

Season salmon fillets with salt and pepper to taste. Sprinkle with lemon juice.

Rub the stone-ground mustard all over the fillets.

Place inside the Slow Cooker and cook on high for 2 Hrs. or on low for 4 Hrs.

An Hr. before the cooking time, pour in the sour cream on top of the fish.

Continue cooking until the fish becomes flaky.

Milky Fish

Servings: 6   Cooking Time: 2 Hrs.

Ingredients:

17 oz. white fish, skinless, boneless and cut into medium chunks
1 yellow onion, chopped
13 oz. milk
14 oz. chicken stock
14 oz. half and half
13 oz. potatoes, peeled and cut into chunks
Salt and black pepper to the taste
14 oz. water

Directions:

In your Slow Cooker, mix fish with onion, potatoes, water, milk and stock, cover and cook on High for 2 Hrs.

Add salt, pepper, half and half, stir, divide into bowls and serve.

Bacon-wrapped Salmon

Servings:2   Cooking Time: 6 Hrs.

Ingredients:

2 salmon fillets
¼ tsp. dried thyme
1 tsp. sunflower oil
1 tsp. liquid honey
2 bacon slices
¼ cup of water

Directions:

Sprinkle the salmon fillets with dried thyme and wrap in the bacon.

Then pour water in the Slow Cooker.

Add sunflower oil and honey.

Then add wrapped salmon and close the lid.

Cook the meal on low for 6 Hrs.

Prosciutto-wrapped Scallops

Servings:4   Cooking Time: 3 Hrs.

Ingredients:

12 large scallops, rinsed and patted dry
1 ¼ oz. prosciutto, cut into 12 long strips
1 tbsp. lemon juice
Salt and pepper to taste
1 tbsp. extra-virgin olive oil

Directions:

Sprinkle individual scallops with salt and pepper to taste.

Wrap a prosciutto around the scallops. Set aside.

Add oil in Slow Cooker and arrange on top the bacon-wrapped scallops.

Pour over the lemon juice.

Cook on low for 1 Hr. or on high for 3 Hrs.

Halfway through the cooking time, flip the scallops.

Continue cooking until scallops are done.

Thyme Mussels

Servings:4   Cooking Time: 2.5 Hrs.

Ingredients:

1-pound mussels
1 tsp. ground black pepper
1 cup of water
1 tsp. dried thyme
½ tsp. salt
½ cup sour cream

Directions:

In the mixing bowl mix mussels, dried thyme, ground black pepper, and salt.

Then pour water in the Slow Cooker.
Add sour cream and cook the liquid on High for 1.5 Hrs.
After this, add mussels and cook them for 1 Hr. on High or until the mussels are opened.

Slow Cooker Smoked Trout

Servings:4 Cooking Time: 2 Hrs.

Ingredients:

2 tbsps. liquid smoke
4 oz. smoked trout, skin removed then flaked
2 tbsps. mustard
2 tbsps. olive oil
Salt and pepper to taste

Directions:

Place all ingredients in the Slow Cooker.
Cook on high for 1 Hr. or on low for 2 Hrs. until the trout flakes have absorbed the sauce.

Creamy Tuna and Scallions

Servings: 2 Cooking Time: 2 Hrs.

Ingredients:

1 lb. tuna fillets, boneless and cubed
½ cup heavy cream
1 tbsp. olive oil
A pinch of salt and black pepper
4 scallions, chopped
½ cup chicken stock
1 tsp. turmeric powder
1 tbsp. chives, chopped

Directions:

In your Slow Cooker, mix the tuna with the scallions, cream and the other ingredients, toss, put the lid on and cook on High for 2 Hrs.
Divide the mix into bowls and serve.

Vinaigrette Dipped Salmon

Servings: 6 Cooking Time: 2 Hrs.

Ingredients:

6 salmon steaks
4 leeks, sliced
2 tbsps. parsley, chopped
2 tbsp. lemon juice
1 tsp. sherry
For the raspberry vinegar:
1-pint cider vinegar
2 tbsps. olive oil
2 garlic cloves, minced
1 cup clam juice
Salt and white pepper to the taste
1/3 cup dill, chopped
2 pints red raspberries

Directions:

Mix raspberries with salmon, and vinegar in a bowl.
Cover the raspberry salmon and refrigerate for 2 Hrs.
Add the raspberry mixture along with the remaining ingredients to the insert of the Slow Cooker.
Put the cooker's lid on and set the cooking time to 2 Hrs. on High settings.
Serve warm.

Slow Cooker Tuna Spaghetti

Servings:3 Cooking Time: 2 Hrs.

Ingredients:

2 stalks of celery, chopped
1 cup full-fat milk
½ lb. ground tuna, boiled
1 tbsps. butter
1/3 cup chicken broth
2 tbsps. parsley flakes
2 zucchinis, spiralized or cut into long strips
Salt and pepper to taste

Directions:

Place all ingredients in the Slow Cooker.
Give a good stir.
Close the lid and cook on high for 1 Hrs. or on low for 2 Hrs.
Garnish with chopped parsley if desired.

Nutmeg Trout

Servings:4 Cooking Time: 3 Hrs.

Ingredients:

1 tbsp. ground nutmeg
1 tsp. dried cilantro
1 tsp. fish sauce
½ cup of water
1 tbsp. butter, softened
1 tsp. dried oregano
4 trout fillets

Directions:

In the shallow bowl mix butter with cilantro, dried oregano, and fish sauce. Add ground nutmeg and whisk the mixture.
Then grease the fish fillets with nutmeg mixture and put in the Slow Cooker.
Add remaining butter mixture and water.
Cook the fish on high for 3 Hrs.

Simple Slow Cooker Steamed Crab

Servings:2 Cooking Time: 3 Hrs.

Ingredients:

2 lbs. medium-sized crabs, cleaned
¼ cup water
4 cloves of garlic, minced
2 bay leaves
Juice from 1 lemon, freshly squeezed
3 tbsps. butter
2 onions, chopped
Salt and pepper to taste

Directions:

Place all ingredients in the Slow Cooker.
Give a good stir.
Close the lid and cook on high for 2 Hrs. or on low for 3 Hrs.

Mussels, Clams and Chorizo Mix

Servings: 4 Cooking Time: 2 Hrs.

Ingredients:

15 small clams
2 chorizo links, sliced
1 yellow onion, chopped
2 tbsps. parsley, chopped
Lemon wedges for serving
30 mussels, scrubbed
1 lb. baby red potatoes, peeled
10 oz. beer
1 tsp. olive oil

Directions:

Grease your Slow Cooker with the oil, add clams, mussels, chorizo, potatoes, onion, beer and parsley, cover and cook on High for 2 Hrs.
Add parsley, stir, divide into bowls and serve with lemon wedges on the side.

Jambalaya

Servings: 8 Cooking Time: 4 Hrs. and 30 Min

Ingredients:

1 lb. chicken breast,
1 lb. shrimp, peeled and deveined

chopped
2 tbsps. extra virgin olive oil
1 lb. sausage, chopped
2 cups onions, chopped
1 and ½ cups rice
2 tbsps. garlic, chopped
2 cups green, yellow and red bell peppers, chopped
3 and ½ cups chicken stock
1 tbsp. Creole seasoning
1 tbsp. Worcestershire sauce
1 cup tomatoes, crushed

Directions:

Add the oil to your Slow Cooker and spread.
Add chicken, sausage, onion, rice, garlic, mixed bell peppers, stock, seasoning, tomatoes and Worcestershire sauce, cover and cook on High for 4 Hrs.
Add shrimp, cover, cook on High for 30 Min. more, divide everything between plates and serve.

Salmon Salad

Servings: 2 Cooking Time: 3 Hrs.

Ingredients:

1 lb. salmon fillets, boneless and cubed
¼ cup chicken stock
1 zucchini, cut with a spiralizer
1 carrot, sliced
1 eggplant, cubed
½ cup cherry tomatoes, halved
1 red onion, sliced
½ tsp. turmeric powder
½ tsp. chili powder
½ tbsp. rosemary, chopped
A pinch of salt and black pepper
1 tbsp. chives, chopped

Directions:

In your Slow Cooker, mix the salmon with the zucchini, stock, carrot and the other ingredients, toss, put the lid on and cook on High for 3 Hrs.
Divide the mix into bowls and serve.

Dill Shrimp Mix

Servings: 4 Cooking Time: 1 Hrs.

Ingredients:

1 lb. shrimp, peeled and deveined
2 tbsps. olive oil
1 tbsp. yellow onion, chopped
1 cup white wine
2 tbsps. cornstarch
¾ cup milk
1 tbsp. dill, chopped

Directions:

In your Slow Cooker, mix oil with onion, cornstarch, milk, wine, dill and shrimp, cover and cook on High for 1 Hr.
Divide everything into bowls and serve.

Mackerel and Lemon

Servings: 4 Cooking Time: 2 Hrs.

Ingredients:

4 mackerels
3 oz. breadcrumbs
Juice and rind of 1 lemon
1 tbsp. chives, finely chopped
Salt and black pepper to the taste
1 egg, whisked
1 tbsp. butter
1 tbsp. vegetable oil
3 lemon wedges

Directions:

In a bowl, mix breadcrumbs with lemon juice, lemon rind, salt, pepper, egg and chives, stir very well and coat mackerel with this mix.
Add the oil and the butter to your Slow Cooker and arrange mackerel inside.
Cover, cook on High for 2 Hrs., divide fish between plates and serve with lemon wedges on the side.

Fish Pudding

Servings: 4 Cooking Time: 2 Hrs.

Ingredients:

1 lb. cod fillets, cut into medium pieces
2 tbsps. parsley, chopped
4 oz. breadcrumbs
2 tsps. lemon juice
2 eggs, whisked
2 oz. butter, melted
½ pint milk
½ pint shrimp sauce
Salt and black pepper to the taste

Directions:

In a bowl, mix fish with crumbs, lemon juice, parsley, salt and pepper and stir.
Add butter to your Slow Cooker, add milk and whisk well.
Add egg and fish mix, stir, cover and cook on High for 2 Hrs.
Divide between plates and serve with shrimp sauce on top.

Onion Cod Fillets

Servings:4 Cooking Time: 3 Hrs.

Ingredients:

1 onion, minced
4 cod fillets
1 tsp. salt
1 tsp. dried cilantro
½ cup of water
1 tsp. butter, melted

Directions:

Sprinkle the cod fillets with salt, dried cilantro, and butter.
Then place them in the Slow Cooker and top with minced onion.
Add water and close the lid.
Cook the fish on high for 3 Hrs.

Butter Crab Legs

Servings:4 Cooking Time: 45 Min

Ingredients:

15 oz. king crab legs
1 tbsp. butter
1 cup of water
1 tsp. dried basil

Directions:

Put the crab legs in the Slow Cooker.
Add basil and water and cook them on High for 45 Min.

Shrimp and Rice Mix

Servings: 2 Cooking Time: 1 Hr. and 30 Min

Ingredients:

1 lb. shrimp, peeled and deveined
1 cup chicken stock
½ cup wild rice
½ cup carrots, peeled and cubed
1 green bell pepper, cubed
½ tsp. turmeric powder
½ tsp. coriander, ground
1 tbsp. olive oil

1 red onion, chopped
1 tbsp. cilantro, chopped
A pinch of salt and black pepper

Directions:

In your Slow Cooker, mix the stock with the rice, carrots and the other ingredients except the shrimp, toss, put the lid on and cook on High for 1 Hr.
Add the shrimp, toss, put the lid back on and cook on High for 30 Min.
Divide the mix between plates and serve.

Chives Shrimp

Servings: 2 Cooking Time: 1 Hr.

Ingredients:

1 lb. shrimp, peeled and deveined
½ tsp. basil, dried
1 tbsp. olive oil
1 tbsp. chives, chopped
1 tsp. turmeric powder
½ cup chicken stock

Directions:

In your Slow Cooker, mix the shrimp with the basil, chives and the other ingredients, toss, put the lid on and cook on High for 1 Hr.
Divide the shrimp between plates and serve with a side salad.

Fish Pie

Servings:6 Cooking Time: 7 Hrs.

Ingredients:

7 oz. yeast dough
8 oz. salmon fillet, chopped
1 tsp. salt
1 tsp. olive oil
1 tbsp. cream cheese
1 onion, diced
1 tbsp. fresh dill

Directions:

Brush the Slow Cooker bottom with olive oil.
Then roll up the dough and place it in the Slow Cooker.
Flatten it in the shape of the pie crust.
After this, in the mixing bowl mix cream cheese, salmon, onion, salt, and dill.
Put the fish mixture over the pie crust and cover with foil.
Close the lid and cook the pie on Low for 7 Hrs.

Shrimp and Pineapple Bowls

Servings: 2 Cooking Time: 1 Hr.

Ingredients:

1 lb. shrimp, peeled and deveined
1 tsp. sweet paprika
3 scallions, chopped
A pinch of salt and black pepper
1 cup pineapple, peeled and cubed
1 tbsp. avocado oil
½ cup chicken stock

Directions:

In your Slow Cooker, mix the shrimp with the pineapple, paprika and the other ingredients, toss, put the lid on and cook on High for 1 Hr.
Divide the mix into bowls and serve.

Mustard Cod

Servings:4 Cooking Time: 3 Hrs.

Ingredients:

4 cod fillets
2 tbsps. sesame oil
4 tsps. mustard
¼ cup of water

Directions:

Mix mustard with sesame oil.
Then brush the cod fillets with mustard mixture and transfer in the Slow Cooker.
Add water and cook the fish on low for 3 Hrs.

Cheesy Fish Dip

Servings:6 Cooking Time: 5 Hrs.

Ingredients:

½ cup cream
8 oz. tuna, canned, shredded
½ cup Mozzarella, shredded
2 oz. chives, chopped

Directions:

Put all ingredients in the Slow Cooker and gently mix.
Then close the lid and cook the fish dip in Low for 5 Hrs.

Salmon, Tomatoes and Green Beans

Servings: 2 Cooking Time: 2 Hrs.

Ingredients:

1 lb. salmon fillets, boneless and cubed
1 cup green beans, trimmed and halved
½ cup chicken stock
1 tbsp. parsley, chopped
1 cup cherry tomatoes, halved
1 cup tomato passata
A pinch of salt and black pepper

Directions:

In your Slow Cooker, mix the salmon with the tomatoes, green beans and the other ingredients, toss, put the lid on and cook on High for 2 Hrs.
Divide the mix into bowls and serve.

Maple Mustard Salmon

Servings: 1 Cooking Time: 2 Hrs.

Ingredients:

1 big salmon fillet
2 tbsp. mustard
1 tbsp. maple extract
Salt and black pepper to the taste
1 tbsp. olive oil

Directions:

Whisk maple extract with mustard in a bowl.
Place the salmon in the insert of Slow Cooker.
Add salt, black pepper and mustard mixture over the salmon.
Put the cooker's lid on and set the cooking time to 2 Hrs. on High settings.
Serve warm.

Thai Style Flounder

Servings:6 Cooking Time: 6 Hrs.

Ingredients:

24 oz. flounder, peeled, cleaned
1 lemon, sliced

1 tsp. ground ginger
½ tsp. chili powder
1 tsp. ground turmeric
1 cup of water
½ tsp. cayenne pepper
1 tsp. salt
1 tbsp. sesame oil

Directions:

Chop the flounder roughly and put in the Slow Cooker.
Add water and all remaining ingredients.
Close the lid and cook the fish on low for 6 Hrs.

Cod with Asparagus

Servings: 4 Cooking Time: 2 Hrs.

Ingredients:

4 cod fillets, boneless
12 tbsp. lemon juice
2 tbsp. olive oil
1 bunch asparagus
Salt and black pepper to the taste

Directions:

Place the cod fillets in separate foil sheets.
Top the fish with asparagus spears, lemon pepper, oil, and lemon juice.
Wrap the fish with its foil sheet then place them in Slow Cooker.
Put the cooker's lid on and set the cooking time to 2 Hrs. on High settings.
Unwrap the fish and serve warm.

Shrimp and Mango Mix

Servings: 2 Cooking Time: 1 Hr.

Ingredients:

1 lb. shrimp, peeled and deveined
½ cup cherry tomatoes, halved
1 tbsp. lime juice
1 tbsp. olive oil
½ cup chicken stock
½ cup mango, peeled and cubed
½ cup shallots, chopped
½ tsp. rosemary, dried
½ tsp. chili powder
A pinch of salt and black pepper
1 tbsp. chives, chopped

Directions:

In your Slow Cooker, mix the shrimp with the mango, tomatoes and the other ingredients, toss, put the lid on and cook on High for 1 Hr.
Divide the mix into bowls and serve.

Sweet and Mustard Tilapia

Servings:4 Cooking Time: 4.5 Hrs.

Ingredients:

16 oz. tilapia fillets
2 tbsps. mustard
¼ cup of water
1 tsp. brown sugar
1 tbsp. sesame oil

Directions:

Mix brown sugar with mustard and sesame oil.
Carefully rub the tilapia fillets with mustard mixture and transfer them in the Slow Cooker.
Add water.
Cook the tilapia on Low for 5 Hrs.

Cod and Broccoli

Servings: 2 Cooking Time: 3 Hrs.

Ingredients:

1 lb. cod fillets, boneless
½ cup veggie stock
2 garlic cloves, minced
½ tsp. rosemary, dried
1 tbsp. chives, chopped
1 cup broccoli florets
2 tbsps. tomato paste
1 red onion, minced
A pinch of salt and black pepper

Directions:

In your Slow Cooker, mix the cod with the broccoli, stock, tomato paste and the other ingredients, toss, put the lid on and cook on Low for 3 Hrs.
Divide the mix between plates and serve.

Broiled Tilapia

Servings: 8 Cooking Time: 5 Hrs. 20 Min

Ingredients:

2 tbsps. avocado mayonnaise
Salt and black pepper, to taste
2 tbsps. tea seed oil
¼ tsp. dried thyme
2 tbsps. fresh lemon juice
½ cup Pecorino Romano cheese, grated
2 lbs. tilapia fillets

Directions:

Mix together all the ingredients except tilapia fillets in a bowl.
Arrange the tilapia fillets in the Slow Cooker and pour in the mixture.
Cover and cook on LOW for about 5 Hrs.
Dish out in a serving platter and immediately serve.

Hot Calamari

Servings:4 Cooking Time: 1 Hr.

Ingredients:

12 oz. calamari, sliced
1 tsp. cayenne pepper
1 tsp. mustard
1 tsp. sesame oil
¼ cup of soy sauce
1 garlic clove, crushed
½ cup of water

Directions:

In the bowl mix slices calamari, soy sauce, cayenne pepper, garlic, mustard, and sesame oil. Leave the ingredients for 10 Min. to marinate.
Then transfer the mixture in the Slow Cooker, add water, and close the lid.
Cook the meal on high for 1 Hr.

Poached Cod and Pineapple Mix

Servings: 2 Cooking Time: 4 Hrs.

Ingredients:

1 lb. cod, boneless
1 small ginger pieces, chopped
1 cup pineapple juice
¼ cup white vinegar
Salt and black pepper to the taste
6 garlic cloves, minced
½ tbsp. black peppercorns
1 cup pineapple, chopped
4 jalapeno peppers, chopped

Directions:

Put the fish in your crock, season with salt and pepper.

Add garlic, ginger, peppercorns, pineapple juice, pineapple chunks, vinegar and jalapenos.
Stir gently, cover and cook on Low for 4 Hrs.
Divide fish between plates, top with the pineapple mix and serve.

Fish Hot Dog Sticks

Servings:4 Cooking Time: 2 Hrs.

Ingredients:

5 oz. salmon fillet, minced
1 egg, beaten
½ tsp. salt
1 tbsp. avocado oil
2 oz. potato, cooked, mashed
2 tbsps. cornflour
1 tsp. dried parsley
¼ cup of water

Directions:

In the mixing bowl mix minced salmon with mashed potato, egg, cornflour, salt, and dried parsley.
Then make the medium size hot dog sticks and put them in the hot skillet.
Add avocado oil and roast them on high heat for 1 minute per side.
Transfer the hot dog sticks in the Slow Cooker.
Add water and close the lid.
Cook the meal on high for 2 Hrs.

Fish Mix

Servings: 4 Cooking Time: 2 Hrs. and 30 Min

Ingredients:

4 white fish fillets, skinless and boneless
Salt and black pepper to the taste
1 tsp. ginger, grated
¼ tsp. cumin, ground
1 small red onion, chopped
¼ cup cilantro, chopped
3 garlic cloves, minced
½ tsp. mustard seeds
2 green chilies, chopped
1 tsp. curry powder
2 tbsps. olive oil
1-inch turmeric root, grated
1 and ½ cups coconut cream

Directions:

Heat up a Slow Cooker with half of the oil over medium heat, add mustard seeds, ginger, onion, garlic, turmeric, chilies, curry powder and cumin, stir and cook for 3-4 Min.
Add the rest of the oil to your Slow Cooker, add spice mix, fish, coconut milk, salt and pepper, cover and cook on High for 2 Hrs. and 30 Min.
Divide into bowls and serve with the cilantro sprinkled on top.

Alaska Salmon with Pecan Crunch Coating

Servings: 6 Cooking Time: 6 Hrs. 30 Min

Ingredients:

½ cup fresh bread crumbs
6 lemon wedges
3 tbsps. butter, melted
5 tsps. honey
3 tsps. fresh parsley, chopped
½ cup pecans, finely chopped
Salt and black pepper, to taste
3 tbsps. Dijon mustard
6 (4 oz) salmon fillets

Directions:

Season the salmon fillets with salt and black pepper and transfer into the Slow Cooker.
Combine honey, mustard and butter in a small bowl.
Mix together the parsley, pecans and bread crumbs in another bowl.
Brush the salmon fillets with honey mixture and top with parsley mixture.
Cover and cook for about 6 Hrs. on LOW.
Garnish with lemon wedges and dish out to serve warm.

Sage Shrimps

Servings:4 Cooking Time: 1 Hr.

Ingredients:

1-pound shrimps, peeled
1 tsp. minced garlic
1 cup tomatoes chopped
1 tsp. dried sage
1 tsp. white pepper
½ cup of water

Directions:

Put all ingredients in the Slow Cooker and close the lid.
Cook the shrimps on High for 1 Hr.

Seabass Ragout

Servings:4 Cooking Time: 3.5 Hrs.

Ingredients:

7 oz. shiitake mushrooms
1 tbsp. coconut oil
½ tsp. salt
12 oz. seabass fillet, chopped
1 onion, diced
1 tsp. ground coriander
1 cup of water

Directions:

Heat the coconut oil in the skillet.
Add onion and mushrooms and roast the vegetables for 5 Min. on medium heat.
Then transfer the vegetables in the Slow Cooker and add water.
Add fish fillet, salt, and ground coriander.
Cook the meal on High for 3.5 Hrs.

Teriyaki Tilapia

Servings:4 Cooking Time: 5 Hrs.

Ingredients:

1 tsp. sesame seeds
¼ cup of water
12 oz. tilapia fillet, roughly chopped
¼ cup teriyaki sauce
1 tbsp. avocado oil

Directions:

Mix water with teriyaki sauce, sesame seeds, and avocado oil.
Pour the liquid in the Slow Cooker.
Add tilapia fillet and close the lid.
Cook the fish on Low for 5 Hrs.

Turmeric Coconut Squid

Servings: 4 Cooking Time: 3 Hrs.

Ingredients:

17 oz. squids
Salt and black pepper to the taste
2 cups of water
4 garlic cloves, minced
3 tbsp. olive oil
1 and ½ tbsp. red chili powder
¼ tsp. turmeric powder
5 pieces coconut, shredded
½ tsp. cumin seeds
¼ tsp. mustard seeds

1-inch ginger pieces, chopped

Directions:

Add squids, turmeric, chili powder, water, black pepper, and salt to the insert of the Slow Cooker.
Put the cooker's lid on and set the cooking time to 2 Hrs. on High settings.
Add ginger, garlic, cumin, and oil to a blender jug and blend well.
Transfer this ginger-garlic mixture to the squids in the cooker.
Cook again for 1 Hr. on High settings.
Serve warm.

Chinese Mackerel

Servings: 4 Cooking Time: 2 Hrs.

Ingredients:

2 lbs. mackerel, cut into medium pieces	1 cup water
1 garlic clove, crushed	1 shallot, sliced
1-inch ginger piece, chopped	1/3 cup sake
1/3 cup mirin	¼ cup miso
1 sweet onion, thinly sliced	2 celery stalks, sliced
1 tbsp. rice vinegar	1 tsp. Japanese hot mustard
Salt to the taste	1 tsp. sugar

Directions:

In your Slow Cooker, mix mirin, sake, ginger, garlic and shallot.
Add miso, water and mackerel, stir, cover the Slow Cooker and cook on High for 2 Hrs.
Put onion and celery in a bowl and cover with ice water.
In another bowl, mix vinegar with salt, sugar and mustard and stir well.
Divide mackerel on plates, drain onion and celery well, mix with mustard dressing, divide next to mackerel and serve.

Thyme and Sesame Halibut

Servings:2 Cooking Time: 4 Hrs.

Ingredients:

1 tbsp. lemon juice	1 tsp. thyme
Salt and pepper to taste	8 oz. halibut or mahi-mahi, cut into 2 portions
1 tbsps. sesame seed, toasted	

Directions:

Line the bottom of the Slow Cooker with a foil.
Mix lemon juice, thyme, salt and pepper in a shallow dish.
Place the fish and allow to marinate for 2 Hrs. in the fish.
Sprinkle the fish with toasted sesame seeds.
Arrange the fish in the foil-lined Slow Cooker.
Close the lid and cook on high for 2 Hrs. or on low for 4 Hrs.

Taco Shrimps

Servings:4 Cooking Time: 40 Min

Ingredients:

1-pound shrimps, peeled	1 tsp. taco seasonings
3 tbsps. lemon juice	1 tsp. dried thyme
1/3 cup water	

Directions:

In the mixing bowl mix shrimps with taco seasonings and dried thyme.
Put the shrimps in the Slow Cooker. Add water.
Cook them on High for 40 Min.
Then drain water and sprinkle the cooked shrimps with lemon juice.

Tuna and Chimichurri

Servings: 4 Cooking Time: 1 Hr. and 15 Min

Ingredients:

½ cup cilantro, chopped	1/3 cup olive oil
1 small red onion, chopped	3 tbsp. balsamic vinegar
2 tbsps. parsley, chopped	2 tbsps. basil, chopped
1 jalapeno pepper, chopped	1 lb. tuna steak, boneless, skinless and cubed
Salt and black pepper to the taste	1 tsp. red pepper flakes
2 garlic cloves, minced	1 tsp. thyme, chopped
A pinch of cayenne pepper	2 avocados, pitted, peeled and sliced
6 oz. baby arugula	

Directions:

In a bowl, mix the oil with jalapeno, vinegar, onion, cilantro, basil, garlic, parsley, pepper flakes, thyme, cayenne, salt and pepper, whisk well, transfer to your Slow Cooker, cover and cook on High for 1 Hr.
Add tuna, cover and cook on High for 15 Min. more.
Divide arugula on plates, top with tuna slices, drizzle the chimichurri sauce and serve with avocado slices on the side.

Spicy Creole Shrimp

Servings: 2 Cooking Time: 1 Hr. and 30 Min

Ingredients:

½ lb. big shrimp, peeled and deveined	2 tsps. Worcestershire sauce
2 tsps. olive oil	Juice of 1 lemon
Salt and black pepper to the taste	1 tsp. Creole seasoning

Directions:

In your Slow Cooker, mix shrimp with Worcestershire sauce, oil, lemon juice, salt, pepper and Creole seasoning, toss, cover and cook on High for 1 Hr. and 30 Min.
Divide into bowls and serve.

Shrimps Boil

Servings:2 Cooking Time: 45 Min

Ingredients:

½ cup of water	1 tbsp. piri piri sauce
1 tbsp. butter	7 oz. shrimps, peeled

Directions:

Pour water in the Slow Cooker.
Add shrimps and cook them on high for 45 Min.
Then drain water and transfer shrimps in the skillet.
Add butter and piri piri sauce.
Roast the shrimps for 2-3 Min. on medium heat.

Thai Salmon Cakes

Servings: 10 Cooking Time: 6 Hrs.

Ingredients:

- 6 oz. squid, minced
- 2 tbsp. chili paste
- 2 oz. lemon leaves
- 2 tsp. fish sauce
- 1 egg yolk
- 1 tsp. salt
- 1 tsp. sugar
- 1/4 cup cream
- 10 oz. salmon fillet, minced
- 1 tsp. cayenne pepper
- 3 tbsp. green peas, mashed
- 2 egg white
- 1 tsp. oyster sauce
- 1/2 tsp. ground coriander
- 2 tbsp. butter
- 3 tbsp. almond flour

Directions:

Mix seafood with chili paste, cayenne pepper, lemon leaves, mashed green peas, fish sauce, whisked egg yolk and egg whites in a bowl.
Stir in sugar, salt, oyster sauce, sugar, almond flour, and ground coriander.
Mix well, then make small-sized fish cakes out of this mixture.
Add cream and butter to the insert of the Slow Cooker.
Place the fish cakes in the butter and cream.
Put the cooker's lid on and set the cooking time to 5 Hrs. on Low settings.
Serve warm with cream mixture.

Pesto Salmon

Servings:4 Cooking Time: 2.5 Hrs.

Ingredients:

- 1-pound salmon fillet
- 1 tbsp. butter
- 3 tbsps. pesto sauce
- 1/4 cup of water

Directions:

Pour water in the Slow Cooker.
Add butter and 1 tbsp. of pesto.
Add salmon and cook the fish on High for 2.5 Hrs.
Chop the cooked salmon and top with remaining pesto sauce.

Fish Pie

Servings:6 Cooking Time: 6 Hrs.

Ingredients:

- 1 tsp. cream cheese
- 1/4 cup fresh dill, chopped
- 1 carrot, diced
- 7 oz. tuna, canned, shredded
- 1 garlic clove, diced
- 1 tsp. butter, softened
- 1 tsp. sesame oil
- 7 oz. puff pastry

Directions:

Brush the Slow Cooker bottom with sesame oil.
Then put the puff pastry inside and flatten it in the shape of the pie crust.
After this, mix garlic with cream cheese, dill, butter, carrot, and tuna.
Put the tuna mixture over the pie crust and flatten it.
Close the lid and cook the pie on Low for 6 Hrs.

Dill Crab Cutlets

Servings: 12 Cooking Time: 1 Hr.

Ingredients:

- 12 oz. crab meat, canned
- 4 tbsp. fresh dill
- 1 tsp. salt
- 1 tbsp. turmeric
- 1/4 cup mashed green peas
- 1 large egg
- 1/2 tsp. cilantro
- 3 tbsp. almond flour
- 1 tsp. olive oil
- 1 tsp. lemon juice

Directions:

Add crab meat, salt, almond flour, turmeric, cilantro, salt, dill to a blender.
Blend this crab mixture then add egg, lemon juice, and mashed green peas.
Beat again for 2 Min. until it forms a smooth dough.
Make small crab cakes out of this mixture.
Grease the insert of Slow Cooker with olive oil.
Place the crab cakes in the cooker.
Put the cooker's lid on and set the cooking time to 1 Hr. on High settings.
Serve warm.

Italian Trout Croquettes

Servings: 8 Cooking Time: 3 Hrs.

Ingredients:

- 14 oz. trout fillet, minced
- 7 tbsp. flour
- 1 tbsp. Italian Seasoning
- 1 tsp. ground black pepper
- 3 tbsp. milk
- 2 tbsp. sesame oil
- 3 tbsp. Worcestershire sauce
- 2 eggs
- 1 tsp. salt
- 6 oz. rice, cooked
- 1 tsp. paprika

Directions:

Mix trout mince with Worcestershire sauce, flour, salt, Italian seasoning, milk, paprika, cooked rice, and black pepper in a bowl.
Whisk in egg and then mix until it forms a smooth mixture.
Make small bowls out of this mixture then add to the Slow Cooker along with sesame oil.
Put the cooker's lid on and set the cooking time to 3 Hrs. on High settings.
Serve warm.

Rice Stuffed Squid

Servings: 4 Cooking Time: 3 Hrs.

Ingredients:

- 3 squids
- 1 cup sticky rice
- 2 tbsps. sake
- 1 tbsp. mirin
- Tentacles from 1 squid, chopped
- 14 oz. dashi stock
- 4 tbsps. soy sauce
- 2 tbsps. sugar

Directions:

Toss the chopped tentacles with rice and stuff the 3 squids with rice mixture.
Seal the squid using toothpicks then place them in the Slow Cooker.
Add soy sauce, stock, sugar, sake, and mirin to the squids.
Put the cooker's lid on and set the cooking time to 3 Hrs. on High settings.
Serve warm.

BBQ Shrimps

Servings:6 Cooking Time: 40 Min

Ingredients:

1/3 cup BBQ sauce
1-pound shrimps, peeled
¼ cup plain yogurt
1 tbsp. butter

Directions:

Melt butter and mix it with shrimps.
Put the mixture in the Slow Cooker.
Add plain yogurt and BBQ sauce.
Close the lid and cook the meal on High for 40 Min.

Herbed Shrimps

Servings: 4 Cooking Time: 40 Min

Ingredients:

4 tbsp. fresh dill
2 tbsp. sugar
1 tbsp. butter
1 tsp. ground ginger
1 tbsp. tomato juice
½ tsp. sage
¼ cup pineapple juice
3 tbsp. mango puree
1 lb. shrimp, peeled
½ tsp. lemon juice
1 cup of water

Directions:

Add shrimp, water, and sage to the insert of Slow Cooker.
Put the cooker's lid on and set the cooking time to 20 Min. on High settings.
Meanwhile, mix melted butter, mango puree, pineapple juice, sugar, lemon juice, ginger ground, dill and tomatoes juice in a bowl.
Add this mixture to the shrimp in the Slow Cooker.
Put the cooker's lid on and set the cooking time to 20 Min. on High settings.
Serve warm.

Salmon Chickpea Fingers

Servings: 8 Cooking Time: 3 Hrs.

Ingredients:

2 large eggs
1 tbsp. turmeric
13 oz. salmon fillet
1 tsp. ground black pepper
1 tsp. onion powder
¼ tsp. ginger
1 cup panko bread crumbs
1 tbsp. butter
1 tsp. salt
¼ cup chickpeas, canned
2 tbsp. semolina

Directions:

Whisk eggs with turmeric, semolina, onion powder, ginger, black pepper, and salt in a bowl.
Blend salmon with chickpeas in a blender then stir in the egg mixture.
Mix well then make medium finger-shaped logs.
Coat the fish fingers with breadcrumbs liberally.
Grease the insert of the Slow Cooker with melted butter then add fish fingers
Put the cooker's lid on and set the cooking time to 3 Hrs. on High settings.
Flip the fish fingers when cooked halfway through.
Serve warm.

Octopus and Veggies Mix

Servings: 4 Cooking Time: 3 Hrs.

Ingredients:

1 octopus, already prepared
1 cup white wine
1 cup olive oil
1 tbsp. hot sauce
1 tbsp. tomato sauce
½ bunch parsley, chopped
1 yellow onion, chopped
1 cup red wine
1 cup water
2 tsps. pepper sauce
1 tbsp. paprika
Salt and black pepper to the taste
2 garlic cloves, minced
4 potatoes, cut into quarters.

Directions:

Put octopus in a bowl, add white wine, red one, water, half of the oil, pepper sauce, hot sauce, paprika, tomato paste, salt, pepper and parsley, toss to coat, cover and keep in a cold place for 1 day.
Add the rest of the oil to your Slow Cooker and arrange onions and potatoes on the bottom.
Add the octopus and the marinade, stir, cover, cook on High for 3 Hrs., divide everything between plates and serve.

Japanese Cod Fillet

Servings: 9 Cooking Time: 1.5 Hrs.

Ingredients:

24 oz. cod fillet
3 oz. pickled jalapeno, chopped
¼ cup of soy sauce
1 tsp. sesame oil
¼ tsp. cayenne pepper
2 tbsp. miso paste
2 tbsp. oyster sauce
¼ cup fish stock
½ tsp. chili flakes
1 tbsp. sugar

Directions:

Whisk miso paste, stock, sesame oil, soy sauce, oyster sauce, sugar, chili flakes, and cayenne pepper in a bowl.
Rub this miso mixture over the cod filet liberally.
Transfer the miso-seasoned cod to the insert of the Slow Cooker.
Top the cod with chopped jalapeno and left-over miso paste.
Put the cooker's lid on and set the cooking time to 1.5 Hrs. on Low settings.
Shred the cooked cod and return to the miso jalapeno sauce.
Serve warm.

Easy Salmon and Kimchi Sauce

Servings: 4 Cooking Time: 2 Hrs.

Ingredients:

2 tbsps. butter, soft
2 oz. Kimchi, finely chopped
1 and ¼ lb. salmon fillet
Salt and black pepper to the taste

Directions:

In your food processor, mix butter with Kimchi, blend well, rub salmon with salt, pepper and Kimchi mix, place in your Slow Cooker, cover and cook on High for 2 Hrs.
Divide between plates and serve with a side salad.

Mackerel Stuffed Tacos

Servings: 6 Cooking Time: 2 Hrs.

Ingredients:

9 oz. mackerel fillet
¼ cup fish stock
1 tsp. paprika
6 corn tortillas
1 tsp. minced garlic
1 tsp. salt
1 tsp. butter
½ tsp. ground white pepper
¼ cup of salsa
½ tsp. mayo

Directions:

Whisk mayo with butter, garlic, white pepper, salt, and paprika in a small bowl.
Rub the mackerel fillet with the mayo garlic mixture.
Place this fish in the insert of Slow Cooker and pour in fish stock.
Put the cooker's lid on and set the cooking time to 2 Hrs. on Low settings.
Meanwhile, layer the corn tortilla with salad evenly.
Shred the cooked mackerel fillet and mix it with 2 tsp. cooking liquid.
Divide the fish shreds on the corn tortillas and wrap them.
Serve warm.

Cod Sticks

Servings:2 Cooking Time: 1.5 Hr.

Ingredients:

2 cod fillets
1 egg, beaten
1 tbsp. coconut oil
1 tsp. ground black pepper
1/3 cup breadcrumbs
¼ cup of water

Directions:

Cut the cod fillets into medium sticks and sprinkle with ground black pepper.
Then dip the fish in the beaten egg and coat in the breadcrumbs.
Pour water in the Slow Cooker.
Add coconut oil and fish sticks.
Cook the meal on High for 1.5 Hrs.

Shrimp and Peas Soup

Servings: 4 Cooking Time: 1 Hr.

Ingredients:

4 scallions, chopped
1 small ginger root, grated
¼ cup soy sauce
Black pepper to the taste
1 lb. shrimp, peeled and deveined
1 tbsp. sesame oil
1 tbsp. olive oil
8 cups chicken stock
5 oz. canned bamboo shoots, sliced
¼ tsp. fish sauce
½ lb. snow peas
½ tbsp. chili oil

Directions:

In your Slow Cooker, mix olive oil with scallions, ginger, stock, soy sauce, bamboo, black pepper, fish sauce, shrimp, peas, sesame oil and chili oil, cover and cook on High for 1 Hr.
Stir soup, ladle into bowls and serve.

Tuna and Brussels Sprouts

Servings: 2 Cooking Time: 3 Hrs.

Ingredients:

1 lb. tuna fillets, boneless
1 tsp. sweet paprika
1 cup Brussels sprouts, trimmed and halved
½ tsp. garlic powder
1 tbsp. cilantro, chopped
½ cup chicken stock
½ tsp. chili powder
1 red onion, chopped
A pinch of salt and black pepper

Directions:

In your Slow Cooker, mix the tuna with the stock, sprouts and the other ingredients, put the lid on and cook on High for 3 Hrs.
Divide the mix between plates and serve.

Creamy Shrimp

Servings: 2 Cooking Time: 1 Hr.

Ingredients:

1 lb. shrimp, peeled and deveined
¼ cup chicken stock
½ cup heavy cream
1 tbsp. ginger, grated
1 tbsp. parsley, chopped
2 scallions, chopped
2 tbsps. avocado oil
1 tsp. garam masala
A pinch of salt and black pepper

Directions:

In your Slow Cooker, mix the shrimp with the scallions, stock and the other ingredients, toss, put the lid on and cook on High for 1 Hr.
Divide the mix into bowls and serve.

Salmon and Berries

Servings: 2 Cooking Time: 3 Hrs.

Ingredients:

1 lb. salmon fillets, boneless and roughly cubed
½ cup blackberries
1 tbsp. avocado oil
½ tsp. Italian seasoning
A pinch of salt and black pepper
Juice of 1 lime
2 scallions, chopped
½ cup fish stock

Directions:

In your Slow Cooker, mix the salmon with the berries, lime juice and the other ingredients, toss, put the lid on and cook on Low for 3 Hrs.
Divide the mix between plates and serve.

Salmon Picatta

Servings:4 Cooking Time: 3.5 Hrs.

Ingredients:

4 salmon fillets
½ lemon, sliced
¼ cup white wine
1 tbsp. flour
½ tsp. minced garlic
1 tbsp. avocado oil
1 tbsp. butter
1 tsp. capers
¼ cup chicken stock

Directions:

In the mixing bowl mix minced garlic and butter.
Put the mixture in the Slow Cooker.
Add chicken stock and flour.
Gently whisk the mixture.
Add lemon, white wine, and avocado oil.
Then add salmon fillets and capers.
Close the lid and cook the meal on High for 3.5 Hrs.

Coconut Catfish

Servings:3 Cooking Time: 2.5 Hrs.

Ingredients:

3 catfish fillets
½ cup of coconut milk
2 tbsps. fish sauce
2 tbsps. soy sauce
1 tsp. coconut shred
1 tsp. sesame seeds
1 cup of water

Directions:

Pour water in the Slow Cooker.
Add soy sauce, fish sauce, sesame seeds, and coconut milk.
Then add coconut shred and catfish fillets.
Cook the fish on high for 2.5 Hrs.

Shrimps and Carrot Saute

Servings:4 Cooking Time: 6 Hrs.

Ingredients:

1 cup carrot, diced
1 cup tomatoes, chopped
1 tsp. fennel seeds
1-pound shrimps, peeled
½ cup of water

Directions:

Put all ingredients in the Slow Cooker.
Gently mix the mixture and close the lid.
Cook the saute on Low for 6 Hrs.

Bigeye Jack Saute

Servings:4 Cooking Time: 6 Hrs.

Ingredients:

7 oz. (bigeye jack) tuna fillet, chopped
1 cup tomato, chopped
1 jalapeno pepper, chopped
1 tsp. ground black pepper
½ cup chicken stock

Directions:

Put all ingredients in the Slow Cooker and close the lid.
Cook the saute on Low for 6 Hrs.

Flounder Cheese Casserole

Servings: 11 Cooking Time: 6 Hrs.

Ingredients:

8 oz. rice noodles
12 oz. flounder fillet, chopped
½ tsp. ground black pepper
3 sweet potatoes, chopped
3 tbsp. chives
7 oz. cream cheese
½ cup fresh cilantro, chopped
2 cups chicken stock
1 cup carrot, cooked
2 sweet peppers, chopped
2 tbsp. butter, melted
4 oz. shallot, chopped
5 oz. Parmesan, shredded
1 cup of water

Directions:

Brush the insert of your Slow Cooker with melted butter.
Place the chopped flounder, carrots, sweet peppers, sweet potatoes, shallots, and chives to the cooker.
Add cilantro, stock, black pepper, cream cheese, and water to the flounder.
Top the flounder casserole with shredded cheese.
Put the cooker's lid on and set the cooking time to 6 Hrs. on Low settings.
Serve warm.

Pineapple Milkfish

Servings:4 Cooking Time: 3 Hrs.

Ingredients:

16 oz. milkfish fillet, chopped
1 cup of coconut milk
½ tsp. curry powder
½ cup pineapple, chopped
1 tsp. white pepper

Directions:

Sprinkle the milkfish fillet with curry powder and white pepper.
Then put it in the Slow Cooker.
Top the fish with pineapple and coconut milk.
Close the lid and cook the fish on High for 3 Hrs.

Mussels Tomato Soup

Servings: 6 Cooking Time: 2 Hrs.

Ingredients:

2 lbs. mussels
28 oz. canned tomatoes, chopped
1 tsp. red pepper flakes, crushed
1 handful parsley, chopped
Salt and black pepper to the taste
28 oz. canned tomatoes, crushed
2 cup chicken stock
3 garlic cloves, minced
1 yellow onion, chopped
1 tbsp. olive oil

Directions:

Toss mussels with tomatoes, stock, parsley, garlic, pepper flakes, oil, black pepper, salt, and onion in the insert of Slow Cooker.
Put the cooker's lid on and set the cooking time to 2 Hrs. on High settings.
Serve warm.

Shrimp and Avocado

Servings: 2 Cooking Time: 1 Hr.

Ingredients:

1 lb. shrimp, peeled and deveined
½ cup chicken stock
Juice of 1 lime
2 tbsps. chili pepper, minced
1 tbsp. chives, chopped
1 cup avocado, peeled, pitted and cubed
½ tsp. sweet paprika
1 tbsp. olive oil
A pinch of salt and black pepper

Directions:

In your Slow Cooker, mix the shrimp with the avocado, stock and the other ingredients, toss, put the lid on and cook on High for 1 Hr.
Divide the mix into bowls and serve.

Cod and Clams Saute

Servings:2 Cooking Time: 4 Hrs.

Ingredients:

1 cod fillet
1 tbsp. fresh parsley, chopped
2 cups tomatoes, chopped
1 tbsp. olive oil
1 cup clams
1 garlic clove, diced
1 jalapeno pepper, diced
1 cup of water

Directions:

Slice the cod fillet and put it in the Slow Cooker.
Add all remaining ingredients and close the lid.
Cook the saute on Low for 4 Hrs.

Shrimp Chicken Jambalaya

Servings: 8 Cooking Time: 4 Hrs. 30 Min

Ingredients:

1 lb. chicken breast,
1 lb. shrimp, peeled and deveined

chopped

2 tbsp. extra virgin olive oil

2 cups onions, chopped

2 tbsp. garlic, chopped

3 and ½ cups chicken stock

1 tbsp. Worcestershire sauce

1 lb. sausage, chopped

1 and ½ cups of rice

2 cups green, yellow and red bell peppers, chopped

1 tbsp. Creole seasoning

1 cup tomatoes, crushed

Directions:

Brush the insert of your Slow Cooker with oil.

Toss in sausage, chicken, bell peppers, garlic, onion, rice, tomatoes, stock, Worcestershire sauce, and seasoning.

Put the cooker's lid on and set the cooking time to 4 Hrs. on High settings.

Stir in shrimp and cook for another 30 Min. on High settings.

Serve warm.

Chili Shrimp and Zucchinis

Servings: 4 Cooking Time: 1 Hr.

Ingredients:

1 lb. shrimp, peeled and deveined

2 scallions, minced

2 green chilies, chopped

1 tbsp. chives, chopped

1 zucchini, cubed

1 cup tomato passata

A pinch of salt and black pepper

Directions:

In your Slow Cooker, mix the shrimp with the zucchini and the other ingredients, toss, put the lid on and cook on High for 1 Hr.

Divide the shrimp mix into bowls and serve.

Sriracha Shrimp

Servings: 6 Cooking Time: 1 Hr. and 30 Min

Ingredients:

¼ cup yellow onion, chopped

1 garlic clove, minced

¼ cup red pepper, roasted and chopped

¼ cup cilantro, chopped

1 cup coconut milk

2 tbsps. lime juice

2 tbsps. olive oil

1 and ½ lbs. shrimp, peeled and deveined

14 oz. canned tomatoes, chopped

2 tbsps. sriracha sauce

Salt and black pepper to the taste

Directions:

Put the oil in your Slow Cooker, add onion, garlic, shrimp, red pepper, tomatoes, cilantro, sriracha sauce, milk, salt, pepper and lime juice, toss, cover and cook on High for 1 Hr. and 30 Min.

Divide into bowls and serve.

Fish Tart

Servings:6 Cooking Time: 4 Hrs.

Ingredients:

1-pound anchovies

1 tsp. ground nutmeg

1 oz. Parmesan, grated

2 tbsps. cornflour

2 eggs, beaten

5 oz. puff pastry

Cooking spray

Directions:

Spray the Slow Cooker bottom with cooking spray.

Then put the puff pastry inside.

Flatten it in the shape of the pie crust.

After this, mix anchovies with cornflour and ground nutmeg.

Put them over the puff pastry in one layer.

Then pour the beaten egg over the anchovies.

Add parmesan and close the lid.

Cook the fish tart on High for 4 Hrs.

Soups & Stews Recipes

Split Pea Sausage Soup

Servings: 8 Cooking Time: 6 1/4 Hrs.

Ingredients:

2 cups split peas, rinsed

4 Italian sausages, sliced

2 carrots, diced

1 garlic clove, chopped

1/2 tsp. dried oregano

Salt and pepper to taste

2 tbsps. chopped parsley

8 cups water

1 sweet onion, chopped

1 celery stalk, diced

1 red chili, chopped

2 tbsps. tomato paste

1 lemon, juiced

Directions:

Combine the split peas, water, sausages, onion, carrots, celery, garlic, red chili, oregano and tomato paste in your Slow Cooker.

Add salt and pepper to taste and cook on low settings for 6 Hrs.

When done, stir in the lemon juice and parsley and serve the soup warm.

Fish Sweet Corn Soup

Servings: 6 Cooking Time: 2 1/4 Hrs.

Ingredients:

2 bacon slices, chopped

2 cups milk

2 potatoes, peeled and diced

Salt and pepper to taste

1 sweet onion, chopped

2 cups frozen sweet corn

1 lb. haddock fillets, cubed

Directions:

Cook the bacon in a skillet and transfer in your Slow Cooker.

Add the remaining ingredients and season with salt and pepper.

cook on high settings for 2 Hrs.

Serve the soup warm.

Tomato and Turkey Chili

Servings:6 Cooking Time: 7 Hrs.

Ingredients:

1-pound turkey fillet, chopped

1 jalapeno pepper, chopped

1 cup chicken stock

2 cup tomatoes, chopped

1 onion, diced

Directions:

Put turkey and tomatoes in the Slow Cooker.

Add jalapeno pepper, onion, and chicken stock.

Close the lid and cook the chili on low for 7 Hrs.

Ham and White Bean Soup

Servings: 8 Cooking Time: 6 1/4 Hrs.

Ingredients:

2 tbsps. olive oil
1 garlic clove, chopped
1 celery stalk, diced
2 cans (15 oz.) white beans, drained
3 cups water
2 tbsps. chopped parsley
1 sweet onion, chopped
1 yellow bell pepper, cored and diced
1 cup diced ham
2 cups chicken stock
Salt and pepper to taste

Directions:

Heat the oil in a skillet and stir in the onion, garlic, celery and bell pepper. Sauté for 5 Min. until softened and transfer in your Slow Cooker.
Add the ham, white beans, stock and water and season with salt and pepper.
Cook on low settings for 6 Hrs.
To serve, pour the soup into bowls and top with parsley. The soup can be served both warm and chilled.

Paprika Noddle Soup

Servings:4 Cooking Time: 4 Hrs.

Ingredients:

3 oz. egg noodles
1 tsp. butter
½ tsp. salt
3 cups chicken stock
1 tsp. ground paprika
2 tbsps. fresh parsley, chopped

Directions:

Put egg noodles in the Slow Cooker.
Add chicken stock, butter, ground paprika, and salt.
Close the lid and cook the soup on High for 4 Hrs.
Then open the lid, add parsley, and stir the soup.

Herbed Chickpea Soup

Servings: 6 Cooking Time: 6 1/4 Hrs.

Ingredients:

1 cup dried chickpeas
1 carrot, diced
1 celery stalk, sliced
2 cups chicken stock
2 tbsps. tomato paste
2 tbsps. chopped cilantro
Salt and pepper to taste
1 shallot, chopped
1 red bell pepper, cored and diced
1 small fennel bulb, chopped
4 cups water
2 tbsps. chopped parsley
1 tbsp. chopped dill

Directions:

Combine the chickpeas, shallot, carrot, bell pepper, celery, fennel, tomato paste, stock and water in your Slow Cooker.
Add salt and pepper to taste and cook on low settings for 6 Hrs.
When done, stir in the chopped herbs and serve the soup warm and fresh.

Shredded Beef Soup

Servings: 8 Cooking Time: 8 1/2 Hrs.

Ingredients:

1 1/2 lbs. beef roast
2 garlic cloves, chopped
2 celery stalks, sliced
1/2 tsp. cumin powder
1/2 tsp. dried basil
2 cups chicken stock
2 jalapenos, chopped
Salt and pepper to taste
1 sweet onion, chopped
2 carrots, sliced
2 red bell peppers, cored and diced
1/2 tsp. dried oregano
1/2 tsp. chili powder
5 cups water
1 cup fire roasted tomatoes

Directions:

Combine the onion, garlic, carrots, celery, bell peppers, cumin powder, oregano, basil, chili powder, stock and water in your Slow Cooker.
Add the jalapenos and tomatoes, as well as salt and pepper then place the beef in the center of the cooker, making sure it's covered in liquid.
Cook on low settings for 8 Hrs.
When done, shred the beef into fine threads and serve the soup warm.

Chicken Sausage Rice Soup

Servings: 6 Cooking Time: 6 1/4 Hrs.

Ingredients:

2 fresh chicken sausages, sliced
1 carrot, sliced
1 yellow bell pepper, cored and diced
2 large potatoes, peeled and cubed
2 cups chicken stock
Salt and pepper to taste
1 shallot, chopped
1 celery stalk, sliced
1 cup diced tomatoes
1/4 cup jasmine rice
4 cups water

Directions:

Combine the chicken, shallot and the rest of the ingredients in your Slow Cooker.
Add salt and pepper to taste and cook on low settings for 6 Hrs.
The soup is best served warm.

Leek Potato Soup

Servings: 8 Cooking Time: 6 1/2 Hrs.

Ingredients:

4 leeks, sliced
4 bacon slices, chopped
4 large potatoes, peeled and cubed
3 cups water
Salt and pepper to taste
1/4 tsp. smoked paprika
1 rosemary sprig
1 tbsp. olive oil
1 celery stalk, sliced
2 cups chicken stock
1 bay leaf
1/4 tsp. cayenne pepper
1 thyme sprig

Directions:

Heat the oil in a skillet and add the bacon. Cook until crisp then stir in the leeks.
Sauté for 5 Min. until softened then transfer in your Slow Cooker.
Add the remaining ingredients and cook on low settings for about 6 Hrs.
Serve the soup warm.

Mussel Stew

Servings:4 Cooking Time: 55 Min

Ingredients:

1-pound mussels
1 tsp. smoked paprika
1 eggplant, chopped
1 tbsp. sesame seeds
2 garlic cloves, diced
½ tsp. chili powder
1 cup coconut cream
1 tsp. tomato paste

Directions:

Put all ingredients from the list above in the Slow Cooker and gently stir.
Close the lid and cook the mussel stew for 55 Min. on High.

Lobster Stew

Servings:4 Cooking Time: 1 Hr.

Ingredients:

7 oz. lobster tail, peeled, chopped
1 onion, roughly chopped
½ tsp. dried lemongrass
3 tomatoes, chopped
1 cup fish stock
2 tbsps. cream cheese

Directions:

Put all ingredients in the Slow Cooker and gently stir.
Close the lid and cook the stew on High for 1 Hr.

Hungarian Goulash Soup

Servings: 8 Cooking Time: 8 1/2 Hrs.

Ingredients:

2 sweet onions, chopped
2 tbsps. canola oil
1/2 celery stalk, diced
1 1/2 lbs. potatoes, peeled and cubed
1 cup diced tomatoes
5 cups water
1/2 tsp. smoked paprika
1 lb. beef roast, cubed
2 carrots, diced
2 red bell peppers, cored and diced
2 tbsps. tomato paste
1/2 cup beef stock
1/2 tsp. cumin seeds
Salt and pepper to taste

Directions:

Heat the oil in a skillet and stir in the beef. Cook for 5 Min. on all sides then stir in the onion. Sauté for 2 additional Min. then transfer in your Slow Cooker.
Add the remaining ingredients and season with salt and pepper.
Cook on low settings for 8 Hrs.
Serve the soup warm.

Hot Lentil Soup

Servings:4 Cooking Time: 24.5 Hrs.

Ingredients:

1 potato, peeled, diced
5 cups chicken stock
1 tsp. chili powder
1 tsp. olive oil
1 cup lentils
1 onion, diced
1 tsp. cayenne pepper
1 tbsp. tomato paste

Directions:

Roast the onion in the olive oil until light brown and transfer in the Slow Cooker.
Add lentils, chicken stock, potato, chili powder, cayenne pepper, and tomato paste.
Carefully stir the soup mixture until the tomato paste is dissolved.
Close the lid and cook the soup on High for 5 Hrs.

Curried Corn Chowder

Servings: 8 Cooking Time: 8 1/4 Hrs.

Ingredients:

1 sweet onion, chopped
2 garlic cloves, chopped
2 cups chicken stock
2 large potatoes, peeled and cubed
1 1/2 cups whole milk
1/4 tsp. cumin seeds
1 can (15 oz.) sweet corn, drained
1/2 chili pepper, chopped
Salt and pepper to taste

Directions:

Combine the onion, garlic, stock, sweet corn, potatoes and chili pepper in your Slow Cooker.
Add the remaining ingredients and season with salt and pepper.
Cook on low settings for 8 Hrs.
Serve the soup warm and fresh.

Salmon Fennel Soup

Servings: 6 Cooking Time: 5 1/4 Hrs.

Ingredients:

1 shallot, chopped
1 fennel bulb, sliced
1 celery stalk, sliced
1 lemon, juiced
Salt and pepper to taste
1 garlic clove, sliced
1 carrot, diced
3 salmon fillets, cubed
1 bay leaf

Directions:

Combine the shallot, garlic, fennel, carrot, celery, fish, lemon juice and bay leaf in your Slow Cooker.
Add salt and pepper to taste and cook on low settings for 5 Hrs.
Serve the soup warm.

Tuscan Kale and White Bean Soup

Servings: 8 Cooking Time: 8 1/2 Hrs.

Ingredients:

1 1/2 cups dried white beans, rinsed
2 carrots, diced
1 tsp. dried oregano
6 cups water
1 tsp. dried basil
Salt and pepper to taste
1 sweet onion, chopped
1 celery stalk, sliced
2 cups chicken stock
1 bay leaf
1 bunch kale, shredded
1 lemon, juiced

Directions:

Combine the beans, onion, carrots, celery, dried herbs, stock and water in your Slow Cooker.
Add salt and pepper to taste and throw in the bay leaf as well.
Cook on low settings for 4 Hrs. then add the kale and lemon juice and cook for 4 additional Hrs.
Serve the soup warm or chilled.

Crock-pot Low-carb Taco Soup

Servings: 8 Cooking Time: 4 Hrs.

Ingredients:

2 lbs. ground pork, beef or sausage
2 10-oz cans of Rotel
4 cups chicken broth
1 can corn kernels, drained
2 8-oz packages of cream cheese
2 tbsps. of taco seasoning
2 tbsps. cilantro, fresh or dried
½ cup cheddar cheese, shredded for garnish (optional)

Directions:

Brown the ground meat until fully cooked over medium-high heat in a pan. While the meat is browning, place cream cheese,

Rotel, corn and taco seasoning in Crock-Pot. Drain grease off meat and place meat in Crock-Pot. Stir and combine. Pour chicken broth over mixture, cover and cook on LOW for 4 Hrs. Just before serving, add in cilantro and garnish with shredded cheddar cheese.

Smoked Sausage Stew

Servings:5 Cooking Time: 3.5 Hrs.

Ingredients:

1-pound smoked sausages, chopped
1 cup tomato juice
1 tsp. butter
¼ cup Cheddar cheese, shredded
1 cup broccoli, chopped
1 cup of water
1 tsp. dried thyme

Directions:

Grease the Slow Cooker bowl with butter from inside.
Put the smoked sausages in one layer in the Slow Cooker.
Add the layer of broccoli and Cheddar cheese.
Then mix water with tomato juice and dried thyme.
Pour the liquid over the sausage mixture and close the lid.
Cook the stew on high for 3.5 Hrs.

Celery Soup with Ham

Servings:8 Cooking Time: 5 Hrs.

Ingredients:

8 oz. ham, chopped
1 tsp. white pepper
2 cups celery stalk, chopped
8 cups chicken stock
½ tsp. cayenne pepper
½ cup corn kernels

Directions:

Put all ingredients in the Slow Cooker and gently stir.
Close the lid and cook the soup on High for 5 Hrs.
When the soup is cooked, cool it to the room temperature and ladle into the bowls.

Fennel Stew

Servings:6 Cooking Time: 5 Hrs.

Ingredients:

1-pound beef sirloin, chopped
3 cups of water
1 tbsp. dried dill
1 cup fennel bulb, chopped
1 yellow onion, chopped
1 tsp. olive oil

Directions:

Roast beef sirloin in the skillet for 2 Min. per side.
Then transfer the meat in the Slow Cooker.
Add olive oil, a fennel bulb, water, onion, and dried dill.
Close the lid and cook the stew on high for 5 Hrs.

Coconut Squash Soup

Servings: 6 Cooking Time: 2 1/4 Hrs.

Ingredients:

1 tbsp. olive oil
1/2 tsp. grated ginger
1 tbsp. curry paste
1 tsp. Worcestershire sauce
2 cups chicken stock
1 cup coconut milk
Salt and pepper to taste
1 shallot, chopped
2 garlic cloves, minced
1 tsp. brown sugar
3 cups butternut squash cubes
2 cups water
1 tbsp. tomato paste

Directions:

Heat the oil in a skillet and stir in the shallot, garlic, ginger and curry paste. Sauté for 1 minute then transfer the mixture in your Slow Cooker.
Add the remaining ingredients and season with salt and pepper.
Cover with its lid and cook on high settings for 2 Hrs.
When done, puree the soup with an immersion blender until smooth.
Pour the soup into serving bowls and serve it warm.

Posole Soup

Servings: 8 Cooking Time: 6 1/4 Hrs.

Ingredients:

1 tbsps. canola oil
1 sweet onion, chopped
1/2 tsp. cumin powder
1/2 tsp. dried basil
1 can (15 oz.) black beans, drained
1 cup diced tomatoes
4 cups chicken stock
Salt and pepper to taste
1 lb. pork tenderloin, cubed
2 garlic cloves, chopped
1/2 tsp. dried oregano
1/4 tsp. chili powder
1 can sweet corn, drained
2 jalapeno peppers, chopped
2 cups water
2 limes, juiced

Directions:

Heat the canola oil in a skillet and stir in the tenderloin. Cook for 5 Min. on all sides.
Add the pork in your Slow Cooker and stir in the remaining ingredients, except the lime juice.
Add salt and pepper to taste and cook on low settings for 6 Hrs.
When done, stir in the lime juice and serve the soup warm or chilled.

Mexican Style Stew

Servings:6 Cooking Time: 6 Hrs.

Ingredients:

1 cup corn kernels
¼ cup white rice
1 tsp. taco seasoning
1 tbsp. butter
1 cup green peas
4 cups chicken stock
1 tsp. dried cilantro

Directions:

Put butter and wild rice in the Slow Cooker.
Then add corn kernels, green peas, chicken stock, taco seasoning, and dried cilantro.
Close the lid and cook the stew on Low for 6 Hrs.

Roasted Garlic Soup

Servings: 6 Cooking Time: 3 ½ Hrs.

Ingredients:

1 tbsp. extra-virgin olive oil
3 shallots, chopped
1 large head of cauliflower, chopped, about 5 cups
Sea salt to taste
2 bulbs of garlic
6 cups gluten-free vegetable broth
Fresh ground pepper to taste

Directions:

Preheat oven to 400°Fahrenheit. Peel the outer layers off garlic bulbs. Cut about 1/4 inch off the top of the bulbs, place into foil pan. Coat bulbs with olive oil, and cook in oven for 35 Min. Once cooked, allow them to cool. Squeeze the garlic out of the bulbs into your food processor. Meanwhile, in a pan, sauté remaining olive oil and chopped shallots over medium-high heat for about 6 Min. Add other ingredients to saucepan, cover and reduce heat to a simmer for 20 Min. or until the cauliflower is softened. Add the mixture to food processor and puree until smooth. Add mix to Slow Cooker, cover with lid, and cook on LOW for 3 ½ Hrs. Serve hot.

Tomato Beef Soup

Servings: 8 Cooking Time: 8 1/4 Hrs.

Ingredients:

2 tbsps. olive oil
2 lbs. beef roast, cubed
2 tomatoes, peeled and diced
1 cup beef stock
Salt and pepper to taste
1 rosemary sprig
2 bacon slices, chopped
2 sweet onions, chopped
2 cups tomato sauce
3 cups water
1 thyme sprig

Directions:

Heat the oil in a skillet and add the bacon. Cook until crisp and stir in the beef roast. Cook for 5 Min. on all sides.
Transfer the beet and bacon in a Slow Cooker.
Add the remaining ingredients and adjust the taste with salt and pepper.
Cook on low settings for 8 Hrs.
Serve the soup warm or chilled.

Chunky Pumpkin and Kale Soup

Servings: 6 Cooking Time: 6 1/2 Hrs.

Ingredients:

1 sweet onion, chopped
1/2 red chili, chopped
2 cups pumpkin cubes
2 cups water
1/2 tsp. cumin seeds
1 red bell pepper, cored and diced
2 tbsps. olive oil
2 cups vegetable stock
1 bunch kale, shredded
Salt and pepper to taste

Directions:

Combine the onion, bell pepper, chili and olive oil in your Slow Cooker.
Add the remaining ingredients and adjust the taste with salt and pepper.
Mix gently just to evenly distribute the ingredients then cook on low settings for 6 Hrs.
Serve the soup warm or chilled.

Butternut Squash Soup

Servings:5 Cooking Time: 7 Hrs.

Ingredients:

2 cups butternut squash, chopped
3 cups chicken stock
1 tsp. ground cardamom
1 cup carrot, chopped
1 cup heavy cream
1 tsp. ground cinnamon

Directions:

Put the butternut squash in the Slow Cooker.
Sprinkle it with ground cardamom and ground cinnamon.
Then add carrot and chicken stock.
Close the lid and cook the soup on High for 5 Hrs.
Then blend the soup until smooth with the help of the immersion blender and add heavy cream.
Cook the soup on high for 2 Hrs. more.

Ham and Sweet Potato Soup

Servings: 6 Cooking Time: 3 1/2 Hrs.

Ingredients:

1 1/2 cups diced ham
1 carrot, diced
1 parsnip, diced
2 cups chicken stock
1 bay leaf
Salt and pepper to taste
1 sweet onion, chopped
1 celery stalk, diced
2 large sweet potatoes, peeled and cubed
2 cups water
1 thyme sprig

Directions:

Combine all the ingredients in your Slow Cooker.
Add salt and pepper to taste and cook on high settings for 3 Hrs.
Serve the soup warm and fresh.

Mexican Style Soup

Servings:6 Cooking Time: 5 Hrs.

Ingredients:

1-pound chicken fillet, cut into strips
6 cups chicken stock
1 cup tomatoes, chopped
¼ cup fresh cilantro, chopped
2 tbsps. enchilada sauce
1 cup black beans, soaked
1 tsp. garlic powder

Directions:

Put all ingredients in the Slow Cooker and close the lid.
Cook the soup on high for 5 Hrs.
When the time is finished, open the lid and carefully mix the soup with the help of the ladle.

Barley Stew

Servings:4 Cooking Time: 9 Hrs.

Ingredients:

½ cup barley
1 cup zucchini, chopped
½ carrot, diced
4 cups chicken stock
1 tbsp. tomato paste
1 tsp. salt

Directions:

Put all ingredients in the Slow Cooker and carefully stir.
Cook the stew on low for 9 Hrs.

Cream Of Broccoli Soup

Servings: 6 Cooking Time: 2 1/4 Hrs.

Ingredients:

2 shallots, chopped
2 tbsps. olive oil
2 potatoes, peeled and cubed
2 cups water
1/2 tsp. dried basil
2 garlic cloves, chopped
1 head broccoli, cut into florets
1 cup chicken stock
Salt and pepper to taste
1/2 tsp. dried oregano

Directions:

Heat the oil in a skillet and stir in the shallots and garlic. Sauté for a few Min. until softened then transfer in your Slow Cooker.
Add the broccoli, potatoes, chicken stock and water, as well as dried herbs, salt and pepper.
Cook on high settings for 2 Hrs. then puree the soup in a blender until creamy and rich.
Pour the soup into bowls in order to serve.

Black Bean Soup

Servings: 8 Cooking Time: 7 1/4 Hrs.

Ingredients:

1/2 lb. black beans, rinsed
5 cups water
2 carrots, diced
1 celery stalk, diced
2 tomatoes, diced
1/2 tsp. cumin powder
1 bay leaf
2 tbsps. chopped cilantro for serving
2 cups chicken stock
1 sweet onion, chopped
1 parsnip, diced
1 red bell peppers, cored and diced
2 tbsps. tomato paste
1/4 tsp. chili powder
Salt and pepper to taste
1/2 cup sour cream for serving

Directions:

Combine the black beans, chicken stock, water and vegetables in your Slow Cooker.
Add the cumin powder, chili powder, bay leaf, salt and pepper and cook the soup on low settings for 7 Hrs.
When done, stir in the cilantro. Pour the soup in bowls and top with sour cream just before serving.

Lamb Stew

Servings:5 Cooking Time: 5 Hrs.

Ingredients:

1 lb. lamb meat, cubed
1 tsp. cayenne pepper
½ tsp. dried thyme
4 cups of water
1 red onion, sliced
1 tsp. dried rosemary
1 cup potatoes, chopped

Directions:

Sprinkle the lamb meat with cayenne pepper, dried rosemary, and dried thyme.
Transfer the meat in the Slow Cooker.
Add water, onion, and potatoes.
Close the lid and cook the stew on high for 5 Hrs.

Tuscan White Bean Soup

Servings: 6 Cooking Time: 6 1/2 Hrs.

Ingredients:

1 cup dried white beans
4 cups water
1 celery stalk, diced
2 tbsps. tomato paste
2 cups spinach, shredded
1 tsp. dried oregano
1/2 lemon, juiced
2 cups chicken stock
1 carrot, diced
4 garlic cloves, chopped
1 bay leaf
Salt and pepper to taste
1 tsp. dried basil

Directions:

Combine the beans, stock, water, carrot, celery, garlic and tomato paste in your Slow Cooker.
Add the bay leaf, dried herbs and lemon juice, as well as salt and pepper.
Cook on low settings for 4 Hrs. then add the spinach and cook for 2 additional Hrs. on low settings.
Serve the soup warm or chilled.

Chicken Wild Rice Soup

Servings: 6 Cooking Time: 6 1/2 Hrs.

Ingredients:

3/4 cup wild rice, rinsed
2 celery stalks, sliced
1 sweet onion, chopped
1/2 tsp. dried oregano
1/2 cup half and half
1 lb. chicken breasts, cubed
2 carrots, sliced
6 cups chicken stock
1 tbsp. butter
Salt and pepper to taste

Directions:

Combine all the ingredients in your Slow Cooker.
Add salt and pepper to taste and cook on low settings for 6 Hrs.
When done, serve the soup warm and fresh.

Summer Vegetable Soup

Servings: 8 Cooking Time: 6 1/2 Hrs.

Ingredients:

1 sweet onion, chopped
2 tbsps. olive oil
1 yellow squash, cubed
1/2 head broccoli, cut into florets
1 carrot, sliced
1/2 cup edamame
5 cups water
1 lemon, juiced
1 garlic clove, chopped
1 zucchini, cubed
1/2 head cauliflower, cut into florets
2 ripe tomatoes, peeled and cubed
1 celery stalk, sliced
2 cups chicken stock
Salt and pepper to taste
1 tbsp. chopped parsley

Directions:

Combine the onion, garlic, olive oil and the rest of the ingredients in your Slow Cooker.
Add salt and pepper to taste and cook on low settings for 6 Hrs.
When done, stir in the lemon juice and parsley and serve the soup warm or chilled.

Tomato Chickpeas Stew

Servings:4 Cooking Time: 7 Hrs.

Ingredients:

2 tbsps. tomato paste
5 cups of water
½ cup fresh parsley, chopped
1 carrot, chopped
1 cup chickpeas, soaked
1 yellow onion, chopped
1 tsp. ground black pepper

Directions:

Mix tomato paste with water and pour in the Slow Cooker.
Add chickpeas, onion, parsley, ground black pepper, and carrot.
Close the lid and cook the stew on Low for 7 Hrs.

Bacon Cheeseburger Soup

Servings: 8 Cooking Time: 6 1/2 Hrs.

Ingredients:

4 bacon slices, chopped
1 large sweet onion, chopped
1 lb. ground beef
2 carrots, diced

1 celery stalk, sliced
1 cup diced tomatoes
1/2 tsp. dried oregano
2 cups beef stock
Salt and pepper to taste
2 potatoes, peeled and cubed
1/2 tsp. dried thyme
1 cup cream cheese
5 cups water
Processed cheese for serving

Directions:

Heat the bacon in a skillet and cook until crisp. Add the beef and cook for a few Min., stirring often.
Add the remaining ingredients and season with salt and pepper.
Cook on low settings for 6 Hrs.
The soup is best served warm, topped with shredded processed cheese.

Broccoli Cheese Soup

Servings: 6 Cooking Time: 6 Hrs. 20 Min

Ingredients:

1½ cups heavy cream
½ cup red bell pepper, chopped
2 tbsps. chives, chopped
2 tbsps. butter
8 oz. cheddar cheese, shredded
¼ tsp. cayenne pepper
2½ cups water
2 cups broccoli, chopped, thawed and drained
¾ tsp. salt
½ tsp. dry mustard
4 cups chicken broth

Directions:

Put all the ingredients in a Slow Cooker except chives and cheese and mix well.
Cover and cook on LOW for about 6 Hrs.
Sprinkle with cheese and cook on LOW for about 30 Min.
Garnish with chives and serve hot.

Creamy Edamame Soup

Servings: 6 Cooking Time: 2 1/4 Hrs.

Ingredients:

1 tbsp. olive oil
2 garlic cloves, chopped
1 celery root, peeled and cubed
Salt and pepper to taste
1 cup water
1/4 tsp. dried marjoram
2 shallots, chopped
1 large potato, peeled and cubed
1 lb. frozen edamame
2 cups chicken stock
1/4 tsp. dried oregano

Directions:

Heat the oil in a skillet and stir in the shallots and garlic. Sauté for 2 Min. until softened then transfer in your Slow Cooker.
Add the remaining ingredients and season with salt and pepper.
Cook on high settings for 2 Hrs.
When done, puree the soup with an immersion blender until creamy.
Serve the soup right away.

Beans Stew

Servings:3 Cooking Time: 5 Hrs.

Ingredients:

½ cup sweet pepper, chopped
1 cup edamame beans
1 tsp. cayenne pepper
¼ cup onion, chopped
1 cup tomatoes
5 cups of water
2 tbsps. cream cheese

Directions:

Mix water with cream cheese and pour the liquid in the Slow Cooker.
Add cayenne pepper, edamame beans, and onion.
Then chop the tomatoes roughly and add in the Slow Cooker.
Close the lid and cook the stew on high for 5 Hrs.

Creamy Potato Soup

Servings: 6 Cooking Time: 6 1/2 Hrs.

Ingredients:

6 bacon slices, chopped
1 can condensed chicken soup
2 cups water
1 1/2 cups half and half
1 sweet onion, chopped
6 medium size potatoes, peeled and cubed
Salt and pepper to taste
1 tbsp. chopped parsley

Directions:

Heat a skillet over medium flame and add the bacon. Cook until crisp then transfer the bacon and its fat in your Slow Cooker.
Add the onion, chicken soup, potatoes, water, salt and pepper and cook on low settings for 4 Hrs.
Add the half and half and continue cooking for 2 additional Hrs.
When done, stir in the chopped parsley and serve the soup warm.

Beef Liver Stew

Servings:3 Cooking Time: 7 Hrs.

Ingredients:

6 oz. beef liver, cut into strips
1 tbsp. olive oil
½ cup of water
1 tsp. ground black pepper
2 tbsps. all-purpose flour
½ cup sour cream
1 onion, roughly chopped

Directions:

Mix beef liver with flour and roast it in the olive oil on high heat for 2 Min. per side.
Then transfer the liver in the Slow Cooker.
Add all remaining ingredients and close the lid.
Cook the stew on low for 7 Hrs.

Mexican Beef Soup

Servings: 6 Cooking Time: 8 1/4 Hrs.

Ingredients:

1 lb. ground beef
2 red bell peppers, cored and diced
2 cups beef stock
1 can (15 oz.) black beans, drained
1/2 cup red salsa
Salt and pepper to taste
2 tbsps. canola oil
1 sweet onion, chopped
1 can (15 oz.) diced tomatoes
3 cups water
1 chipotle pepper, chopped

Directions:

Heat the oil in a skillet and stir in the beef. Cook for 5 Min, stirring often, then transfer the beef in your Slow Cooker.
Add the remaining ingredients and adjust the taste with salt and pepper.
Cook on low settings for 8 Hrs.

Serve the soup warm or chilled.

Spicy Black Bean Soup

Servings: 6 Cooking Time: 6 1/4 Hrs.

Ingredients:

1 tbsp. olive oil
1 carrot, diced
2 cups chicken stock
4 cups water
1/2 tsp. cumin powder
Salt and pepper to taste
1 shallot, chopped
2 jalapeno peppers, chopped
1 can (15 oz.) black beans, drained
1/2 tsp. chili powder
1/2 cup diced tomatoes
1/2 cup sour cream

Directions:

Combine the olive oil, shallot, carrot, jalapeno peppers, stock, beans, water and spices in your Slow Cooker.
Add salt and pepper to taste and cook on low settings for 6 Hrs.
Cook on low settings for6 Hrs.
Serve the soup warm, topped with sour cream.

Garlicky Spinach Soup with Herbed Croutons

Servings: 6 Cooking Time: 2 1/4 Hrs.

Ingredients:

1 lb. fresh spinach, shredded
1 shallot, chopped
1/2 celery stalk, sliced
2 cups chicken stock
1 lemon, juiced
10 oz. one-day old bread, cubed
1 tsp. dried basil
1/2 tsp. dried oregano
4 garlic cloves, chopped
2 cups water
Salt and pepper to taste
1/2 cup half and half
3 tbsps. olive oil
1 tsp. dried marjoram

Directions:

Combine the spinach, oregano, shallot, garlic and celery in your Slow Cooker.
Add the water, stock and lemon juice, as well as salt and pepper to taste and cook on high settings for 2 Hrs.
While the soup is cooking, place the bread cubes in a large baking tray and drizzle with olive oil. Sprinkle with salt and pepper and cook in the preheated oven at 375F for 10-12 Min. until crispy and golden.
When the soup is done, puree it with an immersion blender, adding the half and half while doing so.
Serve the soup warm, topped with herbed croutons.

Jamaican Stew

Servings:8 Cooking Time: 1 Hr.

Ingredients:

1 tbsp. coconut oil
½ cup bell pepper, sliced
1-pound salmon fillet, chopped
½ tsp. ground cumin
1 tsp. garlic powder
½ cup heavy cream
1 tsp. ground coriander

Directions:

Put the coconut oil in the Slow Cooker.
Then mix the salmon with ground cumin and ground coriander and put in the Slow Cooker.
Add the layer of bell pepper and sprinkle with garlic powder.
Add heavy cream and close the lid.
Cook the stew on High for 1 Hr.

Hearty Turkey Chili

Servings: 5 Cooking Time: 8 Hrs. 15 Min

Ingredients:

¼ cup olive oil
½ tsp. salt
2 tsps. dried marjoram
1 green pepper, chopped
2 tbsps. chili powder
1 can no-salt-added tomatoes
1 lb. ground turkey breast
1 can white beans, drained and rinsed
1 large onion, chopped
1 can diced tomatoes
4 garlic cloves, minced

Directions:

Put olive oil, green peppers, onions and garlic in the Slow Cooker and sauté for about 3 Min.
Add rest of the ingredients and cover the lid.
Cook on LOW for about 8 Hrs. and dish out in a bowl to serve hot.

Creamy Tortellini Soup

Servings: 6 Cooking Time: 6 1/4 Hrs.

Ingredients:

1 shallot, chopped
1/2 lb. mushrooms, sliced
2 cups chicken stock
1/2 tsp. dried oregano
1 cup evaporated milk
Salt and pepper to taste
1 garlic clove, chopped
1 can condensed cream of mushroom soup
1 cup water
1/2 tsp. dried basil
7 oz. cheese tortellini

Directions:

Combine the shallot, garlic, mushrooms, cream of mushroom soup, stock, water, dried herbs and milk in your Slow Cooker.
Add the cheese tortellini and season with salt and pepper.
Cook on low settings for 6 Hrs.
Serve the soup warm.

Paprika Hominy Stew

Servings:4 Cooking Time: 4 Hrs.

Ingredients:

2 cups hominy, canned
1 tsp. hot sauce
½ cup ground chicken
1 tbsp. smoked paprika
½ cup full-fat cream
1 cup of water

Directions:

Carefully mix all ingredients in the Slow Cooker and close the lid.
Cook the stew on high for 4 Hrs.

Lentil Soup with Garlic Topping

Servings: 8 Cooking Time: 6 1/2 Hrs.

Ingredients:

Soup:
1/2 cup red lentils, rinsed
1 shallot, chopped
1 carrot, diced
1/2 cup tomato sauce
2 cups water
Salt and pepper to taste
1/2 cup green lentils, rinsed
1 celery stalk, sliced
1 red bell pepper, cored and diced
1 bay leaf
2 cups chicken stock
Topping:

3 garlic cloves, chopped
2 tomatoes, peeled and diced
1 tbsp. olive oil
2 tbsps. chopped parsley
Salt and pepper to taste

Directions:

To make the soup, combine all the ingredients in your Slow Cooker.
Add salt and pepper to taste and cook on low settings for 6 Hrs.
For the topping, mix the garlic, parsley, tomatoes, salt, pepper and olive oil in a bowl.
Pour the warm soup into serving bowls and top with the tomato and garlic topping.
Serve right away.

Clam Soup

Servings:2 Cooking Time:1.5 Hrs.

Ingredients:

¼ tsp. ground black pepper
3 cups fish stock
1 oz. scallions, chopped
½ tsp. dried thyme
¼ tsp. chili flakes
8 oz. clams, canned
2 tbsps. sour cream

Directions:

Pour fish stock in the Slow Cooker.
Add canned clams, chili flakes, ground black pepper, scallions, and dried thyme.
Add sour cream and dried thyme.
Cook the soup on High for 1.5 Hrs.

Creamy Spinach Tortellini Soup

Servings: 8 Cooking Time: 6 1/4 Hrs.

Ingredients:

1 chicken breast, diced
2 shallots, chopped
2 cups tomato sauce
1 can condensed mushroom soup
1 cup water
Salt and pepper to taste
1 tbsp. olive oil
2 garlic cloves, chopped
4 cups chicken stock
2 cups sliced mushrooms
8 oz. spinach tortellini

Directions:

Heat the oil in a skillet and add the chicken. Cook on all sides for 5 Min. then transfer in your Slow Cooker.
Add the remaining ingredients and continue cooking on low settings for 6 Hrs.
The soup is best served warm, either fresh or re-heated.

Cabbage Stew

Servings:2 Cooking Time: 3 Hrs.

Ingredients:

2 cups white cabbage, shredded
1 tsp. ground white pepper
½ cup potato, chopped
½ cup tomato juice
1 cup cauliflower, chopped
1 cup of water

Directions:

Put cabbage, potato, and cauliflower in the Slow Cooker.
Add tomato juice, ground white pepper, and water. Stir the stew ingredients and close the lid.
Cook the stew on high for 3 Hrs.

Chicken Chili

Servings:4 Cooking Time: 5 Hrs.

Ingredients:

2 cups ground chicken
1 yellow onion, chopped
1 tsp. dried basil
3 cups of water
1 chili pepper, chopped
2 tbsps. tomato paste
½ tsp. ground coriander

Directions:

Mix ground chicken with dried basil and ground coriander.
Then transfer the chicken in the Slow Cooker.
Add onion, chili pepper, tomato paste, and water. Carefully stir the mixture and close the lid.
Cook the chili on high for 5 Hrs.

Chunky Potato Ham Soup

Servings: 8 Cooking Time: 8 1/2 Hrs.

Ingredients:

2 cups diced ham
1 garlic clove, chopped
1 celery stalk, sliced
2 lbs. potatoes, peeled and cubed
1/2 tsp. dried basil
3 cups water
1 sweet onion, chopped
1 leek, sliced
2 carrots, sliced
1/2 tsp. dried oregano
2 cups chicken stock
Salt and pepper to taste

Directions:

Combine all the ingredients in your Slow Cooker.
Add salt and pepper to taste and cook on low settings for 8 Hrs.
Serve the soup warm or chilled.

Lemony Salmon Soup

Servings: 6 Cooking Time: 4 1/4 Hrs.

Ingredients:

1 shallot, chopped
1 celery stalk, sliced
1 parsnip, sliced
1/2 tsp. dried oregano
2 cups milk
1 lemon, juiced
1 lb. salmon fillets, cubed
1 garlic clove, chopped
1 carrot, sliced
1 red bell pepper, cored and diced
1/2 tsp. dried basil
2 cups water
1 tsp. lemon zest
Salt and pepper to taste

Directions:

Combine the shallot, garlic, celery, carrot, parsnip and bell pepper in your Slow Cooker.
Add the dried herbs, milk, water, lemon juice and lemon zest and cook for 1 Hr. on high settings.
Add the fish and season with salt and pepper.
Cook for 3 additional Hrs. on low settings.
Serve the soup warm or chilled.

Hot and Sour Soup

Servings: 8 Cooking Time: 7 1/2 Hrs.

Ingredients:

2 oz. dried shiitake mushrooms
1 can (8 oz.) bamboo shoots, drained
1 sweet onion, chopped
1/2 head green cabbage, shredded
1 lb. fresh mushrooms, sliced
2 carrots, sliced
14 oz. tofu, cubed
1 tsp. grated ginger

1/2 tsp. chili flakes
5 cups water
2 tbsps. rice vinegar
2 cups chicken stock
2 tbsps. soy sauce
2 green onions, sliced

Directions:

Place the shiitake mushrooms in a bowl and cover them with boiling water. Allow to rehydrate for 10 Min. then chop and place in your Slow Cooker.

Add the remaining ingredients, except the green onions and cook on low settings for 7 Hrs.

When done, stir in the green onions and serve right away.

Lentil Stew

Servings:4 Cooking Time: 6 Hrs.

Ingredients:

2 cups chicken stock
1 eggplant, chopped
1 cup of water
½ cup red lentils
1 tbsp. tomato paste
1 tsp. Italian seasonings

Directions:

Mix chicken stock with red lentils and tomato paste.

Pour the mixture in the Slow Cooker.

Add eggplants and Italian seasonings.

Cook the stew on low for 6 Hrs.

Light Zucchini Soup

Servings:4 Cooking Time: 30 Min

Ingredients:

1 large zucchini
4 cups beef broth
½ tsp. dried rosemary
1 white onion, diced
1 tsp. dried thyme

Directions:

Pour the beef broth in the Slow Cooker.

Add onion, dried thyme, and dried rosemary.

After this, make the spirals from the zucchini with the help of the spiralizer and transfer them in the Slow Cooker.

Close the lid and cook the sou on High for 30 Min.

Mexican Chicken Stew

Servings: 6 Cooking Time: 9 Hrs. 20 Min

Ingredients:

3 chicken breasts, boneless and skinless
1 can corn
½ cup sour cream
½ cup Mexican cheese, shredded
1 can black beans, not drained
2 cans diced tomatoes and chilies
1 cup onions, optional

Directions:

Place chicken breasts at the bottom of the Slow Cooker and top with tomatoes, beans and corns.

Cover and cook on LOW for about 9 Hrs.

Dish out and serve hot.

French Onion Soup

Servings: 6 Cooking Time: 1 3/4 Hrs.

Ingredients:

4 sweet onions, sliced
2 tbsps. butter
1 tbsp. canola oil
4 cups beef stock
1 tbsp. red wine vinegar
1 thyme sprig
Toasted bread for serving
1 tsp. brown sugar
2 cups water
Salt and pepper to taste
1 rosemary sprig
Grated Gruyere cheese for serving

Directions:

Heat the butter and oil in a skillet and stir in the onion. Cook for 10-15 Min. until they begin to caramelize, adding the brown sugar half way through the cooking time. This step is compulsory as caramelizing the onions improves their taste.

Transfer the onions in your Slow Cooker and add the stock, water, red wine vinegar, thyme and rosemary.

Season with salt and pepper and cook on high settings for 1 1/2 Hrs.

For serving, pour the hot soup into bowls and top right away with a slice of toasted bread and plenty of grated cheese.

Serve right away.

Beef Chili

Servings: 8 Cooking Time: 3 Hrs. 15 Min

Ingredients:

29 oz. canned diced tomatoes, not drained
1 yellow onion, chopped
¼ cup tomato paste
1 jalapeno, minced
2 (16-oz) cans red kidney beans, rinsed and drained
1 tsp. ground cumin
3 tbsps. chili powder
2 lbs. lean ground beef
½ cup saltine cracker crumbs, finely ground
3 garlic cloves, minced
1 tsp. Kosher salt
1 tsp. black pepper

Directions:

Cook onions and beef over medium high heat in a pot until brown.

Transfer to the Slow Cooker along with the rest of the ingredients.

Cover and cook on HIGH for about 3 Hrs. and dish out to serve.

Tomato Fish Soup

Servings: 6 Cooking Time: 3 1/2 Hrs.

Ingredients:

1 shallot, chopped
1 tbsp. olive oil
2 cups vegetable stock
1 bay leaf
Salt and pepper to taste
2 haddock fillets, cubed
2 garlic cloves, chopped
4 ripe tomatoes, pureed
1 cup water
1 lemon, juiced
1 lb. salmon fillets, cubed

Directions:

Heat the oil in a skillet and stir in the shallot and garlic. Sauté for 2 Min. until softened then transfer in your Slow Cooker.

Stir in the tomato puree, stock, water, bay leaf and lemon juice and season with salt and pepper.

Cook on high settings for 1 Hr. then add the fish and continue cooking for 2 additional Hrs.

Serve the soup warm or chilled.

Ginger and Sweet Potato Stew

Servings:3 Cooking Time: 7 Hrs.

Ingredients:

1 cup sweet potatoes, chopped
1 cup bell pepper, cut into the strips
1 tsp. ground cumin
½ tsp. ground ginger
1 apple, chopped
2 cups beef broth

Directions:

Mix ingredients in the Slow Cooker.
Close the lid and cook the stew on Low for 7 Hrs.

Barley Soup

Servings:5 Cooking Time: 8 Hrs.

Ingredients:

¼ cup barley
4 oz. pork tenderloin, chopped
1 tbsp. tomato paste
½ cup heavy cream
5 cups chicken stock
1 tbsp. dried cilantro
3 oz. carrot, grated

Directions:

Put pork tenderloin in the Slow Cooker.
Add barley, chicken stock, tomato paste, carrot, and heavy cream.
Carefully stir the soup mixture and close the lid.
Cook it on Low for 8 Hrs.

Chorizo Soup

Servings:6 Cooking Time: 5 Hrs.

Ingredients:

9 oz. chorizo, chopped
1 cup potato, chopped
1 zucchini, chopped
1 tsp. salt
7 cups of water
1 tsp. minced garlic, chopped
½ cup spinach, chopped

Directions:

Put the chorizo in the skillet and roast it for 2 Min. per side on high heat.
Then transfer the chorizo in the Slow Cooker.
Add water, potato, minced garlic, zucchini, spinach, and salt.
Close the lid and cook the soup on high for 5 Hrs.
Then cool the soup to the room temperature.

Summer Squash Chickpea Soup

Servings: 6 Cooking Time: 2 1/2 Hrs.

Ingredients:

1 sweet onion, chopped
1 carrot, diced
2 summer squashes, cubed
2 cups chicken stock
1 cup diced tomatoes
1 thyme sprig
1 lemon, juiced
1 tbsp. chopped parsley
1 garlic clove, chopped
1 celery stalk, sliced
1 can (15 oz.) chickpeas, drained
3 cups water
1 bay leaf
Salt and pepper to taste
1 tbsp. chopped cilantro

Directions:

Combine the onion, garlic, celery, carrot, summer squash, chickpeas, stock and water in your Slow Cooker.
Add the tomatoes, bay leaf, thyme, salt and pepper and cook on high settings for 2 Hrs.
When done, stir in the lemon juice, parsley and cilantro and serve the soup warm.

Indian Cauliflower Creamy Soup

Servings: 8 Cooking Time: 6 1/2 Hrs.

Ingredients:

2 tbsps. olive oil
1 celery stalk, sliced
1 tbsp. red curry paste
2 medium size potatoes, peeled and cubed
2 cups water
1 pinch red pepper flakes
1 sweet onion, chopped
2 garlic cloves, chopped
1 cauliflower head, cut into florets
2 cups vegetable stock
1/4 tsp. cumin powder
Salt and pepper to taste

Directions:

Heat the oil in a skillet and stir in the onion, celery and garlic. Sauté for 2 Min. until softened. Transfer the mix in your Slow Cooker.
Add the remaining ingredients and cook on low settings for 6 Hrs.
When done, puree the soup with an immersion blender and serve it warm.

Shrimp Soup

Servings: 6 Cooking Time: 6 1/4 Hrs.

Ingredients:

2 tbsps. olive oil
1 fennel bulb, sliced
1 cup dry white wine
2 cup water
1 tsp. dried basil
4 medium size tomatoes, peeled and diced
1/2 lb. cod fillets, cubed
Salt and pepper to taste
1 large sweet onion, chopped
4 garlic cloves, chopped
1/2 cup tomato sauce
1 tsp. dried oregano
1 pinch chili powder
1 bay leaf
1/2 lb. fresh shrimps, peeled and deveined
1 lime, juiced

Directions:

Heat the oil in a skillet and stir in the onion, fennel and garlic. Sauté for 5 Min. until softened.
Transfer the mixture in your Slow Cooker and stir in the wine, tomato sauce, water, oregano, basil, chili powder, tomatoes and bay leaf.
Cook on high settings for 1 Hr. then add the cod and shrimps, as well as lime juice, salt and pepper and continue cooking on low settings for 5 additional Hrs.
Serve the soup warm or chilled.

Ham Potato Chowder

Servings: 8 Cooking Time: 4 1/4 Hrs.

Ingredients:

1 tbsp. olive oil
1 can condensed chicken soup
4 potatoes, peeled and cubed
1 cup sweet corn, drained
1/2 tsp. cumin seeds
1 sweet onion, chopped
2 cups water
1 cup diced ham
1/2 tsp. celery seeds
Salt and pepper to taste

Directions:

Mix the olive oil, onion, chicken soup, water, potatoes, ham and corn in your Slow Cooker.
Add the celery seeds and cumin seeds and season with salt and pepper.

Cook on high settings for 4 Hrs.
Serve the soup warm.

Beef Mushroom Soup

Servings: 8 Cooking Time: 8 1/2 Hrs.

Ingredients:

1 lb. beef roast, cubed
1 sweet onion, chopped
1 lb. mushrooms, sliced
2 cups beef stock
1 bay leaf
1/2 tsp. caraway seeds
2 tbsps. canola oil
2 garlic cloves, chopped
1 can fire roasted tomatoes
5 cups water
1 thyme sprig
Salt and pepper to taste

Directions:

Heat the oil in a skillet and stir in the beef roast. Cook on all sides for a few Min. then transfer in your Slow Cooker.
Add the onion, garlic, mushrooms, tomatoes, stock and water, as well as bay leaf and thyme sprig, plus the caraway seeds.
Season with salt and pepper and cook on low settings for 8 Hrs.
The soup is best served warm.

Taco Soup

Servings:3 Cooking Time: 8 Hrs.

Ingredients:

1 cup ground chicken
1 tomato, chopped
1 jalapeno pepper, sliced
¼ cup black olives, sliced
3 cup chicken stock
¼ cup corn kernels
1 tbsp. taco seasoning
3 corn tortillas, chopped

Directions:

Put the ground chicken in the Slow Cooker.
Add chicken stock, tomato, corn kernels, jalapeno pepper, taco seasoning, and black olives.
Close the lid and cook the soup on low for 8 Hrs.
When the soup is cooked, ladle it in the bowls and top with chopped tortillas.

Pork and Corn Soup

Servings: 8 Cooking Time: 8 1/4 Hrs.

Ingredients:

1 lb. pork roast, cubed
2 bacon slices, chopped
2 carrots, sliced
2 yellow bell peppers, cored and diced
1/2 tsp. cumin seeds
2 cups chicken stock
Salt and pepper to taste
1 sweet onion, chopped
1 garlic clove, chopped
1 celery stalk, sliced
2 cups frozen sweet corn
1/2 red chili, sliced
4 cups water
2 tbsps. chopped cilantro

Directions:

Combine the pork roast, sweet onion, bacon and garlic in a skillet and cook for 5 Min, stirring all the time.
Transfer in your Slow Cooker and add the carrots, celery, bell peppers, sweet corn, cumin seeds, red chili, stock, water, salt and pepper.
Cook on low settings for 8 Hrs.
When done, add the chopped cilantro and serve the soup warm.

Southwestern Turkey Stew

Servings: 6 Cooking Time: 7 Hrs. 15 Min

Ingredients:

½ cup red kidney beans
2 cups diced canned tomatoes
1 cup red bell peppers, sliced
½ cup sour cream
1 garlic clove, minced
½ cup corn
15 oz. ground turkey
½ medium onion, diced
½ cup cheddar cheese, shredded
1½ medium red potatoes, cubed

Directions:

Put all the ingredients in a bowl except sour cream and cheddar cheese.
Transfer into the Slow Cooker and cook on LOW for about 7 Hrs.
Stir in the sour cream and cheddar cheese.
Dish out in a bowl and serve hot.

Bean Medley Soup

Servings: 10 Cooking Time: 8 1/2 Hrs.

Ingredients:

2 sweet onions, chopped
1 celery stalk, sliced
2 red bell peppers, cored and diced
1/4 cup dried kidney beans
1/2 cup dried white beans
1 can fire roasted tomatoes
6 cups water
Salt and pepper to taste
2 carrots, diced
1 parsnip, diced
1/4 cup dried black beans
1/4 cup dried cannellini beans
1/4 cup dried chickpeas
2 cups chicken stock
1 bay leaf

Directions:

Combine all the ingredients in your Slow Cooker.
Add salt and pepper to taste and cook on low settings for 8 Hrs.
Serve the soup warm or chilled.

Kielbasa Kale Soup

Servings: 8 Cooking Time: 6 1/4 Hrs.

Ingredients:

1 lb. kielbasa sausages, sliced
1 carrot, diced
1 red bell pepper, cored and diced
1 cup diced tomatoes
2 cups chicken stock
1/2 tsp. dried oregano
Salt and pepper to taste
1 sweet onion, chopped
1 parsnip, diced
1 can (15 oz.) white beans, drained
1/2 lb. kale, shredded
2 cups water
1/2 tsp. dried basil

Directions:

Combine the kielbasa sausages, onion, carrot, parsnip, bell pepper, white beans, tomatoes and kale in a Slow Cooker.
Add the remaining ingredients and season with salt and pepper.
Cook on low settings for 6 Hrs.
Serve the soup warm or chilled.

Thick Green Lentil Soup

Servings: 8 Cooking Time: 6 1/4 Hrs.

Ingredients:

1 cup dried green lentils, rinsed
1/2 cup red lentils, rinsed
2 cups chicken stock
4 cups water
1/2 tsp. cumin powder
1/4 tsp. chili powder
1/2 tsp. dried oregano
1 celery stalk, chopped
1 shallot, chopped
Salt and pepper to taste
2 tbsps. lemon juice
1 tbsp. chopped parsley

Directions:

Combine the lentils, stock, water, cumin powder, chili, oregano, celery and shallot in your Slow Cooker.
Add salt and pepper to taste and cook on low settings for 6 Hrs.
When done, stir in the lemon juice and parsley and serve right away.

Green Peas Chowder

Servings:6 Cooking Time: 8 Hrs.

Ingredients:

1-pound chicken breast, skinless, boneless, chopped
6 cups of water
1 cup green peas
¼ cup Greek Yogurt
1 tbsp. dried basil
1 tsp. ground black pepper
½ tsp. salt

Directions:

Mix salt, chicken breast, ground black pepper, and dried basil.
Transfer the ingredients in the Slow Cooker.
Add water, green peas, yogurt, and close the lid.
Cook the chowder on Low for 8 Hrs.

Bouillabaisse Soup

Servings: 8 Cooking Time: 6 1/2 Hrs.

Ingredients:

1 shallot, chopped
2 garlic cloves, chopped
1 red bell pepper, cored and diced
1 carrot, diced
1 fennel bulb, sliced
1 cup diced tomatoes
2 cups vegetable stock
2 large potatoes, peeled and cubed
1 celery stalk, sliced
1/2 lemon, juiced
1 lb. haddock fillets, cubed
Salt and pepper to taste
1 tbsp. chopped parsley

Directions:

Combine the shallot, garlic, bell pepper, carrot, fennel, tomatoes and stock in your Slow Cooker.
Add the potatoes, celery, lemon juice, salt and pepper and cook on high settings for 1 Hr.
Add the haddock fillets and continue cooking for 5 Min. on low settings.
Serve the soup warm, topped with chopped parsley

Vegetable & Vegetarian Recipes

Marinated Poached Aubergines

Servings:6 Cooking Time: 4 Hrs.

Ingredients:

½ cup apple cider vinegar
1-pound eggplants, chopped
1 cup of water
¼ cup avocado oil
3 garlic cloves, diced
1 tsp. salt
1 tsp. sugar

Directions:

Put all ingredients in the Slow Cooker.
Cook the meal on Low for 4 Hrs.
Cool the cooked aubergines well.

Rainbow Bake

Servings:4 Cooking Time: 6 Hrs.

Ingredients:

1 zucchini, sliced
1 tomato, sliced
1 eggplant, sliced
1 red onion, sliced
1 tbsp. coconut oil
1 tsp. salt
1 tsp. dried parsley
1 tsp. chili powder
1 cup of water

Directions:

Carefully grease the Slow Cooker bowl with coconut oil.
Then put zucchini, tomato, eggplant, and onion in the Slow Cooker one-by-one.
Sprinkle the vegetables with salt, dried parsley, and chili powder.
Add water and close the lid.
Cook the meal on Low for 6 Hrs.

White Beans Luncheon

Servings: 10 Cooking Time: 4 Hrs.

Ingredients:

2 lbs. white beans
3 celery stalks, chopped
2 carrots, chopped
1 bay leaf
1 yellow onion, chopped
3 garlic cloves, minced
1 tsp. rosemary, dried
1 tsp. oregano, dried
1 tsp. thyme, dried
10 cups water
Salt and black pepper to the taste
28 oz. canned tomatoes, chopped
6 cups chard, chopped

Directions:

Add beans, carrots, and all other ingredients to a Slow Cooker.
Put the cooker's lid on and set the cooking time to 4 Hrs. on High settings.
Serve warm.

Spicy Okra

Servings:2 Cooking Time: 1.5 Hrs.

Ingredients:

2 cups okra, sliced
½ cup vegetable stock
1 tsp. chili powder
½ tsp. ground turmeric
1 tsp. chili flakes
1 tsp. dried oregano
1 tbsp. butter

Directions:

Put okra in the Slow Cooker.
Add vegetable stock, chili powder, ground turmeric, chili flakes, and dried oregano.
Cook the okra on High for 1.5 Hrs.
Then add butter and stir the cooked okra well.

Creamy Puree

Servings:4 Cooking Time: 4 Hrs.

Ingredients:

2 cups potatoes, chopped
1 tbsp. vegan butter
1 tsp. salt
3 cups of water
¼ cup cream

Directions:

Pour water in the Slow Cooker.
Add potatoes and salt.
Cook the vegetables on high for 4 Hrs.
Then drain water, add butter, and cream.
Mash the potatoes until smooth.

Coconut Milk Lentils Bowl

Servings:5 Cooking Time: 9 Hrs.

Ingredients:

2 cups brown lentils
3 cups of water
1 tsp. salt
3 cups of coconut milk
1 tsp. ground nutmeg

Directions:

Mix the brown lentils with salt and ground nutmeg and put in the Slow Cooker.
Add coconut milk and water.
Close the lid and cook the lentils on Low for 9 Hrs.

Cauliflower Mac and Cheese

Servings:6 Cooking Time: 4 Hrs.

Ingredients:

1 large cauliflower, cut into small florets
2 tbsps. butter
2 oz. grass-fed cream cheese
1 tbsp. garlic powder
Salt and pepper to taste
1 ½ cup organic sharp cheddar cheese
1 cup heavy cream
1 ½ tsps. Dijon mustard
½ cup nutritional yeast

Directions:

Place all ingredients in the Slow Cooker.
Give a good stir.
Close the lid and cook on high for 3 Hrs. or on low for 4 Hrs.

Sweet Potato and Lentils Pate

Servings:4 Cooking Time: 6 Hrs.

Ingredients:

1 cup sweet potato, chopped
2.5 cups water
1 tsp. cayenne pepper
½ cup red lentils
1 tbsp. soy milk
½ tsp. salt

Directions:

Put all ingredients in the Slow Cooker.
Close the lid and cook the mixture on low for 6 Hrs.
When the ingredients are cooked, transfer them in the blender and blend until smooth.
Put the cooked pate in the bowl and store it in the fridge for up to 4 days.

Lentil Rice Salad

Servings: 5 Cooking Time: 7 Hrs.

Ingredients:

¼ chili pepper, chopped
½ cup lentils
¼ tsp. minced garlic
¼ tsp. ground ginger
1 tsp. salt
3 tbsp. sour cream
1 red onion, chopped
¼ cup of rice
1 tsp. chili flakes
½ tsp. ground thyme
2 cups chicken stock
1 cup lettuce, torn

Directions:

Add lentils with all other ingredients to the Slow Cooker except the lettuce and sour cream.
Put the cooker's lid on and set the cooking time to 7 Hrs. on High settings.
Stir in torn lettuce leaves and mix gently.
Garnish with sour cream.
Serve warm.

Minestrone Zucchini Soup

Servings: 8 Cooking Time: 4 Hrs.

Ingredients:

28 oz. canned tomatoes, chopped
3 carrots, chopped
1 cup green beans, halved
4 garlic cloves, minced
1 lb. lentils, cooked
1 tsp. curry powder
½ tsp. cumin, ground
2 zucchinis, chopped
1 yellow onion, chopped
3 celery stalks, chopped
10 oz. canned garbanzo beans
4 cups veggie stock
½ tsp. garam masala
Salt and black pepper to the taste

Directions:

Add carrots, zucchinis, and all other ingredients to the Slow Cooker.
Put the cooker's lid on and set the cooking time to 4 Hrs. on High settings.
Serve warm.

Potato Balls

Servings:6 Cooking Time: 1.5 Hrs.

Ingredients:

2 cups mashed potato
3 tbsps. breadcrumbs
2 oz. scallions, diced
2 tbsps. flour
1 tbsp. coconut cream
1 tsp. dried dill
1 egg, beaten
½ cup of coconut milk

Directions:

In the mixing bowl mix mashed potato with coconut cream, breadcrumbs, dried dill, scallions, egg, and flour.
Make the potato balls and put them in the Slow Cooker.
Add coconut milk and cook the meal on High for 1.5 Hrs.

Creamy Corn Chili

Servings: 6 Cooking Time: 6 Hrs.

Ingredients:

2 jalapeno chilies, chopped
1 tbsp. olive oil
4 Anaheim chilies, chopped
1 cup yellow onion, chopped
4 poblano chilies, chopped
3 cups corn

6 cups veggie stock
½ bunch cilantro, chopped
Salt and black pepper to the taste

Directions:

Add jalapenos, oil, onion, poblano, corn, stock, and Anaheim chilies to the Slow Cooker.
Put the cooker's lid on and set the cooking time to 6 Hrs. on Low settings.
Puree the cooked mixture with the help of an immersion blender.
Stir in black pepper, salt and cilantro.
Serve warm.

Asian Broccoli Sauté

Servings:4 Cooking Time: 3 Hrs.

Ingredients:

1 tbsp. coconut aminos or soy sauce
1 tbsp. coconut oil
1 head broccoli, cut into florets
1 tsp. ginger, grated
Salt and pepper to taste

Directions:

Place the ingredients in the Slow Cooker.
Toss everything to combine.
Close the lid and cook on low for 3 Hrs. or on high for an Hr.
Once cooked, sprinkle with sesame seeds or sesame oil.

Bulgur Sauté

Servings:4 Cooking Time: 4 Hrs.

Ingredients:

1 cup bell pepper, chopped
1 white onion, diced
2 tbsps. tomato paste
1 cup bulgur
3 cups vegetable stock
1 tbsp. olive oil
1 tsp. salt
1 tsp. chili flakes

Directions:

Put all ingredients in the Slow Cooker and close the lid.
Cook the meal on low doe 4 Hrs. or until the bulgur is tender.

Cauliflower Curry

Servings:4 Cooking Time: 2 Hrs.

Ingredients:

4 cups cauliflower
1 tbsp. curry paste
2 cups of coconut milk

Directions:

In the mixing bowl mix coconut milk with curry paste until smooth.
Put cauliflower in the Slow Cooker.
Pour the curry liquid over the cauliflower and close the lid.
Cook the meal on High for 2 Hrs.

Cardamom Pumpkin Wedges

Servings:4 Cooking Time: 6 Hrs.

Ingredients:

2-pound pumpkin, peeled
1 tsp. ground cardamom
2 tbsps. lemon juice
1 tsp. lemon zest, grated
2 tbsps. sugar
1 cup of water

Directions:

Cut the pumpkin into wedges and place them in the Slow Cooker.
Add water.
Then sprinkle the pumpkin with ground cardamom, lemon juice, lemon zest, and sugar.
Close the lid and cook the pumpkin on Low for 6 Hrs.
Serve the pumpkin wedges with sweet liquid from the Slow Cooker.

Mushroom Steaks

Servings:4 Cooking Time: 2 Hrs.

Ingredients:

4 Portobello mushrooms
1 tbsp. avocado oil
1 tbsp. lemon juice
2 tbsps. coconut cream
½ tsp. ground black pepper

Directions:

Slice Portobello mushrooms into steaks and sprinkle with avocado oil, lemon juice, coconut cream, and ground black pepper.
Then arrange the mushroom steaks in the Slow Cooker in one layer (you will need to cook all mushroom steaks by 2 times).
Cook the meal on High for 1 Hr.

Spicy Eggplant with Red Pepper and Parsley

Servings:4 Cooking Time: 3 Hrs.

Ingredients:

1 large eggplant, sliced
2 tbsps. parsley, chopped
1 big red bell pepper, chopped
Salt and pepper to taste
2 tbsps. balsamic vinegar

Directions:

Place all ingredients in a mixing bowl.
Toss to coat ingredients.
Place in the Slow Cooker and cook on low for 3 Hrs. or on high for 1 Hr.

Couscous Halloumi Salad

Servings: 5 Cooking Time: 4 Hrs.

Ingredients:

1 cup couscous
1 green sweet pepper, chopped
2 garlic cloves
1 cup beef broth
1 tsp. chives
½ cup cherry tomatoes halved
1 zucchini, diced
7 oz. halloumi cheese, chop
1 tsp. olive oil
1 tsp. paprika
¼ tsp. ground cardamom
1 tsp. salt

Directions:

Add couscous, cardamom, salt, and paprika to the Slow Cooker.
Stir in garlic, zucchini, and beef broth to the couscous.
Put the cooker's lid on and set the cooking time to 4 Hrs. on High settings.
Stir in the remaining ingredients and toss it gently.
Serve.

Teriyaki Kale

Servings:6 Cooking Time: 30 Min

Ingredients:

5 cups kale, roughly chopped
1/2 cup teriyaki sauce
1 tsp. sesame seeds
1 cup of water

1 tsp. garlic powder
2 tbsps. coconut oil

Directions:

Melt the coconut oil and mix it with garlic powder, water, sesame seeds, and teriyaki sauce.
Pour the liquid in the Slow Cooker.
Add kale and close the lid.
Cook the kale on High for 30 Min.
Serve the kale with a small amount of teriyaki liquid.

Jalapeno Corn

Servings:4 Cooking Time: 5 Hrs.

Ingredients:

½ cup Monterey Jack cheese, shredded
1 cup heavy cream
1-pound corn kernels
3 jalapenos, minced
1 tsp. vegan butter
1 tbsp. dried dill

Directions:

Pour heavy cream in the Slow Cooker.
Add Monterey Jack cheese, corn kernels, minced jalapeno, butter, and dried dill.
Cook the corn on Low for 5 Hrs.

Oat Fritters

Servings:4 Cooking Time: 2 Hrs.

Ingredients:

1 cup rolled oats
¼ tsp. ground paprika
1 tsp. salt
2 sweet potatoes, peeled, boiled
1 tbsp. coconut oil
2 tbsps. coconut cream

Directions:

In the mixing bowl mix rolled oats, ground paprika, salt, and potatoes.
When the mixture is homogenous, make the fritters and transfer them in the Slow Cooker.
Add coconut cream and coconut oil.
Cook the fritters in High for 1 Hr.
Then flip the fritters on another side and cook them for 1 Hr. more.

Shredded Cabbage Saute

Servings:4 Cooking Time: 6 Hrs.

Ingredients:

3 cups white cabbage, shredded
1 cup tomato juice
1 tsp. salt
1 tsp. sugar
1 tsp. dried oregano
3 tbsps. olive oil
1 cup of water

Directions:

Put all ingredients in the Slow Cooker.
Carefully mix all ingredients with the help of the spoon and close the lid.
Cook the cabbage saute for 6 Hrs. on Low.

Eggplant Salad

Servings:5 Cooking Time: 3 Hrs.

Ingredients:

4 eggplants, cubed
1 tsp. salt
1 tsp. ground black pepper
1 cup of water
1 tbsp. sesame oil
1 tbsp. apple cider vinegar
1 tsp. sesame seeds
2 cups tomatoes, chopped

Directions:

Mix eggplants with salt and ground black pepper and leave for 10 Min.
Then transfer the eggplants in the Slow Cooker. Add water and cook them for 3 Hrs. on High.
Drain water and cool the eggplants to the room temperature.
Add sesame oil, apple cider vinegar, sesame seeds, and tomatoes.
Gently shake the salad.

Zucchini Mash

Servings:2 Cooking Time: 45 Min

Ingredients:

2 cups zucchini, grated
1 tbsp. olive oil
¼ cup of water
½ tsp. ground black pepper
2 tbsps. sour cream

Directions:

Put all ingredients in the Slow Cooker and gently stir.
Cook the zucchini mash on High for 45 Min.

Chorizo Cashew Salad

Servings: 6 Cooking Time: 4 Hrs. 30 Min

Ingredients:

8 oz. chorizo, chopped
1 tsp. olive oil
1 tsp. cayenne pepper
1 tsp. chili flakes
1 tsp. ground black pepper
1 tsp. onion powder
2 garlic cloves
3 tomatoes, chopped
1 cup lettuce, torn
1 cup fresh dill
1 tsp. oregano
3 tbsp. crushed cashews

Directions:

Add chorizo sausage to the Slow Cooker.
Put the cooker's lid on and set the cooking time to 4 Hrs. on High settings.
Mix chili flakes, cayenne pepper, black pepper, and onion powder in a bowl.
Now add tomatoes to the Slow Cooker and cover again.
Slow Cooker for another 30 Min. on High setting.
Stir in oregano and dill then mix well.
Add sliced garlic and torn lettuce to the mixture.
Garnish with cashews.
Serve.

Garam Masala Potato Bake

Servings:2 Cooking Time: 6 Hrs.

Ingredients:

1 cup potatoes, chopped
1 tsp. garam masala
3 eggs, beaten
½ cup vegan mozzarella, shredded
1 tbsp. vegan butter
2 tbsps. coconut cream

Directions:

Mix potatoes with garam masala.
Then put them in the Slow Cooker.
Add vegan butter and mozzarella.

After this, mix coconut cream with eggs and pour the liquid over the mozzarella.
Close the lid and cook the meal on Low for 6 Hrs.

Broccoli Fritters

Servings:4 Cooking Time: 40 Min

Ingredients:

2 cups broccoli, shredded
1 tsp. salt
1 egg, beaten
1 tbsp. sunflower oil
1 tsp. chili flakes
2 tbsps. semolina
1 tbsp. cornflour
¼ cup coconut cream

Directions:

In the mixing bowl mix shredded broccoli, chili flakes, salt, semolina, egg, and cornflour.
Make the small fritters from the broccoli mixture.
Then pour sunflower in the Slow Cooker.
Out the fritters in the Slow Cooker in one layer.
Add coconut cream.
Cook the fritters on High for 40 Min.

Vegan Kofte

Servings:4 Cooking Time: 4 Hrs.

Ingredients:

2 eggplants, peeled, boiled
1 tsp. ground cumin
½ cup chickpeas, canned
1/3 cup water
1 tsp. minced garlic
¼ tsp. minced ginger
3 tbsps. breadcrumbs
1 tbsp. coconut oil

Directions:

Blend the eggplants until smooth.
Add minced garlic, ground cumin, minced ginger, chickpeas, and blend the mixture until smooth.
Transfer it in the mixing bowl. Add breadcrumbs.
Make the small koftes and put them in the Slow Cooker.
Add coconut oil and close the lid.
Cook the meal on Low for 4 Hrs.

Pumpkin Hummus

Servings:6 Cooking Time: 4 Hrs.

Ingredients:

1 cup chickpeas, canned
1 cup pumpkin, chopped
2 cups of water
1 tbsp. lemon juice
1 tbsp. tahini paste
1 tsp. harissa
2 tbsps. olive oil

Directions:

Pour water in the Slow Cooker.
Add pumpkin and cook it for 4 Hrs. on High or until the pumpkin is soft.
After this, drain water and transfer the pumpkin in the food processor.
Add all remaining ingredients and blend the mixture until smooth.
Add water from pumpkin if the cooked hummus is very thick.

Sauteed Garlic

Servings:4 Cooking Time: 6 Hrs.

Ingredients:

10 oz. garlic cloves, peeled
1 tsp. ground black pepper
1 tbsp. vegan butter
2 tbsps. lemon juice
1 cup of water
1 bay leaf

Directions:

Put all ingredients in the Slow Cooker.
Close the lid and cook the garlic on Low for 6 Hrs.

Rice Stuffed Apple Cups

Servings: 4 Cooking Time: 6 Hrs.

Ingredients:

4 red apples
3 tbsp. raisins
7 tbsp. water
1 tsp. curry powder
1 cup white rice
1 onion, diced
1 tsp. salt
4 tsp. sour cream

Directions:

Remove the seeds and half of the flesh from the center of the apples to make apple cups.
Toss onion with white rice, curry powder, salt, and raisin in a separate bowl.
Divide this rice-raisins mixture into the apple cups.
Pour water into the Slow Cooker and place the stuffed cups in it.
Top the apples with sour cream.
Put the cooker's lid on and set the cooking time to 6 Hrs. on Low settings.
Serve.

Mung Beans Salad

Servings:4 Cooking Time: 3 Hrs.

Ingredients:

½ avocado, chopped
½ cup corn kernels, cooked
3 cups of water
1 tbsp. avocado oil
1 cup cherry tomatoes, halved
1 cup mung beans
1 tbsp. lemon juice

Directions:

Put mung beans in the Slow Cooker.
Add water and cook them on High for 3 Hrs.
Then drain water and transfer the mung beans in the salad bowl.
Add avocado, cherry tomatoes, corn kernels, and shake well.
Then sprinkle the salad with avocado oil and lemon juice.

Creamy Keto Mash

Servings:3 Cooking Time: 4 Hrs.

Ingredients:

1 cauliflower head, cut into florets
2 cloves of garlic, minced
¼ cup butter
½ cup cream cheese
1 white onion, chopped
¼ cup vegetable stock
Salt and pepper to taste

Directions:

Place the all ingredients except for the cream cheese in the Slow Cooker.
Close the lid and cook on high for 3 Hrs. or on low for 4 Hrs.
Place in the food processor and pour in the cream cheese. Pulse until slightly fine.
Garnish with chopped parsley if desired.

Chili Dip

Servings:5 Cooking Time: 5 Hrs.

Ingredients:

5 oz. chilies, canned, chopped
1 tomato, chopped
1 tsp. cornflour
3 oz. Mozzarella, shredded
½ cup milk

Directions:

Mix milk with cornflour and whisk until smooth. Pour the liquid in the Slow Cooker.
Then add chilies, Mozzarella, and tomato.
Close the lid and cook the dip on low for 5 Hrs.

Eggplant Mini Wraps

Servings: 6 Cooking Time: 5 Hrs.

Ingredients:

10 oz. eggplant, sliced into rounds
1 tsp. minced garlic
½ tsp. ground black pepper
1 tsp. paprika
5 oz. halloumi cheese
3 oz. bacon, chopped
1 tsp. salt
1 tomato

Directions:

Season the eggplant sliced with salt, paprika, and black pepper.
Add these slices to the Slow Cooker and spread in a single layer.
Put the cooker's lid on and set the cooking time to 1 Hr. on High settings.
Allow the eggplant to cool then top them with tomato and cheese slices.
And top them with bacon and garlic.
Roll each slice and insert the toothpick to seal them.
Place these wrap in the Slow Cooker carefully.
Put the cooker's lid on and set the cooking time to 4 Hrs. on High settings.
Serve fresh.

Zucchini Spinach Lasagne

Servings: 7 Cooking Time: 5 Hrs.

Ingredients:

1 lb. green zucchini, sliced
½ cup fresh parsley, chopped
1 tbsp. minced garlic
1 onion, chopped
5 oz. mozzarella, shredded
½ cup baby spinach
7 tbsp. tomato sauce
1 tbsp. fresh dill, chopped
7 oz. Parmesan, shredded
4 tbsp. ricotta cheese
2 eggs
1 tsp. olive oil

Directions:

Grease the base of your Slow Cooker with olive oil.
Spread 3 zucchini slices at the bottom of the cooker.
Whisk tomato sauce with garlic, onion, dill, ricotta cheese, parsley, and spinach.
Stir in shredded parmesan, mozzarella, and eggs, then mix well.
Add a layer of this tomato-cheese mixture over the zucchini layer.
Again, place the zucchini slices over this tomato mixture layer.
Continue adding alternating layers of zucchini and tomato sauce
Put the cooker's lid on and set the cooking time to 5 Hrs. on High settings.
Slice and serve warm.

Collard Greens Saute

Servings:4 Cooking Time: 5 Hrs.

Ingredients:

1 cup potato, chopped
1 cup tomatoes, chopped
2 tbsps. coconut oil
1 tsp. salt
8 oz. collard greens, chopped
1 cup of water
1 tsp. dried thyme

Directions:

Put coconut oil in the Slow Cooker.
Then mix chopped potato with dried thyme and salt.
Put the potato in the Slow Cooker and flatten it in one layer.
Add tomatoes, collard greens.
After this, add water and close the lid.
Cook the saute on Low for 5 Hrs.

Corn Pudding

Servings:4 Cooking Time: 5 Hrs.

Ingredients:

3 cups corn kernels
3 tbsps. muffin mix
2 cups heavy cream
1 oz. Parmesan, grated

Directions:

Mix heavy cream with muffin mix and pour the liquid in the Slow Cooker.
Add corn kernels and Parmesan. Stir the mixture well.
Close the lid and cook the pudding on Low for 5 Hrs.

Braised Root Vegetables

Servings:4 Cooking Time: 8 Hrs.

Ingredients:

1 cup beets, chopped
1 tsp. raisins
1 tsp. salt
1 cup carrot, chopped
2 cups vegetable stock
1 tsp. onion powder

Directions:

Put all ingredients in the Slow Cooker.
Close the lid and cook them on Low for 8 Hrs.

Slow Cooker Mediterranean Eggplant Salad

Servings:2 Cooking Time: 4 Hrs.

Ingredients:

1 red onion, sliced
3 extra virgin olive oil
1 cup tomatoes, crushed
2 tsps. cumin
Salt and pepper to taste
2 bell peppers, sliced
1 eggplant, quartered
1 tbsp. smoked paprika
Juice from 1 lemon, freshly squeezed

Directions:

Place all ingredients in the Slow Cooker.
Give a good stir.
Close the lid and cook on high for 3 Hrs. or on low for 4 Hrs.

Bulgur Mushroom Chili

Servings: 4 Cooking Time: 8 Hrs.

Ingredients:

2 cups white mushrooms, sliced
¾ cup bulgur, soaked in 1 cup hot water for 15 Min. and drained

2 cups yellow onion, chopped
½ cup red bell pepper, chopped
1 cup veggie stock
2 garlic cloves, minced
1 cup strong brewed coffee
14 oz. canned kidney beans, drained
14 oz. canned pinto beans, drained
2 tbsp. sugar
2 tbsp. chili powder
1 tbsp. cocoa powder
1 tsp. oregano, dried
2 tsp. cumin, ground
1 bay leaf
Salt and black pepper to the taste

Directions:

Add bulgur with all other ingredients to the base of your Slow Cooker.
Put the cooker's lid on and set the cooking time to 12 Hrs. on Low settings.
Remove the bay leaf from the chili and discard it.
Serve warm.

Warming Butternut Squash Soup

Servings: 9 Cooking Time: 8 Hrs.

Ingredients:

2 lb. butternut squash, peeled and cubed
4 tsp. minced garlic
½ cup onion, chopped
1 tsp. salt
¼ tsp. ground nutmeg
1 tsp. ground black pepper
8 cups chicken stock
1 tbsp. fresh parsley

Directions:

Spread the butternut squash in your Slow Cooker.
Add stock, garlic, and onion to the squash.
Put the cooker's lid on and set the cooking time to 8 Hrs. on Low settings.
Add salt, black pepper, and nutmeg to the squash.
Puree the cooked squash mixture using an immersion blender until smooth.
Garnish with chopped parsley.
Enjoy.

Rice Cauliflower Casserole

Servings: 6 Cooking Time: 8 Hrs. 10 Min

Ingredients:

1 cup white rice
5 oz. broccoli, chopped
4 oz. cauliflower, chopped
1 cup Greek Yogurt
1 cup chicken stock
6 oz. Cheddar cheese, shredded
1 tsp. onion powder
2 yellow onions, chopped
1 tsp. paprika
1 tbsp. salt
2 cups of water
1 tsp. butter

Directions:

Add cauliflower, broccoli, water, chicken stock, salt, paprika, rice, and onion powder to the Slow Cooker.
Top the broccoli-cauliflower mixture with onion slices.
Put the cooker's lid on and set the cooking time to 8 Hrs. on Low settings.
Add butter and cheese on top of the casserole.
Put the cooker's lid on and set the cooking time to 10 Min. on High settings.
Serve warm.

Sweet Pineapple Tofu

Servings:2 Cooking Time: 15 Min

Ingredients:

1/3 cup pineapple juice
1 tsp. brown sugar
1 tsp. ground cinnamon
¼ tsp. ground cardamom
7 oz. firm tofu, chopped
1 tsp. olive oil

Directions:

Put tofu in the mixing bowl.
Then sprinkle it with pineapple juice, brown sugar, ground cinnamon, cardamom, and olive oil. Carefully mix the tofu and leave it for 10-15 Min.
Then transfer the tofu mixture in the Slow Cooker and close the lid.
Cook it on High for 15 Min.

Mushroom Saute

Servings:4 Cooking Time: 2.5 Hrs.

Ingredients:

2 cups cremini mushrooms, sliced
1 white onion, sliced
½ cup fresh dill, chopped
1 cup coconut cream
1 tsp. ground black pepper
¼ cup vegan Cheddar cheese, shredded
1 tbsp. coconut oil

Directions:

Toss the coconut oil in the skillet and melt it.
Add mushrooms and onion.
Roast the vegetables on medium heat for 5 Min.
Then transfer them in the Slow Cooker.
Add all remaining ingredients and carefully mix.
Cook the mushroom saute on High for 2.5 Hrs.

Sweet Onions

Servings:4 Cooking Time: 4 Hrs.

Ingredients:

2 cups white onion, sliced
½ cup vegan butter
¼ cup of water
1 tsp. ground black pepper
1 tbsp. maple syrup
1 tsp. lemon juice

Directions:

Put all ingredients in the Slow Cooker.
Close the lid and cook the onions on low for 4 Hrs.

Potato Parmesan Pie

Servings: 8 Cooking Time: 6 Hrs.

Ingredients:

2 sweet potatoes, peeled and sliced
2 red potatoes, peeled and sliced
6 oz. Parmesan, shredded
1 cup sweet corn
1 tsp. salt
1 tsp. paprika
1 tsp. curry powder
2 red onions, sliced
1 cup flour
1 tsp. baking soda
½ tsp. apple cider vinegar
1 cup Greek Yogurt
3 tomatoes, sliced
¼ tsp. butter

Directions:

Toss the vegetables with curry, salt, paprika, and curry powder for seasoning.
Coat the base of your Slow Cooker with butter.
At first, make a layer of red potatoes in the cooker.
Now add layers of sweet potatoes and onion.
Add corns and tomatoes on top.
Whisk yogurt with baking soda, flour, and apple cider vinegar in a bowl.
Add the yogurt-flour mixture on top of the layers of veggies.
Lastly, drizzle the shredded cheese over it.
Put the cooker's lid on and set the cooking time to 6 Hrs. on High settings.
Slice and serve.

Braised Swiss Chard

Servings:4 Cooking Time: 30 Min

Ingredients:

1-pound swiss chard, chopped
1 tsp. garlic, diced
1 tsp. salt
1 lemon
1 tbsp. sunflower oil
2 cups of water

Directions:

Put the swiss chard in the Slow Cooker.
Cut the lemon into halves and squeeze it over the swiss chard.
After this, sprinkle the greens with diced garlic, sunflower oil, salt, and water.
Mix the mixture gently with the help of the spoon and close the lid.
Cook the greens on High for 30 Min.

Potato Bake

Servings:3 Cooking Time: 7 Hrs.

Ingredients:

2 cups potatoes, peeled, halved
1 tbsp. vegan butter, softened
½ cup vegetable stock
4 oz. vegan Provolone cheese, grated
1 tsp. dried dill
1 carrot, diced

Directions:

Grease the Slow Cooker bottom with butter and put the halved potato inside.
Sprinkle it with dried dill and carrot.
Then add vegetable stock and Provolone cheese.
Cook the potato bake on low for 7 Hrs.

Garlic Gnocchi

Servings:4 Cooking Time: 3 Hrs.

Ingredients:

2 cups mozzarella, shredded
1 tsp. garlic, minced
Salt and pepper to taste
3 egg yolks, beaten
½ cup heavy cream

Directions:

In a mixing bowl, combine the mozzarella and egg yolks.
Form gnocchi balls and place in the fridge to set.
Boil a pot of water over high flame and drop the gnocchi balls for 30 seconds. Take them out and transfer to the Slow Cooker.
Into the Slow Cooker add the garlic and heavy cream.
Season with salt and pepper to taste.
Close the lid and cook on low for 3 Hrs. or on high for 1 Hr.

Sweet Potato Tarragon Soup

Servings: 6 Cooking Time: 5 Hrs. and 20 Min

Ingredients:

5 cups veggie stock
2 celery stalks, chopped
1 cup milk
2 garlic cloves, minced
8 tbsp. almonds, sliced
3 sweet potatoes, peeled and chopped
1 cup yellow onion, chopped
1 tsp. tarragon, dried
2 cups baby spinach
Salt and black pepper to the taste

Directions:

Add potatoes, tarragon, and all other ingredients except spinach and almonds, to the Slow Cooker.
Put the cooker's lid on and set the cooking time to 5 Hrs. on High settings.
Blend the cooked potatoes mixture until smooth and creamy.
Stir in almond and spinach to the cooker.
Mix well and serve warm.

Mushroom Risotto

Servings:4 Cooking Time: 6 Hrs.

Ingredients:

½ cup Arborio rice
1 yellow onion, diced
1 tsp. salt
4 cups vegetable stock
2 cups brown mushrooms, chopped
2 tbsps. avocado oil
1 tsp. ground black pepper

Directions:

Pour the vegetable stock in the Slow Cooker.
Add ground black pepper and salt.
After this, add avocado oil, diced onion, mushrooms, and Arborio rice.
Close the lid and cook the risotto on Low for 6 Hrs.

Chili Okra

Servings:6 Cooking Time: 7 Hrs.

Ingredients:

6 cups okra, chopped
1 tsp. salt
½ tsp. cayenne pepper
1 cup vegetable stock
1 cup tomato juice
½ tsp. chili powder
1 tbsp. olive oil

Directions:

Put all ingredients from the list above in the Slow Cooker.
Mix them gently and cook on Low for 7 Hrs.

Carrot Strips

Servings:2 Cooking Time: 1 Hr.

Ingredients:

2 carrots, peeled
1 tsp. dried thyme
½ cup of water
2 tbsps. sunflower oil
½ tsp. salt

Directions:

Cut the carrots into the strips.
Then heat the sunflower oil in the skillet until hot.

Put the carrot strips in the hot oil and roast for 2-3 Min. per side.
Pour water in the Slow Cooker.
Add salt and dried thyme.
Then add roasted carrot and cook the meal on High for 1 Hr.

Rainbow Carrots

Servings:4 Cooking Time: 3.5 Hrs.

Ingredients:

2-pound rainbow carrots, sliced
1 cup bell pepper, chopped
1 tsp. salt
1 cup vegetable stock
1 onion, sliced
1 tsp. chili powder

Directions:

Put all ingredients in the Slow Cooker.
Close the lid and cook the meal on High for 3.5 Hrs.
Then cool the cooked carrots for 5-10 Min. and transfer in the serving bowls.

Yam Fritters

Servings:1 Cooking Time: 4 Hrs.

Ingredients:

1 yam, grated, boiled
¼ tsp. chili powder
1 egg, beaten
5 tbsps. coconut cream
1 tsp. dried parsley
¼ tsp. salt
1 tsp. flour
Cooking spray

Directions:

In the mixing bowl mix grated yams, dried parsley, chili powder, salt, egg, and flour.
Make the fritters from the yam mixture.
After this, spray the Slow Cooker bottom with cooking spray.
Put the fritters inside in one layer.
Add coconut cream and cook the meal on Low for 4 Hrs.

Cauliflower Stuffing

Servings:4 Cooking Time: 5 Hrs.

Ingredients:

1-pound cauliflower, chopped
1 cup Mozzarella, shredded
2 tbsps. sour cream
½ cup panko breadcrumbs
1 cup of coconut milk
1 tsp. onion powder

Directions:

Put all ingredients in the Slow Cooker and carefully mix.
Then close the lid and cook the stuffing on low for 5 Hrs.
Cool the stuffing for 10-15 Min. and transfer in the bowls.

Arugula and Halloumi Salad

Servings:4 Cooking Time: 30 Min

Ingredients:

1 tbsp. coconut oil
½ tsp. ground turmeric
2 cups arugula, chopped
1 tbsp. olive oil
1 tsp. smoked paprika
½ tsp. garlic powder
1 cup cherry tomatoes
6 oz. halloumi

Directions:

Slice the halloumi and sprinkle with melted coconut oil.
Put the cheese in the Slow Cooker in one layer and cook on high for 15 Min. per side.
Meanwhile, mix arugula with cherry tomatoes in the salad bowl.
Add cooked halloumi, smoked paprika, ground turmeric, garlic powder, and olive oil.
Shake the salad gently.

Zucchini Basil Soup

Servings:8 Cooking Time: 3 Hrs.

Ingredients:

9 cups zucchini, diced
4 cups vegetable broth
1 cup basil leaves
Salt and pepper to taste
2 cups white onions, chopped
8 cloves of garlic, minced
4 tbsps. olive oil

Directions:

Place the ingredients in the Slow Cooker.
Give a good stir.
Close the lid and cook on high for 2 Hrs. or on low for 3 Hrs.
Once cooked, transfer into a blender and pulse until smooth.

Stuffed Okra

Servings:4 Cooking Time: 5 Hrs.

Ingredients:

1-pound okra
1 tsp. curry powder
1 tsp. dried dill
1 tbsp. coconut oil
1 cup cauliflower, shredded
1 tsp. tomato paste
1/3 cup coconut milk

Directions:

Make the cuts in the okra and remove seeds.
Then mix shredded cauliflower with curry powder, tomato paste, and dried dill.
Fill every okra with cauliflower mixture and put in the Slow Cooker.
Add coconut oil and coconut milk in the Slow Cooker and close the lid.
Cook the okra on Low for 5 Hrs.

Hot Sauce Oysters Mushrooms

Servings:4 Cooking Time: 2 Hrs.

Ingredients:

2 tbsps. hot sauce
½ cup of water
1 tsp. dried dill
2 cups oysters mushrooms, sliced
1 tbsp. avocado oil
1 tsp. salt

Directions:

Mix sliced oysters with avocado oil, dried dill, and salt.
Put them in the Slow Cooker.
Add water and cook the mushrooms on High for 2 Hrs.
After this, drain the mushrooms and mix them with hot sauce.

Sautéed Endives

Servings:4 Cooking Time: 40 Min

Ingredients:

1-pound endives, roughly chopped
1 tbsp. avocado oil
2 tbsps. coconut cream
½ cup of water
1 tsp. garlic, diced

Directions:

Pour water in the Slow Cooker.
Add endives and garlic.
Close the lid and cook them on High for 30 Min.
Then add coconut cream and avocado oil.
Cook the endives for 10 Min. more.

Fragrant Jackfruit

Servings:4 Cooking Time: 2 Hrs.

Ingredients:

1-pound jackfruit, canned, chopped
1 tsp. taco seasoning
½ cup coconut cream
1 tsp. tomato paste
1 onion, diced
1 tsp. chili powder

Directions:

In the mixing bowl mix taco seasoning, chili powder, tomato paste, and coconut cream.
Put the jackfruit and diced onion in the Slow Cooker.
Pour the tomato mixture over the vegetables and gently mix them.
Close the lid and cook the meal on High for 2 Hrs.

Eggplant Casserole

Servings:4 Cooking Time: 6 Hrs.

Ingredients:

1 tsp. minced garlic
2 tbsps. sunflower oil
½ cup potato, diced
1 cup vegan Cheddar cheese, shredded
2 cups eggplants, chopped
1 tsp. salt
1 cup of water

Directions:

Brush the Slow Cooker bottom with sunflower oil.
The mix eggplants with minced garlic and salt.
Put the vegetables in the Slow Cooker.
Add potatoes and water.
After this, top the vegetables with vegan Cheddar cheese and close the lid.
Cook the casserole on Low for 6 Hrs.

Sweet Potato Puree

Servings:2 Cooking Time: 4 Hrs.

Ingredients:

2 cups sweet potato, chopped
¼ cup half and half
1 tsp. salt
1 cup of water
1 oz. scallions, chopped

Directions:

Put sweet potatoes in the Slow Cooker.
Add water and salt.
Cook them on High for 4 Hrs.
The drain water and transfer the sweet potatoes in the food processor.
Add half and half and blend until smooth.
Transfer the puree in the bowl, and scallions, and mix carefully.

Fragrant Appetizer Peppers

Servings:2 Cooking Time: 1.5 Hrs.

Ingredients:

4 sweet peppers, seeded
1 red onion, sliced
½ tsp. sugar
1 tbsp. olive oil
¼ cup apple cider vinegar
1 tsp. peppercorns
¼ cup of water

Directions:

Slice the sweet peppers roughly and put in the Slow Cooker.
Add all remaining ingredients and close the lid.
Cook the peppers on high for 1.5 Hrs.
Then cool the peppers well and store them in the fridge for up to 6 days.

Spaghetti Cheese Casserole

Servings: 8 Cooking Time: 7 Hrs.

Ingredients:

1 lb. cottage cheese
5 eggs
5 tbsp. semolina
1 tsp. vanilla extract
1 tsp. lemon zest
7 oz. spaghetti, cooked
1 cup heavy cream
3 tbsp. white sugar
1 tsp. marjoram
1 tsp. butter

Directions:

Start by blending cottage cheese in a blender jug for 1 minute.
Add eggs to the cottage cheese and blend again for 3 Min.
Stir in semolina, cream, sugar, marjoram, vanilla extract, butter and lemon zest.
Blend again for 1 minute and keep the cheese-cream mixture aside.
Spread the chopped spaghetti layer in the Slow Cooker.
Top the spaghetti with 3 tbsp. with the cheese-cream mixture.
Add another layer of spaghetti over the mixture.
Continue adding alternate layers in this manner until all ingredients are used.
Put the cooker's lid on and set the cooking time to 7 Hrs. on Low settings.
Slice and serve.

Vegetable Bean Stew

Servings: 8 Cooking Time: 7 Hrs.

Ingredients:

½ cup barley
¼ cup red beans
1 cup onion, chopped
2 potatoes, peeled and diced
1 tsp. ground black pepper
4 oz. tofu
1 cup fresh cilantro
1 cup black beans
2 carrots, peeled and julienned
1 cup tomato juice
1 tsp. salt
4 cups of water
1 tsp. garlic powder

Directions:

Add black beans, red beans, and barley to the Slow Cooker.
Stir in tomato juice, onion, garlic powder, black pepper, salt, and water.
Put the cooker's lid on and set the cooking time to 4 Hrs. on High settings.
Add carrots, cilantro, and potatoes to the cooker.
Put the cooker's lid on and set the cooking time to 3 Hrs. on Low settings.
Serve warm.

Onion Chives Muffins

Servings: 7 Cooking Time: 8 Hrs.

Ingredients:

1 egg
1 cup flour
1 tsp. baking soda
1 tsp. cilantro
1 tsp. apple cider vinegar
1 tsp. olive oil
5 tbsp. butter, melted
½ cup milk
1 cup onion, chopped
½ tsp. sage
1 tbsp. chives

Directions:

Whisk egg with melted butter, onion, milk, and all other ingredients to make a smooth dough.
Grease a muffin tray with olive oil and divide the batter into its cups.
Pour 2 cups water into the Slow Cooker and set the muffin tray in it.
Put the cooker's lid on and set the cooking time to 8 Hrs. on Low settings.
Serve.

Creamy White Mushrooms

Servings:4 Cooking Time: 8 Hrs.

Ingredients:

1-pound white mushrooms, chopped
1 tsp. chili flakes
1 tbsp. dried parsley
1 cup cream
1 tsp. ground black pepper

Directions:

Put all ingredients in the Slow Cooker.
Cook the mushrooms on low for 8 Hrs.
When the mushrooms are cooked, transfer them in the serving bowls and cool for 10-15 Min.

Paprika Okra

Servings:4 Cooking Time: 40 Min

Ingredients:

4 cups okra, sliced
1 tsp. salt
1 cup organic almond milk
1 tbsp. smoked paprika
2 tbsps. coconut oil

Directions:

Pour almond milk in the Slow Cooker.
Add coconut oil, salt, and smoked paprika.
Then add sliced okra and gently mix the ingredients.
Cook the okra on High for 40 Min. Then cooked okra should be tender but not soft.

Quinoa Fritters

Servings:4 Cooking Time: 1 Hr.

Ingredients:

1 sweet potato, peeled, boiled, grated
1 tsp. chili powder
2 eggs, beaten
1 tbsp. coconut oil, melted
½ cup quinoa, cooked
1 tsp. salt
3 tbsps. cornflour

Directions:

In the mixing bowl mix grated sweet potato, quinoa, chili powder, salt, cornflour, and eggs.
Make the small fritters and put them in the Slow Cooker.
Add coconut oil and close the lid.
Cook the fritters on High for 1 Hr.

Tofu and Cauliflower Bowl

Servings:3 Cooking Time: 2.15 Hrs.

Ingredients:

5 oz. firm tofu, chopped
¼ cup of coconut milk
1 tbsp. sunflower oil
1 cup of water
1 tsp. curry paste
1 tsp. dried basil
2 cups cauliflower, chopped

Directions:

Put cauliflower in the Slow Cooker.
Add water and cook it on High for 2 Hrs.
Meanwhile, mix curry paste with coconut milk, dried basil, and sunflower oil.
Then add tofu and carefully mix the mixture. Leave it for 30 Min.
When the cauliflower is cooked, drain water.
Add tofu mixture and shake the meal well. Cook it on High for 15 Min.

Pumpkin Chili

Servings:6 Cooking Time: 1.5 Hrs.

Ingredients:

½ cup red kidney beans, canned
½ cup bell pepper, chopped
½ cup tomato juice
½ cup of water
1 cup pumpkin puree
1 onion, chopped
1 tsp. chili powder
1 cup lentils, cooked

Directions:

Put all ingredients in the Slow Cooker and carefully mix.
Close the lid and cook chili on High for 1.5 Hrs.

Butter Hasselback Potatoes

Servings:2 Cooking Time: 4 Hrs.

Ingredients:

2 large Russet potatoes
2 tsps. vegan butter
½ cup vegetable stock
1 tbsp. olive oil
1 tsp. onion powder

Directions:

Cut the potatoes in the shape of Hasselback and place it in the Slow Cooker.
Sprinkle them with olive oil, butter, and onion powder.
Add vegetable stock and close the lid.
Cook the potatoes on High for 4 Hrs. or until they are soft.

Parsnip Balls

Servings:4 Cooking Time: 3 Hrs.

Ingredients:

8 oz. parsnip, peeled, grated
1/3 cup coconut flour
1 carrot, boiled, peeled, mashed
1 tsp. chili powder
1 tbsp. coconut cream
1 tbsp. coconut oil
1 tsp. salt

Directions:

In the mixing bowl mix grated parsnip, coconut cream, coconut flour, mashed carrot, salt, and chili powder.
with the help of the scooper make the small balls and freeze them for 10-15 Min.
Then put coconut oil in the Slow Cooker.
Add frozen parsnip balls and cook them on Low for 3 Hrs.

Swedish Style Beets

Servings:4 Cooking Time: 8 Hrs.

Ingredients:

1-pound beets
1 tbsp. olive oil
½ tsp. sugar
¼ cup apple cider vinegar
1 tsp. salt
3 cups of water

Directions:

Put beets in the Slow Cooker.
Add water and cook the vegetables for 8 Hrs. on Low.
Then drain water and peel the beets.
Chop the beets roughly and put in the big bowl.
Add all remaining ingredients and leave the beets for 2-3 Hrs. to marinate.

Fennel Lentils

Servings: 11 Cooking Time: 5 Hrs.

Ingredients:

1 tsp. cumin
10 oz. lentils
7 cups of water
4 oz. onion, chopped
1 oz. bay leaf
1 tsp. salt
1 oz. mustard seeds
1 tsp. fennel seeds
6 oz. tomato, canned
½ tsp. fresh ginger, grated
1 tsp. turmeric
2 cups of rice

Directions:

Add tomatoes, onion, lentils, and all other ingredients to the Slow Cooker.
Put the cooker's lid on and set the cooking time to 5 Hrs. on Low settings.
Serve warm.

Curry Couscous

Servings:4 Cooking Time: 20 Min

Ingredients:

1 cup of water
½ cup coconut cream
1 cup couscous
1 tsp. salt

Directions:

Put all ingredients in the Slow Cooker and close the lid.
Cook the couscous on High for 20 Min.

Zucchini Soup with Rosemary and Parmesan

Servings:6 Cooking Time: 3 Hrs.

Ingredients:

2 tbsps. olive oil
1 onion, chopped
1 tsp. Italian seasoning
2 lbs. zucchini, chopped
Salt and pepper to taste
1 tbsp. butter
1 tsp. minced garlic
4 tsps. rosemary, chopped
8 cups vegetable stock
1 cup grated parmesan cheese

Directions:

Place all ingredients except for the parmesan cheese in the Slow Cooker.
Give a good stir.
Close the lid and cook on high for 3 Hrs. or on low for 4 Hrs.
Place inside a blender and pulse until smooth.
Serve with parmesan cheese on top.

Thyme Tomatoes

Servings:4 Cooking Time: 5 Hrs.

Ingredients:

1-pound tomatoes, sliced
1 tsp. salt
1 tbsp. apple cider vinegar
1 tbsp. dried thyme
2 tbsps. olive oil
½ cup of water

Directions:

Put all ingredients in the Slow Cooker and close the lid.
Cook the tomatoes on Low for 5 Hrs.

Quinoa Casserole

Servings:6 Cooking Time: 3 Hrs.

Ingredients:

1 tsp. nutritional yeast
1 cup bell pepper, chopped
1 cup broccoli florets, chopped
1 tsp. chili flakes
1 cup quinoa
1 tsp. smoked paprika
1 cup cashew cream
3 cups of water

Directions:

Mix quinoa with nutritional yeast and put in the Slow Cooker.
Add bell pepper, smoked paprika, broccoli florets, and chili flakes.
Add cashew cream and water.
Close the lid and cook the casserole for 3 Hrs. on high.

Pumpkin Bean Chili

Servings: 6 Cooking Time: 5 Hrs.

Ingredients:

1 cup pumpkin puree
30 oz. canned roasted tomatoes, chopped
1 cup red lentils, dried
1 jalapeno pepper, chopped
1 tbsp. cocoa powder
2 tsp. cumin, ground
Salt and black pepper to the taste
30 oz. canned kidney beans, drained
2 cups of water
1 cup yellow onion, chopped
1 tbsp. chili powder
½ tsp. cinnamon powder
A pinch of cloves, ground
2 tomatoes, chopped

Directions:

Add pumpkin puree along with other ingredients except for tomatoes, to the Slow Cooker.
Put the cooker's lid on and set the cooking time to 5 Hrs. on High settings.
Serve with tomatoes on top.
Enjoy.

Marinated Jalapeno Rings

Servings:4 Cooking Time: 1 Hr.

Ingredients:

1 cup of water
1 tsp. peppercorns
3 tbsps. sunflower oil
¼ cup apple cider vinegar
1 garlic clove, crushed
5 oz. jalapeno, sliced

Directions:

Put the sliced jalapeno in the plastic vessel (layer by layer).
Then put peppercorns in the Slow Cooker.
Add the garlic clove, sunflower oil, and apple cider vinegar.
Close the lid and cook the liquid on High for 1 Hr.
After this, cool the liquid to the room temperature and pour it over the jalapenos.
Close the plastic vessel and leave it in the fridge for 30-40 Min. before serving.

Tri-bean Chili

Servings: 6 Cooking Time: 8 Hrs.

Ingredients:

15 oz. canned kidney beans, drained
15 oz. canned black beans, drained
30 oz. canned tomatoes, crushed
2 yellow onions, chopped
1 tsp. oregano, dried
Salt and black pepper to the taste
30 oz. canned chili beans in sauce
2 green bell peppers, chopped
2 tbsp. chili powder
2 garlic cloves, minced
1 tbsp. cumin, ground

Directions:

Add kidney beans, black beans, chili beans, and all the spices and veggies to the Slow Cooker.
Put the cooker's lid on and set the cooking time to 8 Hrs. on Low settings.
Serve warm.

Butter Asparagus

Servings:4 Cooking Time: 5 Hrs.

Ingredients:

1 pound asparagus
1 tsp. ground black pepper
2 tbsps. vegan butter
1 cup vegetable stock

Directions:

Pour the vegetable stock in the Slow Cooker.
Chop the asparagus roughly and add in the Slow Cooker.
Close the lid and cook the asparagus for 5 Hrs. on Low.
Then drain water and transfer the asparagus in the bowl.
Sprinkle it with ground black pepper and butter.

Honey Carrot Gravy

Servings: 4 Cooking Time: 2 ½hrs.

Ingredients:

3 tbsp. mustard
1 lb. carrot, peeled and sliced
1 tsp. cinnamon
2 tsp. butter
2 tbsp. honey
1 tsp. white sugar
½ tsp. salt
2 tbsp. water

Directions:

Toss the sliced carrots with cinnamon, water, salt, and sugar in a bowl.
Spread the seasoned carrots in the Slow Cooker.
Put the cooker's lid on and set the cooking time to 2 Hrs. on High settings.
Meanwhile, beat butter with honey and mustard in a separate bowl.
Pour this butter-honey mixture over the cooked carrots.
Cover again and slow cook them for another 30 Min. on the low setting.
Serve.

Zucchini Caviar

Servings:4 Cooking Time: 5 Hrs.

Ingredients:

4 cups zucchini, grated
2 tbsps. tomato paste
1 tsp. ground black pepper
1 tsp. olive oil
2 onions, diced
1 tsp. salt
1 cup of water

Directions:

Put all ingredients in the Slow Cooker.
Close the lid and cook the meal on Low for 5 Hrs.
Then carefully stir the caviar and cool it to the room temperature.

Broccoli Egg Pie

Servings: 7 Cooking Time: 4 Hrs. 25 Min

Ingredients:

7 oz. pie crust
1/3 cup sweet peas
2 tbsp. flour
4 oz. Romano cheese, shredded
1 tsp. salt
1 tomato, chopped
¼ cup broccoli, chopped
¼ cup heavy cream
3 eggs
1 tsp. cilantro
¼ cup spinach, chopped

Directions:

Cover the base of your Slow Cooker with a parchment sheet.
Spread the pie crust in the cooker and press it with your fingertips.
Mix chopped broccoli, sweet peas, flour, cream, salt, and cilantro in a bowl.
Beat eggs and add them to the cream mixture.
Stir in tomatoes and spinach to this mixture.
Spread this broccoli filling in the crust evenly
Put the cooker's lid on and set the cooking time to 4 Hrs. on High settings.
Drizzle cheese over the quiche and cover it again.
Put the cooker's lid on and set the cooking time to 25 Min. on High settings.
Serve warm.

Vegan Pepper Bowl

Servings:4 Cooking Time: 3.5 Hrs.

Ingredients:

2 cups bell pepper, sliced
1 tbsp. apple cider vinegar
5 oz. tofu, chopped
1 tsp. curry powder
1 tbsp. olive oil
4 tbsps. water
½ cup of coconut milk

Directions:

Put the sliced bell peppers in the Slow Cooker.
Sprinkle them with olive oil, apple cider vinegar, and water.

Close the lid and cook the vegetables on low for 3 Hrs.
Meanwhile, mix curry powder with coconut milk. Put the tofu in the curry mixture and leave for 15 Min.
Add the tofu and all remaining curry mixture in the Slow Cooker. Gently mix it and cook for 30 Min. on low.

Pinto Beans with Rice

Servings: 6 Cooking Time: 3 Hrs.

Ingredients:

1 lb. pinto beans, dried
Salt and black pepper to the taste
1 tsp. garlic powder
1 tbsp. chili powder
½ tsp. oregano, dried
1/3 cup hot sauce
1 tbsp. garlic, minced
½ tsp. cumin, ground
3 bay leaves
1 cup white rice, cooked

Directions:

Add pinto beans along with the rest of the ingredients to your Slow Cooker.
Put the cooker's lid on and set the cooking time to 3 Hrs. on High settings.
Serve warm on top of rice.

French Vegetable Stew

Servings: 6 Cooking Time: 9 Hrs.

Ingredients:

2 yellow onions, chopped
4 zucchinis, sliced
2 green bell peppers, cut into medium strips
2 tomatoes, cut into medium wedges
1 tsp. sugar
Salt and black pepper to the taste
¼ cup olive oil
1 eggplant, sliced
2 garlic cloves, minced
6 oz. canned tomato paste
1 tsp. oregano, dried
1 tsp. basil, dried
2 tbsp. parsley, chopped
A pinch of red pepper flakes, crushed

Directions:

Add onions, zucchinis, eggplant, garlic, tomato paste, bell peppers, sugar, basil, salt, black pepper, and oregano to the Slow Cooker.
Put the cooker's lid on and set the cooking time to 9 Hrs. on Low settings.
Stir in parsley and pepper flakes.
Serve warm.

Squash Noodles

Servings:4 Cooking Time: 4 Hrs.

Ingredients:

pound butternut squash, seeded, halved
1 tbsp. vegan butter
½ tsp. garlic powder
1 tsp. salt
3 cups of water

Directions:

Pour water in the Slow Cooker.
Add butternut squash and close the lid.
Cook the vegetable on high for 4 Hrs.
Then drain water and shred the squash flesh with the help of the fork and transfer in the bowl.
Add garlic powder, salt, and butter. Mix the squash noodles.

Beet and Capers Salad

Servings:4 Cooking Time: 4 Hrs.

Ingredients:

2 tsps. capers
2 oz. walnuts, chopped
1 tbsp. sunflower oil
3 cups of water
1 cup lettuce, chopped
1 tbsp. lemon juice
1 tsp. flax seeds
2 cups beets, peeled

Directions:

Pour water in the Slow Cooker and add beets. Cook them on High for 4 Hrs.
Then drain water, cool the beets and chop.
Put the chopped beets in the salad bowl.
Add capers, lettuce, walnuts, lemon juice, sunflower oil, and flax seeds.
Carefully mix the salad.

Rice Stuffed Eggplants

Servings: 4 Cooking Time: 8 Hrs.

Ingredients:

4 medium eggplants
½ cup chicken stock
1 tsp. paprika
3 tbsp. tomato sauce
1 cup rice, half-cooked
1 tsp. salt
½ cup fresh cilantro
1 tsp. olive oil

Directions:

Slice the eggplants in half and scoop 2/3 of the flesh from the center to make boats.
Mix rice with tomato sauce, paprika, salt, and cilantro in a bowl.
Now divide this rice mixture into the eggplant boats.
Pour stock and oil into the Slow Cooker and place the eggplants in it.
Put the cooker's lid on and set the cooking time to 8 Hrs. on Low settings.
Serve warm.

Brussel Sprouts

Servings:4 Cooking Time: 2.5 Hrs.

Ingredients:

1 pound Brussel sprouts
1 tsp. cayenne pepper
1 tbsp. vegan butter
2 oz. tofu, chopped, cooked
2 cups of water

Directions:

Pour water in the Slow Cooker.
Add Brussel sprouts and cayenne pepper.
Cook the vegetables on high for 2.5 Hrs.
Then drain water and mix Brussel sprouts with butter and tofu.
Shake the vegetables gently.

Ranch Broccoli

Servings:3 Cooking Time: 1.5 Hrs.

Ingredients:

3 cups broccoli
2 tbsps. ranch dressing
1 tsp. chili flakes
2 cups of water

Directions:

Put the broccoli in the Slow Cooker.

Add water and close the lid.
Cook the broccoli on high for 1.5 Hrs.
Then drain water and transfer the broccoli in the bowl.
Sprinkle it with chili flakes and ranch dressing. Shake the meal gently.

Aromatic Marinated Mushrooms

Servings:4 Cooking Time: 5 Hrs.

Ingredients:

1 tsp. dried rosemary
1 tsp. onion powder
4 cups mushrooms, roughly chopped
1 tsp. sugar
1 tsp. dried thyme
2 cups of water
1 tsp. salt
½ cup apple cider vinegar

Directions:

Pour water in the Slow Cooker.
Add all remaining ingredients and carefully mix.
Cook the mushrooms on Low for 5 Hrs.
After this, transfer the mushrooms with liquid in the glass cans and cool well.
Store the mushrooms in the fridge for up to 4 days.

Spinach with Halloumi Cheese Casserole

Servings:4 Cooking Time: 2 Hrs.

Ingredients:

1 package spinach, rinsed
Salt and pepper to taste
1 ½ cups halloumi cheese, grated
½ cup walnuts, chopped
1 tbsp. balsamic vinegar

Directions:

Place spinach and walnuts in the Slow Cooker.
Season with salt and pepper. Drizzle with balsamic vinegar.
Top with halloumi cheese and cook on low for 2 Hrs. or on high for 30 Min

Snack Recipes

Bean Dip

Servings: 56 Cooking Time: 3 Hrs.

Ingredients:

16 oz. Mexican cheese
16 oz. canned refried beans
Cooking spray
5 oz. canned green chilies
2 lbs. tortilla chips

Directions:

Grease your Slow Cooker with cooking spray, line it, add Mexican cheese, green chilies and refried beans, stir, cover and cook on Low for 3 Hrs.
Divide into bowls and serve with tortilla chips on the side.

Tacos

Servings: 2 Cooking Time: 4 Hrs.

Ingredients:

13 oz. canned pinto beans, drained
2 oz. chipotle pepper in adobo sauce, chopped
¼ tsp. cinnamon powder
¼ cup chili sauce
½ tbsp. cocoa powder
4 taco shells

Directions:

In your Slow Cooker, mix the beans with the chili sauce and the other ingredients except the taco shells, toss, put the lid on and cook on Low for 4 Hrs.
Divide the mix into the taco shells and serve them as an appetizer.

Tomato and Mushroom Salsa

Servings: 2 Cooking Time: 4 Hrs.

Ingredients:

1 cup cherry tomatoes, halved
1 cup mushrooms, sliced
1 small yellow onion, chopped
1 garlic clove, minced
12 oz. tomato sauce
¼ cup cream cheese, cubed
1 tbsp. chives, chopped
Salt and black pepper to the taste

Directions:

In your Slow Cooker, mix the tomatoes with the mushrooms and the other ingredients, toss, put the lid on and cook on Low for 4 Hrs.
Divide into bowls and serve as a party salsa

Nuts Bowls

Servings: 2 Cooking Time: 2 Hrs.

Ingredients:

2 tbsps. almonds, toasted
2 tbsps. pecans, halved and toasted
2 tbsps. hazelnuts, toasted and peeled
2 tbsps. sugar
½ cup coconut cream
2 tbsps. butter, melted
A pinch of cinnamon powder
A pinch of cayenne pepper

Directions:

In your Slow Cooker, mix the nuts with the sugar and the other ingredients, toss, put the lid on, cook on Low for 2 Hrs., divide into bowls and serve as a snack.

Chickpeas Spread

Servings: 2 Cooking Time: 8 Hrs.

Ingredients:

½ cup chickpeas, dried
1 tbsp. lemon juice
1 tbsp. tahini
1 garlic clove, minced
1 tbsps. olive oil
1 cup veggie stock
A pinch of salt and black pepper
½ tbsp. chives, chopped

Directions:

In your Slow Cooker, combine the chickpeas with the stock, salt, pepper and the garlic, stir, put the lid on and cook on Low for 8 Hrs.

Drain chickpeas, transfer them to a blender, add the rest of the ingredients, pulse well, divide into bowls and serve as a party spread.

Rice Snack Bowls

Servings: 2 Cooking Time: 6 Hrs.

Ingredients:

½ cup wild rice
½ cup brown rice
½ cup baby spinach
2 tbsps. pine nuts, toasted
1 tbsp. chives, chopped
½ tbsp. olive oil
1 red onion, sliced
2 cups veggie stock
½ cup cherry tomatoes, halved
1 tbsp. raisins
1 tbsp. dill, chopped
A pinch of salt and black pepper

Directions:

In your Slow Cooker, mix the rice with the onion, stock and the other ingredients, toss, put the lid on and cook on Low for 6 Hrs.
Divide in to bowls and serve as a snack.

Carrot Broccoli Fritters

Servings: 12 Cooking Time: 4 Hrs.

Ingredients:

2 large carrots, grated
1 tbsp. cream cheese
1 tsp. salt
1 tsp. paprika
4 tbsp. fresh cilantro, chopped
3 oz. celery stalk
4 oz. broccoli, chopped
¼ cup flour
1 tsp. ground black pepper
1 tsp. butter
1 egg

Directions:

Whisk egg with cream cheese, salt, flour, cilantro, black pepper, and paprika in a bowl.
Stir in celery stalk, carrots and broccoli, and mix to well to form a dough.
Divide the broccoli dough into 2 or 4 pieces and roll them into fritters.
Grease the base of Slow Cooker with butter and these fritters inside.
Put the cooker's lid on and set the cooking time to 3 Hrs. on High settings.
Flip the Slow Cooker fritters and again cover to cook for another 1 Hr.
Serve fresh,

Jalapeno Poppers

Servings: 4 Cooking Time: 3 Hrs.

Ingredients:

½ lb. chorizo, chopped
1 small white onion, chopped
¼ tsp. garlic powder
1 tbsp. mustard
10 jalapenos, tops cut off and deseeded
½ lb. beef, ground
1 tbsp. maple syrup
1/3 cup water

Directions:

In a bowl, mix beef with chorizo, garlic powder and onion and stir.
Stuff your jalapenos with the mix, place them in your Slow Cooker, add the water, cover and cook on High for 3 Hrs.
Transfer jalapeno poppers to a lined baking sheet.
In a bowl, mix maple syrup with mustard, whisk well, brush poppers with this mix, arrange on a platter and serve.

Creamy Mushroom Bites

Servings: 10 Cooking Time: 5 Hrs.

Ingredients:

7 oz. shiitake mushroom, chopped
1 tbsp. cream cheese
2 tbsp. flour
1 tsp. salt
1 tsp. olive oil
½ tsp. nutmeg
1 tsp. butter, melted
2 eggs
3 tbsp. panko bread crumbs
1 tsp. minced garlic
½ tsp. chili flakes
1 tsp. ground coriander
1 tbsp. almond flour

Directions:

Toss the mushrooms with salt, chili flakes, olive oil, ground coriander, garlic, and nutmeg in a skillet.
Stir cook for 5 Min. approximately on medium heat.
Whisk eggs with flour, cream cheese, and bread crumbs in a suitable bowl.
Stir in sauteed mushrooms and butter then mix well.
Knead this mushroom dough and divide it into golf ball-sized balls.
Pour the oil from the skillet in the Slow Cooker.
Add the mushroom dough balls to the cooker.
Put the cooker's lid on and set the cooking time to 3 Hrs. on High settings.
Flip the balls and cook for another 2 Hrs. on high heat.
Serve.

Simple Salsa

Servings: 6 Cooking Time: 5 Hrs.

Ingredients:

7 cups tomatoes, chopped
1 red bell pepper, chopped
4 jalapenos, chopped
1 tsp. coriander, ground
3 tbsps. basil, chopped
1 green bell pepper, chopped
2 yellow onions, chopped
¼ cup apple cider vinegar
1 tbsp. cilantro, chopped
Salt and black pepper to the taste

Directions:

In your Slow Cooker, mix tomatoes with green and red peppers, onions, jalapenos, vinegar, coriander, salt and pepper, stir, cover and cook on Low for 5 Hrs.
Add basil and cilantro, stir, divide into bowls and serve.

Salsa Snack

Servings: 6 Cooking Time: 3 Hrs.

Ingredients:

10 roma tomatoes, chopped
1 sweet onion, chopped
3 garlic cloves, minced
Salt and black pepper to the taste
2 jalapenos, chopped
28 oz. canned plum tomatoes
1 bunch cilantro, chopped

Directions:

In your Slow Cooker, mix roma tomatoes with jalapenos, onion, plum tomatoes and garlic, stir, cover and cook on High for 3 Hrs.

Add salt, pepper and cilantro, stir, divide into bowls and serve cold.

Garlicky Bacon Slices

Servings: 9 Cooking Time: 4 Hrs.

Ingredients:

10 oz. Canadian bacon, sliced
2 garlic cloves, peeled and sliced
1 tsp. dried dill
½ tsp. salt
2 tbsp. garlic powder
2 tbsp. whipped cream
1 tsp. chili flakes

Directions:

Season the bacon with garlic powder and spread it in the Slow Cooker.
Whisk the cream with garlic, dill, salt, and chili flakes in a bowl.
Spread this cream mixture over the bacon strips and leave for 10 Min.
Put the cooker's lid on and set the cooking time to 3 Hrs. on High settings.
Flip the bacon slices and remove excess liquid out of the cooker.
Put the cooker's lid on and set the cooking time to 1 Hr. on High settings.
Serve.

Apple Jelly Sausage Snack

Servings: 15 Cooking Time: 2 Hrs.

Ingredients:

2 lbs. sausages, sliced
9 oz. Dijon mustard
18 oz. apple jelly

Directions:

Place sausage slices in your Slow Cooker, add apple jelly and mustard, toss to coat well, cover and cook on Low for 2 Hrs.
Divide into bowls and serve as a snack.

White Cheese & Green Chilies Dip

Servings: 8 Cooking Time: 55 Min

Ingredients:

1 lb. white cheddar, cut into cubes
1 cup cream cheese
2 tbsps. butter, salted
1 can (11 oz.) green chilies, drained
1 tbsps. pepper flake, (optional)
3 tbsps. milk
3 tbsps. water

Directions:

Cut chilies into quarters. Place all the ingredients (except milk and water) in Crock-Pot. Close the lid and cook on HIGH for 30 Min. Stir the mixture until it is well combined and then add water and milk; continue to stir until it reaches desired consistency. Close lid and cook for another 20 Min. Let cool and serve.

Cheeseburger Cream Dip

Servings: 10 Cooking Time: 3 Hrs.

Ingredients:

1 lb. beef, ground
Salt and black pepper to the taste
8 bacon strips, chopped
1 yellow onion, chopped
1 cup sour cream
2 tbsp. mustard
1 and ½ cup cheddar cheese, shredded
1 tsp. garlic powder
2 tbsp. Worcestershire sauce
3 garlic cloves, minced
12 oz. cream cheese, soft
2 tbsp. ketchup
10 oz. canned tomatoes and chilies, chopped
1 cup mozzarella, shredded

Directions:

Add beef, Worcestershire sauce and all other ingredients to the Slow Cooker.
Put the cooker's lid on and set the cooking time to 3 Hrs. on Low settings.
Serve fresh.

Cheese Stuffed Meat Balls

Servings: 9 Cooking Time: 9 Hrs.

Ingredients:

10 oz. ground pork
1 tsp. ground black pepper
1 tsp. paprika
6 oz. Romano cheese, cut into cubes
1 tsp. chili flakes
2 tsp. milk
1 tbsp. minced garlic
1 tsp. salt
1 tsp. oregano
1 cup panko bread crumbs
1 egg
1 tsp. olive oil

Directions:

Mix ground pork with oregano, chili flakes, paprika, salt, garlic, and black pepper in a bowl.
Stir in beaten egg and milk, then mix well with your hands.
Make golf ball-sized meatballs out of this beef mixture and insert one cheese cubes into each ball.
Roll each meatball in the bread crumbs to coat well.
Place these cheese-stuffed meatballs in the Slow Cooker.
Put the cooker's lid on and set the cooking time to 9 Hrs. on Low settings.
Serve warm.

Eggplant Dip

Servings: 4 Cooking Time: 4 Hrs. and 10 Min

Ingredients:

1 eggplant
2 tbsps. olive oil
1 tbsp. parsley, chopped
1 celery stick, chopped
2 tbsps. tomato paste
A pinch of sea salt
1 zucchini, chopped
2 tbsps. balsamic vinegar
1 yellow onion, chopped
1 tomato, chopped
1 and ½ tsps. garlic, minced
Black pepper to the taste

Directions:

Brush eggplant with the oil, place on preheated grill and cook over medium-high heat for 5 Min. on each side.
Leave aside to cool down, chop it and put in your Slow Cooker.
Also add, zucchini, vinegar, onion, celery, tomato, parsley, tomato paste, garlic, salt and pepper and stir everything.
Cover and cook on High for 4 Hrs.
Stir your spread again very well, divide into bowls and serve.

Salsa Corn Dip

Servings: 12 Cooking Time: 2 Hrs. and 30 Min

Ingredients:

2 tsps. cumin, ground
12 oz. corn
4 garlic cloves, minced
1 cup Monterey jack cheese, shredded
½ cup cilantro, chopped
16 oz. salsa Verde
1 yellow onion, chopped
8 oz. cream cheese, soft
pint cherry tomatoes, quartered
Cooking spray

Directions:

Grease your Slow Cooker with cooking spray and mix salsa with cumin, corn, onion, garlic, cream cheese, Monterey Jack cheese, cherry tomatoes and cilantro.
Stir, cover and cook on High for 2 Hrs. and 30 Min.
Divide into bowls and serve as a snack.

Cheesy Potato Dip

Servings: 12 Cooking Time: 5 Hrs.

Ingredients:

1 cup heavy cream
2 tbsp. cornstarch
5 oz. Cheddar cheese, chopped
1 tsp. salt
1 tsp. paprika
1 tbsp. garlic powder
1 cup milk
5 medium potatoes, peeled and diced
1 cup fresh cilantro
1 tsp. black pepper
½ tsp. onion powder
¼ tsp. oregano

Directions:

Add milk, cream, potatoes, salt, paprika, onion powder, oregano, garlic powder, and black pepper to the Slow Cooker.
Put the cooker's lid on and set the cooking time to 3 Hrs. on High settings.
Stir in cilantro and cheese to the cooked potatoes.
Put the cooker's lid on and set the cooking time to 2 Hrs. on High settings.
Mix well and serve.

Chicken Meatballs

Servings: 2 Cooking Time: 7 Hrs.

Ingredients:

A pinch of red pepper flakes, crushed
1 egg, whisked
1 tsp. oregano, dried
½ tsp. rosemary, dried
A pinch of salt and black pepper
½ lb. chicken breast, skinless, boneless, ground
½ cup salsa Verde
½ tsp. chili powder
1 tbsp. parsley, chopped

Directions:

In a bowl, mix the chicken with the egg and the other ingredients except the salsa, stir well and shape medium meatballs out of this mix.
Put the meatballs in the Slow Cooker, add the salsa Verde, toss gently, put the lid on and cook on Low for 7 Hrs.
Arrange the meatballs on a platter and serve.

Crock-pot Coconut Cake

Servings: 8 Cooking Time: 1 Hr. and 50 Min

Ingredients:

½ cup butter
2 ¼ cup coconut flour
1 cup sweetener
1 tsp. baking powder
½ cup coconut oil
½ cup coconut milk
3 eggs
Dash of salt

Directions:

In a large mixing bowl, mix butter, coconut oil, and sweetener. Add eggs, one at a time, and stir well after each addition. Mix together the flour, salt, and baking powder in another bowl. Gradually add the coconut milk; combine with the butter mixture until it is well mixed. Grease ceramic cooker with butter in Crock-Pot and line with baking paper. Spread dough evenly on baking paper. Cover with lid, and put a few layers of kitchen paper on the lid to absorb moisture. Cook on HIGH for about 1 to 1 ½ Hrs. When ready, open the lid and take out the ceramic cooker. Let it cool for about 10 Min. Carefully remove the cake from mold and let it cool for about 1 Hr. Serve.

Curry Pork Meatballs

Servings: 2 Cooking Time: 4 Hrs.

Ingredients:

½ lb. pork stew meat, ground
1 egg, whisked
1 tbsp. cilantro, chopped
¼ tbsp. green curry paste
1 red onion, chopped
Salt and black pepper to the taste
5 oz. coconut milk

Directions:

In a bowl, mix the meat with the onion and the other ingredients except the coconut milk, stir well and shape medium meatballs out of this mix.
Put the meatballs in your Slow Cooker, add the coconut milk, put the lid on and cook on High for 4 Hrs.
Arrange the meatballs on a platter and serve them as an appetizer

Bulgur and Beans Salsa

Servings: 2 Cooking Time: 8 Hrs.

Ingredients:

1 cup veggie stock
1 small yellow onion, chopped
1 garlic clove, minced
½ cup salsa
¼ tsp. oregano, dried
½ cup bulgur
1 red bell pepper, chopped
5 oz. canned kidney beans, drained
1 tbsp. chili powder
Salt and black pepper to the taste

Directions:

In your Slow Cooker, mix the bulgur with the stock and the other ingredients, toss, put the lid on and cook on Low for 8 Hrs.
Divide into bowls and serve cold as an appetizer.

Broccoli Dip

Servings: 2 Cooking Time: 2 Hrs.

Ingredients:

1 green chili pepper, minced
1 cup broccoli florets
2 tbsps. cream cheese, cubed
1 tbsp. chives, chopped
2 tbsps. heavy cream
1 tbsp. mayonnaise
A pinch of salt and black pepper

Directions:

In your Slow Cooker, mix the broccoli with the chili pepper, mayo and the other ingredients, toss, put the lid on and cook on Low for 2 Hrs.
Blend using an immersion blender, divide into bowls and serve as a party dip.

Chicken Taco Nachos

Servings: 10 Cooking Time: 4 Hrs.

Ingredients:

1 tbsp. taco seasoning
1 tsp. salt
1 onion, chopped
2 tbsp. salsa
4 tbsp. tomato sauce
1 tbsp. chives, chopped
7 oz. tortilla chips
16 oz. chicken breast, boneless, diced
1 tsp. paprika
1 chili pepper, chopped
1 tsp. minced garlic
1 tsp. thyme
6 oz. Cheddar cheese, shredded
1 avocado, pitted, peeled and diced

Directions:

Mix taco seasoning, salt, thyme, and paprika in a shallow bowl.
Set the chicken in the Slow Cooker and drizzle the taco mixture over it.
Add tomato sauce, salsa, garlic, chili pepper, and onion to the cooker.
Put the cooker's lid on and set the cooking time to 2 Hrs. on High settings.
Use two forks and shred the slow-cooked chicken.
Spread the tortilla chip on the serving plate and top
Place the tortilla chips on the serving plate and top them with shredded chicken.
Add chives, cheese, and avocado pieces.
Serve.

Peanut Snack

Servings: 4 Cooking Time: 1 Hr. and 30 Min

Ingredients:

1 cup peanuts
12 oz. dark chocolate chips
1 cup chocolate peanut butter
12 oz. white chocolate chips

Directions:

In your Slow Cooker, mix peanuts with peanut butter, dark and white chocolate chips, cover and cook on Low for 1 Hr. and 30 Min.
Divide this mix into small muffin cups, leave aside to cool down and serve as a snack.

Chicken Salad

Servings: 2 Cooking Time: 6 Hrs.

Ingredients:

2 chicken breasts, skinless, boneless and cubed
½ tbsp. olive oil
½ cup mushrooms, sliced
½ cup cherry tomatoes, halved
2 oz. baby spinach
½ tbsp. lemon juice
A pinch of salt and black pepper
½ cup mild salsa
1 red onion, chopped
½ cup kalamata olives, pitted and halved
1 chili pepper, chopped
1 tsp. oregano, chopped
½ cup veggie stock

Directions:

In your Slow Cooker, mix the chicken with the salsa, oil and the other ingredients except the spinach, toss, put the lid on and cook on High for 5 Hrs.
Add the spinach, cook on High for 1 more Hr., divide into bowls and serve as an appetizer.

Crock-pot Citrus Cake

Servings: 10 Cooking Time: 6 Hrs.

Ingredients:

½ tsp. orange rind, grated
1 ½ tbsps. lemon rind, grated
1 ½ cup almond milk
1 cup butter, softened
3 egg yolks
½ cup almond flour
1 tbsp. grapefruit juice (freshly squeezed)
1 cup sweetener
4 egg whites
3 tbsps. lime juice (freshly squeezed)

Directions:

In a bowl, beat sweetener and butter. Mix in flour and stir until well blended. Add the lime, lemon, and orange rinds and all citrus juices. Whisk egg yolks and milk in another bowl; pour into bowl with flour mixture and stir well. In a separate bowl, beat egg whites until they form stiff peaks, then fold into the batter; stir. Spoon the mixture into a lightly greased heat-proof bowl/dish and cover with foil. Pour a cup of water into Crock-Pot and place the batter dish into it. Cover and cook on LOW for 5-6 Hrs.

Beef and Chipotle Dip

Servings: 10 Cooking Time: 2 Hrs.

Ingredients:

8 oz. cream cheese, soft
2 tbsps. mayonnaise
¼ tsp. garlic powder
2 oz. dried beef, chopped
2 tbsps. yellow onion, chopped
2 oz. hot pepper Monterey Jack cheese, shredded
2 chipotle chilies in adobo sauce, chopped
¼ cup pecans, chopped

Directions:

In your Slow Cooker, mix cream cheese with onion, mayo, Monterey Jack cheese, garlic powder, chilies and dried beef, stir, cover and cook on Low for 2 Hrs.
Add pecans, stir, divide into bowls and serve.

Lentils Dip

Servings: 2 Cooking Time: 6 Hrs.

Ingredients:

2 carrots, peeled and grated
A pinch of cayenne pepper
¼ cup lemon juice
2 garlic cloves, minced
2 tbsps. tahini paste
1 cup canned lentils, drained

A pinch of sea salt and black pepper
and rinsed
½ tbsp. rosemary, chopped

Directions:

In your Slow Cooker, mix the lentils with the carrots, garlic and the other ingredients, toss, put the lid on and cook on Low for 6 Hrs.
Transfer to a blender, pulse well, divide into bowls and serve.

Zucchini Spread

Servings: 2 Cooking Time: 6 Hrs.

Ingredients:

1 tbsp. walnuts, chopped
1 cup heavy cream
1 tbsp. tahini paste
2 zucchinis, grated
1 tsp. balsamic vinegar
1 tbsp. chives, chopped

Directions:

In your Slow Cooker, combine the zucchinis with the cream, walnuts and the other ingredients, whisk, put the lid on and cook on Low for 6 Hrs.
Blend using an immersion blender, divide into bowls and serve as a party spread.

Zucchini Sticks

Servings: 13 Cooking Time: 2 Hrs.

Ingredients:

9 oz. green zucchini, cut into thick sticks
4 oz. Parmesan, grated
1 tsp. salt
1 tsp. olive oil
1 egg
1 tsp. ground white pepper
2 tbsp. milk

Directions:

Grease of the base of your Slow Cooker with olive oil.
Whisk egg with milk, white pepper, and salt in a bowl.
Dip the prepared zucchini sticks in the egg mixture then place them in the Slow Cooker.
Put the cooker's lid on and set the cooking time to 2 Hrs. on High settings.
Spread the cheese over the zucchini sticks evenly.
Put the cooker's lid on and set the cooking time to 2 Hrs. on High settings.
Serve.

Macadamia Nuts Snack

Servings: 2 Cooking Time: 2 Hrs.

Ingredients:

½ lb. macadamia nuts
¼ cup water
½ tsp. oregano, dried
1 tbsp. avocado oil
½ tbsp. chili powder
½ tsp. onion powder

Directions:

In your Slow Cooker, mix the macadamia nuts with the oil and the other ingredients, toss, put the lid on, cook on Low for 2 Hrs., divide into bowls and serve as a snack.

Stuffed Peppers Platter

Servings: 2 Cooking Time: 4 Hrs.

Ingredients:

1 red onion, chopped
½ tsp. sweet paprika
1 garlic clove, minced
½ cup corn
2 colored bell peppers, tops and insides scooped out
1 tsps. olive oil
½ tbsp. chili powder
1 cup white rice, cooked
A pinch of salt and black pepper
½ cup tomato sauce

Directions:

In a bowl, mix the onion with the oil, paprika and the other ingredients except the peppers and tomato sauce, stir well and stuff the peppers the with this mix.
Put the peppers in the Slow Cooker, add the sauce, put the lid on and cook on Low for 4 Hrs.
Transfer the peppers on a platter and serve as an appetizer.

Calamari Rings Bowls

Servings: 2 Cooking Time: 6 Hrs.

Ingredients:

½ lb. calamari rings
½ tbsp. soy sauce
1 cup veggie stock
½ tsp. sweet paprika
1 tbsp. balsamic vinegar
1 tbsp. sugar
½ tsp. turmeric powder
½ cup chicken stock

Directions:

In your Slow Cooker, mix the calamari rings with the vinegar, soy sauce and the other ingredients, toss, put the lid on and cook on High for 6 Hrs.
Divide into bowls and serve right away as an appetizer.

Mixed Nuts

Servings: 6 Cooking Time: 40 Min

Ingredients:

½ tsp. cooking spray
1 tsp. ground cinnamon
1 tsp. salt
1 cup cashew
3 tbsp. maple syrup
1 tsp. chili flakes
2 oz. butter, melted
1 cup peanuts
1 cup walnuts

Directions:

Toss cashew, peanuts, and walnuts in a baking sheet and bake for 10 Min. at 350 degrees F.
Toss the nuts after every 2 Min. of cooking.
Mix chili flakes, salt, and cinnamon ground in a bowl.
Transfer the nuts to the Slow Cooker and drizzle spice mixture on top.
Whisk maple syrup and melted butter in a bowl and pour over the nuts.
Put the cooker's lid on and set the cooking time to 20 Min. on High settings.
Stir the nuts well, then continue cooking for another 20 Min. on High setting.
Serve.

Spicy Mussels

Servings: 4 Cooking Time: 1 Hr.

Ingredients:

2 lbs. mussels, scrubbed and debearded

2 tbsps. olive oil
½ tsp. red pepper flakes
2 tsps. garlic, minced
2 tsps. oregano, dried
1 yellow onion, chopped
14 oz. tomatoes, chopped
½ cup chicken stock

Directions:

In your Slow Cooker, mix oil with onions, pepper flakes, garlic, stock, oregano, tomatoes and mussels, stir, cover and cook on High for 1 Hr.

Divide between bowls and serve.

Piquant Mushrooms

Servings: 3 Cooking Time: Low Setting-4 Hrs. Or High-2 Hrs.

Ingredients:

2 tbsps. ghee/butter
Ginger, grated
2 cloves garlic, chopped
1 tsp. chili powder
2 cups water
1 tbsp. fresh lemon juice
1 lb. mushrooms, fresh
1 onion, chopped
1 tbsp. olive oil
Basil, oregano, parsley, and thyme, to taste
Salt and pepper to taste

Directions:

Rinse and slice mushrooms. Peel and grate ginger. Place mushrooms and all remaining ingredients in Crock-Pot. Stir in the water. Cover with lid and cook on LOW for 3-4 Hrs. or on HIGH for 1-2 Hrs. Just before serving, sprinkle with fresh lemon juice and parsley. Serve with steak bites.

Almond Spread

Servings: 2 Cooking time: 8 Hrs.

Ingredients:

¼ cup almonds
½ tsp. nutritional yeast flakes
1 cup heavy cream
A pinch of salt and black pepper

Directions:

In your Slow Cooker, mix the almonds with the cream and the other ingredients, toss, put the lid on and cook on Low for 8 Hrs.

Transfer to a blender, pulse well, divide into bowls and serve.

Black Bean Salsa Salad

Servings: 6 Cooking Time: 4 Hrs.

Ingredients:

1 tbsp. soy sauce
1 cup canned black beans
6 cups romaine lettuce leaves
½ tsp. cumin, ground
1 cup salsa
½ cup avocado, peeled, pitted and mashed

Directions:

In your Slow Cooker, mix black beans with salsa, cumin and soy sauce, stir, cover and cook on Low for 4 Hrs.

In a salad bowl, mix lettuce leaves with black beans mix and mashed avocado, toss and serve.

Apple Sausage Snack

Servings: 15 Cooking Time: 2 Hrs.

Ingredients:

2 lbs. sausages, sliced
9 oz. Dijon mustard
18 oz. apple jelly

Directions:

Add sausage slices, apple jelly, and mustard to the Slow Cooker.

Put the cooker's lid on and set the cooking time to 2 Hrs. on Low settings.

Serve fresh.

Black Eyes Peas Dip

Servings: 4 Cooking Time: 5 Hrs.

Ingredients:

1 ½ cups black-eyed peas
1 tsp. Cajun seasoning
½ tsp. garlic powder
Salt and black pepper to the taste
½ tsp. Tabasco sauce
3 cups of water
½ cup pecans, toasted
½ tsp. jalapeno powder
¼ tsp. liquid smoke

Directions:

Add water, salt, Cajun seasoning, black pepper, and black eye peas to the Slow Cooker.

Put the cooker's lid on and set the cooking time to 5 Hrs. on High settings.

Drain and transfer the black-eyed peas to a blender jug.

Add jalapeno powder, tabasco sauce, pecans, garlic, liquid smoke, salt and black pepper, to taste.

Blend this black-eyes pea dip until smooth.

Serve.

Mozzarella Basil Tomatoes

Servings: 8 Cooking Time: 30 Min

Ingredients:

3 tbsp. fresh basil
5 oz. Mozzarella, sliced
1 tbsp. olive oil
½ tsp. onion powder
1 tsp. chili flakes
4 large tomatoes, sliced
1 tsp. minced garlic
½ tsp. cilantro

Directions:

Whisk olive oil with onion powder, cilantro, garlic, and chili flakes in a bowl.

Rub all the tomato slices with this cilantro mixture.

Top each tomato slice with cheese slice and then place another tomato slice on top to make a sandwich.

Insert a toothpick into each tomato sandwich to seal it.

Place them in the base of the Slow Cooker.

Put the cooker's lid on and set the cooking time to 20 Min. on High settings.

Garnish with basil.

Enjoy.

Fava Bean Onion Dip

Servings: 6 Cooking Time: 5 Hrs.

Ingredients:

1 lb. fava bean, rinsed
4 and ½ cups of water
¼ cup olive oil
2 tbsp. lemon juice
1 cup yellow onion, chopped
1 bay leaf
1 garlic clove, minced
Salt to the taste

Directions:

Add 4 cups water, bay leaf, salt, and fava beans to the Slow Cooker.
Put the cooker's lid on and set the cooking time to 3 Hrs. on low settings.
Drain the Slow Cooker beans and discard the bay leaf.
Return the cooked beans to the cooker and add onion, garlic, and ½ cup water.
Put the cooker's lid on and set the cooking time to 2 Hrs. on Low settings.
Blend the slow-cooked beans with lemon juice and olive oil.
Serve.

Potato Cups

Servings: 8 Cooking Time: 8 Hrs.

Ingredients:

5 tbsp. mashed potato
3 tbsp. green peas
3 tbsp. sour cream
7 oz. puff pastry
4 oz. Parmesan, shredded
1 carrot, boiled, cubed
1 tsp. paprika
1 tsp. minced garlic
1 egg yolk, beaten

Directions:

Mix mashed potato with carrot cubes in a bowl.
Stir in sour cream, paprika, green peas, and garlic, then mix well.
Spread the puff pastry and slice it into 2x2 inches squares.
Place the puff pastry square in the muffin cups of the muffin tray.
Press the puff pastry and in the muffin cups and brush it with egg yolk.
Divide the potatoes mixture into the muffin cups
Place the muffin tray in the Slow Cooker.
Put the cooker's lid on and set the cooking time to 8 Hrs. on Low settings.
Serve.

Cauliflower Bites

Servings: 2 Cooking Time: 4 Hrs.

Ingredients:

2 cups cauliflower florets
1 tbsp. sweet paprika
1 tsp. sweet paprika
¼ cup veggie stock
1 tbsp. Italian seasoning
2 tbsps. tomato sauce
1 tbsp. olive oil

Directions:

In your Slow Cooker, mix the cauliflower florets with the Italian seasoning and the other ingredients, toss, put the lid on and cook on Low for 4 Hrs.
Divide into bowls and serve as a snack.

Wild Rice Pilaf

Servings: 8 Cooking Time: 3 Hrs. and 10 Min

Ingredients:

2 green onions, chopped
1 cup whole tomatoes, sliced
4 cups water
4 tbsps. olive oil
2 cups long grain wild rice
1 tsp. seasonings, thyme, basil, rosemary
1 lemon rind, finely grated
Sea salt and fresh cracked pepper to taste

Directions:

Place all the ingredients in Crock-Pot except the seasonings and lemon rind, and give it a good stir. Close the lid and cook on HIGH for 1 ½ Hrs. or on LOW for 3 Hrs. After done cooking add seasoning to taste. Sprinkle with lemon rind and serve hot.

Potato Onion Salsa

Servings: 6 Cooking Time: 8 Hrs.

Ingredients:

1 sweet onion, chopped
2 tbsp. mustard
1 and ½ lbs. gold potatoes, cut into medium cubes
1 cup celery, chopped
¼ cup white vinegar
Salt and black pepper to the taste
¼ cup dill, chopped
Cooking spray

Directions:

Grease the base of the Slow Cooker with cooking spray.
Add onion, potatoes and all other ingredients to the cooker.
Put the cooker's lid on and set the cooking time to 8 Hrs. on Low settings.
Mix well and serve.

Almond Bowls

Servings: 2 Cooking Time: 4 Hrs.

Ingredients:

1 tbsp. cinnamon powder
2 cups almonds
½ tsps. vanilla extract
1 cup sugar
½ cup water

Directions:

In your Slow Cooker, mix the almonds with the cinnamon and the other ingredients, toss, put the lid on and cook on Low for 4 Hrs.
Divide into bowls and serve as a snack.

Caramel Corn

Servings: 13 Cooking Time: 2 Hrs.

Ingredients:

½ cup butter
¼ cup corn syrup
1 tsp. baking soda
1 cup mixed nuts
1 tsp. vanilla extract
1 cup brown sugar
12 cups plain popcorn
Cooking spray

Directions:

Grease your Slow Cooker with cooking spray, add butter, vanilla, corn syrup, brown sugar and baking soda, cover and cook on High for 1 Hr., stirring after 30 Min.
Add popcorn, toss, cover and cook on Low for 1 Hr. more.
Add nuts, toss, divide into bowls and serve as a snack.

Eggplant Salsa

Servings: 4 Cooking Time: 7 Hrs.

Ingredients:

1 and ½ cups tomatoes, chopped
2 tsps. capers
4 garlic cloves, minced
1 tbsp. basil, chopped
3 cups eggplant, cubed
6 oz. green olives, pitted and sliced
2 tsps. balsamic vinegar
Salt and black pepper to the

taste

Directions:

In your Slow Cooker, mix tomatoes with eggplant cubes, capers, green olives, garlic, vinegar, basil, salt and pepper, toss, cover and cook on Low for 7 Hrs.

Divide salsa into bowls and serve.

Queso Dip

Servings: 10 Cooking Time: 1 Hr.

Ingredients:

16 oz. Velveeta
½ cup cotija
2 tsps. sweet paprika
A pinch of cayenne pepper
1 cup whole milk
2 jalapenos, chopped
2 garlic cloves, minced
1 tbsp. cilantro, chopped

Directions:

In your Slow Cooker, mix Velveeta with milk, cotija, jalapenos, paprika, garlic and cayenne, stir, cover and cook on High for 1 Hr.

Stir the dip, add cilantro, divide into bowls and serve as a dip.

Cauliflower Dip

Servings: 2 Cooking Time: 5 Hrs.

Ingredients:

1 cup cauliflower florets
1 tbsp. tahini paste
2 garlic cloves, minced
1 tbsp. basil, chopped
A pinch of salt and black pepper
½ cup heavy cream
½ cup white mushrooms, chopped
2 tbsps. lemon juice
1 tsp. rosemary, dried

Directions:

In your Slow Cooker, mix the cauliflower with the cream, tahini paste and the other ingredients, toss, put the lid on and cook on Low for 5 Hrs.

Transfer to a blender, pulse well, divide into bowls and serve as a party dip.

Cashew Dip

Servings: 10 Cooking Time: 3 Hrs.

Ingredients:

1 cup water
10 oz. hummus
¼ tsp. onion powder
¼ tsp. mustard powder
1 cup cashews
¼ tsp. garlic powder
A pinch of salt and black pepper
1 tsp. apple cider vinegar

Directions:

In your Slow Cooker, mix water with cashews, salt and pepper, stir, cover and cook on High for 3 Hrs.

Transfer to your blender, add hummus, garlic powder, onion powder, mustard powder and vinegar, pulse well, divide into bowls and serve.

Cheesy Corn Dip

Servings: 12 Cooking Time: 4 Hrs.

Ingredients:

3 cups corn
1 and ½ cup cheddar cheese, shredded
2 oz. black olives, pitted and sliced
Cooking spray
8 oz. cream cheese, soft
½ cup salsa Verde
1 tsp. chives, chopped

Directions:

Grease your Slow Cooker with the cooking spray, add corn, cream cheese, cheddar, salsa Verde, olives and chives, stir, cover and cook on Low for 4 Hrs.

Divide into bowls and serve as a snack.

Lemony Artichokes

Servings: 4 Cooking Time: 4 Hrs. and 10 Min

Ingredients:

4 artichokes
3 tbsps. lemon juice
Ground black pepper to taste
2 tbsps. coconut butter, melted
1 tsp. sea salt

Directions:

Wash the artichokes. Pull off the outermost leaves until you get to the lighter yellow leaves. Cut off the top third or so of the artichokes. Trim the bottom of the stems. Place in Crock-Pot. Mix together lemon juice, salt, and melted coconut butter and pour over artichokes. Cover and cook on LOW for 6-8 Hrs. or on HIGH for 3-4 Hrs. Serve.

Lentils Hummus

Servings: 2 Cooking Time: 4 Hrs.

Ingredients:

1 cup chicken stock
2 tbsps. tahini paste
¼ cup heavy cream
¼ tsp. turmeric powder
1 cup canned lentils, drained
¼ tsp. onion powder
A pinch of salt and black pepper
1 tsp. lemon juice

Directions:

In your Slow Cooker, mix the lentils with the stock, onion powder, salt and pepper, toss, put the lid on and cook on High for 4 Hrs.

Drain the lentils, transfer to your blender, add the rest of the ingredients, pulse well, divide into bowls and serve.

Buffalo Meatballs

Servings: 36 Cooking Time: 3 Hrs. and 10 Min

Ingredients:

1 cup breadcrumbs
2 eggs
½ cup yellow onion, chopped
Salt and black pepper to the taste
¼ cup butter, melted
2 lbs. chicken, ground
¾ cup buffalo wings sauce
3 garlic cloves, minced
2 tbsps. olive oil
1 cup blue cheese dressing

Directions:

In a bowl, mix chicken with breadcrumbs, eggs, onion, garlic, salt and pepper, stir and shape small meatballs out of this mix.

Heat up a pan with the oil over medium-high heat, add meatballs, brown them for a few Min. on each side and transfer them to your Slow Cooker.

Add melted butter and buffalo wings sauce, cover and cook on Low for 3 Hrs.

Arrange meatballs on a platter and serve them with the blue cheese dressing on the side.

Thyme Pepper Shrimp

Servings: 5 Cooking Time: 25 Min

Ingredients:

1 tsp. sage
1 tsp. thyme
2 tbsp. heavy cream
¼ cup butter
½ cup fresh parsley
1 tbsp. Piri Piri sauce
1 tbsp. cayenne pepper
1 tsp. salt
1 lb. shrimp, peeled

Directions:

Blend butter with Piri Piri, thyme, sage, cayenne pepper, salt, and cream in a blender until smooth.
Add this buttercream mixture to the Slow Cooker.
Put the cooker's lid on and set the cooking time to 10 Min. on High settings.
Now add the shrimp to the Slow Cooker and cover again to cook for another 15 Min.
Serve warm.

Cinnamon Pecans Snack

Servings: 2 Cooking Time: 3 Hrs.

Ingredients:

½ tbsp. cinnamon powder
½ tbsp. avocado oil
2 cups pecans
¼ cup water
½ tsp. chili powder

Directions:

In your Slow Cooker, mix the pecans with the cinnamon and the other ingredients, toss, put the lid on and cook on Low for 3 Hrs.
Divide the pecans into bowls and serve as a snack.

Onion Dip

Servings: 6 Cooking Time: 1 Hr.

Ingredients:

8 oz. cream cheese, soft
1 cup cheddar cheese, shredded
2 yellow onions, chopped
¾ cup sour cream
10 bacon slices, cooked and chopped

Directions:

In your Slow Cooker, mix cream cheese with sour cream, cheddar cheese, bacon and onion, stir, cover and cook on High for 1 Hr.
Divide into bowls and serve.

Veggie Spread

Servings: 4 Cooking Time: 7 Hrs.

Ingredients:

1 cup carrots, sliced
1/3 cup cashews
2 and ½ cups water
1 tsp. garlic powder
¼ tsp. smoked paprika
A pinch of salt
1 and ½ cups cauliflower florets
½ cup turnips, chopped
1 cup almond milk
Salt and black pepper to the taste
¼ tsp. mustard powder

Directions:

In your Slow Cooker, mix carrots with cauliflower, cashews, turnips and water, stir, cover and cook on Low for 7 Hrs.
Drain, transfer to a blender, add almond milk, garlic powder, paprika, mustard powder, salt and pepper, blend well, divide into bowls and serve as a snack.

Stuffed Mushrooms

Servings: 2 Cooking Time: 3 Hrs.

Ingredients:

¼ lb. chorizo, chopped
1 red onion, chopped
¼ tsp. garlic powder
4 Portobello mushroom caps
Salt and black pepper to the taste
¼ cup tomato sauce

Directions:

In a bowl, mix the chorizo with the onion, garlic powder, salt and pepper, stir and stuff the mushroom caps with this mix.
Put the mushroom caps in the Slow Cooker, add the tomato sauce, put the lid on and cook on High for 3 Hrs.
Arrange the stuffed mushrooms on a platter and serve.

Crab Dip

Servings: 6 Cooking Time: 2 Hrs.

Ingredients:

12 oz. cream cheese
½ cup mayonnaise
2 garlic cloves, minced
1 and ½ tbsp. Worcestershire sauce
12 oz. crabmeat
½ cup parmesan, grated
½ cup green onions, chopped
Juice of 1 lemon
1 and ½ tsps. old bay seasoning

Directions:

In your Slow Cooker, mix cream cheese with parmesan, mayo, green onions, garlic, lemon juice, Worcestershire sauce, old bay seasoning and crabmeat, stir, cover and cook on Low for 2 Hrs.
Divide into bowls and serve as a dip.

Beef Meatballs

Servings: 8 Cooking Time: 8 Hrs.

Ingredients:

1 and ½ lbs. beef, ground
16 oz. canned tomatoes, crushed
¼ cup parsley, chopped
1 yellow onion, chopped
1 egg, whisked
14 oz. canned tomato puree
2 garlic cloves, minced
Salt and black pepper to the taste

Directions:

In a bowl, mix beef with egg, parsley, garlic, black pepper and onion, stir well and shape 16 meatballs.
Place them in your Slow Cooker, add tomato puree and crushed tomatoes on top, cover and cook on Low for 8 Hrs.
Arrange them on a platter and serve.

Sweet Potato Dip

Servings: 2 Cooking Time: 4 Hrs.

Ingredients:

2 sweet potatoes, peeled and
½ cup coconut cream

cubed
½ tsp. turmeric powder
2 garlic cloves, minced
1 cup basil leaves
1 tbsp. lemon juice
½ tsp. garam masala
½ cup veggie stock
2 tbsps. olive oil
A pinch of salt and black pepper

Directions:

In your Slow Cooker, mix the sweet potatoes with the cream, turmeric and the other ingredients, toss, put the lid on and cook on High for 4 Hrs.
Blend using an immersion blender, divide into bowls and serve as a party dip.

Jalapeno Onion Dip

Servings: 6 Cooking Time: 4 Hrs.

Ingredients:

7 cups tomatoes, chopped
1 red onion, chopped
1 red bell pepper, chopped
¼ cup apple cider vinegar
1 tbsp. sage, chopped
Salt to the taste
1 yellow onion, chopped
3 jalapenos, chopped
1 green bell pepper, chopped
1 tbsp. cilantro, chopped
3 tbsp. basil, chopped

Directions:

Add tomatoes, onion and all other ingredients to the Slow Cooker.
Put the cooker's lid on and set the cooking time to 4 Hrs. on Low settings.
Puree the cooked mixture in a blender until smooth.
Serve.

Paprika Cod Sticks

Servings: 2 Cooking Time: 2 Hrs.

Ingredients:

1 egg whisked
½ cup almond flour
½ tsp. coriander, ground
A pinch of salt and black pepper
Cooking spray
½ lb. cod fillets, cut into medium strips
½ tsp. cumin, ground
½ tsp. turmeric powder
¼ tsp. sweet paprika

Directions:

In a bowl, mix the flour with cumin, coriander and the other ingredients except the fish, eggs and cooking spray.
Put the egg in another bowl and whisk it.
Dip the fish sticks in the egg and then dredge them in the flour mix.
Grease the Slow Cooker with cooking spray, add fish sticks, put the lid on, cook on High for 2 Hrs., arrange on a platter and serve.

Spicy Dip

Servings: 10 Cooking Time: 3 Hrs.

Ingredients:

20 oz. canned tomatoes and green chilies, chopped
1 lb. spicy sausage, chopped
8 oz. sour cream
8 oz. cream cheese, soft

Directions:

In your Slow Cooker, mix sausage with cream cheese, sour cream and tomatoes and chilies, stir, cover and cook on Low for 3 Hrs.
Divide into bowls and serve as a snack.

Potato Salsa

Servings: 6 Cooking Time: 8 Hrs.

Ingredients:

1 sweet onion, chopped
2 tbsps. mustard
1 and ½ lbs. gold potatoes, cut into medium cubes
1 cup celery, chopped
¼ cup white vinegar
Salt and black pepper to the taste
¼ cup dill, chopped
Cooking spray

Directions:

Spray your Slow Cooker with cooking spray, add onion, vinegar, mustard, salt and pepper and whisk well.
Add celery and potatoes, toss them well, cover and cook on Low for 8 Hrs.
Divide salad into small bowls, sprinkle dill on top and serve.

Mushroom Salsa

Servings: 4 Cooking Time: 5 Hrs.

Ingredients:

2 cups white mushrooms, sliced
1 cup spring onions, chopped
½ tsp. rosemary, dried
½ cup black olives, pitted and sliced
1 cup mild salsa
1 cup cherry tomatoes halved
½ tsp. chili powder
½ tsp. oregano, dried
3 garlic cloves, minced
Salt and black pepper to the taste

Directions:

In your Slow Cooker, mix the mushrooms with the cherry tomatoes and the other ingredients, toss, put the lid on and cook on Low for 5 Hrs.
Divide into bowls and serve as a snack.

Butter Stuffed Chicken Balls

Servings: 9 Cooking Time: 3.5 Hrs.

Ingredients:

3 oz. butter, cubed
1 tsp. cayenne pepper
1 tsp. salt
2 oz. white bread
1 tsp. olive oil
1 tsp. dried dill
½ tsp. olive oil
1 tbsp. mayonnaise
1 tsp. ground black pepper
1 egg
4 tbsp. milk
1 tbsp. almond flour
14 oz. ground chicken

Directions:

Whisk mayonnaise with black pepper, dill, chicken, salt, and cayenne pepper in a bowl.
Stir in egg, milk, and white bread then mix well.
Grease the base of the Slow Cooker with cooking oil.
Make small meatballs ours of this mixture and insert one butter cubes into each ball.

Dust the meatballs with almond then place them in the Slow Cooker.
Put the cooker's lid on and set the cooking time to 3.5 Hrs. on High settings.
Serve warm.

Tostadas

Servings: 4 Cooking Time: 4 Hrs.

Ingredients:

4 lbs. pork shoulder, boneless and cubed
Salt and black pepper to the taste
2 cups coca cola
1/3 cup brown sugar
½ cup hot sauce
2 tsps. chili powder
2 tbsps. tomato paste
¼ tsp. cumin, ground
1 cup enchilada sauce
Corn tortillas, toasted for a few Min. in the oven
Mexican cheese, shredded for serving
4 shredded lettuce leaves, for serving
Salsa
Guacamole for serving

Directions:

In your Slow Cooker, mix 1 cup coke with hot sauce, salsa, sugar, tomato paste, chili powder, cumin and pork, stir, cover and cook on Low for 4 Hrs.
Drain juice from the Slow Cooker, transfer meat to a cutting board, shred it, return it to Slow Cooker, add the rest of the coke and enchilada sauce and stir.
Place tortillas on a working surface, divide pork mix, lettuce leaves, Mexican cheese and guacamole and serve as a snack.

Hummus

Servings: 10 Cooking Time: 8 Hrs.

Ingredients:

1 cup chickpeas, dried
2 tbsps. olive oil
3 cups water
A pinch of salt and black pepper
1 garlic clove, minced
1 tbsp. lemon juice

Directions:

In your Slow Cooker, mix chickpeas with water, salt and pepper, stir, cover and cook on Low for 8 Hrs.
Drain chickpeas, transfer to a blender, add oil, more salt and pepper, garlic and lemon juice, blend well, divide into bowls and serve.

Ginger Chili Peppers

Servings: 7 Cooking Time: 3 Hrs.

Ingredients:

2 tbsp. balsamic vinegar
10 oz. red chili pepper, chopped
4 garlic cloves, peeled and sliced
1 white onion, chopped
3 tbsp. water
1 tsp. oregano
1 tsp. ground black pepper
4 tbsp. olive oil
1 tsp. ground nutmeg
½ tsp. ground ginger

Directions:

Spread the red chili peppers in the Slow Cooker.
Mix onion and garlic with remaining ingredients and spread on top of chili peppers.
Put the cooker's lid on and set the cooking time to 3 Hrs. on High settings.
Serve.

Crumbly Chickpeas Snack

Servings: 9 Cooking Time: 4 Hrs.

Ingredients:

1 lb. chickpea, canned, drained
4 oz. white onion, peeled and grated
1 tbsp. minced garlic
1 tbsp. chili flakes
½ tsp. thyme
½ tsp. ground coriander
1 tsp. salt
12 oz. chicken stock
½ cup fresh dill, chopped
1 tsp. butter, melted
3 tbsp. bread crumbs

Directions:

Mix onion with garlic, salt, butter, cinnamon, thyme, and chili flakes.
Spread the chickpeas in the Slow Cooker and top it with onion mixture.
Pour the chicken stock over the chickpeas.
Put the cooker's lid on and set the cooking time to 4 Hrs. on High settings.
Strain the cooked chickpeas and transfer to the bowl.
Top them with breadcrumbs and chopped dill.
Serve.

Spinach Dip

Servings: 2 Cooking Time: 1 Hr.

Ingredients:

2 tbsps. heavy cream
½ cup Greek yogurt
½ lb. baby spinach
2 garlic cloves, minced
Salt and black pepper to the taste

Directions:

In your Slow Cooker, mix the spinach with the cream and the other ingredients, toss, put the lid on and cook on High for 1 Hr.
Blend using an immersion blender, divide into bowls and serve as a party dip.

White Bean Spread

Servings: 4 Cooking Time: 7 Hrs.

Ingredients:

½ cup white beans, dried
2 tbsps. cashews, chopped
1 tsp. apple cider vinegar
1 cup veggie stock
1 tbsp. water

Directions:

In your Slow Cooker, mix beans with cashews and stock, stir, cover and cook on Low for 6 Hrs.
Drain, transfer to your food processor, add vinegar and water, pulse well, divide into bowls and serve as a spread.

Pork Stuffed Tamales

Servings: 24 Cooking Time: 8 Hrs. 30 Min

Ingredients:

8 oz. dried corn husks, soaked for 1 day and drained
4 cups of water

3 lbs. pork shoulder, boneless and chopped
1 yellow onion, chopped
2 garlic cloves, crushed
1 tbsp. chipotle chili powder
2 tbsp. chili powder
Salt and black pepper to the taste
1 tsp. cumin, ground
4 cups masa harina
¼ cup of corn oil
¼ cup shortening
1 tsp. baking powder

Directions:

Add 2 cups water, onion, black pepper, salt, garlic, chili powder, pork, cumin, and chipotle powder to the Slow Cooker.
Put the cooker's lid on and set the cooking time to 7 Hrs. on Low settings.
Shred the slow-cooked meat using 2 forks then mix it with 1 tbsp. cooking liquid, black pepper, and salt.
Mix masa harina with baking powder, oil, shortening, black pepper, and salt in a mixer.
Add the cooking liquid from the cooker and blend well until smooth.
Spread the corn husks on the working surface and add ¼ cup harina mixture to the top of each husk.
Add 1 tbsp. shredded pork to each husk and fold it from the top, bottom, and sideways to make a roll.
Place these tamales in the Slow Cooker and pour in the remaining water.
Put the cooker's lid on and set the cooking time to 1.5 Hrs. on High settings.
Serve.

Tamales

Servings: 24 Cooking Time: 8 Hrs. and 30 Min

Ingredients:

8 oz. dried corn husks, soaked for 1 day and drained
3 lbs. pork shoulder, boneless and chopped
4 cups water
1 yellow onion, chopped
2 garlic cloves, crushed
1 tbsp. chipotle chili powder
2 tbsps. chili powder
Salt and black pepper to the taste
1 tsp. cumin, ground
4 cups masa harina
¼ cup corn oil
¼ cup shortening
1 tsp. baking powder

Directions:

In your Slow Cooker, mix 2 cups water with salt, pepper, onion, garlic, chipotle powder, chili powder, cumin and pork, stir, cover the Slow Cooker and cook on Low for 7 Hrs.
Transfer meat to a cutting board, shred it with2 forks, add to a bowl, mix with 1 tbsp. of cooking liquid, more salt and pepper, stir and leave aside.
In another bowl, mix masa harina with salt, pepper, baking powder, shortening and oil and stir using a mixer.
Add cooking liquid from the instant Slow Cooker and blend again well.
Unfold corn husks, place them on a work surface, add ¼ cup masa mix near the top of the husk, press into a square and leaves 2 inches at the bottom.
Add 1 tbsp. pork mix in the center of the masa, wrap the husk around the dough, place all of them in your Slow Cooker, add the rest of the water, cover and cook on High for 1 Hr. and 30 Min.
Arrange tamales on a platter and serve.

Side Dish Recipes

Green Beans with Mushrooms

Servings: 4 Cooking Time: 3 Hrs.

Ingredients:

1 lb. fresh green beans, trimmed
1 small yellow onion, chopped
6 oz. bacon, chopped
1 garlic clove, minced
1 cup chicken stock
8 oz. mushrooms, sliced
Salt and black pepper to the taste
A splash of balsamic vinegar

Directions:

Add green beans, onion, stock and rest of the ingredients to the Slow Cooker.
Put the cooker's lid on and set the cooking time to 3 Hrs. on Low settings.
Serve warm.

Berry Wild Rice

Servings: 4 Cooking Time: 5 Hrs. 30 Min

Ingredients:

2 cups wild rice
4 cups of water
1 tsp. salt
6 oz. cherries, dried
1 tbsp. chives
1 tbsp. butter
2 tbsp. heavy cream

Directions:

Add wild rice, salt, water, and dried cherries to the Slow Cooker.
Put the cooker's lid on and set the cooking time to 5 Hrs. on High settings.
Stir in cream and butter, then cover again to cook for 30 Min. on the low setting.
Serve.

Herbed Balsamic Beets

Servings: 4 Cooking Time: 7 Hrs.

Ingredients:

6 medium assorted-color beets, peeled and cut into wedges
2 tbsp. balsamic vinegar
2 tbsp. olive oil
2 tbsp. chives, chopped
1 tbsp. tarragon, chopped
Salt and black pepper to the taste
1 tsp. orange peel, grated

Directions:

Add beets, tarragon, and rest of the ingredients to the Slow Cooker.
Put the cooker's lid on and set the cooking time to 7 Hrs. on Low settings.
Serve warm.

Tomato and Corn Mix

Servings: 2 Cooking Time: 4 Hrs.

Ingredients:

1 red onion, sliced
1 cup corn
1 tbsp. olive oil
½ cup tomato sauce
½ tsp. cumin, ground
Salt and black pepper to the taste
2 spring onions, chopped
1 cup tomatoes, cubed
½ red bell pepper, chopped
¼ tsp. sweet paprika
1 tbsp. chives, chopped

Directions:

Heat up a pan with the oil over medium-high heat, add the onion , spring onions and bell pepper and cook for 10 Min.
Transfer the mix to the Slow Cooker, add the corn and the other ingredients, toss, put the lid on and cook on Low for 4 Hrs.
Divide the mix between plates and serve as a side dish.

Zucchini Casserole

Servings: 10 Cooking Time: 2 Hrs.

Ingredients:

7 cups zucchini, sliced
2 tbsps. melted butter
1 cup cheddar cheese, shredded
1/3 cup sour cream
1 tbsp. parsley, chopped
2 cups crackers, crushed
1/3 cup yellow onion, chopped
1 cup chicken stock
Salt and black pepper to the taste
Cooking spray

Directions:

Grease your Slow Cooker with cooking spray and arrange zucchini and onion in the pot.
Add melted butter, stock, sour cream, salt and pepper and toss.
Add cheese mixed with crackers, cover and cook on High for 2 Hrs.
Divide zucchini casserole on plates, sprinkle parsley all over and serve as a side dish.

Italian Black Beans Mix

Servings: 2 Cooking Time: 5 Hrs.

Ingredients:

2 tbsps. tomato paste
2 cups black beans
1 red onion, sliced
1 tsp. Italian seasoning
½ red bell pepper, chopped
¼ tsp. mustard seeds
2 oz. canned corn, drained
Cooking spray
¼ cup veggie stock
Cooking spray
½ celery rib, chopped
½ sweet red pepper, chopped
Salt and black pepper to the taste
1 tbsp. cilantro, chopped

Directions:

Grease the Slow Cooker with the cooking spray, and mix the beans with the stock, onion and the other ingredients inside.
Put the lid on, cook on Low for 5 Hrs., divide between plates and serve as a side dish.

Barley Mix

Servings: 2 Cooking Time: 6 Hrs.

Ingredients:

1 red onion, sliced
½ tsp. turmeric powder
½ tsp. sweet paprika
1 cup barley
1 cup veggie stock
1 garlic clove, minced
A pinch of salt and black pepper

Directions:

In your Slow Cooker, mix the barley with the onion, paprika and the other ingredients, toss, put the lid on and cook on Low for 6 Hrs.
Divide between plates and serve as a side dish.

Cauliflower Rice and Spinach

Servings: 8 Cooking Time: 3 Hrs.

Ingredients:

2 garlic cloves, minced
1 yellow onion, chopped
3 cups veggie stock
6 oz. coconut cream
2 cups cauliflower rice
2 tbsps. butter, melted
¼ tsp. thyme, dried
20 oz. spinach, chopped
Salt and black pepper to the taste

Directions:

Heat up a pan with the butter over medium heat, add onion, stir and cook for 4 Min.
Add garlic, thyme and stock, stir, cook for 1 minute more and transfer to your Slow Cooker.
Add spinach, coconut cream, cauliflower rice, salt and pepper, stir a bit, cover and cook on High for 3 Hrs.
Divide between plates and serve as a side dish.

Chicken with Sweet Potato

Servings: 6 Cooking Time: 3 Hrs.

Ingredients:

16 oz. sweet potato, peeled and diced
1 tbsp. salt
2 tbsp. cream cheese
3 cups chicken stock
3 tbsp. margarine

Directions:

Add sweet potato, chicken stock, and salt to the Slow Cooker.
Put the cooker's lid on and set the cooking time to 5 Hrs. on High settings.
Drain the slow-cooked potatoes and transfer them to a suitable bowl.
Mash the sweet potatoes and stir in cream cheese and margarine.
Serve fresh.

Slow-cooked White Onions

Servings: 5 Cooking Time: 9 Hrs.

Ingredients:

½ cup bread crumbs
¼ cup cream cheese
3 oz. butter
5 large white onions, peeled and wedges
1 tsp. garlic powder
5 oz. Romano cheese, shredded
¼ cup half and half
1 tbsp. salt
1 tsp. ground black pepper

Directions:

Add onion wedges to the insert of the Slow Cooker.
Mix breadcrumbs and shredded cheese in a suitable bowl.
Whisk the half and half cream with remaining ingredients.

Spread this mixture over the onion and then top it with breadcrumbs mixture.
Put the cooker's lid on and set the cooking time to 9 Hrs. on Low settings.
Serve warm.

Okra and Corn

Servings: 4 Cooking Time: 8 Hrs.

Ingredients:

3 garlic cloves, minced
1 small green bell pepper, chopped
1 small yellow onion, chopped
1 cup water
16 oz. okra, sliced
2 cups corn
1 and ½ tsp. smoked paprika
28 oz. canned tomatoes, crushed
1 tsp. oregano, dried
1 tsp. thyme, dried
1 tsp. marjoram, dried
A pinch of cayenne pepper
Salt and black pepper to the taste

Directions:

In your Slow Cooker, mix garlic with bell pepper, onion, water, okra, corn, paprika, tomatoes, oregano, thyme, marjoram, cayenne, salt and pepper, cover, cook on Low for 8 Hrs., divide between plates and serve as a side dish.

Summer Squash Mix

Servings: 4 Cooking Time: 2 Hrs.

Ingredients:

¼ cup olive oil
2 tbsps. basil, chopped
2 tbsps. balsamic vinegar
2 garlic cloves, minced
2 tsps. mustard
Salt and black pepper to the taste
3 summer squash, sliced
2 zucchinis, sliced

Directions:

In your Slow Cooker, mix squash with zucchinis, salt, pepper, mustard, garlic, vinegar, basil and oil, toss a bit, cover and cook on High for 2 Hrs.
Divide between plates and serve as a side dish.

Marjoram Rice Mix

Servings: 2 Cooking Time: 6 Hrs.

Ingredients:

1 cup wild rice
2 cups chicken stock
1 carrot, peeled and grated
2 tbsps. marjoram, chopped
1 tbsp. olive oil
A pinch of salt and black pepper
1 tbsp. green onions, chopped

Directions:

In your Slow Cooker, mix the rice with the stock and the other ingredients, toss, put the lid on and cook on Low for 6 Hrs.
Divide between plates and serve.

Summer Squash Medley

Servings: 4 Cooking Time: 2 Hrs.

Ingredients:

¼ cup olive oil
2 tbsp. basil, chopped
2 tbsp. balsamic vinegar
2 garlic cloves, minced
2 tsp. mustard
Salt and black pepper to the taste
3 summer squash, sliced
2 zucchinis, sliced

Directions:

Add squash, zucchinis, and all other ingredients to the Slow Cooker.
Put the cooker's lid on and set the cooking time to 2 Hrs. on High settings.
Serve.

Cream Cheese Macaroni

Servings: 6 Cooking Time: 3.5 Hrs.

Ingredients:

12 oz. elbow macaroni
1 cup cream cheese
3 tbsp. fresh parsley
1 tbsp. fresh dill
3 cups chicken stock
1 tsp. salt
1 egg
¼ tsp. turmeric

Directions:

Whisk egg with cream cheese and chicken stock in a mixer.
Spread the macaroni in the Slow Cooker then pour the stock mixture on top.
Drizzle parsley, dill, turmeric, and salt on top.
Put the cooker's lid on and set the cooking time to 3.5 Hrs. on High settings.
Serve warm.

Saucy Macaroni

Servings: 6 Cooking Time: 3.5 Hrs.

Ingredients:

8 oz. macaroni
1 cup tomatoes, chopped
1 garlic clove, peeled
1 tsp. butter
1 cup heavy cream
3 cups of water
1 tbsp. salt
6 oz. Parmesan, shredded
1 tbsp. dried basil

Directions:

Add macaroni, salt, and water to the Slow Cooker.
Put the cooker's lid on and set the cooking time to 3 Hrs. on High settings.
Meanwhile, puree tomatoes in a blender then add cheese, cream, butter, and dried basil.
Drain the cooked macaroni and return them to the Slow Cooker.
Pour in the tomato-cream mixture.
Put the cooker's lid on and set the cooking time to 30 Min. on High settings.
Serve warm.

Paprika Green Beans and Zucchinis

Servings: 2 Cooking Time: 3 Hrs.

Ingredients:

1 lb. green beans, trimmed and halved
1 cup zucchinis, cubed
1 cup tomato sauce
1 tsp. smoked paprika
½ tsp. cumin , ground
Salt and black pepper to the taste
½ tsp. garlic powder
¼ tbsp. chives, chopped

Directions:

In your Slow Cooker, mix the green beans with the zucchinis, tomato sauce and the other ingredients, toss, put the lid on and cook on Low for 3 Hrs.
Divide the mix between plates and serve as a side dish.

Peas and Carrots

Servings: 12 Cooking Time: 5 Hrs.

Ingredients:

1 yellow onion, chopped
16 oz. peas
1/4 cup water
4 garlic cloves, minced
1 tsp. marjoram, dried
1 lb. carrots, sliced
1/4 cup melted butter
1/4 cup honey
A pinch of salt and black pepper

Directions:

In your Slow Cooker, mix onion with carrots, peas, butter, water, honey, garlic, salt, pepper and marjoram, cover and cook on Low for 5 Hrs.
Stir peas and carrots mix, divide between plates and serve as a side dish.

White Beans Mix

Servings: 4 Cooking Time: 6 Hrs.

Ingredients:

1 celery stalk, chopped
1 carrot, chopped
1/2 cup canned tomatoes, crushed
1/2 tbsp. Italian seasoning
1 tbsp. parsley, chopped
2 garlic cloves, minced
1 cup veggie stock
1/2 tsp. chili powder
15 oz. canned white beans, drained

Directions:

In your Slow Cooker, mix the beans with the celery, garlic and the other ingredients, toss, put the lid on and cook on Low for 6 Hrs.
Divide the mix between plates and serve.

Cabbage and Kale Mix

Servings: 2 Cooking Time: 2 Hrs.

Ingredients:

1 red onion, sliced
1 cup baby kale
1/2 tsp. hot paprika
A pinch of salt and black pepper
1 cup green cabbage, shredded
1/2 cup canned tomatoes, crushed
1/2 tsp. Italian seasoning
1 tbsp. dill, chopped

Directions:

In your Slow Cooker, mix the cabbage with the kale, onion and the other ingredients, toss, put the lid on and cook on High for 2 Hrs.
Divide between plates and serve right away as a side dish.

Sweet Potato and Cauliflower Mix

Servings: 2 Cooking Time: 4 Hrs.

Ingredients:

2 sweet potatoes, peeled and cubed
1 cup cauliflower florets
1/2 cup coconut milk
A pinch of salt and black pepper
1 tbsp. red curry paste
2 tbsps. cilantro, chopped
1 tsps. sriracha sauce
1/2 tbsp. sugar
3 oz. white mushrooms, roughly chopped

Directions:

In your Slow Cooker, mix the sweet potatoes with the cauliflower and the other ingredients, toss, put the lid on and cook on Low for 4 Hrs.
Divide between plates and serve as a side dish.

Zucchini Mix

Servings: 2 Cooking Time: 6 Hrs.

Ingredients:

1 lb. zucchinis, sliced
1/2 tsp. sweet paprika
1/2 cup heavy cream
1 tbsp. olive oil
1/2 tsp. Italian seasoning
Salt and black pepper
1/2 tsp. garlic powder

Directions:

In your Slow Cooker, mix the zucchinis with the seasoning, paprika and the other ingredients, toss, put the lid on and cook on Low for 6 Hrs.
Divide between plates and serve as a side dish.

Savoy Cabbage Mix

Servings: 2 Cooking Time: 2 Hrs.

Ingredients:

1 lb. Savoy cabbage, shredded
1 tbsp. olive oil
A pinch of salt and black pepper
1/2 cup tomatoes, cubed
1/2 inch ginger, grated
1 red onion, sliced
1/2 cup veggie stock
1 carrot, grated
1/2 tsp. sweet paprika

Directions:

In your Slow Cooker, mix the cabbage with the onion, oil and the other ingredients, toss, put the lid on and cook on High for 2 Hrs.
Divide the mix between plates and serve as a side dish.

Carrot and Beet Side Salad

Servings: 6 Cooking Time: 7 Hrs.

Ingredients:

1/2 cup walnuts, chopped
1/2 cup olive oil
1 tsp. Dijon mustard
Salt and black pepper to the taste
2 carrots, peeled and sliced
5 oz. arugula
1/4 cup lemon juice
1 shallot, chopped
1 tbsp. brown sugar
2 beets, peeled and cut into wedges
1 cup parsley

Directions:

In your Slow Cooker, mix beets with carrots, salt, pepper, sugar, mustard, shallot, oil, lemon juice and walnuts, cover and cook on Low for 7 Hrs.
Transfer everything to a bowl, add parsley and arugula, toss, divide between plates and serve as a side dish.

Tangy Red Potatoes

Servings: 4 Cooking Time: 8 Hrs.

Ingredients:

1 lb. red potato
1 garlic clove
4 tbsp. mayo
3 tbsp. fresh dill, chopped
2 tbsp. olive oil
1 tsp. sage
1 tsp. minced garlic
1 tsp. paprika

Directions:

Add potatoes, olive oil, garlic cloves, garlic, and sage to the Slow Cooker.
Put the cooker's lid on and set the cooking time to 8 Hrs. on Low settings.
Whisk mayo and minced garlic in a suitable bowl.
Transfer the slow-cooked potatoes to a bowl and mash them using a fork.
Stir in the mayo-garlic mixture then mix well.
Serve fresh.

Ramen Noodles

Servings: 5 Cooking Time: 25 Min

Ingredients:

1 tbsp. ramen seasoning
4 cups chicken stock
3 tbsp. soy sauce
1 tbsp. butter
10 oz. ramen noodles
1 tsp. salt
1 tsp. paprika

Directions:

Add chicken stock, butter, ramen, paprika, noodles and all other ingredients to the Slow Cooker.
Put the cooker's lid on and set the cooking time to 25 Min. on High settings.
Serve warm.

Mexican Rice

Servings: 8 Cooking Time: 4 Hrs.

Ingredients:

1 cup long grain rice
½ cup cilantro, chopped
Salt and black pepper to the taste
1 and ¼ cups veggie stock
½ avocado, pitted, peeled and chopped
¼ cup green hot sauce

Directions:

Put the rice in your Slow Cooker, add stock, stir, cover, cook on Low for 4 Hrs., fluff with a fork and transfer to a bowl.
In your food processor, mix avocado with hot sauce and cilantro, blend well, pour over rice, toss well, add salt and pepper, divide between plates and serve as a side dish.

Cinnamon Applesauce

Servings: 5 Cooking Time: 6 Hrs.

Ingredients:

1 lb. red apples, peeled and chopped
1 tsp. ground ginger
1 tsp. ground cinnamon
½ tsp. salt
2 oz. cinnamon stick
½ tsp. nutmeg
4 oz. water
1 tbsp. lime juice

Directions:

Add red apples, cinnamon stick, salt, cinnamon ground, water, lime juice, nutmeg, and ginger to the Slow Cooker.
Put the cooker's lid on and set the cooking time to 6 Hrs. on High settings.
Discard the cinnamon sticks from the apples.
Serve fresh.
Transfer the dish to the serving bowls and serve it or keep in the fridge for not more than 3 days. Enjoy!

Rice with Artichokes

Servings: 4 Cooking Time: 4 Hrs.

Ingredients:

1 tbsp. olive oil
2 garlic cloves, minced
1 tbsp. white wine
1 and ¼ cups of water
16 oz. cream cheese
1 and ½ tbsp. thyme, chopped
5 oz. Arborio rice
1 and ¼ cups chicken stock
6 oz. graham crackers, crumbled
15 oz. canned artichoke hearts, chopped
1 tbsp. parmesan, grated
Salt and black pepper to the taste

Directions:

Add oil, rice, artichokes, garlic, water, wine, crackers, and stock to the Slow Cooker.
Put the cooker's lid on and set the cooking time to 4 Hrs. on Low settings.
Stir in cream cheese, salt, parmesan, thyme, and black pepper.
Mix well and serve warm.

Balsamic Okra Mix

Servings: 4 Cooking Time: 2 Hrs.

Ingredients:

2 cups okra, sliced
1 tbsp. olive oil
½ cup canned tomatoes, crushed
2 tbsps. basil, chopped
1 cup cherry tomatoes, halved
½ tsp. turmeric powder
2 tbsps. balsamic vinegar
1 tbsp. thyme, chopped

Directions:

In your Slow Cooker, mix the okra with the tomatoes, crushed tomatoes and the other ingredients, toss, put the lid on and cook on High for 2 Hrs.
Divide between plates and serve as a side dish.

Cauliflower and Broccoli Mix

Servings: 10 Cooking Time: 7 Hrs.

Ingredients:

4 cups broccoli florets
7 oz. Swiss cheese, torn
1 yellow onion, chopped
1 tsp. thyme, dried
4 cups cauliflower florets
14 oz. Alfredo sauce
Salt and black pepper to the taste
½ cup almonds, sliced

Directions:

In your Slow Cooker, mix broccoli with cauliflower, cheese, sauce, onion, salt, pepper and thyme, stir, cover and cook on Low for 7 Hrs.
Add almonds, divide between plates and serve as a side dish.

Parsley Mushroom Mix

Servings: 2 Cooking Time: 4 Hrs.

Ingredients:

1 lb. brown mushrooms, halved
2 garlic cloves, minced
A pinch of basil, dried
A pinch of oregano, dried
½ cup veggie stock
Salt and black pepper to the taste
1 tbsp. olive oil
1 tbsp. parsley, chopped

Directions:

In your Slow Cooker, mix the mushrooms with the garlic, basil and the other ingredients, toss, put the lid on and cook on Low for 4 Hrs.
Divide everything between plates and serve.

Glazed Baby Carrots

Servings: 6 Cooking Time: 6 Hrs.

Ingredients:

½ cup peach preserves
½ cup butter, melted
2 lbs. baby carrots
2 tbsp. sugar
1 tsp. vanilla extract
A pinch of salt and black pepper
A pinch of nutmeg, ground
½ tsp. cinnamon powder
2 tbsps. water

Directions:

Put baby carrots in your Slow Cooker, add butter, peach preserves, sugar, vanilla, salt, pepper, nutmeg, cinnamon and water, toss well, cover and cook on Low for 6 Hrs.
Divide between plates and serve as a side dish.

Mexican Avocado Rice

Servings: 8 Cooking Time: 4 Hrs.

Ingredients:

1 cup long-grain rice
1 and ¼ cups veggie stock
½ cup cilantro, chopped
½ avocado, pitted, peeled and chopped
Salt and black pepper to the taste
¼ cup green hot sauce

Directions:

Add rice and stock to the Slow Cooker.
Put the cooker's lid on and set the cooking time to 4 Hrs. on Low settings.
Meanwhile, blend avocado flesh with hot sauce, cilantro, salt, and black pepper.
Serve the cooked rice with avocado sauce on top.

Spinach Mix

Servings: 2 Cooking Time: 1 Hr.

Ingredients:

1 lb. baby spinach
½ cup cherry tomatoes, halved
½ tbsp. olive oil
½ cup veggie stock
1 small yellow onion, chopped
¼ tsp. coriander, ground
¼ tsp. cumin, ground
¼ tsp. garam masala
¼ tsp. chili powder
Salt and black pepper to the taste

Directions:

In your Slow Cooker, mix the spinach with the tomatoes, oil and the other ingredients, toss, put the lid on and cook on High for 1 Hr.
Divide between plates and serve as a side dish.,

Carrot Beet Salad

Servings: 6 Cooking Time: 7 Hrs.

Ingredients:

½ cup walnuts, chopped
¼ cup lemon juice
½ cup olive oil
1 shallot, chopped
1 tsp. Dijon mustard
1 tbsp. brown sugar
Salt and black pepper to the taste
2 beets, peeled and cut into wedges
2 carrots, peeled and sliced
1 cup parsley
5 oz. arugula

Directions:

Add beets, carrots, and rest of the ingredients to the Slow Cooker.
Put the cooker's lid on and set the cooking time to 7 Hrs. on Low settings.
Serve warm.

Veggies Rice Pilaf

Servings: 4 Cooking Time: 5 Hrs.

Ingredients:

2 cups basmati rice
1 cup mixed carrots, peas, corn, and green beans
2 cups of water
½ tsp. green chili, minced
½ tsp. ginger, grated
3 garlic cloves, minced
2 tbsp. butter
1 cinnamon stick
1 tbsp. cumin seeds
2 bay leaves
3 whole cloves
5 black peppercorns
2 whole cardamoms
1 tbsp. sugar
Salt to the taste

Directions:

Add water, rice, veggies and all other ingredients to the Slow Cooker.
Put the cooker's lid on and set the cooking time to 5 Hrs. on Low settings.
Discard the cinnamon and serve warm.

Mint Farro Pilaf

Servings: 2 Cooking Time: 4 Hrs.

Ingredients:

½ tbsp. balsamic vinegar
½ cup whole grain farro
A pinch of salt and black pepper
1 cup chicken stock
½ tbsp. olive oil
1 tbsp. green onions, chopped
1 tbsp. mint, chopped

Directions:

In your Slow Cooker, mix the farro with the vinegar and the other ingredients, toss, put the lid on and cook on Low for 4 Hrs.
Divide between plates and serve.

Cornbread Cream Pudding

Servings: 8 Cooking Time: 8 Hrs.

Ingredients:

11 oz. cornbread mix
3 cups heavy cream
3 eggs
1 tsp. salt
2 oz. pickled jalapeno
1 tsp. butter
1 cup corn kernels
1 cup sour cream
1 chili pepper
1 tsp. ground black pepper
¼ tbsp. sugar

Directions:

Whisk eggs in a suitable bowl and add cream and cornbread mix. Mix it well then add salt, chili pepper, sour cream, sugar, butter, and black pepper.
Add corn kernels and pickled jalapeno then mix well to make a smooth dough.
Spread this dough in the insert of a Slow Cooker.
Put the cooker's lid on and set the cooking time to 8 Hrs. on Low settings.
Slice and serve.

Zucchini Crackers Casserole

Servings: 10 Cooking Time: 2 Hrs.

Ingredients:

7 cups zucchini, sliced
2 tbsp. melted butter
1 cup cheddar cheese, shredded
1/3 cup sour cream
1 tbsp. parsley, chopped
2 cups crackers, crushed
1/3 cup yellow onion, chopped
1 cup chicken stock
Salt and black pepper to the taste
Cooking spray

Directions:

Grease the insert of your Slow Cooker with cooking spray.
Spread the zucchini and onion in the cooker.
Top the veggies with stock, sour cream, butter, black pepper, and salt.
Spread cheese and crackers over the veggies.
Put the cooker's lid on and set the cooking time to 2 Hrs. on High settings.
Garnish with parsley.
Serve warm.

Potatoes and Leeks Mix

Servings: 2 Cooking Time: 4 Hrs.

Ingredients:

2 leeks, sliced
½ cup veggie stock
1 tbsp. chives, chopped
½ lb. sweet potatoes, cut into medium wedges
½ tbsp. balsamic vinegar
½ tsp. pumpkin pie spice

Directions:

In your Slow Cooker, mix the leeks with the potatoes and the other ingredients, toss, put the lid on and cook on High for 4 Hrs.
Divide between plates and serve as a side dish.

Garlic Squash Mix

Servings: 2 Cooking Time: 3 Hrs.

Ingredients:

1 lb. butternut squash, peeled and cubed
1 cup veggie stock
½ tsp. turmeric powder
3 garlic cloves, minced
2 spring onions, chopped
½ tsp. red pepper flakes, crushed
A pinch of salt and black pepper

Directions:

In your Slow Cooker, mix the squash with the garlic, stock and the other ingredients, toss, put the lid on and cook on Low for 3 Hrs.
Divide squash mix between plates and serve as a side dish.

Garlic Mushrooms

Servings: 6 Cooking Time: 8 Hrs.

Ingredients:

2 lbs. cremini mushrooms, quartered
½ cup fresh parsley
1 tsp. ground black pepper
1 tsp. thyme
1 tsp. turmeric
1 lemon, chopped
1 tsp. salt
1/3 cup half and half
1 tsp. coriander
3 tbsp. garlic, chopped

Directions:

Spread the mushrooms in the insert of Slow Cooker.
Whisk the half and half cream with remaining ingredients.
Top the mushrooms with the cream sauce.
Put the cooker's lid on and set the cooking time to 8 Hrs. on Low settings.
Serve warm.

Butter Green Beans

Servings: 2 Cooking Time: 2 Hrs.

Ingredients:

1 lb. green beans, trimmed and halved
½ cup veggie stock
1 tbsp. chives, chopped
¼ tsp. soy sauce
2 tbsps. butter, melted
1 tsp. rosemary, dried
Salt and black pepper to the taste

Directions:

In your Slow Cooker, combine the green beans with the melted butter, stock and the other ingredients, toss, put the lid on and cook on Low for 2 Hrs.
Divide between plates and serve as a side dish.

Beets Side Salad

Servings: 12 Cooking Time: 7 Hrs.

Ingredients:

5 beets, peeled and sliced
1/3 cup honey
2 tbsps. olive oil
2 garlic cloves, minced
¼ cup balsamic vinegar
1 tbsp. rosemary, chopped
Salt and black pepper to the taste

Directions:

In your Slow Cooker, mix beets with vinegar, honey, oil, salt, pepper, rosemary and garlic, cover and cook on Low for 7 Hrs.
Divide between plates and serve as a side dish.

Okra Side Dish

Servings: 4 Cooking Time: 4 Hrs.

Ingredients:

1 lb. okra, sliced
6 oz. tomato sauce
Salt and black pepper to the taste
2 garlic cloves, minced
1 tomato, chopped
1 cup water
1 yellow onion, chopped

Directions:

In your Slow Cooker, mix okra with tomato, tomato sauce, water, salt, pepper, onion and garlic, stir, cover and cook on Low for 4 Hrs.
Divide between plates and serve as a side dish.

Stewed Okra

Servings: 4 Cooking Time: 3 Hrs.

Ingredients:

2 cups okra, sliced
6 oz. tomato sauce
A pinch of cayenne peppers
Salt and black pepper to the taste
2 garlic cloves, minced
1 red onion, chopped
1 tsp. liquid smoke

Directions:

In your Slow Cooker, mix okra with garlic, onion, cayenne, tomato sauce, liquid smoke, salt and pepper, cover, cook on Low for 3 Hrs.
Divide between plates and serve as a side dish.

Maple Brussels Sprouts

Servings: 12 Cooking Time: 3 Hrs.

Ingredients:

1 cup red onion, chopped
2 lbs. Brussels sprouts, trimmed and halved
Salt and black pepper to the taste
1/4 cup apple juice
3 tbsps. olive oil
1/4 cup maple syrup
1 tbsp. thyme, chopped

Directions:

In your Slow Cooker, mix Brussels sprouts with onion, salt, pepper and apple juice, toss, cover and cook on Low for 3 Hrs.
In a bowl, mix maple syrup with oil and thyme, whisk really well, add over Brussels sprouts, toss well, divide between plates and serve as a side dish.

Minty Peas and Tomatoes

Servings: 2 Cooking Time: 3 Hrs.

Ingredients:

1 lb. okra, sliced
1 tbsp. olive oil
1/2 tsp. chili powder
1 tbsp. mint, chopped
1 tbsp. chives, chopped
1/2 lb. tomatoes, cut into wedges
1/2 cup veggie stock
Salt and black pepper to the taste
3 green onions, chopped

Directions:

Grease your Slow Cooker with the oil, and mix the okra with the tomatoes and the other ingredients inside.
Put the lid on, cook on Low for 3 Hrs., divide between plates and serve as a side dish.

Scalloped Potatoes

Servings: 6 Cooking Time: 6 Hrs.

Ingredients:

Cooking spray
2 and 1/2 lbs. gold potatoes, sliced
10 oz. canned cream of potato soup
1 yellow onion, roughly chopped
8 oz. sour cream
1 cup Gouda cheese, shredded
1/2 cup blue cheese, crumbled
1/2 cup parmesan, grated
1/2 cup chicken stock
Salt and black pepper to the taste
1 tbsp. chives, chopped

Directions:

Grease your Slow Cooker with cooking spray and arrange potato slices on the bottom.
Add cream of potato soup, onion, sour cream, Gouda cheese, blue cheese, parmesan, stock, salt and pepper, cover and cook on Low for 6 Hrs.
Add chives, divide between plates and serve as a side dish.

Butternut Squash and Eggplant Mix

Servings: 2 Cooking Time: 4 Hrs.

Ingredients:

1 butternut squash, peeled and roughly cubed
1 eggplant, roughly cubed
Cooking spray
1/4 cup tomato paste
Salt and black pepper to the taste
1 red onion, chopped
1/2 cup veggie stock
1/2 tbsp. parsley, chopped
2 garlic cloves, minced

Directions:

Grease the Slow Cooker with the cooking spray and mix the squash with the eggplant, onion and the other ingredients inside.
Put the lid on and cook on Low for 4 Hrs.
Divide between plates and serve as a side dish.

Balsamic Cauliflower

Servings: 2 Cooking Time: 5 Hrs.

Ingredients:

2 cups cauliflower florets
1 tbsp. balsamic vinegar
2 spring onions, chopped
Salt and black pepper to the taste
1/2 cup veggie stock
1 tbsp. lemon zest, grated
1/4 tsp. sweet paprika
1 tbsp. dill, chopped

Directions:

In your Slow Cooker, mix the cauliflower with the stock, vinegar and the other ingredients, toss, put the lid on and cook on Low for 5 Hrs.
Divide the cauliflower mix between plates and serve.

Hot Zucchini Mix

Servings: 2 Cooking Time: 2 Hrs.

Ingredients:

1 lb. zucchinis, roughly cubed
1/2 tsp. chili powder
1/2 tbsp. olive oil
1 garlic clove, minced
A pinch of salt and black pepper
1/4 cup carrots, grated
1 tsp. hot paprika
2 spring onions, chopped
1/2 tsp. curry powder
1/2 tsp. ginger powder
1 tbsp. cilantro, chopped

Directions:

In your Slow Cooker, mix the carrots with the zucchinis, paprika and the other ingredients, toss, put the lid on and cook on Low for 2 Hrs.
Divide between plates and serve as a side dish.

Thai Side Salad

Servings: 8 Cooking Time: 3 Hrs.

Ingredients:

8 oz. yellow summer squash, peeled and roughly chopped
2 cups button mushrooms, quartered
2 leeks, sliced
2 garlic cloves, minced
1 tbsp. ginger, grated
¼ cup basil, chopped
12 oz. zucchini, halved and sliced
1 red sweet potatoe, chopped
2 tbsps. veggie stock
2 tbsp. Thai red curry paste
1/3 cup coconut milk

Directions:

In your Slow Cooker, mix zucchini with summer squash, mushrooms, red pepper, leeks, garlic, stock, curry paste, ginger, coconut milk and basil, toss, cover and cook on Low for 3 Hrs.
Stir your Thai mix one more time, divide between plates and serve as a side dish.

Nut and Berry Side Salad

Servings: 4 Cooking Time: 1 Hr.

Ingredients:

2 cups strawberries, halved
1/3 cup raspberry vinegar
1 tbsp. canola oil
4 cups spinach, torn
¼ cup walnuts, chopped
2 tbsps. mint, chopped
2 tbsps. honey
Salt and black pepper to the taste
½ cup blueberries
1 oz. goat cheese, crumbled

Directions:

In your Slow Cooker, mix strawberries with mint, vinegar, honey, oil, salt, pepper, spinach, blueberries and walnuts, cover and cook on High for 1 Hr.
Divide salad on plates, sprinkle cheese on top and serve as a side dish.

Mashed Potatoes

Servings: 12 Cooking Time: 4 Hrs.

Ingredients:

3 lbs. gold potatoes, peeled and cubed
6 garlic cloves, minced
1 cup milk
Salt and black pepper to the taste
1 bay leaf
28 oz. chicken stock
¼ cup butter

Directions:

In your Slow Cooker, mix potatoes with bay leaf, garlic, salt, pepper and stock, cover and cook on Low for 4 Hrs.
Drain potatoes, mash them, mix with butter and milk, blend really, divide between plates and serve as a side dish.

Veggie Medley

Servings: 2 Cooking Time: 3 Hrs.

Ingredients:

1 zucchini, cubed
½ cup baby carrots, peeled
1 cup cherry tomatoes, halved
1 tbsp. olive oil
1 tsp. Italian seasoning
1 cup yellow squash, peeled and cut into wedges
1 tbsp. cilantro, chopped
1 eggplant, cubed
½ cup baby kale
1 tsp. sweet paprika
1 cup tomato sauce
A pinch of salt and black pepper
1 tsp. garlic powder
A pinch of salt and black pepper

Directions:

Grease your Slow Cooker with the oil, and mix the zucchini with the eggplant, carrots and the other ingredients inside.
Toss, put the lid on and cook on Low for 3 Hrs.
Divide the mix between plates and serve as a side dish.

Cider Dipped Farro

Servings: 6 Cooking Time: 5 Hrs.

Ingredients:

1 tbsp. apple cider vinegar
1 tsp. lemon juice
3 cups of water
½ cup cherries, dried and chopped
10 mint leaves, chopped
1 cup whole-grain farro
Salt to the taste
1 tbsp. olive oil
¼ cup green onions, chopped
2 cups cherries, pitted and halved

Directions:

Add water and farro to the Slow Cooker.
Put the cooker's lid on and set the cooking time to 5 Hrs. on Low settings.
Toss the cooker farro with salt, cherries, mint, green onion, lemon juice, and oil in a bowl.
Serve fresh.

Apples and Potatoes

Servings: 10 Cooking Time: 7 Hrs.

Ingredients:

2 green apples, cored and cut into wedges
1 cup coconut cream
1 cup apple butter
3 lbs. sweet potatoes, peeled and cut into medium wedges
½ cup dried cherries
1 and ½ tsp. pumpkin pie spice

Directions:

In your Slow Cooker, mix sweet potatoes with green apples, cream, cherries, apple butter and spice, toss, cover and cook on Low for 7 Hrs.
Toss, divide between plates and serve as a side dish.

Farro

Servings: 6 Cooking Time: 5 Hrs.

Ingredients:

1 tbsp. apple cider vinegar
1 tsp. lemon juice
3 cups water
½ cup cherries, dried and chopped
10 mint leaves, chopped
1 cup whole grain farro
Salt to the taste
1 tbsp. olive oil
¼ cup green onions, chopped
2 cups cherries, pitted and halved

Directions:

Put the water in your Slow Cooker, add farro, stir, cover, cook on Low for 5 Hrs., drain and transfer to a bowl.
Add salt, oil, lemon juice, vinegar, dried cherries, fresh cherries, green onions and mint, toss, divide between plates and serve as a side dish.

Cabbage Mix

Servings: 2 Cooking Time: 6 Hrs.

Ingredients:

1 lb. red cabbage, shredded
A pinch of salt and black pepper to the taste
1 tbsp. mustard
1 apple, peeled, cored and roughly chopped
1/4 cup chicken stock
1/2 tbsp. olive oil

Directions:

In your Slow Cooker, mix the cabbage with the apple and the other ingredients, toss, put the lid on and cook on Low for 6 Hrs.
Divide between plates and serve as a side dish.

Spinach Rice

Servings: 2 Cooking Time: 2 Hrs.

Ingredients:

2 scallions, chopped
1 cup Arborio rice
6 oz. spinach, chopped
2 oz. goat cheese, crumbled
1 tbsp. olive oil
1 cup chicken stock
Salt and black pepper to the taste

Directions:

In your Slow Cooker, mix the rice with the stock and the other ingredients, toss, put the lid on and cook on High for 2 Hrs.
Divide between plates and serve as a side dish.

BBQ Beans

Servings: 2 Cooking Time: 8 Hrs.

Ingredients:

1/4 lb. navy beans, soaked overnight and drained
1 cup BBQ sauce
1 tbsp. ketchup
1 tbsp. apple cider vinegar
1 tbsp. soy sauce
1 tbsp. sugar
1 tbsp. water
1 tbsp. olive oil

Directions:

In your Slow Cooker, mix the beans with the sauce, sugar and the other ingredients, toss, put the lid on and cook on Low for 8 Hrs.
Divide between plates and serve as a side dish.

Eggplants with Mayo Sauce

Servings: 8 Cooking Time: 5 Hrs.

Ingredients:

2 tbsp. minced garlic
1 sweet pepper, chopped
1 tsp. olive oil
1/2 tsp. ground black pepper
2 tbsp. sour cream
1 chili pepper, chopped
4 tbsp. mayo
1 tsp. salt
18 oz. eggplants, peeled and diced

Directions:

Blend chili pepper, sweet peppers, salt, garlic, and black pepper in a blender until smooth.
Add eggplant and this chili mixture to the Slow Cooker then toss them well.
Now mix mayo with sour cream and spread on top of eggplants.
Put the cooker's lid on and set the cooking time to 5 Hrs. on High settings.
Serve warm

Lime Beans Mix

Servings: 2 Cooking Time: 8 Hrs.

Ingredients:

1/2 lb. lima beans, soaked for 6 Hrs. and drained
1 tbsp. olive oil
2 scallions, chopped
1 carrot, chopped
2 tbsps. tomato paste
1 garlic cloves, minced
A pinch of salt and black pepper to the taste
3 cups water
A pinch of red pepper, crushed
2 tbsps. parsley, chopped

Directions:

In your Slow Cooker, mix the beans with the scallions, oil and the other ingredients, toss, put the lid on and cook on Low for 8 Hrs.
Divide between plates and serve as a side dish/

Zucchini Onion Pate

Servings: 6 Cooking Time: 6 Hrs.

Ingredients:

3 medium zucchinis, peeled and chopped
6 tbsp. tomato paste
1 tsp. salt
1 tbsp. brown sugar
1 tsp. paprika
2 red onions, grated
1/2 cup fresh dill
1 tsp. butter
1/2 tsp. ground black pepper
1/4 chili pepper

Directions:

Add zucchini to the food processor and blend for 3 Min. until smooth.
Transfer the zucchini blend to the Slow Cooker.
Stir in onions and all other ingredients.
Put the cooker's lid on and set the cooking time to 6 Hrs. on Low settings.
Serve warm.

Parmesan Spinach Mix

Servings: 2 Cooking Time: 2 Hrs.

Ingredients:

2 garlic cloves, minced
1/4 cup veggie stock
Salt and black pepper to the taste
2 tbsps. parmesan cheese, grated
1 lb. baby spinach
A drizzle of olive oil
4 tbsps. heavy cream

Directions:

Grease your Slow Cooker with the oil, and mix the spinach with the garlic and the other ingredients inside.
Toss, put the lid on and cook on Low for 2 Hrs.
Divide the mix between plates and serve as a side dish.

Sweet Potatoes with Bacon

Servings: 6 Cooking Time: 5 Hrs.

Ingredients:

4 lbs. sweet potatoes, peeled and sliced
3 tbsps. brown sugar
½ cup orange juice
½ tsp. sage, dried
½ tsp. thyme, dried
4 bacon slices, cooked and crumbled
2 tbsps. soft butter

Directions:

Arrange sweet potato slices in your Slow Cooker, add sugar, orange juice, sage, thyme, butter and bacon, cover and cook on Low for 5 Hrs.
Divide between plates and serve them as a side dish.

Thyme Mushrooms and Corn

Servings: 2 Cooking Time: 4 Hrs.

Ingredients:

4 garlic cloves, minced
1 tbsp. olive oil
1 lb. white mushroom caps, halved
1 cup corn
1 cup canned tomatoes, crushed
¼ tsp. thyme, dried
½ cup veggie stock
A pinch of salt and black pepper
2 tbsps. parsley, chopped

Directions:

Grease your Slow Cooker with the oil, and mix the garlic with the mushrooms, corn and the other ingredients inside.
Toss, put the lid on and cook on Low for 4 Hrs.
Divide between plates and serve as a side dish.

Italian Eggplant

Servings: 2 Cooking Time: 2 Hrs.

Ingredients:

2 small eggplants, roughly cubed
½ cup heavy cream
Salt and black pepper to the taste
1 tbsp. olive oil
A pinch of hot pepper flakes
2 tbsps. oregano, chopped

Directions:

In your Slow Cooker, mix the eggplants with the cream and the other ingredients, toss, put the lid on and cook on High for 2 Hrs.
Divide between plates and serve as a side dish.

Nut Berry Salad

Servings: 4 Cooking Time: 1 Hr.

Ingredients:

2 cups strawberries, halved
2 tbsp. mint, chopped
1/3 cup raspberry vinegar
2 tbsp. honey
1 tbsp. canola oil
Salt and black pepper to the taste
4 cups spinach, torn
½ cup blueberries
¼ cup walnuts, chopped
1 oz. goat cheese, crumbled

Directions:

Toss strawberries with walnuts, spinach, honey, oil, salt, black pepper, blueberries, vinegar, and mint in the Slow Cooker.
Put the cooker's lid on and set the cooking time to 1 Hr. on High settings.
Serve warm with cheese on top.

Corn and Bacon

Servings: 20 Cooking Time: 4 Hrs.

Ingredients:

10 cups corn
24 oz. cream cheese, cubed
½ cup milk
½ cup melted butter
½ cup heavy cream
¼ cup sugar
A pinch of salt and black pepper
4 bacon strips, cooked and crumbled
2 tbsps. green onions, chopped

Directions:

In your Slow Cooker, mix corn with cream cheese, milk, butter, cream, sugar, salt, pepper, bacon and green onions, cover and cook on Low for 4 Hrs.
Stir the corn, divide between plates and serve as a side dish.

Mustard Brussels Sprouts

Servings: 2 Cooking Time: 3 Hrs.

Ingredients:

1 lb. Brussels sprouts, trimmed and halved
1 tbsp. olive oil
1 tbsp. mustard
1 tbsp. balsamic vinegar
Salt and black pepper to the taste
¼ cup veggie stock
A pinch of red pepper, crushed
2 tbsps. chives, chopped

Directions:

In your Slow Cooker, mix the Brussels sprouts with the oil, mustard and the other ingredients, toss, put the lid on and cook on High for 3 Hrs.
Divide the mix between plates and serve as a side dish.

Mac Cream Cups

Servings: 6 Cooking Time: 8 Hrs.

Ingredients:

6 oz. puff pastry
1 cup fresh basil
7 oz. elbow macaroni, cooked
1 egg
¼ cup heavy cream
1 tbsp. flour
1 tbsp. cornstarch
1 tsp. salt
1 tbsp. turmeric
1 tsp. olive oil

Directions:

Roll the puff pastry and cut it into 6 squares.
Layer a muffin tray with olive oil and place one square into each muffin cup.
Press the puff pastry square into the muffin cup.
Beat egg with cream, flour, salt, cornstarch, and turmeric in a suitable bowl.
Stir in macaroni then divide this mixture into the muffin cups.
Place this muffin tray in the Slow Cooker.
Put the cooker's lid on and set the cooking time to 8 Hrs. on Low settings.
Serve warm.

Corn Sauté

Servings: 2 Cooking Time: 2 Hrs.

Ingredients:

3 cups corn
1 carrot, peeled and grated
2 tbsps. butter, melted
2 bacon strips, cooked and crumbled
2 tbsp. whipping cream
1 tbsp. chives, chopped
Salt and black pepper to the taste
1 tbsp. green onions, chopped

Directions:

In your Slow Cooker, combine the corn with the cream, carrot and the other ingredients, toss, put the lid on and cook on Low for 2 Hrs.
Divide between plates, and serve.

Kale Mix

Servings: 2 Cooking Time: 2 Hrs.

Ingredients:

1 lb. baby kale
½ cup chicken stock
A pinch of salt and black pepper
1 small yellow onion, chopped
½ tbsp. tomato paste
½ tsp. chili powder
1 tbsp. olive oil
1 tbsp. apple cider vinegar

Directions:

In your Slow Cooker, mix the kale with the tomato paste, stock and the other ingredients, toss, put the lid on and cook on Low for 2 Hrs.
Divide between plates and serve as a side dish.

Orange Squash

Servings: 6 Cooking Time: 5 Hrs.

Ingredients:

1 lb. butternut squash, peeled and diced
1 tsp. brown sugar
1 tbsp. salt
1 orange, sliced
1 Poblano pepper,chopped
1 tsp. ground cinnamon
1 cup heavy cream
¼ tsp. ground cardamom

Directions:

Toss the butternut squash with poblano pepper, salt, cream, cardamom, sugar, and cardamom.
Spread the orange slices in the insert of the Slow Cooker.
Spread the butternut squash-poblano pepper mixture over the orange slices.
Put the cooker's lid on and set the cooking time to 5 Hrs. on Low settings.
Serve warm.

Mashed Potatoes

Servings: 2 Cooking Time: 6 Hrs.

Ingredients:

1 lb. gold potatoes, peeled and cubed
1 cup milk
2 tbsps. butter
2 garlic cloves, chopped
1 cup water
A pinch of salt and white pepper

Directions:

In your Slow Cooker, mix the potatoes with the water, salt and pepper, put the lid on and cook on Low for 6 Hrs.
Mash the potatoes, add the rest of the ingredients, whisk and serve.

Bean Medley

Servings: 12 Cooking Time: 5 Hrs.

Ingredients:

2 celery ribs, chopped
1 green bell pepper, chopped
1 sweet red pepper, chopped
½ cup Italian dressing
1 tbsp. cider vinegar
16 oz. kidney beans, drained
15 oz. canned black-eyed peas, drained
15 oz. canned corn, drained
15 oz. canned black beans, drained
1 and ½ cups ketchup
1 yellow onion, chopped
½ cup brown sugar
½ cup water
2 bay leaves
Salt and black pepper to the taste
15 oz. canned northern beans, drained
15 oz. canned lima beans, drained

Directions:

In your Slow Cooker, mix celery with ketchup, red and green bell pepper, onion, sugar, Italian dressing, water, vinegar, bay leaves, kidney beans, black-eyed peas, northern beans, corn, lima beans and black beans, stir, cover and cook on Low for 5 Hrs.
Divide between plates and serve as a side dish.

Italian Squash and Peppers Mix

Servings: 4 Cooking Time: 1 Hr. and 30 Min

Ingredients:

12 small squash, peeled and cut into wedges
2 green bell peppers, cut into wedges
1 red onion, cut into wedges
1 tbsp. parsley, chopped
2 red bell peppers, cut into wedges
1/3 cup Italian dressing
Salt and black pepper to the taste

Directions:

In your Slow Cooker, mix squash with red bell peppers, green bell peppers, salt, pepper and Italian dressing, cover and cook on High for 1 Hr. and 30 Min.
Add parsley, toss, divide between plates and serve as a side dish.

Dessert Recipes

Lavender Blackberry Crumble

Servings: 6 Cooking Time: 2 1/4 Hrs.

Ingredients:

1 1/2 lbs. fresh blackberries
1 tsp. vanilla extract
1 tsp. dried lavender buds
1 pinch salt
2 tbsps. cornstarch
1/4 cup white sugar
1 cup all-purpose flour
1/2 cup butter, chilled and cubed

Directions:

Mix the blackberries, cornstarch, vanilla, sugar and lavender in your Slow Cooker.
Combine the flour, salt and butter in a bowl and rub them well with your fingertips until the mixture looks grainy.
Spread the mixture over the veggies and cook on high settings for 2 Hrs.
Serve the crumble chilled.

Granola Apples

Servings:6 Cooking Time: 2.5 Hrs.

Ingredients:

6 apples, cored
3 tsps. maple syrup
6 tsps. granola
½ cup of water

Directions:

Mix maple syrup with granola.
Fill the apples with granola mixture and transfer in the Slow Cooker.
Add water and close the lid.
Cook the apples on High for 2.5 Hrs.

Grain Free Chocolate Cake

Servings: 10 Cooking Time: 6 1/4 Hrs.

Ingredients:

2 cups almond flour
1/4 cup cocoa powder
1 tsp. baking soda
1/4 tsp. salt
1/2 cup coconut oil, melted
1 tsp. vanilla extract
1 cup shredded coconut
1/2 cup xylitol powder
1 tsp. baking powder
4 eggs
1 cup coconut milk

Directions:

Mix the dry ingredients in your Slow Cooker.
Add the remaining ingredients and mix well with a spatula.
Cover the pot and bake for 6 Hrs. on low settings.
Allow the cake to cool completely before slicing and serving.

Pumpkin Bars

Servings:6 Cooking Time: 5 Hrs.

Ingredients:

1 tsp. pumpkin spices
1 cup flour
1 tsp. lime zest, grated
4 tbsps. flax meal
½ cup pumpkin puree
½ tsp. baking powder
¼ cup of sugar
2 tbsps. olive oil

Directions:

Put all ingredients in the mixing bowl. Mix the mixture until smooth.
Then line the Slow Cooker with baking paper.
Transfer the pumpkin mixture in the Slow Cooker.
Close the lid and cook it on Low for 5 Hrs.
Then cool the dessert and cut into bars.

Chia Muffins

Servings:4 Cooking Time: 2.5 Hrs.

Ingredients:

2 eggs, beaten
1 tsp. ground nutmeg
¼ cup plain yogurt
1 tbsp. brown sugar
½ cup flour
1 tsp. butter, melted
1 tbsp. chia seeds

Directions:

Mix eggs with plain yogurt, ground nutmeg, brown sugar, flour, and butter.
Whisk the mixture until you get a smooth batter.
Then add chia seeds and mix the batter with the help of the spoon.
Pour the batter in the silicone muffin molds (fill ½ part of every mold).
Place the muffins in the Slow Cooker.
Close the lid and cook them on High for 2.5 Hrs.

Lemon Poppy Seed Cake

Servings: 8 Cooking Time: 4 1/2 Hrs.

Ingredients:

3/4 cup butter, softened
1 large lemon, zested and juiced
1 cup all-purpose flour
1 tsp. baking soda
1/2 tsp. salt
1 cup buttermilk
3/4 cup white sugar
2 eggs
1/2 cup fine cornmeal
1/2 tsp. baking powder
2 tbsps. poppy seeds

Directions:

Mix the flour, cornmeal, baking soda, baking powder, salt and poppy seeds in a bowl.
Combine the butter, sugar and lemon zest in a bowl and mix well for 5 Min.
Add the eggs and lemon zest and mix well.
Fold in the flour mixture, alternating it with the buttermilk.
Spoon the batter in your Slow Cooker and cook on low settings for 4 Hrs.
Allow the cake to cool in the pot before slicing and serving.

Raisin-flax Meal Bars

Servings: 8 Cooking Time: 3.5 Hrs.

Ingredients:

¼ cup raisins
1 egg, whisked
5 oz. milk
1 tsp. ground cinnamon
1 tbsp. lemon juice
1 tbsp. flour
1 cup oat flour
4 oz. banana, mashed
1 tbsp. flax meal
½ tsp. baking soda
1 tbsp. butter

Directions:

Whisk egg with mashed banana, oat flour, milk, flax meal, raising in a bowl.
Stir in cinnamon, lemon juice, baking soda, and flour, then knead well.
Grease the insert of the Slow Cooker with butter.
Make big balls out of this raisin dough and shape them into 3-4 inches bars.
Place these bars in the insert of the Slow Cooker.
Put the cooker's lid on and set the cooking time to 3 Hrs. on Low settings.
Serve when chilled.

Prune Bake

Servings:4 Cooking Time: 3 Hrs.

Ingredients:

2 cups of cottage cheese
1 cup prunes, chopped
5 eggs, beaten
4 tsps. butter

Directions:

Mix cottage cheese with eggs and blend the mixture until smooth and fluffy.
Then put the butter into 4 ramekins.
Mix cottage cheese mixture with prunes and transfer in the ramekins with butter.
Transfer the ramekins in the Slow Cooker and close the lid.
Cook the meal on High for 3 Hrs.

Dark Chocolate Almond Cake

Servings: 10 Cooking Time: 4 1/2 Hrs.

Ingredients:

1 1/2 cups almond flour
3/4 cup white sugar
1/4 tsp. salt
2 eggs
1 tsp. vanilla extract
1/2 cup cocoa powder
1 1/2 tsps. baking powder
1/2 cup butter, melted
1 cup almond milk
1/4 cup sliced almonds

Directions:

Mix the almond flour, cocoa powder, sugar, baking powder and salt in a bowl.
Stir in the wet ingredients and mix well.
Pour the batter in a greased Slow Cooker and top with sliced almonds.
Bake for 4 Hrs. on low settings.
Allow the cake to cool completely before slicing and serving.

Coconut Poached Pears

Servings: 6 Cooking Time: 6 1/4 Hrs.

Ingredients:

6 ripe but firm pears
2 cups water
1 star anise
2 lemon rings
2 cups coconut milk
1 cinnamon stick
3/4 cup coconut sugar

Directions:

Carefully peel and core the pears and place them in your Slow Cooker.
Add the rest of the ingredients and cover with a lid. Cook on low settings for 6 Hrs.
Allow the pears to cool in the pot before serving.

Peach Cobbler

Servings: 8 Cooking Time: 6 1/2 Hrs.

Ingredients:

2 lbs. ripe peaches, pitted and sliced
2 tbsps. brown sugar
1/2 tsp. baking powder
1/4 cup sugar
2/3 cup buttermilk, chilled
1 tbsp. cornstarch
1 1/2 cups all-purpose flour
1/4 tsp. salt
1/2 cup butter, chilled and cubed

Directions:

Mix the peaches, cornstarch and brown sugar in your Slow Cooker.
Combine the flour, baking powder, salt, sugar and butter in a bowl and rub the mixture well until sandy.
Stir in the buttermilk and give it a quick mix then spoon the batter over the peaches.
Cover and cook on low settings for 6 Hrs.
The cobbler is best served slightly warm or chilled.

Lemon Cream

Servings: 4 Cooking Time: 1 Hr.

Ingredients:

1 cup heavy cream
¼ cup lemon juice
1 tsp. lemon zest, grated
8 oz. mascarpone cheese

Directions:

In your Slow Cooker, mix heavy cream with mascarpone, lemon zest and lemon juice, stir, cover and cook on Low for 1 Hr.
Divide into dessert glasses and keep in the fridge until you serve.

Cardamom Plums

Servings:6 Cooking Time: 5 Hrs.

Ingredients:

4 cups plums, pitted, halved
¼ cup of sugar
1 cup of water
1 tsp. ground cardamom
1 tsp. lemon juice

Directions:

Put plums in the Slow Cooker and sprinkle them with ground cardamom, sugar, and lemon juice.
Add water and close the lid.
Cook the plums on Low for 5 Hrs.
Carefully stir the cooked dessert and transfer in the serving ramekins.

Orange and Apricot Jam

Servings:4 Cooking Time: 3 Hrs.

Ingredients:

2 oranges, peeled, chopped
1 tbsp. orange zest, grated
1 cup apricots, chopped
4 tbsps. sugar

Directions:

Put all ingredients in the bowl and blend them until smooth with the help of the immersion blender.
Then pour the mixture in the Slow Cooker and cook it on High for 3 Hrs.
Transfer the hot jam in the glass cans and close with a lid.
Cool the jam well.

Cinnamon Rice Milk Cocktail

Servings:6 Cooking Time: 1.5 Hrs.

Ingredients:

1 cup long-grain rice
3 cups of water
1 banana, chopped
½ cup agave syrup
1 tsp. ground cinnamon

Directions:

Put rice in the food processor.
Add water and blend the mixture until smooth.
Then sieve the liquid and transfer it in the Slow Cooker.
Add agave syrup and ground cinnamon. Cook the liquid on High for 1.5 Hrs.
After this, transfer the hot liquid in the food processor.
Add banana and blend until smooth.

Matcha Shake

Servings:4 Cooking Time: 40 Min

Ingredients:

1 tsp. matcha green tea
2 bananas, mashed
2 cups of coconut milk
¼ cup agave nectar

Directions:

Mix agave nectar with coconut milk and matcha green tea. Mix the mixture until smooth and pour it in the Slow Cooker.
Cook the mixture on high for 40 Min.
Then transfer the mixture in the blender, add mashed bananas and blend the liquid until smooth.
Pour the cooked shake in the glasses and cool to room temperature.

Cinnamon Rolls

Servings: 8 Cooking Time: 6 Hrs.

Ingredients:

4 cups all-purpose flour
1 1/4 tsps. active dry yeast
1 3/4 cups milk
1/4 cup white sugar
1 tsp. cinnamon powder
1/2 tsp. salt
2 eggs
1/4 cup sour cream
1 cup light brown sugar
1/2 cup butter, softened

Directions:

Mix the flour, salt and yeast in a bowl.
Add the eggs, milk, sour cream and white sugar and mix well with a spoon then knead for 10 Min. until elastic and smooth.
Allow the dough to rise for 40 Min.
Transfer the dough on a floured working surface and roll it into a thin rectangle.
Spread the softened butter over the dough and top with brown sugar and cinnamon.
Roll the dough as tight as possible then cut the roll into thick slices and arrange them all in your Slow Cooker.
Allow to rise for 20 additional Min. then bake for 4 1/2 Hrs. on low settings.
Serve warm or chilled.

Rhubarb Stew

Servings: 2 Cooking Time: 2 Hrs.

Ingredients:

½ lb. rhubarb, roughly sliced
½ tsp. vanilla extract
1 tbsp. lemon juice
2 tbsps. sugar
½ tsp. lemon extract
¼ cup water

Directions:

In your Slow Cooker, mix the rhubarb with the sugar, vanilla and the other ingredients, toss, put the lid on and cook on Low for 2 Hrs.
Divide the mix into bowls and serve cold.

Raspberry Nutmeg Cake

Servings: 8 Cooking Time: 7 Hrs.

Ingredients:

4 eggs
1 cup flour
1 cup raspberry
1 tbsp. butter
1 tbsp. cornstarch
1 cup sugar
1 tsp. vanilla extract
1/3 cup sugar, brown
¼ tsp. nutmeg

Directions:

Separate the egg yolks from egg whites and keep them in a separate bowl.
Beat egg yolks with sugar, vanilla extract, cornstarch and nutmeg in a mixer.
Now beat the egg whites in an electric mixer until it forms peaks.
Add this egg white foam to the egg yolk mixture.
Mix gently, then add brown sugar and raspberry and blend again.
Grease the insert of your Slow Cooker with butter.
Spread the raspberry batter in the cooker.
Put the cooker's lid on and set the cooking time to 7 Hrs. on Low settings.
Slice and serve when chilled.

Greek Cream

Servings: 2 Cooking Time: 1 Hr.

Ingredients:

1 cup heavy cream
2 tbsps. brown sugar
½ tsp. ginger powder
1 cup Greek yogurt
½ tsp. vanilla extract

Directions:

In your Slow Cooker, mix the cream with the yogurt and the other ingredients, whisk, put the lid on and cook on High for 1 Hr.
Divide the cream into bowls and serve cold.

Citron Vanilla Bars

Servings: 10 Cooking Time: 4 Hrs.

Ingredients:

6 tbsp. sugar
1 ½ cup flour
1 tbsp. lemon zest
1 large egg, beaten
9 tbsp. butter
7 oz. lemon curd
¼ tsp. olive oil
1 tsp. vanilla extract

Directions:

Mix softened butter with lemon zest, egg, sugar, and flour in a bowl.
Stir in vanilla extract, then mix well until it forms a smooth dough.
Spread this dough into a sheet then place this dough in the insert of Slow Cooker.
Add lemon curd over the dough evenly.
Put the cooker's lid on and set the cooking time to 4 Hrs. on High settings.
Slice and serve.

Berry Marmalade

Servings: 12 Cooking Time: 3 Hrs.

Ingredients:

1 lb. cranberries
½ lb. blueberries
2 lbs. sugar
2 tbsp. water
1 lb. strawberries
3.5 oz. black currant
Zest of 1 lemon

Directions:

In your Slow Cooker, mix strawberries with cranberries, blueberries, currants, lemon zest, sugar and water, cover, cook on High for 3 Hrs., divide into jars and serve cold.

Apricot and Peaches Cream

Servings: 2 Cooking Time: 2 Hrs.

Ingredients:

1 cup apricots, pitted and chopped
1 cup heavy cream
1 tsp. vanilla extract
1 cup peaches, pitted and chopped
3 tbsps. brown sugar

Directions:

In a blender, mix the apricots with the peaches and the other ingredients, and pulse well.
Put the cream in the Slow Cooker, put the lid on, cook on High for 2 Hrs., divide into bowls and serve.

Mint Summer Drink

Servings:6 Cooking Time: 3 Hrs.

Ingredients:

1 cup fresh mint, chopped
1 orange, sliced
1 cup agave syrup
7 cups of water
1 lemon, sliced
1 cup strawberries

Directions:

Put all ingredients in the Slow Cooker.
Close the lid and cook the drink on High for 3 Hrs.
Then refrigerate the drink until cool.

Dark Cherry Chocolate Cake

Servings: 8 Cooking Time: 4 1/2 Hrs.

Ingredients:

2/3 cup butter, softened
3 eggs
2/3 cup all-purpose flour
1/4 tsp. salt
1 1/2 cups dark cherries, pitted
1/2 cup dark chocolate chips
2/3 cup white sugar
1 tsp. vanilla extract
1 tsp. baking powder
1/4 cup cocoa powder
1/2 cup water

Directions:

Mix the butter and sugar in a bowl until creamy.
Stir in the eggs and vanilla and mix well then fold in the flour, baking powder, salt, baking powder and cocoa.
Pour the batter in your Slow Cooker and top with dark cherries.
Mix the water and chocolate chips in a saucepan and cook over low heat until melted and smooth.
Pour the hot sauce over the cherries and cook the cake on low settings for 4 Hrs.
Allow the cake to cool in the pot before serving.

Fudgy Raspberry Chocolate Bread Pudding

Servings: 8 Cooking Time: 6 1/4 Hrs.

Ingredients:

6 cups bread cubes
2 cups whole milk
1 1/2 cups fresh raspberries
1/4 cup cocoa powder
1 cup heavy cream
1/2 cup white chocolate chips

Directions:

Mix the bread cubes, raspberries and white chocolate chips in your Slow Cooker.
Combine the cocoa powder, milk and cream in a bowl and give it a good mix. Pour this mix over the bread cubes.
Cover the pot with its lid and cook on low settings for 6 Hrs.
Allow to cool slightly before serving.

Banana Cake

Servings: 6 Cooking Time: 2 Hrs.

Ingredients:

¾ cup sugar
1 tsp. vanilla
3 bananas, mashed
1 and ½ cups flour
1/3 cup milk
1/3 cup butter, soft
1 egg
1 tsp. baking powder
½ tsps. baking soda
Cooking spray

Directions:

In a bowl, mix butter with sugar, vanilla extract, eggs, bananas, baking powder, flour, baking soda and milk and whisk.
Grease your Slow Cooker with the cooking spray, add the batter, spread, cover and cook on High for 2 Hrs.
Leave the cake to cool down, slice and serve.

Red Muffins

Servings:8 Cooking Time: 2 Hrs.

Ingredients:

5 oz. carrot, grated
3 tbsps. coconut oil, softened
1 cup flour
¼ cup of sugar
2 eggs, beaten
2 tbsps. cream cheese
¼ cup skim milk
1 tsp. baking powder

Directions:

In the bowl mix eggs, coconut oil, cream cheese, flour, skim milk, sugar, and baking powder.
Carefully stir the mixture until you get a smooth batter.
Then add carrot and stir the mixture with the help of the spoon.
Pour the batter in the muffin molds (fill ½ part of every mold) and place it in the Slow Cooker.
Cook the muffins on high for 2 Hrs.

Hazelnut Liqueur Cheesecake

Servings: 8 Cooking Time: 6 1/2 Hrs.

Ingredients:

Crust:
1 cup graham crackers, crushed
1/4 cup butter, melted
1 cup ground hazelnuts
Filling:
20 oz. cream cheese
1/4 cup hazelnut liqueur
1/2 cup white sugar
1/2 cup hazelnut butter
1/4 cup light brown sugar
4 eggs

1/2 cup heavy cream
1 tsp. vanilla extract
1 pinch salt

Directions:

For the crust, mix the crackers, hazelnuts and butter in a bowl.
Transfer the mix in your Slow Cooker and press it well on the bottom of the pot.
For the filling, mix the cream cheese, hazelnut butter, liqueur, sugars, eggs, cream, salt and vanilla and mix well.
Pour the mixture over the crust and cook in the covered pot for 6 Hrs. on low settings.
Serve the cheesecake chilled.

Coconut and Macadamia Cream

Servings: 4 Cooking Time: 1 Hr. and 30 Min

Ingredients:

4 tbsps. vegetable oil
2 tbsps. sugar
5 tbsps. coconut powder
3 tbsps. macadamia nuts, chopped
1 cup heavy cream

Directions:

Put the oil in your Slow Cooker, add nuts, sugar, coconut powder and cream, stir, cover, cook on Low for 1 Hr. and 30 Min.
Stir well, divide into bowls and serve.

Creamy Rhubarb and Plums Bowls

Servings: 2 Cooking Time: 2 Hrs.

Ingredients:

1 cup plums, pitted and halved
1 cup coconut cream
½ cup sugar
1 tsp. almond extract
1 cup rhubarb, sliced
½ tsp. vanilla extract
½ tbsp. lemon juice

Directions:

In your Slow Cooker, mix the plums with the rhubarb, cream and the other ingredients, toss, put the lid on and cook on High for 2 Hrs.
Divide the mix into bowls and serve.

Berries Salad

Servings: 2 Cooking Time: 1 Hr.

Ingredients:

2 tbsps. brown sugar
1 tbsp. lime zest, grated
½ cup cranberries
1 cup strawberries
1 tbsp. lime juice
1 cup blueberries
1 cup blackberries
½ cup heavy cream

Directions:

In your Slow Cooker, mix the berries with the sugar and the other ingredients, toss, put the lid on and cook on High for 1 Hr.
Divide the mix into bowls and serve.

Cottage Cheese Ramekins

Servings:4 Cooking Time: 3 Hrs.

Ingredients:

4 tsps. semolina
1 tsp. vanilla extract
2 tbsps. butter, melted
2 oz. raisins, chopped
2 cups of cottage cheese

Directions:

Mix semolina with cottage cheese, vanilla extract, butter, and raisins.
Transfer the mixture into ramekins and place the ramekins in the Slow Cooker.
Close the lid and cook the meal on High for 3 Hrs.

Spiced Plum Butter

Servings: 8 Cooking Time: 8 1/2 Hrs.

Ingredients:

6 lbs. ripe plums, pitted
2 star anise
4 cardamom pods, crushed
3 cups white sugar
2 cinnamon stick
2 whole cloves

Directions:

Combine all the ingredients in your Slow Cooker.
Cover the pot and cook on low settings for 8 Hrs.
Remove and discard the spices then pour the hot butter into glass jars and seal them with a lid.

Cardamom Lemon Pie

Servings: 6 Cooking Time: 7 Hrs.

Ingredients:

3 lemons, sliced
5 eggs, whisked
½ cup cottage cheese
1 tsp. baking powder
1 cup of sugar
2 tsp. ground ginger
1 tsp. ground cardamom
1 cup whey
2 cups flour
1 tbsp. lemon juice
1 tsp. lime zest

Directions:

Start by mixing whey, lemon juice, baking powder, cottage cheese, sugar, ground cardamom, lime zest, and ground ginger in a mixer.
Stir in flour and whisk until it forms a smooth whey batter.
Fold in the sliced lemons and mix gently.
Layer the base of the insert of Slow Cooker with a parchment sheet.
Spread the lemon-whey batter in the insert of Slow Cooker.
Put the cooker's lid on and set the cooking time to 7 Hrs. on Low settings.
Slice and serve chilled.

Amaranth Bars

Servings:7 Cooking Time: 1 Hr.

Ingredients:

½ cup amaranth
¼ cup of coconut oil
4 oz. peanuts, chopped
3 oz. milk chocolate, chopped

Directions:

Put all ingredients in the Slow Cooker and cook on High for 1 Hr.
Then transfer the melted amaranth mixture in the silicone mold, flatten it, and refrigerate until solid.
Cut the dessert into bars.

Apricot Spoon Cake

Servings:10 Cooking Time: 2.5 Hrs.

Ingredients:

2 cups cake mix 1 cup milk
1 cup apricots, canned, pitted, chopped, with juice
2 eggs, beaten 1 tbsp. sunflower oil

Directions:

Mix milk with cake mix and egg.
Then sunflower oil and blend the mixture until smooth.
Then place the baking paper in the Slow Cooker.
Pour the cake mix batter in the Slow Cooker, flatten it gently, and close the lid.
Cook the cake on High for 2.5 Hrs.
Then transfer the cooked cake in the plate and top with apricots and apricot juice.
Leave the cake until it is warm and cut into servings.

Butterscotch Self Saucing Pudding

Servings: 6 Cooking Time: 2 1/4 Hrs.

Ingredients:

1/2 cup butter, melted
1 tsp. vanilla extract
1 1/2 cups all-purpose flour
2 cups hot water
2 tbsps. golden syrup
1 cup whole milk
1 cup white sugar
1/4 tsp. salt
3/4 cup dark brown sugar
2 tbsps. butter

Directions:

Make the butterscotch sauce by mixing the hot water, brown sugar, golden syrup and 2 tbsps. of butter in a saucepan. Cook over medium flame for 5-6 Min. until thickened then place aside.
For the pudding, mix 1/2 cup butter, milk, vanilla, white sugar, flour and salt in a bowl. Pour the batter in a Slow Cooker.
Drizzle the butterscotch sauce on top and cook on high settings for 2 Hrs.
Serve the pudding slightly warm.

Chocolate Cake

Servings: 10 Cooking Time: 3 Hrs.

Ingredients:

1 cup flour
½ cup cocoa powder
1 and ½ tsps. baking powder
4 tbsps. vegetable oil
2/3 cup milk
3 egg whites, whisked
½ cup sugar
3 eggs
¾ tsp. vanilla extract
1/3 cup dark chocolate chips

Directions:

In a bowl, mix sugar with flour, egg whites, cocoa powder, baking powder, milk, oil, eggs, chocolate chips and vanilla extract and whisk really well.
Pour this into your lined and greased Slow Cooker and cook on Low for 2 Hrs.
Leave the cake aside to cool down, slice and serve.

Vanilla Bean Caramel Custard

Servings: 6 Cooking Time: 6 1/4 Hrs.

Ingredients:

1 cup white sugar for melting
1 cup heavy cream
4 eggs
2 tbsps. white sugar
4 cups whole milk
2 egg yolks
1 tbsp. vanilla bean paste

Directions:

Caramelize 1 cup of sugar in a thick saucepan until it has an amber color. Pour the caramel in your Slow Cooker and swirl to coat the bottom and sides as much as possible.
Mix the milk, cream, egg yolks, eggs, vanilla bean paste and sugar in a bowl. Pour this mixture over the caramel.
Cover the pot and cook on low settings for 6 Hrs.
Serve the custard chilled.

Monkey Bread

Servings: 8 Cooking Time: 5 1/4 Hrs.

Ingredients:

3 cups all-purpose flour
1/4 cup white sugar
1 1/4 cups warm milk
3/4 cup butter, melted
1 1/2 tsps. cinnamon powder
4 eggs
1 tsp. vanilla extract
1 tsp. active dry yeast
1 cup white sugar

Directions:

Mix the flour, salt, eggs, 1/4 cup white sugar, warm milk, vanilla and active dry yeast in the bowl of your mixer and knead for 10 Min. Allow the dough to rise for 1 Hr.
Transfer the dough on a floured working surface and cut it into 24-30 small pieces of dough. Roll each piece of dough into a ball.
Mix the sugar with cinnamon powder.
To finish the bread, dip each ball of dough into melted butter then roll through the cinnamon sugar.
Grease your Slow Cooker and place the dough balls in the pot.
Cook on low settings for 4 Hrs.
Allow to cool before serving.

Pears and Sauce

Servings: 4 Cooking Time: 4 Hrs.

Ingredients:

4 pears, peeled and cored
¼ cup maple syrup
1 tbsp. ginger, grated
2 cups orange juice
2 tsps. cinnamon powder

Directions:

In your Slow Cooker, mix pears with orange juice, maple syrup, cinnamon and ginger, cover and cook on Low for 4 Hrs.
Divide pears and sauce between plates and serve warm.

Mint Cookies

Servings:6 Cooking Time: 3.5 Hrs.

Ingredients:

1 tsp. dried mint
1 tbsp. olive oil
1 cup flour
4 tbsps. flax meal
½ cup buttermilk
2 eggs, beaten
4 tbsps. brown sugar
1 tsp. baking powder

Directions:

Put all ingredients in the mixing bowl.
Knead the soft dough.
Then line the Slow Cooker with baking paper.
Cut the dough into small pieces and roll them in the balls.
Put the balls in the Slow Cooker one-by-one.
Close the lid and cook the cookies on High for 3.5 Hrs.

Cinnamon Plum Jam

Servings:6 Cooking Time: 6 Hrs.

Ingredients:

4 cups plums, pitted, halved
½ cup brown sugar
1 tbsp. ground cinnamon
1 tsp. vanilla extract

Directions:

Put all ingredients in the Slow Cooker and gently mix.
Close the lid and cook it on Low for 6 Hrs.

Chocolate Mocha Bread Pudding

Servings: 6 Cooking Time: 4 1/4 Hrs.

Ingredients:

6 cups bread cubed
1 cup whole milk
2 egg yolks
1/2 cup white sugar
1 cup heavy cream
1 cup brewed coffee
2 whole eggs

Directions:

Mix the cream, milk, coffee, egg yolks, eggs and sugar in a bowl.
Place the bread cubes in a Slow Cooker and pour the coffee mixture over it.
Cover and cook on low settings for 4 Hrs.
Allow the pudding to cool slightly before serving.

Creamy Dark Chocolate Dessert

Servings: 6 Cooking Time: 1 Hr.

Ingredients:

½ cup heavy cream
4 oz. dark chocolate, unsweetened and chopped

Directions:

Add cream with chocolate in the insert of Slow Cooker.
Put the cooker's lid on and set the cooking time to 1 Hr. on High settings.
Allow this mixture to cool.
Serve.

Coffee Cinnamon Roll

Servings: 4 Cooking Time: 4 Hrs.

Ingredients:

3 tbsp. butter
1 tbsp. instant coffee powder
3 tbsp. sugar, brown
¼ cup whey
¼ tsp. salt
1 egg yolk
3 tbsp. ground cinnamon
1 tsp. vanilla extract
½ tsp. yeast
½ cup flour
1 tsp. white sugar
½ tsp. canola oil

Directions:

Whisk yeast with sugar and whey in a bowl.
Stir in flour, salt, vanilla, and enough water to make a smooth dough.
Roll this dough into ¼ inch thick sheet.
Mix cinnamon with coffee powder, brown sugar, and butter in a small bowl.
Spread this cinnamon-butter mixture over the dough sheet.
Start rolling the dough from one to make a cinnamon roll.
Grease the insert of your Slow Cooker with canola oil and place the cinnamon roll it.
Brush the top of this roll with whisked egg yolk.
Put the cooker's lid on and set the cooking time to 4 Hrs. on High settings.
Slice the roll and serve.

Caramelized Bananas

Servings:6 Cooking Time: 2 Hrs. 15 Min

Ingredients:

6 bananas, peeled
3 tbsps. caramel
2 tbsps. butter

Directions:

Put butter in the Slow Cooker.
Add bananas and cook them on High for 15 Min.
Then add caramel and cook the dessert on Low for 2 Hrs.
Carefully mix the cooked dessert and transfer it into the plates.

Cardamom Rice Porridge

Servings:2 Cooking Time: 4 Hrs.

Ingredients:

¼ cup basmati rice
½ cup of water
1 tsp. ground cardamom
1 cup milk
1 tsp. butter

Directions:

Put all ingredients in the Slow Cooker.
Close the lid and cook the dessert on high for 4 Hrs.
Cool the cooked meal and add sugar if desired.

Golden Syrup Pudding

Servings: 8 Cooking Time: 4 1/4 Hrs.

Ingredients:

1/2 cup golden syrup
1/4 cup light brown sugar
1 1/2 cups all-purpose flour
1/2 tsp. baking soda
1/2 cup butter, softened
2 eggs
1/4 tsp. salt
3/4 cup whole milk

Directions:

Mix the dry ingredients in a bowl and the wet ingredients in another bowl. Combine the dry and wet ingredients in a bowl and give it a quick mix.
Spoon the batter in your Slow Cooker and bake on low settings for 4 Hrs.
Allow the pudding cool before serving.

Cherry Dump Cake

Servings: 8-10 Cooking Time: 6 1/4 Hrs.

Ingredients:

1 1/2 lbs. dark cherries, pitted
1/4 cup white sugar
1 cup all-purpose flour
1/4 tsp. salt
1 tbsp. cornstarch
1 tsp. lemon juice
1 cup ground almonds
1/2 cup butter, drizzled

Directions:

Mix the cherries, cornstarch, sugar and lemon juice in your Slow Cooker.

Mix the flour, almonds and salt in a bowl. Spread this mixture over the cherries then drizzle with melted butter.
Bake for 6 Hrs. on low settings.
Allow the cake to cool in the pot before serving.

Honey Yogurt Cake

Servings: 8 Cooking Time: 5 1/2 Hrs.

Ingredients:

1/2 cup butter, softened
1/2 cup light brown sugar
2 eggs
1 tsp. baking powder
1/4 cup Greek yogurt
1/4 cup honey
1 tsp. lemon zest
1 cup all-purpose flour
1/4 tsp. salt

Directions:

Mix the butter, honey and sugar in a bowl for 5 Min. until pale and creamy.
Stir in the lemon zest and eggs and mix well.
Fold in the flour, baking powder and salt then add the yogurt.
Spoon the batter in a greased Slow Cooker and bake for 5 Hrs. on low settings.
Allow the cake to cool in the pot before slicing and serving.

Mocha Chocolate Brioche Pudding

Servings: 8 Cooking Time: 4 1/2 Hrs.

Ingredients:

8 cups brioche bread cubes
1 cup dark chocolate chips
4 eggs
1/4 cup light brown sugar
1/4 cup white chocolate chips
1 cup heavy cream
1 1/2 cups whole milk
2 tsps. instant coffee
1 tsp. orange zest

Directions:

Heat the cream in a saucepan to the boiling point then remove from heat and add the chocolate. Mix until melted then pour the mixture in a bowl and add the milk, eggs, coffee powder and sugar. Mix well.
Combine the brioche cubes with white chocolate chips in your Slow Cooker.
Pour the milk and egg mixture over the brioche and cook on low settings for 4 Hrs.
Serve the pudding slightly warm.

Banana Muffins

Servings:2 Cooking Time: 2.5 Hrs.

Ingredients:

2 eggs, beaten
4 tbsps. flour
½ tsp. baking powder
2 bananas, chopped
½ tsp. vanilla extract

Directions:

Mash the chopped bananas and mix them with eggs.
Then add vanilla extract and baking powder.
Add flour and stir the mixture until smooth.
Pour the banana mixture in the muffin molds (fill ½ part of every muffin mold) and transfer in the Slow Cooker.
Cook the muffins on High for 2.5 Hrs.

Butternut Squash Pudding

Servings: 8 Cooking Time: 3 Hrs.

Ingredients:

2 lbs. butternut squash, steamed, peeled and mashed
2 eggs
¾ cup maple syrup
½ tsp. ginger powder
1 tbsp. cornstarch
1 cup milk
1 tsp. cinnamon powder
¼ tsp. cloves, ground
Whipped cream for serving

Directions:

Toss squash with milk, eggs, maple syrup, cornstarch, cinnamon, cloves ground, and ginger in the insert of Slow Cooker.
Put the cooker's lid on and set the cooking time to 2 Hrs. on Low settings.
Serve with whipped cream on top.

Classic Apple Pie

Servings:6 Cooking Time: 2 Hrs.

Ingredients:

1 cup apples, chopped
4 eggs, beaten
1 tbsp. butter, melted
1 cup flour
1 cup of sugar
1 tsp. vanilla extract

Directions:

Blend the sugar with eggs until you get a lemon color mixture.
Then add flour, butter, vanilla extract, and mix until smooth.
Add apples and carefully stir the mixture until homogenous.
After this, line the Slow Cooker bottom with baking paper and pour the dough inside.
Cook the pie on High for 2 Hrs. on High.
Cook the cooked pie well.

Mango Cream

Servings: 4 Cooking Time: 1 Hr.

Ingredients:

1 mango, sliced
14 oz. coconut cream

Directions:

In your Slow Cooker, mix mango with the cream, cover and cook on High for 1 Hr.
Divide into bowls and serve right away.

Lemony Orange Marmalade

Servings: 8 Cooking Time: 3 Hrs.

Ingredients:

Juice of 2 lemons
3 lbs. sugar
1 lb. oranges, peeled and cut into segments
pint water

Directions:

Whisk lemon juice, sugar, water, and oranges in the insert of Slow Cooker.
Put the cooker's lid on and set the cooking time to 3 Hrs. on High settings.
Serve when chilled.

Rich Bread Pudding

Servings: 6 Cooking Time: 6 1/2 Hrs.

Ingredients:

6 cups bread cubes
1/2 cup dark chocolate chips
4 eggs
1/2 cup heavy cream
1 pinch cinnamon powder
1/4 cup golden raisins
1/4 cup butter, melted
1 1/2 cups whole milk
1 tsp. vanilla extract
2 tbsps. dark rum

Directions:

Mix the bread cubes, raisins and chocolate chips in your Slow Cooker.
Combine the butter, eggs, milk, cream, vanilla, cinnamon and dark rum and give it a good mix.
Pour the mixture over the bread and bake on low settings for 6 Hrs.
Serve the bread pudding slightly warm.

Pear Crumble

Servings:2 Cooking Time: 3 Hrs.

Ingredients:

4 tbsps. oatmeal
2 tbsps. sugar
½ tsp. ground cardamom
¼ cup of coconut milk
1 pear, chopped
1 tbsp. coconut oil
1 tbsp. dried apricots, chopped

Directions:

Mix oatmeal with chopped pear, sugar, coconut oil, ground cardamom, dried apricots, and coconut milk.
Then put the mixture in the Slow Cooker and close the lid.
Cook the crumble on Low for 3 Hrs.

Fig Bars

Servings:6 Cooking Time: 2.5 Hrs.

Ingredients:

1 cup coconut flour
1 egg, beaten
5 oz. figs, diced
¼ cup of coconut oil
1 tsp. baking powder
1 tsp. liquid honey

Directions:

Mix coconut flour and coconut oil and egg.
Add baking powder and knead the soft dough.
Then line the Slow Cooker bottom with baking paper.
Put the dough inside and flatten it in the shape of the pie crust.
After this, mix liquid honey with diced figs and transfer them on the dough. Flatten it well.
Close the lid and cook the fig bars on High for 2.5 Hrs.

Milk Fondue

Servings:3 Cooking Time: 4 Hrs.

Ingredients:

5 oz. milk chocolate, chopped
1 tsp. vanilla extract
1 tbsp. butter
¼ cup milk

Directions:

Put the chocolate in the Slow Cooker in one layer.
Then top it with butter, vanilla extract, and milk.
Close the lid and cook the dessert on Low for 4 Hrs.
Gently stir the cooked fondue and transfer in the ramekins.

Pear Apple Jam

Servings: 12 Cooking Time: 3 Hrs.

Ingredients:

8 pears, cored and cut into quarters
½ cup apple juice
2 apples, peeled, cored and quartered
1 tsp. cinnamon, ground

Directions:

Toss pears, apples, apple juice, and cinnamon in the insert of Slow Cooker.
Put the cooker's lid on and set the cooking time to 3 Hrs. on High settings.
Blend this cooked pears-apples mixture to make a jam.
Allow it to cool them divide in the jars.
Serve.

Summer Fruits Compote

Servings:6 Cooking Time: 3 Hrs.

Ingredients:

1 cup apricots, pitted, chopped
1 cup strawberries
½ cup of sugar
½ cup cherries, pitted
¼ cup blackberries
8 cups of water

Directions:

Put all ingredients in the Slow Cooker.
Cook compote on High for 3 Hrs.
Cool it and serve with ice cubes.

Cherry Bowls

Servings: 2 Cooking Time: 1 Hr.

Ingredients:

1 cup cherries, pitted
½ cup red cherry juice
1 tbsp. sugar
2 tbsps. maple syrup

Directions:

In your Slow Cooker, mix the cherries with the sugar and the other ingredients, toss gently, put the lid on, cook on High for 1 Hr., divide into bowls and serve.

Baked Goat Cheese Balls

Servings:6 Cooking Time: 1 Hr.

Ingredients:

8 oz. goat cheese
1 tsp. of sugar powder
1 tbsp. breadcrumbs
4 tbsps. sesame seeds
1 tsp. butter

Directions:

Mix goat cheese with sugar powder and breadcrumbs.
Make the medium size balls and coat them in the sesame seeds.
Melt the butter and pour it in the Slow Cooker.
Put the balls in the Slow Cooker in one layer and close the lid.
Cook the dessert on high for 1 Hr.

Sweet Milk Souffle

Servings:4 Cooking Time: 10 Hrs.

Ingredients:

2 cups of milk
5 eggs, beaten
1 cup condensed milk

Directions:

Mix eggs with milk and pour the mixture in the Slow Cooker.
Add condensed milk.
Carefully mix the mixture and close the lid.
Cook the soufflé on Low for 10 Hrs.

Quinoa Pudding

Servings: 2 Cooking Time: 2 Hrs.

Ingredients:

1 cup quinoa
½ cup sugar
½ tbsp. almonds, chopped
2 cups almond milk
½ tbsp. walnuts, chopped

Directions:

In your Slow Cooker, mix the quinoa with the milk and the other ingredients, toss, put the lid on and cook on High for 2 Hrs.
Divide the pudding into cups and serve.

Spongy Banana Bread

Servings: 6 Cooking Time: 3 Hrs.

Ingredients:

¾ cup of sugar
1 tsp. vanilla extract
2 bananas, mashed
1 and ½ cups flour
1/3 cup milk
Cooking spray
1/3 cup butter, soft
1 egg
1 tsp. baking powder
½ tsp. baking soda
1 and ½ tsp. cream of tartar

Directions:

Whisk milk with cream of tartar, sugar, egg, butter, bananas, and vanilla in a bowl.
Beat well, then add flour, baking soda, baking powder, and salt.
Again, mix well until it forms a smooth tartar-banana batter,
Grease the insert of Slow Cooker with cooking spray and spread the bread batter in it.
Put the cooker's lid on and set the cooking time to 3 Hrs. on High settings.
Slice and serve.

Cinnamon Apples

Servings: 2 Cooking Time: 2 Hrs.

Ingredients:

2 tbsps. brown sugar
1 tbsp. cinnamon powder
A pinch of nutmeg, ground
¼ cup water
1 lb. apples, cored and cut into wedges
2 tbsps. walnuts, chopped
½ tbsp. lemon juice
2 apples, cored and tops cut off

Directions:

In your Slow Cooker, mix the apples with the sugar, cinnamon and the other ingredients, toss, put the lid on and cook on High for 2 Hrs.
Divide the mix between plates and serve.

Saucy Peach and Apple Dessert

Servings: 4 Cooking Time: 4 1/4 Hrs.

Ingredients:

2 Granny Smith apples, peeled, cored and sliced
1 cinnamon stick
1 tsp. orange zest
1 tsp. cornstarch
2 ripe peaches, pitted and sliced
1 cup fresh orange juice
3 tbsps. honey
Ice cream or whipped cream for serving

Directions:

Combine all the ingredients in your Slow Cooker.
Cover the pot and cook for 4 Hrs. on low settings.
Allow the dessert to cool in the pot before serving.
Ice cream or whipped cream can be a great match for this dessert.

Caramel Apple Crisp

Servings: 8 Cooking Time: 6 1/2 Hrs.

Ingredients:

6 Granny Smith apples, peeled, cored and sliced
1/2 cup caramel sauce
1/2 tsp. cinnamon powder
1/2 cup rolled oats
1 pinch salt
1 tbsp. cornstarch
1 cup all-purpose flour
1/4 cup butter, chilled

Directions:

Mix the apples, caramel sauce, cinnamon and cornstarch in your Slow Cooker.
For the topping, mix the flour, oats, butter and salt in a bowl until grainy.
Spread the topping over the apples and cook on low settings for 6 Hrs.
Allow the crisp to cool in the pot before serving.

Pavlova

Servings:6 Cooking Time: 3 Hrs.

Ingredients:

5 egg whites
1 tsp. lemon juice
½ cup whipped cream
1 cup of sugar powder
1 tsp. vanilla extract

Directions:

Mix egg whites with sugar powder, lemon juice, and vanilla extract and whisk until you get firm peaks.
Then line the Slow Cooker with baking paper and put the egg white mixture inside.
Flatten it and cook for 3 Hrs. on low.
When the egg white mixture is cooked, transfer it in the serving plate and top with whipped cream.

Pumpkin Croissant Pudding

Servings: 6 Cooking Time: 5 1/4 Hrs.

Ingredients:

6 large croissants, cubed
1 1/2 cups pumpkin puree
1 tsp. cinnamon powder
1 cup skim milk
3 eggs
1/4 cup white sugar

Directions:

Place the croissants in your Slow Cooker.
Mix the milk, pumpkin puree, eggs, cinnamon and sugar in a bowl. Pour this mixture over the croissants.

Cover the pot with its lid and cook on low settings for 5 Hrs.
Serve the pudding chilled.

Vanilla Buns

Servings:4 Cooking Time: 3 Hrs.

Ingredients:

1 cup flour
3 tbsps. sugar
2 tbsps. olive oil
½ tsp. fresh yeast
¼ cup milk
1 tsp. vanilla extract

Directions:

Mix sugar with fresh yeast and leave for 5 Min.
Then mix the mixture with milk, flour, and vanilla extract.
Knead it and add olive oil.
Knead the dough until smooth and cut into 4 buns.
Leave the buns for 30 Min. in a warm place to rise.
Then line the Slow Cooker bowl with baking paper.
Put the buns inside and close the lid.
Cook them on High for 3 Hrs.

Classic Banana Foster

Servings:3 Cooking Time: 3 Hrs.

Ingredients:

3 bananas, peeled chopped
2 tbsps. butter, melted
1 tbsp. rum
2 tbsps. sugar
1 tsp. vanilla extract
3 ice cream balls

Directions:

Put the bananas in the Slow Cooker in one layer.
Then sprinkle them with sugar, butter, vanilla extract, and rum.
Close the lid and cook on Low for 3 Hrs.
Transfer the cooked bananas in the ramekins and top with ice cream balls.

Blueberry Tapioca Pudding

Servings:4 Cooking Time: 3 Hrs.

Ingredients:

4 tsps. blueberry jam
2 cups of milk
4 tbsps. tapioca

Directions:

Mix tapioca with milk and pour it in the Slow Cooker.
Close the lid and cook the liquid on low for 3 Hrs.
Then put the blueberry jam in 4 ramekins.
Cool the cooked tapioca pudding until warm and pour over the jam.

Bread and Berries Pudding

Servings: 2 Cooking Time: 3 Hrs.

Ingredients:

2 cups white bread, cubed
2 tbsps. butter, melted
1 cup almond milk
2 eggs, whisked
¼ tsp. vanilla extract
1 cup blackberries
2 tbsps. white sugar
¼ cup heavy cream
1 tbsp. lemon zest, grated

Directions:

In your Slow Cooker, mix the bread with the berries, butter and the other ingredients, toss gently, put the lid on and cook on Low for 3 Hrs.
Divide pudding between dessert plates and serve.

Peanut Sweets

Servings:8 Cooking Time: 4 Hrs.

Ingredients:

1 cup peanuts, roasted, chopped
¼ cup heavy cream
1 cup of chocolate chips

Directions:

Put chocolate chips and heavy cream in the Slow Cooker.
Cook the mixture on low for 4 Hrs.
Then mix the mixture until smooth and add roasted peanuts.
Carefully mix the mixture again.
Line the baking tray with baking paper.
with the help of the spoon, make the medium size balls (sweets) and put on the baking paper.
Cool the sweets until they are solid.

Cranberry Cookies

Servings:6 Cooking Time: 2.5 Hrs.

Ingredients:

2 oz. dried cranberries, chopped
1 cup flour
3 tbsps. sugar
3 tbsps. peanut butter
1 tsp. baking powder
1 tbsp. cream cheese

Directions:

Mix peanut butter with flour, baking powder, and sugar.
Add cream cheese and cranberries and knead the dough.
Make the small balls and press them gently to get the shape of the cookies.
After this, line the Slow Cooker bowl with baking paper.
Put the cookies inside and close the lid.
Cook the cookies on high for 2.5 Hrs.

Recipe index

A

Alaska Salmon with Pecan Crunch Coating....91
Almond and Quinoa Bowls....20
Almond Bowls....130
Almond Spread....129
Amaranth Bars....151
Apple Breakfast Rice....20
Apple Chicken Bombs....80
Apple Crumble....16
Apple Jelly Sausage Snack....125
Apple Sausage Snack....129
Apples and Potatoes....143
Apricot and Peaches Cream....150
Apricot Butter....22
Apricot Spoon Cake....151
Apricots Bread Pudding....27
Artichoke Bread Pudding....49
Artichoke Dip....51
Artichoke Pepper Frittata....21
Artichoke Soup....35
Arugula and Halloumi Salad....117
Asiago Chickpea Stew....31
Asian Broccoli Sauté....111
Asian Sesame Chicken....73
Asparagus Barley Stew....37
Asparagus Egg Casserole....28

B

Baba Ganoush....45
Baby Carrots In Syrup....22
Bacon and Egg Casserole....16
Bacon Baked Potatoes....52
Bacon Black Bean Dip....46
Bacon Cheeseburger Soup....102
Bacon Chicken Sliders....47
Bacon Chicken Stew....42
Bacon Chicken....78
Bacon Crab Dip....55
Bacon Eggs....25
Bacon New Potatoes....44
Bacon Potatoes....19
Bacon Swiss Pork Chops....68
Bacon Tater....25
Bacon Wrapped Dates....52
Bacon-wrapped Salmon....86
Baguette Boats....27
Baked Eggs....20
Baked Goat Cheese Balls....155
Balsamic Beef Cheeks....59
Balsamic Beef....63
Balsamic Cauliflower....142
Balsamic Lamb Mix....66
Balsamic Okra Mix....139
Balsamico Pulled Pork....52
Banana Cake....150
Banana Muffins....154
Barley and Bean Tacos....43
Barley Mix....136
Barley Soup....107
Barley Stew....101
Basil Chicken Wings....81
Basil Chicken....82
Bavarian Beef Roast....32
BBQ Beans....144
BBQ Beer Beef Tenderloin....56
BBQ Bratwurst....56
BBQ Pulled Chicken....72
BBQ Shrimps....93
Bean Dip....123
Bean Medley Soup....108
Bean Medley....146
Bean Queso....54
Beans and Peas Bowl....38
Beans Chili....35
Beans Stew....103
Beans-rice Mix....34
Beef and Chipotle Dip....127
Beef and Pancetta....58
Beef and Parsnip Saute....66
Beef and Peas....65
Beef and Sauce....62
Beef and Veggie Stew....29
Beef Barbacoa....42
Beef Brisket and Turnips Mix. 65
Beef Brisket In Orange Juice....66
Beef Burger....65
Beef Casserole....56
Beef Chili....106
Beef In Sauce....68
Beef Liver Stew....103
Beef Mac & cheese....61
Beef Meatballs....132
Beef Mushroom Soup....108
Beef Roast with Cauliflower....58
Beef Saute with Endives....64
Beef Soup....57
Beef Stroganoff....39
Beef Stuffing....57
Beef with Yams....61
Beer BBQ Meatballs....53
Beet and Capers Salad....122
Beets Side Salad....141
Berries Salad....151
Berry Marmalade....150
Berry Wild Rice....135
Bigeye Jack Saute....96
Black Bean Salsa Salad....129
Black Bean Soup....102
Black Eyes Peas Dip....129
Blue Cheese Chicken Wings....53
Blue Cheese Chicken....31
Blueberry Tapioca Pudding....157
Boiled Peanuts with Skin On....49
Bouillabaisse Soup....109
Bourbon Baked Beans....37
Bourbon Glazed Sausages....51
Bourbon Honey Chicken....72
Braised Root Vegetables....114
Braised Swiss Chard....116
Bread and Berries Pudding....157
Breakfast Casserole....16
Breakfast Pork Ground....19
Breakfast Zucchini Oatmeal....28
Brisket Turnips Medley....57
Broccoli Cheese Soup....103
Broccoli Dip....126
Broccoli Egg Pie....121
Broccoli Fritters....113
Broiled Tilapia....90
Brussel Sprouts....122
Buffalo Chicken....81
Buffalo Meatballs....131
Bulgur and Beans Salsa....126
Bulgur Mushroom Chili....114
Bulgur Sauté....111
Burgers....55
Butter Asparagus....121
Butter Crab Legs....88
Butter Crab....83
Butter Dipped Crab Legs....84
Butter Green Beans....141
Butter Hasselback Potatoes....119

Butter Oatmeal........................... 18
Butter Stuffed Chicken Balls... 133
Buttered Broccoli....................... 35
Butternut Squash Pate............. 22
Butternut Squash Pudding...... 154
Butternut Squash Soup............ 101
Butterscotch Self Saucing Pudding152

C

Cabbage and Kale Mix..............138
Cabbage Mix............................. 144
Cabbage Stew............................105
Cajun Beef.................................. 58
Calamari Rings Bowls...............128
Candied Kielbasa........................47
Cannellini Chicken.....................76
Caramel Apple Crisp.................156
Caramel Corn.............................130
Caramelized Bananas............... 153
Caramelized Onion Dip............50
Cardamom Lemon Pie..............151
Cardamom Plums..................... 148
Cardamom Pumpkin Wedges..111
Cardamom Rice Porridge.........153
Caribbean Pork Chop.............. 67
Carne Adovada.......................... 29
Carne Asada Nachos.................44
Carrot and Beet Side Salad...... 138
Carrot Beet Salad...................... 140
Carrot Broccoli Fritters........... 124
Carrot Oatmeal..........................28
Carrot Strips............................. 116
Cashew Chicken........................ 40
Cashew Dip............................... 131
Cauliflower and Broccoli Mix.. 139
Cauliflower Bites...................... 130
Cauliflower Casserole.............. 20
Cauliflower Chicken.................80
Cauliflower Curry......................111
Cauliflower Dip..........................131
Cauliflower Mac and Cheese... 110
Cauliflower Rice and Spinach. 136
Cauliflower Rice Pudding........ 28
Cauliflower Stuffing..................117
Celery Soup with Ham..............100
Charred Tomato Salsa..............55
Cheddar Eggs.............................22
Cheese and Beer Fondue...........51
Cheese and Turkey Casserole.. 23
Cheese Stuffed Meat Balls....... 125
Cheeseburger Cream Dip.........125
Cheeseburger Dip......................48
Cheeseburger Meatballs...........44
Cheesy Bacon Dip..................... 51
Cheesy Cauliflower Hash......... 25
Cheesy Chicken Breasts........... 75
Cheesy Chicken Chili................39
Cheesy Chicken Pasta...............38
Cheesy Corn Dip........................131
Cheesy Egg Bake....................... 23
Cheesy Eggs.............................. 18
Cheesy Fish Dip.........................89
Cheesy Mushroom Dip.............46
Cheesy Potato Dip....................126
Cheesy Three Bean Chili......... 41
Cherry Bowls.............................155
Cherry Dump Cake.................. 153
Chia Muffins............................. 147
Chicken and Apples Mix.......... 70
Chicken and Asparagus............81
Chicken and Beans....................74
Chicken and Chickpeas............ 75
Chicken and Peppers................74
Chicken and Rice.......................44
Chicken and Tomatillos........... 71
Chicken Bowl.............................77
Chicken Broccoli Casserole......82
Chicken Cabbage Medley.........19
Chicken Cacciatore.................. 74
Chicken Casserole.................... 81
Chicken Cauliflower Gratin..... 34
Chicken Chili.............................105
Chicken Chowder......................73
Chicken Curry...........................71
Chicken In Apricots.................72
Chicken In Onion Rings...........82
Chicken Meatballs....................126
Chicken Parm........................... 78
Chicken Pepper Chili................72
Chicken- Pork Meatballs..........29
Chicken Potato Sandwich........ 73
Chicken Salad........................... 127
Chicken Sausage Rice Soup.....98
Chicken Stroganoff.................. 69
Chicken Stuffed with Beans.....76
Chicken Taco Nachos.............. 127
Chicken Tacos...........................33
Chicken Thighs and Mushrooms74
Chicken Thighs Delight............82
Chicken Thighs Mix..................43
Chicken Tomato Salad..............76
Chicken Vegetable Pot Pie....... 77
Chicken Wild Rice Soup...........102
Chicken with Corn and Wild Rice40
Chicken with Couscous............ 40
Chicken with Sweet Potato...... 136
Chicken with Vegetables..........77
Chickpea Tikka Masala............ 38
Chickpeas Spread.....................123
Chickpeas Stew..........................41
Chili Chicken Liver.................. 73
Chili Chicken Wings................ 53
Chili Corn Cheese Dip............. 50
Chili Dip.................................... 114
Chili Okra..................................116
Chili Shrimp and Zucchinis..... 97
Chili Tamarind Mackerel......... 84
Chili Verde................................ 35
Chinese Cod.............................. 85
Chinese Hot Pot........................30
Chinese Mackerel......................92
Chinese Mushroom Pork......... 57
Chipotle BBQ Meatballs...........47
Chives Shrimp.......................... 89
Chocolate Cake.........................152
Chocolate Chicken Mole...........71
Chocolate French Toast............24
Chocolate Toast........................24
Chopped Chicken Liver Balls.. 70
Chorizo Cashew Salad............. 112
Chorizo Eggs............................. 19
Chorizo Soup.............................107
Chunky Potato Ham Soup....... 105
Cider Dipped Farro..................143
Cider Pork Roast.......................56
Cilantro Salmon....................... 83
Cinnamon and Cumin Chicken Drumsticks................................72
Cinnamon Apples.....................156
Cinnamon Applesauce..............139
Cinnamon French Toast...........19
Cinnamon Lamb........................56
Cinnamon Pecans Snack..........132
Cinnamon Plum Jam................153
Cinnamon Pork Ribs................ 43
Cinnamon Pumpkin Oatmeal..24
Cinnamon Rice Milk Cocktail..148
Cinnamon Rolls........................149
Citron Vanilla Bars...................149
Citrus Chicken..........................80
Citrus Glazed Chicken............. 70
Clam Soup................................. 105
Classic Apple Pie...................... 154
Classic Banana Foster..............157
Classic Osso Buco.....................33
Cocktail Beef Meatballs............68
Cocktail Meatballs.....................49
Cocoa and Berries Quinoa....... 19
Cocoa Pork Chops.................... 60

Coconut Beef.............................58
Coconut Catfish.........................95
Coconut Milk Lentils Bowl...... 110
Coconut Poached Pears............148
Coconut Squash Soup...............100
Cod and Broccoli.......................90
Cod and Clams Saute................96
Cod Sticks..................................95
Cod with Asparagus..................90
Coffee Cinnamon Roll.............. 153
Collard Greens Saute................114
Collard Greens Stew................. 40
Corn and Bacon.........................145
Corn and Chicken Saute...........77
Corn Pudding............................114
Corn Sauté.................................146
Cornbread Cream Pudding......140
Corned Beef with Sauerkraut.. 42
Corned Beef................................61
Cottage Cheese Ramekins........151
Couscous Halloumi Salad........ 111
Crab Dip.................................... 132
Cranberry Cookies.................... 157
Cranberry Maple Oatmeal....... 20
Cranberry Quinoa..................... 24
Cranberry Sauce Meatballs......45
Cream Cheese Macaroni.......... 137
Cream Chicken with Spices..... 75
Cream Of Broccoli Soup...........101
Cream White Fish..................... 85
Creamed Sweet Corn............... 39
Creamy Asparagus Chicken..... 18
Creamy Bacon Chicken............ 73
Creamy Breakfast......................24
Creamy Chicken Dip.................50
Creamy Chicken Soup............. 36
Creamy Corn Chili....................110
Creamy Duck Breast................ 78
Creamy Edamame Soup...........103
Creamy Keto Mash....................113
Creamy Mushroom Bites......... 124
Creamy Onion Casserole..........86
Creamy Potato Soup................ 103
Creamy Potatoes...................... 47
Creamy Puree........................... 110
Creamy Quinoa with Nuts....... 28
Creamy Shrimp Bowls.............20
Creamy Shrimp........................ 95
Creamy Spinach Dip.................55
Creamy Spinach Tortellini Soup105
Creamy Tortellini Soup............ 104
Creamy Tuna and Scallions..... 87
Creamy Turkey Mix.................. 72
Creamy White Mushrooms......119
Creamy Yogurt...........................21
Crock-pot Breakfast Casserole 29
Crock-pot Citrus Cake............. 127
Crock-pot Coconut Cake.......... 126
Crock-pot Low-carb Taco Soup99
Crumbly Chickpeas Snack....... 134
Cuban Flank Steaks.................. 37
Cucumber and Pork Cubes Bowl58
Cumin Pork Chops....................64
Curried Beef Short Ribs........... 30
Curried Chicken Wings............ 51
Curried Corn Chowder............. 99
Curry Braised Chicken............. 32
Curry Couscous......................... 120
Curry Drumsticks......................78
Curry Pork Meatballs................126

D

Dark Cherry Chocolate Cake... 150
Dark Chocolate Almond Cake. 148
Dates Quinoa............................ 24
Dill Crab Cutlets........................93
Dill Shrimp Mix.........................88
Duck and Mushrooms............. 72
Duck Breast and Veggies..........81
Duck Saute................................ 69
Dumplings with Polenta...........38

E

Easy Slow Cooker Pulled Pork 64
Egg Bake....................................17
Egg Salad with Ground Pork... 59
Eggplant Casserole...................118
Eggplant Caviar.........................47
Eggplant Dip.............................125
Eggplant Mini Wraps.............. 114
Eggplant Salad..........................112
Eggplant Salsa.......................... 130
Eggplant Tapenade.................. 34
Eggplants with Mayo Sauce.....144
Eggs and Sausage Casserole.... 19
Eggs with Spinach and Yogurt 27

F

Farro.. 143
Fava Bean Onion Dip...............129
Fennel Lentils...........................120
Fennel Stew...............................100
Fennel Tomato Pasta Sauce.....30
Fig Bars......................................155
Fish Hot Dog Sticks................. 91
Fish Mix.....................................91
Fish Pie...................................... 89
Fish Pie...................................... 93
Fish Pudding.............................88
Fish Sweet Corn Soup..............97
Fish Tart................................... 97
Five-spice Tilapia..................... 84
Five-spiced Chicken Wings......54
Flounder Cheese Casserole......96
Four Cheese Dip.......................47
Fragrant Appetizer Peppers.....118
Fragrant Jackfruit....................118
French Breakfast Pudding....... 17
French Onion Dip.................... 51
French Onion Soup..................106
French Toast............................. 19
French Vegetable Stew............ 122
Fried Apple Slices.....................23
Fruity Veal Shanks...................39
Fudgy Raspberry Chocolate Bread Pudding.................................... 150

G

Garam Masala Potato Bake..... 112
Garlic Chipotle Lime Chicken. 77
Garlic Gnocchi.......................... 116
Garlic Lamb Chilli.................... 60
Garlic Mushrooms................... 141
Garlic Pork Ribs....................... 66
Garlic Squash Mix.................... 141
Garlicky Bacon Slices...............125
Garlicky Spinach Soup with Herbed Croutons.................................. 104
Ginger and Sweet Potato Stew 106
Ginger Apple Bowls................. 28
Ginger Beef.............................. 66
Ginger Chili Peppers................134
Ginger Turkey Mix...................79
Ginger Turkey..........................77
Glazed Baby Carrots................ 140
Glazed Peanuts.........................51
Golden Syrup Pudding............ 153
Goose Mix.................................74
Goose with Mushroom Cream 79
Grain Free Chocolate Cake..... 147
Granola Apples........................147
Greek Cream............................149
Greek Orzo Chicken.................41
Green Beans with Mushrooms 135
Green Peas Chowder................109
Green Vegetable Dip................45

H

Ham and Sweet Potato Soup... 101
Ham and Swiss Cheese Dip..... 49
Ham and White Bean Soup..... 98
Ham Omelet.............................16
Ham Pockets............................22
Ham Potato Chowder.............. 107
Hamburger Beef Casserole...... 35
Hash Browns Casserole...........18
Hazelnut Liqueur Cheesecake. 150
Hearty Turkey Chili................. 104
Herbed and Cinnamon Beef.... 58
Herbed Balsamic Beets........... 135
Herbed Chickpea Soup............98
Herbed Egg Scramble..............20
Herbed Shrimps.......................94
Hoisin Chicken Wings.............48
Honey Apple Pork Chops.........37
Honey Carrot Gravy.................121
Honey Orange Glazed Chicken Drumsticks..............................40
Honey Orange Glazed Tofu..... 34
Honey Yogurt Cake..................154
Horseradish Chicken Wings.... 69
Hot and Sour Soup...................105
Hot Calamari........................... 90
Hot Eggs Mix........................... 25
Hot Lamb Strips.......................57
Hot Lentil Soup........................ 99
Hot Sauce Oysters Mushrooms117
Hot Zucchini Mix..................... 142
Hummus..................................134
Hungarian Goulash Soup.........99

I

Indian Fish...............................83
Indian Spiced Quinoa Stew..... 41
Italian Black Beans Mix........... 136
Italian Eggplant........................145
Italian Pork Chops................... 57
Italian Style Pork Shoulder......36
Italian Style Scrambled Eggs...18
Italian Trout Croquettes.......... 93

J

Jalapeno Corn...........................112
Jalapeno Mississippi Roast..... 59
Jalapeno Muffins..................... 21
Jalapeno Onion Dip.................133
Jalapeno Poppers.....................124
Jamaican Jerk Chicken............ 42
Jamaican Pork Shoulder.......... 67
Jamaican Stew.........................104
Jambalaya................................ 87
Japanese Cod Fillet..................94
Jerk Chicken............................ 82

K

Kale & Feta Breakfast Frittata. 21
Kale Mix...................................146
Kielbasa Kale Soup.................. 108

L

Lamb and Cabbage................... 68
Lamb and Eggs Mix................. 27
Lamb and Kale..........................63
Lamb and Lime Zucchinis....... 61
Lamb and Onion Stew.............34
Lamb Bacon Stew.....................85
Lamb Cashews Tagine............. 63
Lamb Leg and Sweet Potatoes.59
Lamb Meatballs........................65
Lamb Shanks........................... 67
Lamb Stew................................102
Lavender and Orange Lamb.... 60
Lavender Blackberry Crumble 146
Leek Bake................................. 18
Leek Casserole.......................... 28
Leek Eggs................................. 24
Leek Potato Soup..................... 98
Lemon Chicken.........................31
Lemon Cream.......................... 148
Lemon Poppy Seed Cake..........147
Lemon Vegetable Pork Roast.. 35
Lemongrass Chicken Thighs... 83
Lemony Artichokes..................131
Lemony Orange Marmalade....154

Lemony Salmon Soup...............105
Lentil Rice Salad....................... 110
Lentil Stew................................ 106
Lentils and Quinoa Mix...........17
Lentils Curry............................. 41
Lentils Dip.................................127
Lentils Hummus........................131
Lentils Soup.............................. 35
Lettuce and Pork Wraps...........65
Light Zucchini Soup.................106
Lime and Pepper Chicken........78
Lime Bean Stew........................42
Lime Beans Mix........................144
Lobster Stew............................. 99
London Broil.............................63

M

Mac Cream Cups....................... 145
Macadamia Nuts Snack...........128
Mackerel and Lemon................88
Mackerel Stuffed Tacos...........94
Madras Lentils..........................41
Mango Cream........................... 154
Maple Brussels Sprouts...........142
Maple Ginger Chicken.............75
Maple Mustard Salmon...........89
Marinated Jalapeno Rings.......120
Marjoram Rice Mix..................137
Marmalade Glazed Meatballs..52
Mashed Potatoes......................143
Mashed Potatoes......................146
Matcha Shake........................... 149
Mayo Pork Salad...................... 63
Mayo Sausage Rolls.................. 17
Meat Buns................................. 23
Mediterranean Chicken...........69
Mediterranean Dip.................. 48
Mexican Avocado Rice............ 140
Mexican Beef Soup...................103
Mexican Carne Adovada.......... 62
Mexican Chicken Stew............ 106
Mexican Chili Dip.................... 48
Mexican Dip..............................50
Mexican Lamb Fillet................67
Mexican Pork Roast.................64
Mexican Rice.............................139
Mexican Shredded Chicken.....30
Mexican Style Soup..................101
Mexican Style Stew.................. 100
Milk Fondue..............................155
Milk Oatmeal............................ 17
Milky Fish.................................86
Minestrone Zucchini Soup.......110
Mint Cookies.............................152
Mint Farro Pilaf........................140
Mint Summer Drink................. 150
Minty Peas and Tomatoes........142
Mixed Nuts................................128
Mixed Olive Dip........................48
Mixed Pork and Beans.............30
Molasses Lime Meatballs.........46
Monkey Bread...........................152
Morning Muesli........................20
Morning Pie.............................. 26
Moscow Bacon Chicken...........81
Mozzarella Basil Tomatoes......129
Mozzarella Stuffed Meatballs..54
Mung Beans Salad....................113
Mushroom Chicken Casserole.22
Mushroom Pork Stew..............31
Mushroom Risotto................... 116
Mushroom Salsa.......................133
Mushroom Saute......................115
Mushroom Steaks.................... 111
Mussaman Curry......................64
Mussel Stew.............................. 98
Mussels Tomato Soup............. 96
Mustard Brussels Sprouts........145
Mustard Chicken Mix..............73
Mustard Cod............................. 89
Mustard-crusted Salmon......... 86

N

Naked Beef Enchilada in A Slow Cooker.......................................59
Nut and Berry Side Salad.........143
Nut Berry Salad........................ 145
Nutmeg Banana Oatmeal.........26
Nutmeg Trout........................... 87
Nuts Bowls................................ 123

O

Oat Fritters................................112
Oats Granola............................. 23
Octopus and Veggies Mix.........94
Okra and Corn.......................... 137
Okra Chicken Saute................. 82
Okra Side Dish..........................142
Omelet with Greens................. 16
Onion and Bison Soup.............62
Onion Beef............................... 65
Onion Chives Muffins..............119
Onion Cod Fillets..................... 88
Onion Dip.................................132
Onion Pork Chops with Creamy Mustard Sauce..........................37
Orange and Apricot Jam..........148
Orange Duck Fillets................. 71
Orange Squash......................... 146
Oregano Pork Chops................68
Oregano Turkey and Tomatoes70
Oriental Chicken Bites.............50

P

Paprika Cod Sticks................... 133
Paprika Hominy Stew..............104
Paprika Noddle Soup................98
Paprika Okra.............................119
Parmesan Biscuit Pot Pie.........43
Parmesan Rosemary Potato.... 67
Parmesan Spinach Mix............144
Parsley Chicken Mix................ 74
Parsley Mushroom Mix...........140
Parsley Salmon.........................83
Parsley Turkey Breast..............78
Parsnip Balls.............................119

Party Mix....48
Pavlova....156
Peach Cobbler....148
Peach Oats....27
Peach, Vanilla and Oats Mix....16
Peanut Snack....127
Peanut Sweets....157
Pear Apple Jam....155
Pear Crumble....155
Pear Roasted Chicken....34
Pears and Sauce....152
Peas and Carrots....138
Peppercorn Beef Steak....59
Pesto Pork Chops....62
Pesto Salmon....93
Pickled Pulled Beef....61
Pineapple Milkfish....96
Pinto Beans with Rice....122
Piquant Mushrooms....129
Pizza Dip....50
Pork and Beans Mix....60
Pork and Chilies Mix....56
Pork and Chorizo Lunch Mix.. 39
Pork and Corn Soup....108
Pork and Eggplant Casserole...23
Pork and Tomatoes Mix....32
Pork Ham Dip....55
Pork Roast in Slow Cooker....62
Pork Roast with Apples....62
Pork Sirloin Salsa Mix....65
Pork Stew....41
Pork Stuffed Tamales....134
Pork Tomatoes....63
Posole Soup....100
Potato Bake....116
Potato Balls....110
Potato Cups....130
Potato Omelet....23
Potato Onion Salsa....130
Potato Parmesan Pie....115
Potato Salsa....133
Potatoes and Leeks Mix....141
Poultry Stew....73
Pretzel Party Mix....53
Prosciutto-wrapped Scallops...86
Prune Bake....148
Pulled Maple Chicken....77
Pumpkin Bars....147
Pumpkin Bean Chili....120
Pumpkin Chili....119
Pumpkin Croissant Pudding... 156
Pumpkin Hummus....113

Q

Queso Dip....131
Queso Verde Dip....46
Quick Layered Appetizer....45
Quick Parmesan Bread....47
Quinoa and Oats Mix....26
Quinoa Bars....26
Quinoa Casserole....120
Quinoa Cauliflower Medley....25
Quinoa Fritters....119
Quinoa Oats Bake....25
Quinoa Pudding....156
Quinoa Tofu Veggie Stew....43

R

Rainbow Bake....109
Rainbow Carrots....117
Raisin-flax Meal Bars....147
Raisins and Rice Pudding....26
Ramen Noodles....139
Ranch Broccoli....122
Ranch Turkey Bites....46
Raspberry Chia Porridge....22
Raspberry Nutmeg Cake....149
Raspberry Oatmeal....26
Red Muffins....150
Red Salsa Chicken....43
Rhubarb Stew....149
Rice Cauliflower Casserole....115
Rice Snack Bowls....124
Rice Stuffed Apple Cups....113
Rice Stuffed Eggplants....122
Rice Stuffed Squid....93
Rice with Artichokes....139
Rich Bread Pudding....154
Rich Lamb Shanks....64
Roast with Pepperoncini....67
Roasted Bell Peppers Dip....45
Roasted Garlic Soup....100
Rosemary Lamb Shoulder....56
Russian Chicken....80

S

Sage Shrimps....91
Salmon and Berries....95
Salmon Chickpea Fingers....94
Salmon Croquettes....86
Salmon Fennel Soup....99
Salmon Picatta....95
Salmon Salad....88
Salsa Corn Dip....126
Salsa Meat....59
Salsa Snack....124
Sauce Goose....69
Saucy Chicken Thighs....75
Saucy Macaroni....137
Saucy Sriracha Red Beans....29
Sausage and Eggs Mix....27
Sausage and Pepper Appetizer 55
Sausage Dip....46
Sausage Frittata....21
Sautéed Endives....117
Sauteed Garlic....113
Savoy Cabbage Mix....138
Scalloped Potato Casserole....60
Scalloped Potatoes....142
Schweinshaxe....64
Seabass Ragout....91
Seafood Chowder....84
Seafood Soup....33
Sheriff Chicken Wings....79
Shredded Beef Soup....98
Shredded Cabbage Saute....112
Shrimp and Avocado....96
Shrimp and Mango Mix....90
Shrimp and Peas Soup....95
Shrimp and Pineapple Bowls.. 89
Shrimp and Rice Mix....88
Shrimp Chicken Jambalaya....96
Shrimp Mix....84
Shrimp Omelet....17
Shrimp Soup....107
Shrimp Stew....42
Shrimps and Carrot Saute....96
Shrimps Boil....92

Sichuan Chicken........................74
Simple Pork Chop Casserole... 62
Simple Salsa..............................124
Slow Cooked Turkey Delight... 79
Slow Cooker Beef Rendang......61
Slow Cooker Caesar Chicken... 71
Slow Cooker Chicken Breasts.. 83
Slow Cooker Fajita Chicken.....70
Slow Cooker Greek Snapper.... 83
Slow Cooker Jambalaya........... 36
Slow Cooker Pork Carnitas...... 65
Slow Cooker Salsa Chicken......70
Slow Cooker Smoked Trout..... 87
Slow Cooker Tuna Spaghetti... 87
Slow-cooked White Onions..... 136
Smoked Sausage Stew............. 100
Snapper Ragout........................85
Sour Cream Roast.................... 58
Southwestern Turkey Stew...... 108
Soy Beef Steak.......................... 66
Soy Braised Chicken................ 34
Spaghetti Cheese Casserole..... 118
Spanish Chorizo Dip................49
Spiced Buffalo Wings................54
Spiced Butter Chicken.............31
Spiced Mackerel....................... 84
Spiced Plum Butter..................151
Spicy Almond-crusted Chicken Nuggets......................................78
Spicy Asian Style Mushroom...49
Spicy Black Bean Soup............ 104
Spicy Cajun Scallops................85
Spicy Chicken Taquitos...........52
Spicy Creole Shrimp................ 92
Spicy Dip.................................. 133
Spicy Eggplant with Red Pepper and Parsley...................................... 111
Spicy Enchilada Dip.................46
Spicy Glazed Pecans................ 50
Spicy Monterey Jack Fondue.. 45
Spicy Mussels............................128
Spicy Okra................................ 109
Spinach Dip...............................134
Spinach Mix............................. 140
Spinach Potato Stew................38
Spinach Rice............................. 144
Spinach with Halloumi Cheese Casserole.................................. 123
Split Pea Sausage Soup........... 97
Spongy Banana Bread............. 156
Squash and Chicken Soup........40
Squash Bowls............................21
Squash Butter.......................... 23
Squash Noodles........................122
Sriracha Shrimp....................... 97
Stewed Okra.............................142
Strawberry Yogurt Oatmeal.....27
Stuffed Artichokes....................48
Stuffed Chicken Fillets............ 81
Stuffed Mushrooms................. 132
Stuffed Okra.............................117
Stuffed Peppers Platter........... 128
Succulent Pork Ribs.................59
Summer Fruits Compote..........155
Summer Squash Chickpea Soup107
Summer Squash Medley.......... 137
Summer Squash Mix............... 137
Summer Vegetable Soup.........102
Sun-dried Tomato Chicken......71
Swedish Style Beets................. 120
Sweet and Mustard Tilapia......90
Sweet Corn Jalapeno Dip.........51
Sweet Milk Souffle................... 155
Sweet Onions........................... 115
Sweet Pineapple Tofu.............. 115
Sweet Potato and Lentils Pate. 110
Sweet Potato Dip......................132
Sweet Potato Puree.................. 118
Sweet Potato Tarragon Soup... 116
Sweet Potatoes with Bacon......145
Sweet Quinoa........................... 28

T

Tabasco Halibut........................ 85
Taco Dip.................................... 52
Taco Shrimps............................ 92
Taco Soup..................................108
Tacos... 123
Tahini Cheese Dip.....................53
Tamales..................................... 135
Tangy Italian Shredded Beef... 43
Tangy Red Potatoes................. 139
Tempeh Carnitas.......................38
Teriyaki Kale.............................111
Teriyaki Tilapia........................ 91
Thai Salmon Cakes.................. 93
Thai Side Salad.........................143
Thai Style Flounder................. 89
Thick Green Lentil Soup.......... 108
Three Cheese Artichoke Sauce 49
Three Pepper Roasted Pork Tenderloin.................................33
Thyme and Sesame Halibut.....92
Thyme Beef.............................. 60
Thyme Mushrooms and Corn. 145
Thyme Mussels.........................86
Thyme Pepper Shrimp............ 132
Thyme Tomatoes......................120
Tofu and Cauliflower Bowl...... 119
Tofu Chickpea Curry................32
Tofu Eggs..................................25
Tomato and Corn Mix............. 136
Tomato and Mushroom Salsa. 123
Tomato and Turkey Chili........ 97
Tomato Beef Chowder.............56
Tomato Beef Soup....................101
Tomato Bulgur..........................39
Tomato Chickpeas Stew.......... 102
Tomato Fish Soup....................106
Tomato Sauce Pork Roast........32
Tostadas................................... 134
Tri-bean Chili............................121
Tropical Meatballs................... 53
Tuna and Brussels Sprouts...... 95
Tuna and Chimichurri............. 92
Tuna Loin Mix.......................... 85
Turkey and Avocado................ 83
Turkey Breakfast Casserole..... 22
Turkey Cranberry Stew........... 76
Turkey Meatloaf....................... 52
Turkey Wings and Sauce..........75
Turkey with Olives and Corn... 69
Turkey with Plums................... 69
Turkey with Rice...................... 82
Turkish Meat Saute..................68
Turmeric Coconut Squid.......... 91
Turnip and Beans Casserole.... 36
Tuscan White Bean Soup......... 102

V

Vanilla Bean Caramel Custard 152
Vanilla Buns..............................157
Vanilla Quinoa..........................24
Vegan Kofte...............................113
Vegan Pepper Bowl..................121
Vegetable Bean Stew................118
Vegetable Beef Roast with Horseradish............................. 36
Vegetable Pot Pie......................36

Veggie Medley....................143
Veggie Spread....................132
Veggies Casserole....................29
Veggies Rice Pilaf....................140
Vinaigrette Dipped Salmon..... 87

W

White Bean Hummus....................54
White Bean Spread....................134
White Beans Luncheon....................109
White Beans Mix....................138
White Chicken Cassoulet.........31
Whole Roasted Cauliflower..... 32
Wild Rice Pilaf....................130
Wine Chicken....................77
Winter Pork with Green Peas..62

Z

Zesty Lamb Meatballs....................54
Zesty Pumpkin Cubes....................18
Zucchini Basil Soup....................117
Zucchini Casserole....................136
Zucchini Caviar....................121
Zucchini Chicken....................74
Zucchini Crackers Casserole....141
Zucchini Mash....................112
Zucchini Mix....................138
Zucchini Onion Pate....................144
Zucchini Soup with Rosemary and Parmesan....................120
Zucchini Spinach Lasagne....... 114
Zucchini Spread....................128
Zucchini Sticks....................128

Made in the USA
Las Vegas, NV
12 December 2021

37401031R00092